Lecture Notes in Economics and Mathematical Systems 449

Springer
Berlin
Heidelberg
New York
Barcelona
Budapest
Hong Kong
London
Milan
Paris
Santa Clara
Singapore
Tokyo

Fukang Fang · Michèle Sanglier (Eds.)

Complexity and Self-Organization in Social and Economic Systems

Proceedings of the International Conference
on Complexity and Self-Organization
in Social and Economic Systems
Beijing, October 1994

Springer

Editors

Prof. Fukang Fang
Beijing Normal University
Beijing 100875
People's Republic of China

Prof. Michèle Sanglier
Instituts Internationaux de Physique et de
Chimie Fondés par E. Solvay
Université Libre de Bruxelles
Campus Plaine CP 231
Bd. du Triomphe
B-1050 Brussels, Belgium

Library of Congress Cataloging-in-Publication Data

Complexity and self-organization in social and economic systems : proceedings, Beijing, China, October 1994 / Fang Fukang, Michèle Sanglier (eds.).
p. cm. -- (Lecture notes in economics and mathematical systems ; 449)
Contains the proceedings of the International Conference on Complexity and Self-Organization in Social and Economics Systems, held at Beijing, October 1994.
Includes bibliographical references (p.).

ISBN-13: 978-3-540-62400-4 e-ISBN-13: 978-3-642-48406-3
DOI: 10.1007/978-3-642-48406-3

1. Economics--Mathematical models--Congresses. 2. Social sciences--Mathematical models--Congresses. 3. China--Economic conditions--1976- --Mathematical models--Congresses. I. Fang, Fukang, 1946- . II. Sanglier, M. III. International Conference on Complexity and Self-Organization in Social and Economics Systems (1994 : Peking, China) IV. Series.
HB141.C623 1997
330'.01'5118--dc21

Typesetting: Camera ready by author/editor
SPIN: 10546723 42/3142-543210 - Printed on acid-free paper

Foreword

The *Instituts Internationaux de Physique et de Chimie fondés par E. Solvay* and the *Institute of Nonequilibrium systems* of Beijing Normal University jointly sponsored a conference on "The Complexity and Self-organization in Socio-economic Systems" on October 17-20, 1994 at Beijing, China. The purpose of the conference was to explore the complexity and evolutionary laws of socio-economic systems through nonlinear dynamic systems and self-organization theory. The conference was chaired by Professor M. Sanglier and Professor Fang Fukang and was introduced by the Nobel prize winner, Professor I. Prigogine and the vice director of the Chinese National System Reform Committee, Mr. Wu Jie.

The conference was held at an important time. On the one hand, the research in the natural sciences about the evolution of complex systems has made great progress, modern scientific theories such as nonlinear dynamic system theory and self-organization theory are becoming more and more mature and a series of methods dealing with these complex systems are being developed which enable us to understand and study non equilibrium, uncertainty and instability. On the other hand, human societies around the world witness a general increase of connectedness, interactivity and an increase of reaction speeds to decisions. In this context, the deterministic, linear way of thinking becomes more and more inadequate and this stimulates the development of non linear science.

The idea and method of dynamic evolution appear in the study of microeconomic phenomena, economic fluctuations, cycles and even of important macroeconomic problems such as economic growth and development. The idea that there could exist a specific dynamic mechanism behind the evolution of economic systems is becoming more and more accepted.

Although P. Samuelson had already predicted this stage of development of economic thinking and its importance half a century ago, its realization today depends upon developments in the natural sciences. Obviously, this is not the first time that economic science borrows from physics and other natural sciences, but this time there are good chances that previous errors of direct transposition from physics to economics might be avoided. Indeed, both disciplines could benefit greatly from this recent cross-fertilisation :

a) economics could benefit by retraining its own complexity levels where agents have subjective intentions, representations of their macroscopic environments, memories thereof, and where behaviours seem so unstable or random (i.e. learning abilities abilities are so powerful) that no experimentation can be reproduced with identical conditions, as in the case in the natural sciences; this could generate scientific hypotheses paying more attention to human specific

III. Microeconomics: technological change, market structure and regional economics

IV. Stochastic Approach and Data Analysis

I. Introduction

In a sense, instability and chaos is the rule in the human sciences.

Now let me go briefly to cultural problems to close this introduction. There is a different view of nature in the West and the East, in Europe and in China. In the West, the description of nature is based on the idea of "laws of nature". The most famous example is Newton's law which relates force to acceleration, and it forms the basis of classical dynamics. We know today how to generalize it to include quantum effects. The western concept of laws of nature has been foreign to the eastern ideas of nature, as accepted in Japan and China. Western laws of nature implied a kind of obligation. In addition the laws of nature implied that the future is already given. In contrast for China, nature means spontaneity, therefore the future is not completely predictable.

I believe that there is a possibility to overcome this "schism" to derive a view of nature which has room both for laws of nature and for creativity and the emergence of novelty. Indeed we have succeeded to include instability into the fundamental laws of physics. This is precisely the extension of classical and quantum mechanics which I already mentioned. In this extension, past and future play different roles and there is an "arrow of time". Also, laws of nature no longer express certitudes. They express possibilities. I think that this view describes the universe which we cannot dominate in the same way as we could dominate nature in classical physics. It is important that at the end of this century science may present a more universal message that is consistent with the view of nature of both the East and the West.

This conference is a good opportunity for an academic exchange with scholars from the West and the East meeting in China. Chinese scholars have already achieved significant advances in the field of non-equilibrium systems, and China's reality presents an attractive background for studying self-organization and complexity of socio-economic systems. So I believe this conference will be a great success.

I. P.

Market Economy and Systematic Management

Wu Jie

Deputy Minister
State Commission for Restructuring the Economic Systems, China

1 Economy Is a System

The national economy of a country is a system. It has both the general and specific character of system. In this paper, economic system is analyzed from five different perspectives.

A . It is the whole of various elements and relations between them.

Economic system, complicated in nature and enormous in size, is one kind of social systems, Complexity is an outstanding feature economic system possessed. This complexity can be understood as three different facets. Firstly, it has many essential elements; secondly, its structure is complex; and thirdly, its essential elements are all interacted. Like biosystem and other complex systems, economic system is of multistructure with all internal essential elements mutually and closely related, and therefore, this multistructure finds itself in a whole ONE with a nature of being more than the sheer sum of its parts. Just as Marx says in *On Capital*, three types of capital rotation (P-G-W) constitute the movement of whole capital. In other words, the three subsystems-production, circulation and consumption-form a greater system with the nature of being a complete whole. The three subsystems interact as prerequisite and conditions for one another. They are interrelated and mutually influenced and mutually act upon each other, thus making up a three-dimensional and network-like structure. We can use mathematical symbols to describe it in the following way: $1 + 2 > 3$

B . It sustains intrinsic internal structure.

The structure of a system is realized in the relations between its essential elements. The structure of economic system has two properties-hierarchical and ordered (in other words, *organized*). It is hierarchical because there are different levels inside economic system, which can be roughly divided into three categories: macrolevel, which refers to the state or government; intermediate level, which is market; and microlevel, which consists of individual enterprises. Each of these levels forms an essential structural element, or, in other words, subsystem within economic system, and each level itself is composed of lower levels (or smaller elements). For example, the unitarity of macroeconomy and microeconomy is further strengthened by the present tendency towards economic internationalization.

Due to the extensive application of new technology and the upgrading and updating of industrial structures, traditional boundary between macroeconomy and microeconomy is becoming vaguer and vaguer and their unitarity, on the contrary, is becoming clearer and clearer. If microeconomy is not going on well, the stability and development of macroeconomy will inevitably be affected. The misguidance of macroeconomy, whereas, might exert direct negative influence on microeconomy. How to handle the relation between macroeconomy and microeconomy has presented a great challenge to international economic circles. We are sure that between macroeconomy (macromanagement) and microeconomy (micromanagement) there is an intermediate level, which is intermediate economy. This intermediate economy is now functioning to make an integrated economic whole of macroeconomy and microeconomy. Before Keynes J.M. microeconomics led the main stream, and after the publication of *The General Theory of Employment, Interest and Money*, macroeconomics began to take shape. At the present, these two levels of economics have found in international economic integration a practical common basis on which they merge. This merger gives birth to system economics.

It is ordered because different economic levels and elements are combined not disorderly but in a highly organized and ordered manner. The structure of economic system can be analyzed in three different terms-quality, quantity and order. Quality is its internal defining and specific characteristics that distinguish it from other systems; quantity displays its elements as well as the relations between the elements in quantitative ways; and order indicates the positions of its elements in time and space.

C. It is also the subsystem within a larger system (a system at a higher level) when analyzed from its specific external social environment.

First the economic system of a country forms a part of, and a subsystem in, the economic system of the whole world. Second, it is a subsystem in the whole system of society, which is made up of political system, cultural system, etc. along with economic system. Economic system and its social environment, the former being the latter's subsystem, form a system at a higher level. Like any other objective systems, economic system is open to its environment and is always in the process of communicating material, energy and information with its environment. China is now trying to rejoin GATT and her purpose is to have communication and cooperation with international economic system and to gain the right for fair competition within the larger system.

D. It has specific functions and purposes.

Just like biological organism, objective economic system, being a highly organized object, is purpose-oriented. First, it is of objective teleonomy. It has to maintain its existence and stability and prevent itself from dissolved and disintegrating. In other words, its purpose, considered from the system itself, is to exist. Meanwhile, the system has to evolve, that is to say, it has to develop and improve itself. Second, from the perspective of relation between economic system and its environment, it has to serve the needs of social system, a system of higher level, that is, to serve the needs of human beings. This is its purpose relevant to human beings. To be more specific, this purpose is to seek the maximum benefits of the system and its environment. All activities that economic system is engaged in to realize the above mentioned purposes are its functions.

E. It evolves.

Like other systems, economic system is dynamic. It is never absolutely stable and immutable. On the contrary it is always in motion and is always changing towards becoming more and more highly organized and ordered, that is to say, it is evolvable. Some of its parts might disintegrate and degenerate, but the system as a whole will evolve. The basic prerequisite of evolution is that the system must be open to its environment.

2 What Does Management Mean to Economic System?

What significance does management have for economic system? To answer this question, we have to analyze firstly the properties of economic system itself.

Economic system is neither a pure objective system nor a pure artificial one, and therefore, its dynamic mechanisms depend not only on automatic adjustment of the system itself but also on artificial stimulation.

Automatic adjustment is realized in two processes. One includes self-feedback process, self-catalyzing process and self-stimulating process, which can be all collectively called self-organizing. For example, market prices spontaneously go up and down due to the changes in supply and demand; resources are spontaneously distributed according to benefit principle; and only the fittest of the enterprises (microcomponents) within economic system will survive because of the functions of competition mechanism. The other process is caused by the functions of economic system environment, referring to the spontaneous adjustment and changes in the structures and functions of economic system itself as results from its communication and interaction with its environment by exchange of material, energy and information. For example, Economic system will react to the changes in political and cultural situations, to the changes in natural ecological environment, and to the influence of international economic system, i.g., structural and functional changes in economic system itself caused by international trade, international division of labor, import and export of technology, flow and distribution of funds, regional economic effect, shifting of economic center, etc.. Automatic adjustment (referring to market adjustment) has the characteristics of being slow, contingent and spontaneous.

Artificial stimulation refers to purposeful actions consciously and selectively made by the government in order to cause some changes in the structure and functions of economic system and to guide its development according to the government's rationally proportioned; (3) All industries should be gradually upgraded and updated so as to improve their qualities.

C. Scientificalty and stability of micropolicies

The term macropolicies refers here to policies on planning, financial and monetary matters, taxes and prices etc.. Macropolicies are a major factor in artificial stimulation approach of economic system's dynamic mechanisms and are essential to the survival and evolution of economic system. At the present the following points should be emphasized: (1) Overall strategies and overall planning should be made; (2) Policies on mediumterm and long-term industrial structures should be made; (3) There should be five-year plans and annual plans; (4) The policies should be mutually supportive.

Intermediate management (structural management) is the management of all economic aspects related to market and is important to the order and structural optimization of the internal elements and their relations of economic system. The goal of intermediate management is to bring about the rational distribution of economic system's internal resources and the ordered flow of manpower, materials, funds and information. Intermediate management can be further divided into two categories-production element market management and commodity market management. The objectives of intermediate management are to make it possible for the elements such as commodity, land, funds, manpower, technology etc. to flow and combine in an ordered manner. The purposes of comprehensive laws, intermediary service and the management of social security systems are to realize a normalized, quick and smooth flow of the elements.

Micro-management refers to the management of the microcomponents (enterprises) of economic system and it deals with the production and trade activities of enterprises. The objectives of enterprise management are to bring about the optimized combination and ordered function of production elements (such as manpower, funds, land, technology, etc.) and, as a result, to increase the economic benefits of enterprises by means of the reasonable structure of the five major essential factors-planning, organizing, directing, coordinating and controlling.

System management is the important guarantee of the sustained stable healthy development of national economy. System management, as the trinity of macromanagement, intermediate management and micromanagement, combine effectively and organically the visible *hands of government*, the invisible *hands of market* and the hands of entrepreneurs so as to bring about the ordered structure and optimized function of economic system. In contrast with the skipping and intermittent development of the Western economy, the economy of Eastern Asia, or even that of the whole Asia, has rapidly and steadily developed. One of the reasons for this Asian success is that system management has effectively been used on a national scale in those successful countries. System management level has gradually become a weatherglass indicating a country's economic order and development. The competition about overall management between countries has now become a new arena of rivalry for international economy. The outcome of competition between countries ultimately depends on the level and qualities of their macromanagement, intermediate management and micromanagement. The Greek word for economy is *Oikonomia*, which consists of two radicals, *Oikos* meaning family and *Nomos* meaning management. Analyzed from the perspective of etymology, therefore, economy initsessence is the extension of *family management* to *state management*. Economy, in its final analysis, is management. This profound idea, I think, is still correct in modern times. The most fundamental intention of *economics* is *management*, and is how to manage economic system. We should now understand what economy really means and vigorously advocate the idea of scientific system management and its corresponding specific methods.

II. Macroeconomics: Economic growth and development, business cycles and chaos

Macroeconomic Dynamic Model and Economic Evolution*

Fang Fukang

Beijing Normal University, Beijing 100875, People's Republic of China

Abstract. This paper discusses the complicated evolution of macroeconomic system and its mechanism. It points out that the evolution of macroeconomic system is a nonlinear dynamic process in constant growth and oscillation that are either strengthening or weakening. This theoretical analysis agrees with the practical economic development. Besides, the unity of constant growth and oscillation generated and decided by the complicated internal interactions is the basic characteristic of the evolution, which is not solely decided by the push from changes in the external environment. Finally, the nonlinear interactions and coupling among economic variables and those between economic variables and parameters make the system evolution characterized by growth and oscillation much complicated and diversified. The impact of parameters on evolution is not monotonous and cannot be viewed directly.

The major task of macroeconomics is to describe the complicated macroeconomic evolution as a whole and to explain the growth and oscillation in the process of economic development. This paper starts with the equilibria and their interactions among the three markets of product, labor and money which constitute the macroeconomic system. Through the analysis of the forming mechanism of the market equilibrium and the dynamic process of the equilibrium transition, the paper explores the dynamic law in the complicated macroeconomic system evolution. In the first part, we discuss our views of the core issues of macroeconomic evolution and propose the relevant methods and ways of dealing those issues. In the second and the third parts, we create nonlinear dynamic models and discuss the evolution behavior and laws in the macroeconomic system that includes the product and money markets as well as the product and labor markets. In the fourth part, we establish the total system dynamic model that contains major variables and parameters in the macroeconomy and their interactions. We use concrete numerical experiments to explore the evolution of macroeconomy. In the fifth part, we analyze and process relevant economic data in China's economic development and the practical economic evolution is observed in this way. The paper finally summarize the major work and results and discuss the possibility and direction of future developments.

*Supported by College Doctoral Project Funds of China.

1 Introduction

Different schools like Keynesian School, Currency School, Neo-classical School and New Keynesian School exist in the filed of macroeconomics. Many new schools will undoubtedly appear in the future. Different schools have different opinions and methods of research. The discussions among them have brought macroeconomics to the frontier of economic studies. Behind the complicated controversies and discussions, there are two basic facts that seem to be conflicting to each other, i.e. the ever-increasing interest of economists to macroeconomics and the ever-changing difficulties macroeconomics has encountered in the process of development. On the one hand, the attention to the growth and oscillation in the aggregates such as production, employment, income and price urges economists study macroeconomics, particularly macroeconomic dynamics so as to explain and illustrate the constant changing economic facts. On the other, the differences and controversies over theories show that economists have not yet reached a common understanding to the description and illustration of the process and mechanism of evolution of economic systems. Each school explains the laws and facts in the evolution of macroeconomic system separately, but there is no unified and complete theoretical basis by now. The publication of "the General Theory of Employment, Interest and Money" marked Keynesian economics as the leading theory in macroeconomics. Yet in the past decades, it has been increasingly criticized by different schools. The global economic growth after World War II challenges the economists. How to overcome the contradictions and controversies? How to establish a theory to explain the coexistence of growth and oscillation as well as inflation and unemployment? These have become questions macroeconomics has to answer.

People have reasons to set high requirements for macroeconomics. Since 1970s, the economy in South-eastern Asian countries has boomed. The reform and development in China in the past ten years needs economist provide reasonable explanations. So does the economic situation in former Soviet Union and Eastern European countries after the change in their political system. The fore-mentioned phenomena and the stimulus behind are not only the objects of study of politicians and policy-makers, but also those of macroeconomic dynamics.

Macroeconomics treats the national economy as a whole with its functions and evolution. Its objects of study are output, labor, price and other aggregates of macroeconomy that change with time and their specification. Macroeconomics tends to solve the major issues in social economy such as GNP and its growth rate, employment rate, price level and inflation rate etc. If we view with a deeper insight, the core issue of macroeconomics is the interaction of the equilibria of product, money and labor markets which form the total macroeconomic system, as well as the nonequilibrium dynamic process of the transition and evolution of these market equilibria. First of all, the total equilibrium of product, money and labor markets decide the balance level of GNP, employment and price as well as the mechanism that forms the equilibrium. A separate study of the properties in certain market equilibrium and the market factors that have impacts on the equilibrium constitute the local and quasi-static analysis by macroeconomics to the evolution behavior of the system. In addition, because the interactions of the markets are complicated and nonlinear, the local equilibrium will be influenced by the changes in the other markets. The change in one market caused by other markets will in return shows impact on other markets. This makes the three major markets in macroeconomics be in the interactive, inter-constraint state that is non-synchronous. The local equilibrium of each market is both associated and independent, which makes the macroeconomics constantly adjusts its system in order to satisfy the total equilibrium of the three balancing markets. The nonlinear interaction may lead to multiple local equilibria that form the manifold patterns of the total equilibrium and will finally show impacts over the transition and evolution of the equilibrium of the economic system. The nonequilibrium evolution process explains the constant growth and oscillations of economic aggregates.

The major task of macroeconomic dynamics is to use mathematical and particularly quantitative model methods to analyze the core issues mentioned above. Macroeconomic dynamic model that illustrates the evolution process of the macroeconomic system can be traced back to the time of Keynes' Model based on the theory of "effective demand controls supply". Such models have been criticized and modified by many Keynesian and non-Keynesian schools since the time of Hicks. By now a complete frame of model based on the Keynes' Model has been formed and has so far solved many core issues. The traditional IS-LM model bases itself on the equilibrium point of the product market and money market and discusses the specification of macroeconomic equilibrium and the quasi-static change when system diverges the equilibrium on the basis of full employment and fixed capital stock. Boldrin (1988) improved the traditional model by discussing the nonequilibrium process in which output, interest rate and capital stock interact and change together. He also provided the existence of the limit cycle under large-scale parameter value. Boldrin thus described the economic growth and oscillation under the situation of fixed price level and salary. Zhang Weibin (1992) further considered the changes in output and capital stock with technical progress.

The afore-mentioned work has different emphasis. But as a whole they cannot describe properly the total macroeconomic behavior that includes product, money and labor market. They cannot describe properly the nonequilibrium evolution process that is characterized by persistent growth and oscillation. Therefore they are partial or static models. In my opinion, in order to have a deeper understanding of the core issues of macroeconomic evolution, a macroeconomic evolution model that consists of product, money and labor markets should be created. The changes in demand and supply and the interactions among the three markets should be studied comprehensively. The properties and evolution law that governs individual market equilibrium and the total macroeconomic equilibrium should be analyzed. In this way, such major national economic variables as GNP, employment, inflation, salary and money supply can be identified. On this basis, the macroeconomic growth and oscillation and its dynamic evolution process can be explained. Due to the complicity of macroeconomic system, this work of building a reasonable total model is no doubt both difficult and challenging. In order to approach to this goal, we proceed from the following aspects.

First, the total model that includes product, money and labor markets becomes much complicated due to the nonlinear interactions. Therefore it is very difficult to use quantitative methods to solve such issues. We use analytic methods to analyze the interactions between two of the markets and then establish a dynamic model of system evolution. With the improvements in the equations to the direction of practical economic development, we have made some detailed descriptions of different aspects of the evolution of the macroeconomic system. Our aim is to provide an understanding of the complete law of macroeconomic evolution. We proceed from two aspects: on the one hand, we take into consideration of product market and money market that form the macroeconomic system. Then we introduce variable money supply and total supply and associate them with the fluctuation of capital stock. So the constant growth and fluctuation caused by the changes in the economic environment such as changes in technology and the interactions between products and money markets are reflected. We also introduce difference equations to describe the sticky change in the practical price level. Through numerical simulations, the unity of constant growth and oscillation---the two basic phenomena in the macroeconomic evolution is clarified. On the other hand, we consider the macroeconomic system formed by the product and labor markets. We put emphasis on the decisive impact of interactions between demand and supply on the economic equilibrium and evolution. We introduce production potential, possible production demand, possible labor demand and labor resources. We also used logistic equations that can finely reflect the constrained dynamic growth to form the dynamic system model that describes the macroeconomic growth and oscillation decided by demand and supply.

In addition, we use the methods of numerical experiments to understand system evolution laws and characteristics. All the works above-mentioned use theoretical analysis to explore the dynamic mechanism of macroeconomic system evolution. Due to the complicity and difficulty of the issue, the models established by using these methods can only partly describe the system evolution as a whole. We cannot fully understand the internal interactions of macroeconomic systems. In order to have a full understanding of the nonequilibrium dynamic process, we must use both theoretical analysis and numerical experiments. Through simulating macroeconomic evolution process, we can understand the interactions among the internal variables and those between internal and external environments. In this way, the theoretical studies become deeper than before. We use the numerical experiments of system dynamics and the integrated computer software to create a total model that includes such major macroeconomic variables and parameters as output, capital stock, investment, labor, price, interest rate and salary level. Through observing macroeconomic evolution, we abstract the laws and interactions so as to recognize the complicity of the economic system.

At last, we move our attention to the practical economic growth. We notice that the study of macroeconomic system evolution mechanism benefit not only theoretical studies but also practical work. The changing economic reality constantly challenges macroeconomic studies and examines the authenticity and feasibility of the theories. We collect China's GNP growth rate, price index, interest rate and many other major economic index numbers and data. We use index regression analysis and Fourier transformation to observe the growth and oscillation in Chinese macroeconomic evaluation. We also examined and improved the dynamic model for macroeconomic system through this application.

2 The Dynamic Model under Changes in Supply and Price

In the early works of nonlinear analysis, Richard Goodwin (1951) used the limit cycle in a two-dimensional dynamic model to illustrate the constant economic oscillation under multiple accelerations. In 1980s, Guguo/Montoarchio (1983) introduced constant price changes on the basis of Kaldor's Model and Boldrin's Model (1983). They used the Hopf's bifurcation theory to prove the existence of periodical solution of economic system. We consider a macroeconomic system that includes both product market and money market by analyzing interactions among markets and by creating nonlinear dynamic models that depict system evolution(Di, Z./Fang, F.(1994)). In comparison with other works, there are two characteristics of our model. First, other works assume the stability of money supply and total supply. Therefore, they can only describe the short-term oscillation. We introduce changeable external environments that may lead to long-term growth and changing total supply and capital stock as well as their interactions. We discuss the impact of interactions between the evolving product market and money market on the macroeconomic growth and oscillation. In addition, in Cuguo and Montoarchio's models, the description of price change is continuous while actual price adjustment is mostly sticky. Therefore it has relative stability in the short-term. We have introduced difference-differential equation system to reflect the changing property of the actual price level. We have formed the following models:

$$dY/dt = \alpha[I(Y,K,R) - S(Y,R)] \tag{2.1}$$

$$I(Y,K,R) = a\{(1-bR) + 1 - \exp[-(\tfrac{Y}{K})^2/2\mu^2]\}Y \tag{2.2}$$

$$S(Y,R) = cRY \tag{2.3}$$

where Y denotes actual output and I denotes investment, $\partial I/\partial Y > 0, \partial I/\partial R < 0, \partial I/\partial K < 0$, a, b, α, μ are positive parameters. S denotes savings which satisfies $\partial S/\partial Y > 0, \partial S/\partial R > 0$, c is a positive constant.

$$dK/dt = I - \beta K \tag{2.4}$$

$$dR/dt = v[M_d(Y,R,P) - M(t)] \tag{2.5}$$

$$M_d(Y,R,P) = PY \cdot \varphi(R+\pi) \tag{2.6}$$

where K is capital stock, R is actual interest rate, P is price level and M_d is money demand. π denotes inflation rate and $M(t)$ is changing money supply. $\varphi(R+\pi) = 1 - d(R+\pi)$ and d, β, v are positive parameters.

$$Y^* = AK^m L^{1-m} \tag{2.7}$$

where Y^* is total supply and L is labor supply. A is a positive constant.

$$dP/dt = fP(Y - Y^*) \qquad \text{elastic} \tag{2.8}$$

$$P_t = P_{t-1} + fP_{t-1}(Y_{t-1} - Y^*_{t-1})$$

$$\pi = (1/P)\cdot dP/dt$$

$$\pi = (P_t - P_{t-1})/P_{t-1}$$

The six equations in actual output, capital stock, intere
level and inflation rate together with other functions c
dynamic evolution of the macroeconomic system. Mone
supply $L(t)$ provided, under some initial conditions
discuss core issues like growth in the macroeconomic sys
and inflation within full employment. Through mathem
get different evolution processes when parameters α,
adjustment speed of total output, interest rate and price le
values.

If $Y^* = 1$ and $M = 0.8$, price adjusts elastically and th
four-dimensional differential dynamic system. If α=
$f = 0.13$, the model shows stable periodical oscillati
without growth. This result, like theoretical analysi
assumption that total supply and money supply are fixed.

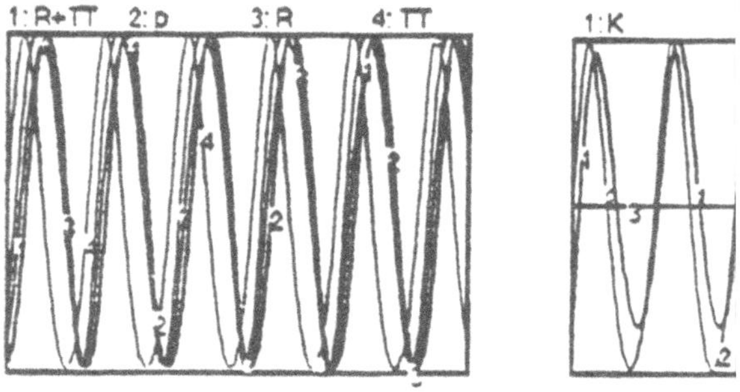

Figure 2.1. a=0.1 n=0.1 f=0.13

3 Dynamic Model Created by Demand and

Among the factors that have impact on macroecon
addition to the changing total supply, money supply a
the interactions of product market and money market,
market's internal supply and demand are also very
consider the conflicts between effective demand theory
and restraint by demand and supply to the economic gr
economists. From the view of interactions, economic
demand and supply. Under certain economic conditi
realized by using the maximum products and labor pr
resources in the society. Whereas within the pos
production demand is realized by the maximum need t
by consumption and investment. The demand and sup
situation together decide the actual quantity of
macroeconomic system at a certain time, i.e. actual o
interactions and constraints between capital and
consumption and investment pull and constrain econo
output and employment. Through analysis of model
among production potential, labor resources and possi
of factors that have impact on production potential a
describe the evolution process of the macroeconomic
We take into consideration of the economic system
market and the labor market by using logistic equa
dynamic evolution process created by the interactio
demand and supply in the two markets(Li, K./
assumption of sufficient use of capital stock and no
the following:

$$dY/dt = \alpha Y[1-(1/2)(1/Y_d + 1/Y_s)Y]$$

$$dL/dt = \beta L[1-(1/2)(1/L_d + 1/L_s)L]$$

$$dP/dt = \eta P(1 - Y/Y_d)$$

$$dK/dt = Y - C - \xi K$$

$$Y_d = Y_d(Y, M)$$

$$Y_s = Y_s(K, P)$$

$$C = C(Y)$$

$$L_d = L_d(K, Y)$$

where Y denotes actual output, L denotes employmen
and K denotes capital stock. Y_d is possible productic
potential, L_s is labor resources and L_d is possible
consumption and M denotes money supply and $\alpha, \beta,$

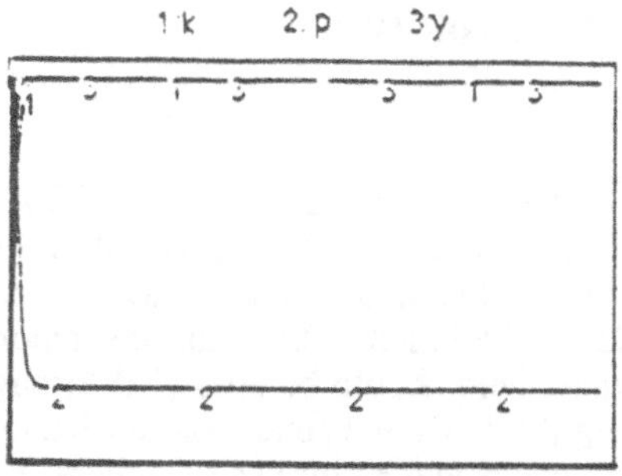

Figure 3.1. Stability

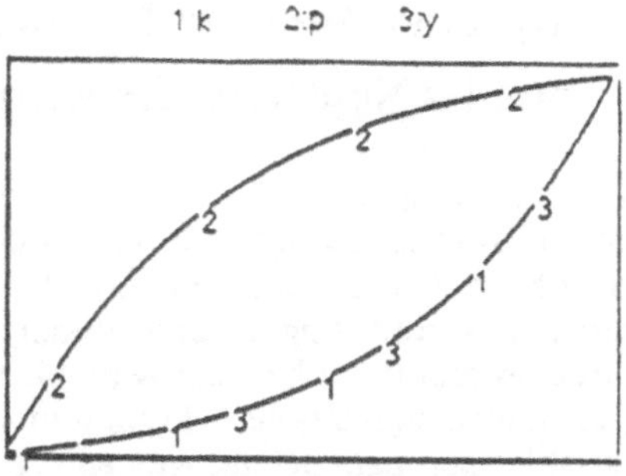

Figure 3.2. Growth

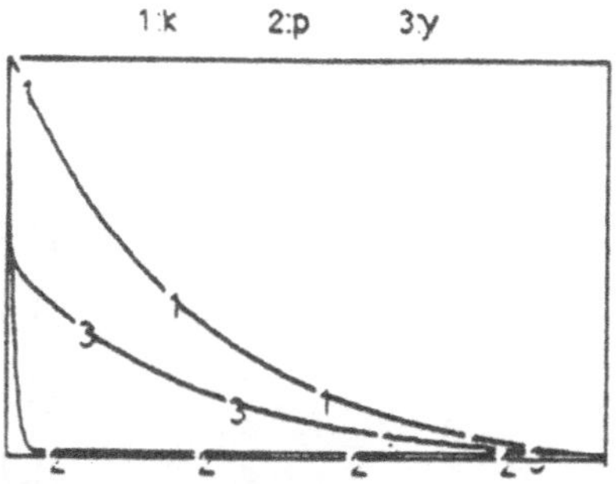

Figure 3.3. Decay

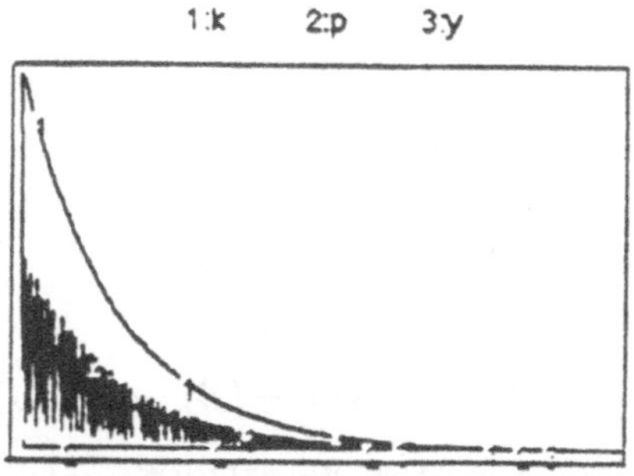

Figure 3.4. Oscillation

The first four equations depict the dynamic evolution process respectively in actual output, employment level, price level and capital stock decided by the interactions of demand and supply. If possible production demand Y_d, production potential Y_s, possible labor demand L_d and consumption level C are embodied with concrete functions, we can discuss the evolution process within adequate use of capital. In order to facilitate the description of deciding factors of interactions of demand and supply to the actual output, we do not consider equation (3.2) first. If we assume the equilibrium in labor market, under certain parameters, we may obtain the evolution behavior of actual output Y, capital stock K and price level P in the macroeconomic system.

Under different initial conditions and parameters, the system shows complicated dynamic behaviors, such as stability, growth, decay and fluctuation. Refer to Figure 3.1., 3.2., 3.3. and 3.4.

4 Dynamic Model of Macroeconomic Evolution and Its Numerical Experiments

It is not enough to have a theoretical model limited in analytical mode. In addition, for the macroeconomic evolution studies, there should be a descriptive model of the total system based on numerical simulations. In this model, major variables and parameters reflecting macroeconomy should be included. The relations among variables and those between variables and parameters should be specified through quantitative simulations. Through investigating the roles and functions of different variables and parameters, we can provide references and examples of general law and mechanism of macroeconomic evolution. Parallel to the afore-mentioned theoretical model analysis, we establishe a total model that depicts product, money and labor markets by using numerical experiment in system dynamics and Ithink software(Li, H./Fang, F.(1994)).

$$dK/dt = I - d_c K \tag{4.1}$$

$$Y_s = Y_s(K, L) = \min(b_k K, L \cdot pL) = b_k K \tag{4.2}$$

$$dpL/dt = gpl \cdot pL \tag{4.3}$$

$$Y_d = C + I \tag{4.4}$$

$$Y = \min(Y_s, Y_d) \tag{4.5}$$

$$C_t = (1-s)[(1-h)Y_{t-1} + dM/p] + hY_{t-1} \tag{4.6}$$

$$I = (d_c + glp)\exp[a(R_{t-1} - r_{t-1})] \tag{4.7}$$

$$dLp/dt = glp \cdot Lp \tag{4.8}$$

$$R = (Y - wL/p)/K \tag{4.9}$$

$$r = l_0/(M/k_c pY - 1) \tag{4.10}$$

$$1/p \cdot dp/dt = j_1 ip_{t-1} + j_2(Y_d - Y_s)/Y_s \tag{4.11}$$

$$L = Y/b_k \tag{4.12}$$

$$u = 1 - L/N \tag{4.13}$$

$$gw = ip_t - j_3(u - u_0) + gpl \tag{4.14}$$

$$dM/dt = gmM \tag{4.15}$$

where K denotes capital stock; Y_s denotes production potential; pL denotes output per capita; Y_d is effective demand; Y is actual output; C_t is consumption; I is investment; Lp is labor resources and R is average profit rate. r denotes interest rate; p denotes price level; L is employment; u is unemployment rate; gw is salary increase rate and M is money stock. d_c is depreciation rate; b_k is capital output; gpl is output increase rate per labor; glp is labor increase rate; s is the rate of savings; *ip* is inflation rate; *w* is salary; *h* is tax ratio in GNP; *gm* is real money stock increase rate, k_c is the reciprocal of capital circulation rate; j_1, j_2, j_3, a are positive parameters and *gy* is GNP growth rate.

The above model is built on the following framework: money market decides interest rate and decides investment together with the expected profit in product market. Therefore the present effective demand and future supply will be increased. Present demand and supply together decide present output and can further decide present employment rate.

Numerical experiment simulates the evolution process at different parameters and initial stages. Figure 4.1. and 4.2. provide a evolution result.

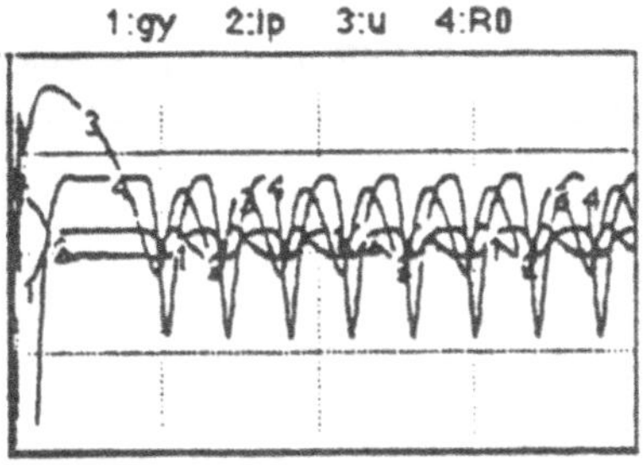

Figure 4.1.

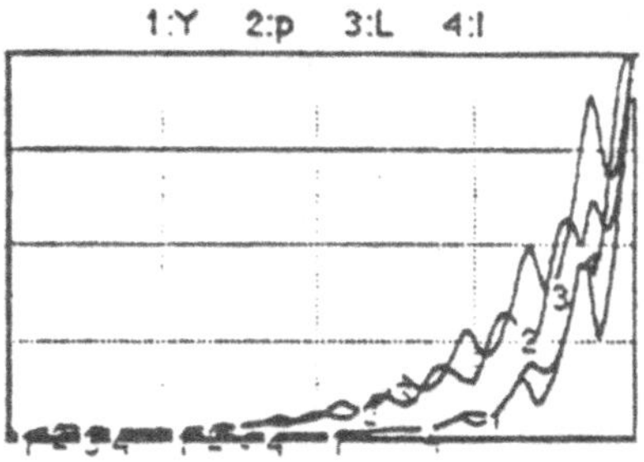

Figure 4.2.

This result reflects the complicity and diversity of macroeconomic system evolution. On the one hand, the nonlinear relation among variables and between variables and parameters has become the internal stimulus of system evolution. It illustrates the basic evolution characteristic of the unity of fluctuation and growth. Besides, due to the endogenuity of evolution, economic growth and fluctuation have a strong lasting effect. It is not like those in the multiplier-acceleration model (Gabisch/Lorenz (1987)) that are easy to diverge or slow down. On the other hand, the nonlinear interactions between variables and parameters in the system make the concrete mode of evolution complicated and diversified. In specific parameters, the change in the parameter shows a non-monotonous impact on the periodical behavior of variables. This complicated association between variable, parameter states and system evolution results decides the importance of making suitable response and selecting good state and policy parameters through improving economic environment and adjusting economic structure and policy. We can see from the simulation that proper parameters selected are decisive in a stable and fast economic development.

References

Boldrin, M. (1983): Applying Bifurcation Theory: Some Simple Results on the Keynesian Business Cycle. Note di Lavoro #8403, Dip. di Scienze Economiche, Univ. di Venezia.

Boldrin, M. (1988): Persistent Oscillations and Chaos in Dynamic Economic Models: Notes for a Survey. in Anderson, P./Arrow, K./Pines, D. (eds.): *The Economy as an Evolving Complex System.* Addison Wesley

Chang, W./Smith, D. J. (1971): The Existence and Persistence of Cycles in a Nonlinear Model: Kaldor's 1940 Model Reexamined. *Review of Economic Studies 38*

Cugno, F./Montrucchio, L. (1983): Disequilibrium Dynamics in a Multidimensional Macroeconomic Model: A Bifurcation Approach. *Richerche Economiche XXXVII*

Di, Z./Fang, F. (1994): An Dynamic Economic Model with Changeable Supply and Prices. Manuscript.

Goodwin, R. M. (1951): The Nonlinear Accelerator and the Persistence of Business Cycles. *Econometrica 19*

Han, Z./Fang, F. (1994): Growth and Fluctuation Analysis of Chinese Economy. Submitted to IC^2S^3

Li, H./Fang, F. (1994): A Dynamic Model and Numerical Experiment on the Evolution of Macroeconomic. Submitted to Inter. confer. on the Complexity and Self-organization in Socioeconomic Systems. Beijing. (IC^2S^3)

Li, K./Fang, F. (1994): A Macroeconomic Dynamic Model under Supply-Demand Interaction. Submitted to IC^2S^3

Gabisch, G./Lorenz, H. (1987): *Business Cycle Theory.* Springer Verlag

Zhang, W. (1992): *Synergetic Economics.* Springer Verlag

Economic Cycles in a Behavioral Disequilibrium Perspective

Erik Mosekilde[1] and John D. Sterman[2]
[1]Physics Department, Technical University of Denmark, 2800 Lyngby, Denmark
[2]Sloan School of Management, MIT, Cambridge, MA 02139, USA

Abstract. We review the characteristic features of the main economic cycles and discuss the behavioral foundation for each mode at the microlevel. The analysis continues to illustrate some of the nonlinear dynamic phenomena that can arise through interaction between the various modes and through coupling between the different sectors of the economy.

Keywords. Entrainment, economic cycles, bounded rationality, nonlinear phenomena

1 Introduction

Cyclical fluctuations are characteristic and persistent features of economic life. Throughout the century economic statisticians have identified several distinct modes of behavior, including the 3-7 year business cycle (Mitchell, 1927; Moore, 1961; Zarnowitz, 1985), the 15-25 year construction or Kuznets cycle (Riggleman, 1933; Long, 1940; Kuznets, 1973), and the 40-60 year Kondratieff cycle or economic long wave (Kondratieff, 1935; van Duijn, 1983). The existence of these cycles is not without controversy, however. Debate continues today about the causes of the short-term business cycle, and the causes or even the existence of the longer cycles are still more controversial.

In part the controversy is empirical. Business cycles are not at all regular and constant in amplitude and period. At certain times they almost seem to disappear to emerge again and cause significant variations in industrial production, capacity utilization, unemployment, and other indices. As an illustration, Figure 1 shows the variation in capacity utilization for US manufacturing industries over the period from 1947 through 1989. In this plot we observe a series of minima, perhaps with five such minima between 1947 and 1965 (average period between minima app. 3 years) and with three significantly larger minima from 1967 to 1989 (average period between minima app. 6 years). As measured in terms of the distance to the saturation level at 100% capacity utilization, the amplitude of these fluctuations is clearly so large that nonlinear phenomena must be expected. The presence of such effects are also evident from the lack of symmetry between the maxima and the minima.

Figure 2 illustrates the corresponding variation in US civilian unemployment rate. There is a clear relation between high values of unemployment and low values of capacity utilization. However, the problem here is not only whether the business cycle itself is produced by systematic mechanisms related to the

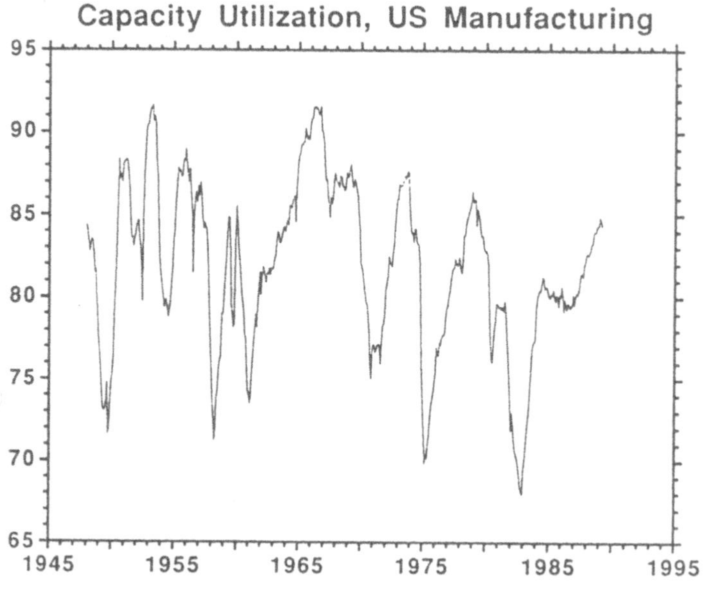

Fig. 1. Capacity utilization in US manufacturing industries. Note the recurrent minima, but also the variation in the period between these. With characteristic amplitudes and phase shifts, the short-term business cycle manifests clearly in a host of aggregate and industrial level data, including inventory coverage, help wanted advertising, interest rates, etc.

Fig. 2. Variation in US civilian unemployment. The apparent shift in behavior from the first two decades to the last two decades may be related to the changing phases of the economic long wave.

structure of the economy. The question is also whether the observed variations in periodicity and amplitude of this cycle have systematic causes, related, for instance, to its interaction with other modes of the economy.

Is there a tendency for the business cycles to be relatively small and fast during the upswing phases of the economic long wave to grow in amplitude and duration during the downswing phases? As soon as we start to ask such questions, conventional linear identification methods are no longer useful, and a completely new perspective for the behavior of the economic system arises.

For the long wave itself, the empirical difficulties are even more pronounced: At its best, 3-4 cycles of the wave can be documented (Kleinknecht, 1984; Rasmussen et al., 1989), and they have occurred over such a long time span that almost every aspect of economic life has changed. Despite these difficulties, the inability of conventional policies to reduce the unacceptable unemployment numbers and balance the enormous public deficits that have below the level required for replacements until the excess has been fully depreciated and room for a new expansion created.

In its simplest form the Sterman model is meant to isolate the minimal structure required to produce 40-60 year oscillations with economically realistic mechanisms and parameters. In a series of papers (Mosekilde et al. 1992 and 1993) we have analysed how mode-locking and other nonlinear dynamic phenomena may arise by forcing the simple long wave model with a sinusoidal signal representing the influence of other modes in the economy. An early study by Kampmann (1984) took a first step in the direction of studying the interaction of several capital producing sectors with different parameters. Kampmann showed how the multi-sector model could produce a range of different behaviors, at times quite different from the original one-sector model. We are presently pursuing this problem in more detail (Haxholdt et al., 1995) by determining the type of behavior which arises for different sets of parameter values. For many such sets within the range of realistic values, the model produces deterministic chaos. Hence, we are led to the conclusion that relatively simple and well documented economic mechanisms can lead to extremely complex dynamics, emphasizing the need for new approaches in the study of economic behavior.

2 The Behavioral Foundation

To clarify the mechanisms by which oscillations arise in the economy let us consider a manufacturing company in equilibrium with its various markets (Sterman and Mosekilde, 1994). Let us assume that the firm is small enough relative to its labor, capital and other input markets, so that factor prices can be considered constant. Interaction with these markets as well as with the financial and public sector provides some of the main mechanisms by which individual firms become entrained with one another so as to produce coherent aggregate cycles. It is of interest, however, first to consider the behavioral foundations of these cycles at the microlevel. Now consider the firm's response to a step increase in incoming orders. The company may eventually expand material consumption, work force, capital stock, etc. to meet orders. The interesting point, however, is how the transient towards the new equilibrium unfolds.

If all inputs could be adjusted immediately, the transient would be fast and nonoscillatory. However, factor inputs cannot change right away. Backlogs and inventories buffer the production line from short-term variations in demand to provide time for efficient adjustment of inputs. In fact, immediately following the unanticipated demand increase, the firm may not change production at all, until it becomes clear that the incoming orders will remain at the new, higher level. During this period inventories necessarily fall while, on the other hand, desired inventory may increase as the expected throughput rises. To restore inventories, the firm must now increase production above the rate of incoming orders for at least some time. As a consequence, orders for materials and intermediate goods must also increase above the rate of incoming orders, passing a larger disturbance on to the supplying industries. This process, the familiar inventory accelerator (Forrester, 1976; Thomsen et al., 1992; Towill, 1992), provides an explanation for the amplification of the business cycle from consumer goods sector through the intermediate goods and finally to the raw materials sector.

Provided that the needed materials are available, small changes in output may be accomplished quickly through more intensive use of existing employees (overtime). From a control theoretic point of view, the use of workweek to regulate inventory creates an effective first-order negative feedback loop which is non-oscillatory and adds damping to the system (Sterman, 1988). However, the workweek response is limited by the cost of overtime and by decreasing worker productivity after long workweeks. Thus, while small amplitude changes in demand can be accommodated through overtime, larger and more persistent changes require expansion of the work force.

Expansion of the work force, however, involves significant delays. Vacancies must be authorized, new employees hired and trained, and time must pass before productivity rises to that of experienced workers (comparable delays exist in the case of an unexpected decrease in demand). The use of employment to control inventory levels and respond to demand shocks creates a negative feedback loop, but unlike the workweek loop, this loop involves delays on the order of several months or more. Negative feedback loops with such phase lag elements tend to be oscillatory. The characteristic behavior of models that portray workweek and work force adjustments with realistic decision parameters is damped oscillations with a period of 3 to 7 years (Forrester, 1982). These models also generate the phase and amplitude relationships observed in data for output, employment, inventories, delivery delay, vacancies, labor accession, and other variables. The business cycle these models generate is robust as the boundary of the model expands to include consumer demand, interest rates, monetary and fiscal policies, and other elements of the traditional aggregate supply/aggregate demand models (Mass, 1975).

Regulation of output by work force adjustment is also limited due to diminishing returns as labor expands relative to existing plant and equipment. In the long run, capital stocks must also be increased. However, capital investment involves even longer delays arising from the processes of planning for, ordering, and constructing new plant and equipment. Adjustment of capital stocks thus involves a negative feedback loop with substantially longer delays. Models that integrate capital investment with inventory and work force management tend to produce oscillations with periods of 15-20 years in addition to the short-term cycle (Mass, 1975; Forrester, 1982).

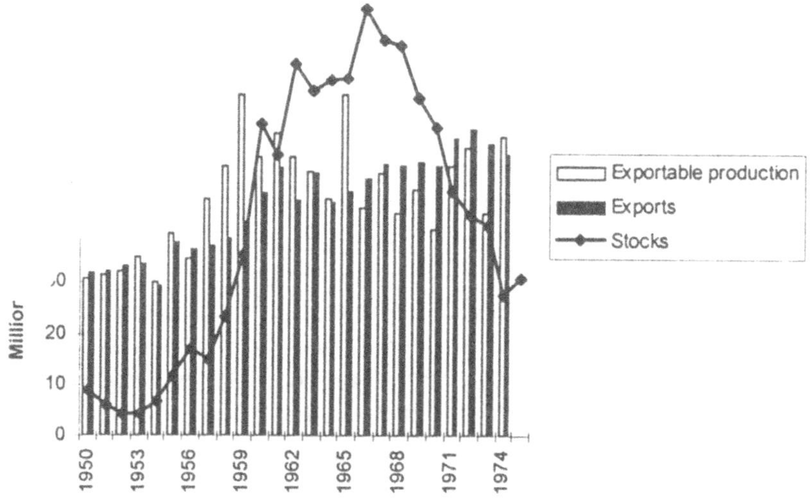

Fig. 4. Variation in exportable production and exports of coffee. Also shown is the variation in producers' stocks. (Sources: United Nations Commodity Survey and Pan American Coffee Bureau: Annual Coffee Statistics).

As an illustration of this phenomenon, Figure 4 shows the variation in total exportable production and actual exports from the coffee producing countries during the period 1950-1975. For comparison we have also plotted the variation in the producers' stocks of coffee in millions of bags each weighing 60 kg. Figure 5 shows the corresponding variation in the New York spot prices for coffee of quality "Other Milds". The spot price is given in 1975 US c/lb. The conversion from current prices was made by means of the US wholesale price index.

As revealed by these figures, the period up till 1956 was characterized by relatively low stocks and high prices. During this period the market was expanding partly as a result of the rapidly improving conditions in Europe after the first postwar years. As a consequence of the favorable conditions, a considerable expansion of the production capacity (coffee fields) took place in Latin America as well as in many African countries. Five to six years

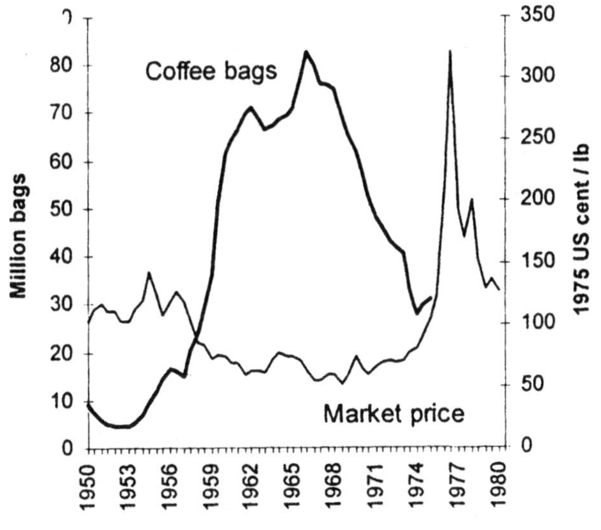

Fig. 5. Variation in coffee prices vis-à-vis the development in producers' stocks. Faced with the low prices, the producers acquired very little new capacity between 1957 and 1975, and by the time prices started to rise, the market had been operating with insufficient production capacity for more than a decade.

production capacity was too small, a price signal to invest in new capacity did not occur until nearly a decade later.

Our behavioral description of the adjustment processes assumes that decision makers have bounded rationality in the sense of Simon (1979, 1982). At the same time it recognizes that firms partition the problem of optimizing the enterprise into subproblems. Production and worktime is typically influenced by decisions at the plant level, while prizing may be the responsibility of senior divisional management, and capital investment may be decided at corporate headquarters. Due to limitations in time, information availability, and attentional resources, management of the subsystems may be imperfectly coordinated.

The theory of bounded rationality does not assume that the individual managers are irrational, but rather locally or intendedly rational - that is, they use heuristics which would work well if the couplings among subsystems were weak, and the separability assumption implicit in task factoring within the firm were valid. Agents seek to take appropriate decisions. However, by virtue of the complexity of the high order, nonlinear, randomly exited dynamic system in which they operate, agents are not assumed to possess the cognitive and other resources necessary to operate optimally.

3 Nonlinear Interactions

Linear theories are applicable to small variations around a stable equilibrium point. However, the excursions we observe in time series for many economic variables are so large that linear descriptions clearly will not suffice. Nonlinear phenomena show up as deformations of the wave form of the individual modes or as interactions between these modes. Such interactions can again give rise to a range of different phenomena including synchronization and frequency-locking between the modes or changes in the behavioral characteristics of the shorter term modes dependent on the phase of the longer term modes. Frequency-locking is a universal phenomenon by which oscillatory components of different periodicities in nonlinear systems may adjust themselves until the periods become commensurate. In the locked state one mode will complete precisely p cycles each time the other mode completes q cycles, where p and q are integers.

Examples of nonlinear distortions in the wave forms of the various economic modes are illustrated in the variation of the capacity utilization in US manufacturing industries (Figure 1), the variation of US civilian unemployment (Figure 2), and the variation of New York spot prices for coffee (Figure 5). Clearly, the maxima in unemployment tend to be sharper than the minima. This asymmetry implies that the system operates differently in the two phases of the business cycle. A simple explanation could be that the system saturates as the unemployment approaches a certain lower limit and that the corresponding elasticity therefore changes. In a completely analogous manner, the minima in the capacity utilization tend to be sharper than the maxima, and also the variation in coffee prices is very different from the simple sinusoidal wave form characteristic of linear systems.

We have already discussed the indications that the business cycle is weaker in amplitude and shorter in period during phases of long wave expansion than during stagnation or recession phases. This is an example of a variation in the behavioral characteristics of one mode in dependence of the phase of another. This type of interaction makes it extremely difficult to use conventional statistical methods to identify the economic modes. A related phenomenon appears in the form of a shift in the amplitude of the short term modulation between the quantity variable and the corresponding price variable. Typically, the short term inventory-workforce cycle will be most pronounced in production volume during periods of low capacity utilization for the construction cycle and most pronounced in the price variable during periods of high capacity utilization. This has been observed, for instance, for the tanker and paper markets (Mosekilde et al., 1993). A more detailed examination of the variation in coffee prices confirms this picture.

If the economic system were linear, the cyclic responses to external perturbations produced by different firms, industries, and nations would evolve independently of one another, and the total behavior would be a linear superposition of the individual responses. The frequency and damping in these responses would clearly depend of the structure of the company, its production and inventory coverage times, the life time of its capital components, the composition of its workforce, the hiring and instruction times for new employees, etc. Hence, while individual companies might experience relatively large fluctuations, the aggregate over many independent oscillatory modes is likely to exhibit a noise-like, low amplitude character, and there would not be a business cycle.

Recognizing this problem many business cycle theories rely on a synchronization between the responses via common external variables such as government monetary or fiscal policies, changes in aggregate demand, or highly correlated external shocks. Nonlinear interactions between the oscillatory subunits clearly offer an alternative, endogenous explanation. Unfortunately, macroeconomic theory has so far been largely silent about this possibility.

Frequency-locking is well documented for a variety of different physical, chemical, technical and biological systems (Glass et al., 1986; Togeby and Mosekilde, 1988). As previously mentioned, we have performed a series of investigations of a sinusoidal forced version of the simple long wave model (Mosekilde et al., 1992; Mosekilde et al., 1993). This has provided us with an impression of how the economic long wave might frequency-lock with the shorter term Kuznets and business cycles. However, frequency-locking and synchronization may be even more important in understanding how the various sectors of the economy interact to produce the observed complicated variations in the aggregate economic variables.

As an example of nonlinear mode-interaction in the economy, Figure 6 shows a phase diagram for the distribution of modes in a two sector economic long wave model (Haxholdt et al., 1995). The model describes the interaction between two capital producing sectors. One sector might represent the construction of buildings and infrastructure capital with long lifetimes, while the other represents production of machinery, transport means, computers, etc., with much shorter lifetimes. Due to the positive feedback associated with capital self-ordering, each sector in isolation produces a self-sustained oscillation with a period and amplitude determined by the characteristics of that sector.

However, machinery production requires buildings and infrastructure, and construction of buildings and infrastructure involves machinery and transport means. When these dependencies are taken into account, the self-ordering loop weakens. At the same time, however, the system acquires the ability to exhibit a broad variety of highly nonlinear dynamical phenomena. The production capacity in each sector is assumed to be described by a constant-returns-to-scale Cobb-Douglas function of the stocks of the two capital types with a factor share α of the other sector's capital type and a share $1-\alpha$ of the sector's own capital type. This defines the coupling parameter $\alpha \in [0, 1]$. The other parameter in the phase diagram is the difference in lifetimes between the two types of capital. The average capital lifetime is taken to be $\tau = 20$ years, and with a lifetime difference $\Delta\tau$, the lifetimes of the two capital types are defined to be $\tau_1 = \tau + \Delta\tau/2$ and $\tau_2 = \tau - \Delta\tau/2$, respectively.

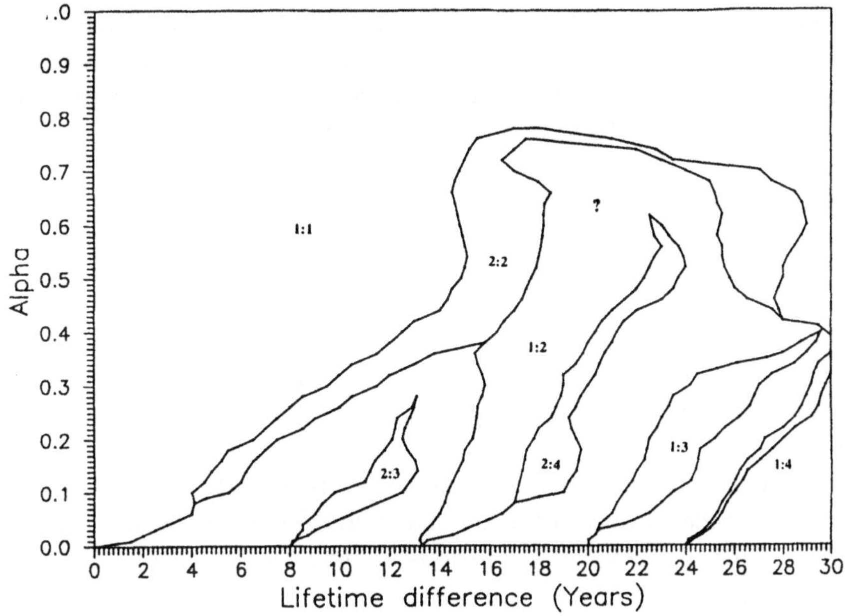

Fig. 6. Phase diagram for the two-sector long wave model. The parameters are the coupling strength α and the difference in lifetimes between the capital produced by the two sectors.

In the phase diagram we have plotted the regions of the main frequency-locking zones (the so-called Arnol'd tongues). The diagram was obtained by simulating the coupled model for a very large set of parameter combinations and determining in each case the character of the final stationary behavior. This technique is sometimes referred to as carpet bombing. We are presently redoing the diagram with the means of continuation techniques which allow a more precise determination of the bifurcation curves in parameter space.

Interaction between the various modes and sectors of the economy clearly play a major role in generating the apparent complexity.

In this connection it is worth emphasizing that although deterministic chaos may be indistinguishable from random noise in certain simple statistical tests, the two types of behavior are very different. First of all chaos is a deterministic phenomenon which is predictable over a certain time horizon. As a consequence, chaotic dynamics can be stabilized and controlled through policies which are fundamentally different from the policies that one would apply to reduce the fluctuations of a random system. For the same reason, the popular notion that deterministic chaos implies that planning is in vain is incorrect. Actually, the opposite is true. If the fluctuations we see in economic time series were completely random, planning would be difficult. As soon as the fluctuations have a deterministic component, we can start to predict, control, plan, or speculate.

Secondly, chaos is a nonlinear phenomenon. We have previously noted that the response of a chaotic system to en external perturbation can depend crucially on the phase of the system. On the other hand, with an appropriate model we can predict when the system is moving into a particularly fragile regime, and hence take our precautions. Another characteristics of nonlinear systems which distinguishes them from linear systems is the infinite detail in their parameter variation. This is clearly illustrated by the bifurcation diagrams in figure 7. A small change in a parameter can qualitatively change the behavior of the system, e.g., from being chaotic into being periodic.

Actual economic systems are seldom stationary. If they exhibit complex nonlinear dynamics phenomena we must picture them as drifting slowly in parameter space, presumably crossing a bifurcation plane from time to time. This makes any form of time series analysis extremely difficult. In particular, the common practice of detrending economic time series is likely to produce results which are hard to interpret.

Acknowledgment

Thanks are due to Henrik Mosekilde for preparing the figures. C. Haxholdt and C. Kampmann have performed the analysis of the two-sector long-wave model.

References

Dosi, G. et al. (1988), *Technical Change and Economic Theory*, Pinter, London.

Forrester, J.W. (1976), Business Structure, Economic Cycles, and National Policy, *Futures* 8, 195-214.

Forrester, N. (1982), *A Dynamic Synthesis of Basic Macroeconomic Theory: Implications for Stabilization Policy Analysis*, Ph.D. Dissertation, Sloan School of Management, MIT, Cambridge, MA.

Glass, L., A. Schrier and J. Belair (1986), Chaotic Cardiac Rhythms, *Chaos* (A. Holden, ed.), Manchester University Press, Manchester.

Haxholdt, C., C. Kampmann, E. Mosekilde and J.D. Sterman (1995), Entrainment in a Disaggregated Economic long Wave Model, *System Dynamics Review* 11, 177-198.

Haxholdt, C., C. Kampmann, E. Mosekilde and J.D. Sterman (1996), *Dynamic Phenomena of Coupled Economic Sectors*, in preparation.

Kampmann, C.E. (1984), *Disaggregating a Simple Model of the Economic Long Wave*, Working Paper # D-3641, Sloan School of Management, MIT, Cambridge, MA.

Kleinknecht, A. (1984), *Prosperity, Crises, and Innovation Patterns*, Cambridge Journal of Economics 8 (3).

Kondratieff, N.D. (1928/1984), *The Long Wave Cycle*, (G. Daniels, tr.), Richardson and Snyder, New York.

Kuznets, S. (1973), *Modern Economic Growth: Findings and Reflections*, American Economic Review 63, 247-258.

Long, C.D. Jr. (1940), *Building Cycles and the Theory of Investment*, Princeton University Press, New Jersey.

Mass, N. (1975), *Economic Cycles: An Analysis of Underlying Causes*, MIT Press /Productivity Press, Cambridge, MA.

Mitchell, W.C. (1927), *Business Cycles: The Problem ans Its Setting*, National Bureau of Economic Research, New York.

Moore, H.G. (ed.) (1961), *Business Cycle Indicators*, National Bureau of Economic Research, Princeton University Press, New Jersey.

Mosekilde, E., E.R. Larsen, J.D. Sterman, and J.S. Thomsen (1992), *Nonlinear Mode-Interaction in the Macroeconomy*, Annals of Operations Research 37, 185-215.

Mosekilde, E., E.R. Larsen, J.D. Sterman, and J.S. Thomsen (1993), *Mode-Locking and Nonlinear Entrainment of Macroeconomic Cycles*, Nonlinear Dynamics and Evolutionary Economics (R.H. Day and P. Chen, eds.), Oxford University Press.

Mosekilde, E. and S. Rasmussen (1986), *Technical Economic Succession and the Economic Long Wave*, European Journal of Operational Research 25, 27-38.

Rasmussen, S., E. Mosekilde, and J. Holst (1989), *Empirical Indication of Economic Long Waves in Aggregate Production*, European Journal of Operational Research 42, 279-293.

Riggleman, J.R. (1933), *Building Cycles in the United States,1897 - 1932*, Journal of the American Statistical Association 28, 182.

Silverberg, G. (1988), *Modeling Economic Dynamics and Technical Change: Mathematical Approach to Self-Organization and Evolution*, in Dosi et al. (eds.) Technical Change and Economic Theory. Pinter, London.

Simon, H. (1979), *Rational Decisionmaking in Business Organizations*, American Economic Review 69, 493-513.

Simon, H. (1982), *Models of Bounded Rationality*, MIT Press, Cambridge, MA.

Sterman, J.D. (1985), *A Behavioral Model of the Economic Long Wave*, Journal of Economic Behavior and Organization 6, 17-53.

Sterman, J.D. (1986), *The Economic Long Wave: Theory and Evidence*, Systems Dynamics Review 2, 87-125.

Sterman, J.D. (1988), *Nonlinear Dynamics in the World Economy: The Economic Long Wave*, Structure, Coherence and Chaos in Dynamical Systems (P.L. Christiansen and R. Parmentier, eds.), Manchester University Press, Manchester.

Stermann, J.D. and E. Mosekilde (1994), *Business Cycles and Long Waves: A Behavioral Disequilibrium Perspective*, in Semmler (ed.) Business Cycles: Theory and Empirical Methods. Kluwer Academic Publishers, Dordrecht.

Thomsen, J.S., E. Mosekilde, and J.D. Sterman (1992), *Hyperchaotic Phenomena in Dynamic Decision Making*, Journal of System Analysis and Modeling Simulation 9, 137-156.

Togeby, M. and E. Mosekilde (1988), *Frequency-Locking in a Model of Two Coupled Thermostatically Controlled Radiators*, Proc. Winter Annual Meeting of the American Society of Mechanical Engineers, 88-WA/DSC-14.

Towill, D.R. (1992), *Supply Chain Dynamics - the Engineering Challenge of the Mid 1990s,* Proc. Instr. Mech. Engrs. 206, 233-245.

van Duijn, J.J. (1983), *The Long Wave in Economic Life*, George Allen and Unwin, London.

Zarnowitz, V. (1985), *Recent Work on Business Cycles in Historical Perspective: A Review of Theory and Evidence*, Journal of Economic Literature 23, 523-80.

The Evolution of Economic System and the Development of Economy in China

Jinglian Wu

National Social Science Academy
Beijing, China, 100732

Chinese economy, as a typical unbalanced system, matches with the regular pattern for the development of a complex system. Along with the changes in China's economic reforms and opening up policy, some characteristics in the evolutionary process of an unbalanced system are observed clearly. This paper presents some facts of China's economic development as well as an analysis on these issues and ends up with a brief discussion on China's economic development under the theory of a complex system's evolution.

1 The Achievements and Loopholes of China's Reform from Late 1970s to Early 1990s

The great achievements China has made since late 1970s in reforming its economic system and promoting economic growth has been widely noticed in the world. The strategy responsible for the success in economic reform was not the one characterized by *gradual movement of the system as a whole*, as some may suggest. It was more tactful: While transformation of the *inside-the-system sector*, i.e. the sector owned by the state and under the control of the central planning system , was carried on very slowly, great efforts were made to speed up the reform of the *outside-the-system sector*, roughly the non-state owned sector, with a contemplation that this would in turn pull the *inside-the-system sector* towards a new system. Three major measures were taken:

A.Giving strong government support to the non-state sector in its rapid expansion;

B. Exposing the domestic economy to international market by implementing the opening up policy;

C. Allowing *coastal regions moving on first* by combining **A** and **B** in some carefully selected coastal regions.

The advantages of this strategy have become clear. By early 1990s, 1/2 of the country's total value of industrial output and 2/3 of GNP were produced by the non-state sector. Even more important, as the economic activities in this sector were primarily directed by market forces and there was great progress in the formation of the commodity market, market factors began to exercise much stronger influence than ever before in allocating resources in the whole economy. This helped to release vigor and energy everywhere in the economy which have clearly contributed to the sustained prosperity and rapid growth in the past 15 years. In the 1980s. GNP in mainland China grew at an annual rate of 9 per cent while export at 11.7 per cent. Economic success made the market-oriented reform process a nonreversible one, both economically and politically.

From the point of view of the whole economic transformation, however, this strategy is no more than a tactical arrangement. It was adopted to neutralize resistance to reform and cultivate reformers' force so that the process of the reform can be completed in a shorter period. The destination is to transform the whole economy into a market economy. With this in mind, it is obvious that when the reform in the *outside sector* provided necessary foundations for the reform in the *inside sector*, the opportunity should be taken immediately to launch a major reform campaign in the *inside sector* which was, after all. the backbone of the national economy. In particular, a set of integrated reform measures should be taken to solve those problems which have been regarded as fortified point of the old system for a long time, e.g. the problem of pricing system, and this would have put in place the main cornerstones of the market system.

Unfortunately, many opportunities were missed or given up and no significant breakthrough was made in the *inside sector* for quite a long period. This gave rise to a dual system with numerous loopholes. As a result, the stability and development of the economy were constantly threatened by

A. Inflation pressure stemmed from the failure in improving efficiency;

B. Rent-seeking activities and various corruption which found it easier to survive and expand under the dual system;

C. Distributional problems. On one hand, populations in different regions across the country enjoyed quite different levels of economic development and the gaps became larger as time went on; on the other hand, there was also enlarging gaps between the income levels of different social classes or groups.

It is apparent that fundamental reforms in the key sectors and the establishment of the basic framework of the market system are absolutely needed in order to solve these problems. Along with these problems were, however, vested interests and their social representatives newly developed under the dual system. These pressure groups tended to, as one might predict, use their economic, social and political influences in such a way that the distortions and chaos in the economy can be maintained and intensified. Thus, reformers often found it difficult to take any step forward and the economy was on its way to some kind of corruptive economy, as those in Latin America.

2 New Economic Upsurge and Loopholes Left in 1992 and 1993

Economic reform regained its momentum after Deng Xiaoping's speeches in the south in early 1992. Progresses were made in the following aspects.

A. Pricing system reform was accelerated;

B. Further opening up to the world; and

C. Rapid expansion of the non-state sector.

And again, the new wave of reform brought about the economic prosperity and growth in 1992-93.

But what a few regions, industries and firms can do alone is very limited in the transformation of the whole system of the national economy, esp. the system of the state owned sector. After 14 years reform, there were very few tasks left that can be completed by a region or an industry alone. In 1992, due to the lack of progress in those aspects of the reform which required unified design, regulation and measures from the central government, three parts of the state sector lagged far behind the other parts of the economic system, they were the fiscal and taxation system, the banking system and the internal organization of state owned firms.

The fiscal and taxation system in 1992 was still in the form which had been adopted to serve the central planning system. Fiscal revenue was collected in the forms of profit or tax from producers and distributors by the state which took advantages of its power to set prices and the monopolistic position of the state owned firms. After 14 years reform, these advantages no long existed. While the state had to hold responsibility for most the expenditures it had been financing in the past, fiscal revenue declined year by year in respect to the level of national income. Consequently, deficit run up quickly and the government frequently found itself unable to finance even the basic public services.

As to the banking system, the only bank under the old system, the People's Bank, was nothing but a cashier for the government: its function was no more than distributing cash among various uses in accordance with the direction of a comprehensive fiscal plan. Although central bank and *specialized banks* were separated in 1984, none of them got rid of the characteristics of the bank under the planning system. The central bank found it difficult to formulate and implement monetary policies it regarded as proper. And the banking system exhibited strong expansionary tendency. Allocation of capital resources could hardly be efficient, while *rent--seeking activities* brooded by low-interest-rate even negative-interest-rate bank loans were rampant.

There were problems with the same nature in the internal organization of the state owned large-and medium-size firms. On one hand, managers did not have sufficient power to run their firms efficiently, on the other hand, the operations of their firms were not subject to any hard budget constraint (property rights constraint). There would be a long way to go before these firms are transformed into independent corporations as required by a market system.

3 The Comprehensive Reform Launched in 1994

In November 1993, the 3rd Session of the 14th Central Committee of the Chinese Communist Party adopted a comprehensive program of transformation into market economy. Soon after, fundamental reforms were launched in the three fields mentioned in the previous section.

3.1 Establish a New Fiscal and Taxation System

3.1.1 Taxation System Reform

The basic requirement of the taxation reform in 1994 is to standardize the taxation system in line with the following principles: tax burden should be allocated fairly among tax payers; taxation system should be simplified; and the relevant powers should be divided properly between national and sub-national authorities. It is expected that by doing so, a new taxation system can be established to meet the requirement of a market economy; income distribution can be put in proper order and fair competition can be encouraged. The major measures to be taken are
A. Replace the old system of indirect taxes with the new system of indirect tax, mainly value-added-tax (VAT);
B. Unify the corporate tax for firms with domestic capital and foreign capital;
C. Standardize personal income tax;
D. Improve the collection and administration of tax.

3.1.2 Fiscal System Reform

The target of the fiscal system reform is to replace the current fiscal system of central-local-revenue-sharing with a tax-sharing system which will have powers and responsibilities properly divided between central and local (provinces and counties) authorities.

3.2 Establish a New Financial System

The financial system reform is designed to establish a system of financial institutions consisting of a wide range of financial organizations with the state owned banks in a dominate position and having the policy--oriented financing and commercial financing separated. It is also expected that the reform will lead to the establishment of a set of financial markets which will be integrated, opening, competitive and well regulated. Three measures are to be taken:
A. Transform the Chinese People's Bank into a real central bank;
B. Transform the state owned specialized banks into real commercialized banks which operate in accordance with common rules of the banking industry in market economies, while investing and financing instruments are to be developed for government to carry out its policies.
C. Have interest rates liberalized.

3.3 Foreign Exchange Administration Reform

The target of the reform in the foreign exchange administration system is full convertibility of the RMB.

In light of the successful experiences in other countries and the current situation at home, the government decided to carry on the reform by taking two successive steps. Firstly, abolish the dual exchange rate system and make the RMB conditionally convertible in current accounts. Secondly, lift the control over capital flows and make the RMB fully convertible.

3.4 Accelerate the State Owned Enterprises Reform While Keep Encouraging the Development of Non-state Sector

Firms operating as independent entities are absolutely indispensable for a market economic system to be established. To bring about such firms, the development of various non-state owned firms, including those with mixed ownership, should be encouraged as before. There is , however, a problem in this respect that one can not sidestep, namely, reform of the state owned firms. With reference to industries and scales, different measures should be taken in reforming state owned firms. Medium-and small-size firms can be transformed into *state-owned and privately-run* or *privately-owned and privately-run* firms by *contracting, leasing* and *selling* them to individuals. Large- and medium-size firms, on the other hand, should be corporatized, that is, transformed into corporations.

3.5 Establish a New Social Security System

The transformation into a market economy requires supports from reforms in many other fields, among which is that of social security. The old regime serving the central planning system is characterized by a *trinity* of employment, welfare and social security which every single firm has to provide to its employees and to which, accordingly, rural population is not entitled. This is , of course, incompatible with a market system. In fact, reforms in fields such as state owned firms and financial system are often restrained either by the presence of the old social security system or by the absence of a new one. It is, therefore, of strategic importance that a new social security system should be in place of the old one . Five major tasks have been identified in setting up new social security system.

A. Starting from urban population, a national fund for unemployment insurance should be created.

B. The current health system in which the state pays for all medical cares of the urban population should be replaced by health insurance institutions which can be established with references to industries and regions.

C. Trial implementation of pension fund system.

D. A national fund should be created for the purpose of poverty releasing.

E. The existing life insurance and property insurance industries which have been in rapid expansion for years should become more competitive by encouraging establishment or entry of new companies and break-up of the old ones.

The effect of the reforms started this year in the fields of fiscal and taxation, finance and state owned firms will, to a large extent, pass a judgment on the program of building a socialist market economy. Measures taken this year are closely related. Failure in one aspect will bring about a chain reaction and distort others. It is therefore absolutely necessary that reforms in all aspects are well coordinated so that weak links can be strengthened and disturbances arising from some links' being out of line can be avoided. The present situation suggests that the reform of fiscal and taxation system and current account foreign exchange administration are going well on the way scheduled. But the reforms in financial system and enterprises are moving slowly, to some extent, the delay in these fields may endanger the macro-stability of the economy and the transformation process itself. Every effort is being made by Chinese reformers to remove these obstacles.

4 Conclusion

We have discussed the reality of the development and reformation of China's economy. Viewing the above discussion as background, now that let us switch to the common law of the evolution of a complex system.

As an unbalanced system, the evolution of economy can be viewed as a process constantly moving towards the equilibrium. Furthermore, it is more important that the equilibrium of the system is movable as well. During the movement of the equilibrium under certain conditions in the economic system, two kinds of phenomena can be observed: Under certain conditions, changes only take place in quantity inside the original system; while under other conditions, the original structure may lose stability and become dissolved. In this case, qualitative changes will happen and a new structure will be formed.

Furthermore, as we know, changes of a systematic structure greatly depend on certain critical conditions. When the system is positioned far from the critical point, there is absolutely no structure change even if the balanced movement inside the system is going on. As the system is passing through the critical point, structure change happens right away in the system. The branches of the structure may turn up, therefore, the whole system is facing different new ways of development. For this reason, when government is trying to adjust and regulate the economic development through macro-adjusting measure, it should be able to recognize the existence and position of the critical point. If the system is far away from the critical point, the economic transformation can be carried in the original frame of reformation. When the economy has not reached the critical point, to subjectively enforce the transformation of system will definitely violate the common law of the evolution of a complex system. On the contrary, as soon as the economy is getting close to the critical point, the economy will face the transformation of the structure. At this moment, government should guide the transformation of the economic structure, otherwise the evolution of the system will halt and block the economic development. In addition, near the critical point, the transformation of the structure makes the system have many alternatives of measures. In this case, government should be more careful and more active before it can make decision to select a proper alternative, like an old Chinese saying goes: *Neglect of millimeter leads to the mistake thousands of miles away*. In the process of evolution, monitoring is very much necessary. It can instantly have the out-of-way problems solved and make the transformation back to the prosperous road. By this way, a lock-in economic structure, as well as the economic recession and deteriorate economic environment will be out of the question.

We may consider that China's economy has reached a critical point of evolution and faced a fundamental transformation of the structure. Encourage and knowledge of government are needed (encourage surely backed up by knowledge) so as to hold the opportunity to carry on the structural transformation of market-oriented economy and select a proper economic structure as well as a suitable route for development.

THE COMPLEXITY OF ECONOMIC EVOLUTION
- Change Speeds and Time Scales

Wei-Bin Zhang

Institute for Futures Studies, Drottninggatan 33, 2tr., Box 591, 101 31, Stockholm, Sweden

Abstract: The purpose of this study is to discuss the relationship between change speeds of economic variables and time scales in economic dynamics in the light of nonlinear theory. Firstly, it is argued that economic variables have different change speeds in different societies. Secondly, the significance of time scales in dynamic economic analysis is emphasized. Thirdly, the relationship between change speeds and time scales in dynamic analysis is examined. Fourthly, it is shown that it is possible to classify the traditional economic theories according to the relationship between change speeds and time scales. Finally, the study is concluded.

1. The Complexity of Economic Evolution

> **Consequently: he who wants to have right without wrong, order without disorder, does not understand the principles of heaven and earth. He does not know how things hang together.**
>
> **- Chuang Tzu**

Nonlinear theory has recently found an enormous spectrum of areas of applications in natural and social sciences. The great variety of applied fields manifests a possibly unifying methodological factor in sciences. This study is to further show how general ideas in nonlinear theory may be applied to theoretical economics.

Our inquiry is specially based on a new field of economics, nonlinear economics (e.g., Zhang, 1990b, 1991e, Allen and Sanglier, 1979, Andersson, 1986, Dendrinos and Sonis, 1990, Chiarella, 1990, Rosser, 1991, Puu, 1989). The construction of nonlinear economics is much influenced, except traditional economics, by self-organization (e.g., Nicolis and Prigogine, 1977, Prigogine, 1980, synergetics (e.g., Haken, 1977, 1983), nonlinear theory in mathematics. Synergetic economics is the study of cooperativity among the parts of open economic systems. It attempts to provide a new vision of economic dynamics: a vision toward the multiple, the temporal, the unpredictable, and the complexity. Economic dynamics are considered to resemble a turbulent movement of liquid in which varied and relatively stable forms of current and whirlpools, constantly change one another. It argues that social and economic changes consist of dynamic processes of self-organization along with the spontaneous formation of increasingly subtle and complicated structures. The accidental nature and the presence of structural changes like catastrophes and bifurcations, which are characteristic of nonlinear systems and whose further trajectory is determined by chance, make dynamics irreversible, i.e., deprive the evolution process of a time symmetry. Synergetic economics mainly examines the spontaneous formation of new macroscopic structures associated with discontinuous processes. It shows how parts of a system can organize themselves into new structures at certain instability points. The instabilities can form hierarchies leading to complicated patterns of structure and behavior. The range of applications of synergetic methods to economic problems includes many topics, such as catastrophes, bifurcations, trade cycles, economic chaos, urban pattern formation, the role of stochastic noise upon economic structures, fast and slow economic processes, and relationship between microscopic and macroscopic economics. Although it is possible to examine different aspects of social and economic evolution in the light of synergetic economics, this study is mainly concerned with the relationship between change speeds of economic variables and time scales in analysis in this study.

The complexity of social and economic reality is constantly increasing in modern time. This is partially because of the expanded capital and knowledge stocks of mankind. Time is, as Marshall rightly argued in the Principles of Economics, the center of the chief difficulty of almost every economic problem. As time passes, the economic issues with which economists are concerned are shifted. Even since the time of Adam Smith, the main variables that economists have dealt with appear not to have changed significantly. But as the way in which these variables are combined and speeds at which they change have constantly varied and the dominant economic doctrines have shifted over time and space.

The complexity of economic dynamics is also reflected in the fact that when economists are concerned with genuine economic evolution, their points of view tend to be diverged, rather than converged. Although equilibrium economists have exhibited a certain harmony of viewpoints, we can hardly find such a happy convergence among the economists who are deeply concerned with economic evolution. For instance, although Smith, Marx and Schumpeter have one common point of view about the capitalist system which is that competitive capitalism plays a significant (positive) role in improving western civilization at least during certain period of history, they have different visions of actual processes of the system. Smith was mainly concerned with agricultural and commercial exchange economies. He could hardly foresee possible instabilities and serious social and cultural problems possibly associated with capital and knowledge accumulation in capitalist dynamics. Both Marx and Schumpeter foresaw the possibility of self-destruction of capitalism due to capital accumulation and technological improvement. But they could not foresee how people and government could make adjustment in life styles and institutions under changed social and economic conditions.

It may be argued that a main factor for the differences in vision about capitalist processes among the three economists may be that they understood dynamic processes of capitalist systems differently. Each of them highly appreciated positive aspects of capitalism. Each of them developed their theory in order to explain social and economic reality of their time. In certain sense, the differences in their conclusions about capitalist systems might not be so much due to differences in their ideologies, than due to differences in understanding of dynamic processes of capitalist systems. For instance, if Marx could have foreseen the possibility of class transformations and effective intervention of government in education, infrastructure and welfare systems in a capitalist society, he might not have suggested socialism as a replacement of capitalism in order to solve social conflicts of an industrialized society.

Although economists have varied points of view about economic evolution, it is obviously important to ask whether it is possible to provide a general unifying methodology for analyzing the complexity of economic evolution. Synergetic economics proves that nonlinear theory is potentially quietly useful for this purpose. We now show the significance of distinction of speeds of change in reality and time scales in scientific investigation and thus provide some hints on how to find out validity, limitations and relationships of different economic theories.

2. Economic Dynamics with Different Speeds

> **Primitive organisms have slow neural systems. The more evolved human nervous system processes signals faster. The same is true of primitive and advanced economies. Historically, power has shifted from the slow to the fast - whether we speak of species or nations.**
>
> **- Alvin Toffler (1990)**

Although it is difficult to accurately identify the time when they begin and when end, it may be claimed that mankind has experienced three economic structural transformations - from hunting society to agricultural one, agricultural society to industrial one, industrial society to information/knowledge-based one. These transformations are still occurring in different nations in different forms at different speeds. Each of these economic systems has certain corresponding dominant ideologies such as religions, socialism and capitalism. At each turning point there tend to be great conflicts among different social classes, though their forms are much affected by geographical conditions, cultural traditions, international environment, and other factors.

It may be argued that the general tendency of social evolution can be described as a transforming process from a simple structure into a more complex one, from a lower level to a higher one, from few types into multiple types and from slowness into quickness in adaptability. Comparing a society at stage of initial industrialization (e.g., China) and a society at stage of mature industrialization (e.g., Japan), we can find great differences in diversity of social and economic activities between the two societies.

Although they are so different from each other, societies may still be described by some common variables. Synergetic economics tries to examine possible behavior and structures of social and economic systems with different combinations of the following variables:

i) monetary variables - e.g., prices, wages, interest rates (monetary) incomes and profits;
ii) material variables - e.g., output of different agents, capital, natural resources, infrastructures and wealth distribution;
iii) knowledge-related variables - e.g., knowledge, education level, skill, technology, information;
iv) population - e.g., the population, the structure of the population by age, birth and death rates, sex, skill, preferences (or tastes), family or other criteria;
v) social and cultural variables - e.g., habits or customs, morals, institutions including laws, tax systems, education systems, and the like.

These variables have different change speeds under different social and cultural circumstances. For instance, prices may be determined quickly in a competitive economy; construction of transportation and communication infrastructures may take a long time. For convenience of discussion, let us introduce time-dependent vector variables. Let X denote consumption components, P monetary variables, N population, K capital, Z knowledge, M institutions, Q the other variables (e.g., globally political, military and natural environment). It should be remarked that we will not further classify components of a vector. For instance, the wage rate and price of commodities, which are elements of P, may have different speeds. The speeds of P are obviously affected by the structure of institutions. We may generally describe dynamic interactions of these variables in the following way

$$dX/dt = s^{a} F_{x}(X,P,N,K,Z,M,Q),$$

$$dP/dt = s^{ß} F_{p}(X,P,N,K,Z,M,Q),$$

$$dN/dt = s^{t} F_{n}(X,P,N,K,Z,M,Q),$$

$$dK/dt = s^{\pi} F_{k}(X,P,N,K,Z,M,Q),$$

$$dZ/dt = s^{E}F_{z}(X,P,N,K,Z,M,Q),$$

$$dM/dt = s^{-}F_{m}(X,P,N,K,Z,M,Q),$$

$$dQ/dt = s^{\partial}F_{q}(X,P,N,K,Z,M,Q), \qquad (2.1)$$

in which t is time, s (<< 1) is a parameter for classifying adjustment speeds of variables, and a, ß, t, π E, _, and ∂ are integral numbers. The parameters, a, ß, t, π E, _, and ∂ describe the order of time dimensions of the corresponding variables. Here, we neglect spatial dimensions. It is quite natural to think of s as an endogenous variable. We thus may further introduce the corresponding functions, s_x, s_p, x_n, s_k, s_z, s_m and s_q, of X, P, N, K, Z, M and Q to take account of influences of the endogenous variables upon adjustment speeds. We will omit any further discussion on this issue.

It may be argued that different historical, social and economic theories are descriptions of interactions of these variables over time and space under various assumptions. In some abstract sense, these different theories tend to find some specified functional forms of (2.1) and use different methods to solve them. To investigate how these variables interact upon each other over time and space is the main purpose of synergetic economics. To simplify our illustration, we use three basic variables - the population, capital and knowledge - to describe long-run economic development. As shown Table 1, these three variables may be roughly considered to be changed at different speeds in different societies.

Table 1. Change Speeds of the Economic Variables

society variables	agricultural	industrial	knowledge- based
population	fast	fast/slow	slow
capital	slow	slow/fast	fast
knowledge	slow	slow/fast	fast

It may be thus argued that if an agricultural economy is to be analyzed, an economist may get an appropriate explanation of economic reality by concentrating on population (and power struggle) dynamics. But the analytical conclusions about agricultural economies cannot be applied to explain economic dynamics of industrialized economies as capital is a dominant variable of industrial economies (with the population "enslaved"). Similarly the analytical conclusions about capital-based societies cannot be applied to economic phenomena of knowledge-based societies. In fact, from the studies of history of economic analysis (e.g., Schumpeter, 1954, Blaug, 1985, Morishima, 1989), it is clear that many economic ideas were created at the time when the societies were faced with new economic problems and thus required new ideas to solve those problems. We may thus expect certain correspondence between creation of economists' ideas and social conditions. In section 5, we will briefly discuss the issue.

3. Time Scales in Dynamics Analysis

To realize the unimportance of time is the gate of wisdom.

- Bertrand Russell

Natural scientists in different fields, like men from different cultures or social scientists specified in different subjects, have various images of time scales. A physician of elementary particle physics is involved in physical dimensions of order of 10^{-15} cm and time scales of the order 10^{-22} second; a physician of cosmology is concerned with time scales of the order of 10^{10}. But from a point of view of an economist, all physicians are dealing with the same objective world. Similarly, a physician may imagine that all economists are dealing with the same market, though there are hundreds of subjects of economics dealing with different economic phenomena. For instance, financial economists and economic historians may obviously have varied visions about time.

Like scientists in any other fields, economists have been faced with analytical problems with different time scales since the very beginning of economics. The father of economics, Adam Smith, not only analyzed actual temporary functioning of markets, he was also deeply concerned with the significance of morality in a competitive market system for civilization (in the long term). Irrespective of the fact that economists has implicitly or explicitly different viewpoints about time scales, this does not imply that the economist has theories for examining the role of time scales in dynamic analysis. In fact, it is only through recent works, e.g., in fields of nonlinear dynamics, Prigogine's self-organization theory, Haken's slaving principle, and synergetic economics that we can relatively effectively handle some cases of nonlinear dynamic systems with different time scales.

4. Adjustment Speeds and Time Scales in Dynamic Analysis

In section 2 we classified endogenous variables according to their speeds of change and in section 3 we emphasized time scales in scientific investigation. This section examines the relationship between speeds of change and time scales of our investigation. As shown later on, this relationship is a key point for us to understand validity and limitations of different schools in economics under given circumstances and to recognize similarity and difference among these schools.

It has been proved that the macroscopic time-dependent behavior of multicomponent systems may be governed by the dynamics of a few order parameters only. The slaving principle developed by Haken (1983) shows that the dynamic behavior of a huge number of microscopic degrees of freedom is slaved by a small number of order parameters. As the system can be described by a self-contained dynamics of a few order parameters alone, it is often analytically possible to get sufficient information about the entire system consisting of multiple units just by examine behavior of a low-dimensional dynamics.

Social and economic variables are changeable, but changed at different speeds. Prices may be determined very quickly in a competitive economy, but fixed in a planned economy. Speeds, at which transactions take place, decisions are made, new ideas are created in laboratories, and data, information and new knowledge affect economic systems, are obviously different among peoples, regions, and nations. Even ideologies, morals, habits, which are often treated as parameters in analysis and thought of "being fixed" in diary life, are subjected to changes. The loss of the absolute power of the Church and the current collapse of the state-planned economies show that ideologies are long-run endogenous variables of social evolution.

To illustrate how to analyze dynamic processes with different speeds, we consider the following system

$$dx_{ij}/dt = s^{m_i} F_i(x), \qquad (4.1)$$

in which s (<< 1) is a parameter used to classify speeds of variables, x_{ij} (as defined in (2.1) are variables, such as prices, wages, capital, population and knowledge, describing the state of a dynamic system, and m_i are parameters describing "speed order" of the variables. For simplicity of discussion, the remainder of this section is only concerned with a two-dimensional case.

The two-dimensional problem is defined by

$$dx/dt = f(x,y), \quad dy/dt = sg(x,y), \qquad (4.2)$$

in which f, g E C^2 and $0 \leq s << 1$. We call x and y fast and slow variables, respectively.

As a first approximation, assume dy/dt = 0, i.e., treating y as a constant in a short-run dynamic analysis. The entire system is thus reduced to

$$dx/dt = f^*(x), \qquad (4.3)$$

in which $f^* = f(x,y)$ with y fixed.

Making a transformation, T = st, of our "conscience of time", (4.2) is rewritten as

$$sdx/dT = f(x,y), \quad dy/dT = g(x,y). \qquad (4.4)$$

The slow variable is thus described by

$$dy/dT = g(h(y),y) = g^*(y), \qquad (4.5)$$

where x = h(y) determined by f(x,y) = 0. Accordingly, the fast variable disappears as an explicit variable in the long-run analysis.

The above illustration tells why it is often reasonable for economists to neglect studies by historians, while a historian without a profound knowledge of economics can never really understand history. Many economic variables are fast, e.g., prices. This implies that it is acceptable for an economist to "forget" slow variables such as institutions as the latter can be treated as parameters in the short-run dynamic analysis. But (4.5) tells that the slow variable is constantly affected by the fast variable x even in long-run dynamics.

It must be emphasized that the reduction of dimensions of a nonlinear dynamic system is not often as simple as in the illustrated model. The validity of the above discussion is dependent upon the stability of the system. From the literature of modern dynamic analysis, we know that a small change in a parameter may cause structural changes in an unstable nonlinear system. This implies that even when s is very small, we cannot safely omit its effects upon the reduced system in a dynamic analysis. The methods for analyzing this kind of dynamic problems with different speeds are referred to, e.g., Haken (1983), Carr (1981), Kevorkian and Cole (1981), Chow and Hale (1982), O'Malley (1988), and Pliss and Sell (1991).

5. A Simplified Classification of Some Schools in Economics

Economic theory learns nothing from economic history, and economic history is as much corrupted as enriched by economic theory.
- Robert Solow (1985)

The previous sections emphasized the significance of speeds of change and time scales and provided some general ideas about the relationship between speeds of change and time scales. This section applies these ideas to the existing economic theories.

An important issue in economic dynamics is related to the adjustment speeds of variables. For some (in particular, middle twentieth century equilibrium) economists a competitive economic system adjusts smoothly and quickly to disturbances in its way toward to the long-run equilibrium. For others a competitive economic system can hardly simultaneously guarantee both (social, political and cultural) stability and economic efficiency because the assumption of a perfectly competitive market structure, perfect information and perfect expectations cannot be accepted in real world. Some economists don't accept the possibility of simultaneously achieving social harmony and economic efficiency which has been claimed by liberal economists. From the economic history it may be argued that each school in economics has its own time - the time for it to be valid and the time for it to be wrong. Keynesian economics and Multhasian economics provide suitable examples of "there is a time for everything" (Ecclesiastes). Although we have different economic theories which are developed under certain cultural and historical circumstances, unfortunately there is not yet a general theory to take account of main ideas of the current economic theories within a compact framework.

There are different indicators for classifying schools in economics. For instance, whether wages are fixed or not is an important indicator to distinguish Keynesian/Marxian and neo-classical economics from a purely analytical economic point of view. We will soon show that it is possible to analytically classify different, such as Keynesian, neo-classical, Schumpeterian, and Marxian economic systems according to change speeds of variables of prices (including interest rates and wages), capital, resources, institutions, knowledge, innovation and creativity assumed in these schools.

Adam Smith (1723-1790)

He was the founder of the classical school of economics. He was living in times of extremely unusual economic change - the stage of initial industrialization. This partly explained his neglect of fixed capital and for the conviction that agriculture and not manufacture was the principal source of Britain's wealth. He noted that industry generally affords greater scope for specialization than does agriculture and insisted that division of labor is necessary to increase wealth and that exchanges and the system of prices are necessary as the division of labor develops. His theory on economic equilibrium has been accurately proved by modern competitive equilibrium approach; while his theory on division of labor is still not well formed, even though many efforts have been made in the literature on human capital accumulation. It should remarked that Smith did not believe in a rigid subsistence wage supply of labor in the short and intermediate run as Marx did.

If we classify monetary variables such as prices and wages as fast variables and skills and morals as slow variables, we may claim, in a broad sense, that analytical economists have not succeeded in forming a compact and logic framework to analyze Adam Smith's "rudimentary" social and economic system as a whole.

Ricardo (1772-1823)

Ricardo's fame relies on his Principles (1817). Although his interest in economics began with reading Adam Smith and was greatly influenced by the Wealth of Nations, Ricardo emphasized more on manufacturing than Adam Smith. He tried to establish laws which regulate what proportion of the whole produce of the society will be allotted to each of three - landowner, capitalist and worker - under the names of rent, profit and wages, respectively. These laws show how the distribution will change at different stages of society. He was concerned with an economic system consisting of agriculture and industry. Different aspects of Ricardo's system are mathematically formulated by different authors (e.g., Morishima, 1989).

Malthus (1766-1834)

Although Malthus was not the first to examine demographic problems, he was the first to succeed in developing a theory of population growth. By emphasizing the interdependence of population growth and food supply, his theory lent support to the subsistence theory of wages which had important influences upon Ricardo, Marx and Keynes. By explaining poverty in terms of a simple interdependence between the population and the means of subsistence, the theory still provides important suggestions for poor countries' economic policy. It should be remarked that although Malthus did not deeply discuss capital accumulation, he analyzed the possibility of social progresses as checking forces of population and poverty.

In the simplest form of "Malthusian growth model" the population grows at a constant rate times the population present, with no limitations on its resources. That is, $dN/dt = aN$, where N is the population at time t and a is a positive parameter. Such a population growth may be valid for a short time, but it clearly cannot go on forever. There are limitations of natural resources which prevent population from limitlessly growing. The logistic growth model, which is defined by $dN/dt = aN(1 - bN)$, takes account of checking effects of natural resources upon population growth. However, for human society resources are not given, but "endogenous variables". To analyze how production affects population growth, Haavelmo (1954) suggested the following extension of Malthus' system

$$dN/dt = aN(1 - bN/Y), \quad a, b > 0, \qquad (5.1)$$

$$Y = AN^{a}, \quad A > 0, \; 0 < a < 1, \qquad (5.2)$$

in which Y is real output. Substituting (5.2) into (5.1) yields

$$dN/dt = N(a_1 - a_2 N^{1-a}). \qquad (5.3)$$

We see that the growth law is a generalization of the familiar logistic form widely used in biological population and economic analysis. It is not difficult to see that the dynamics of this system are very simple with the parameter choices made.

Marx (1818-1883)

As Marx created a system that embraced almost all fields of social sciences, his ideas about economic dynamics are quite beyond the scope of this study. A mistake he made was that he neglected the possibility of class transformation and government's "positive interventions". For instance, by providing education opportunities to children of working classes, the government may make class transformation possible in the long term. If we introduce endogenous classes transformation in an industrialized capitalist society within the framework of endogenous knowledge and capital accumulation, Marx's conclusion about capitalism may be invalid in a long-run perspective. According to Schumpeter (p.596, 1954), "Ricardo, the most unmetaphysical of theoretists, introduced the labor-quantity theory of value simply as a hypothesis that was to explain the actual relative prices - or rather the actual long-run normals of relative prices - that we observe in real life. But for Marx, the most metaphysical of theoretists, the labor-quantity theory was no mere hypothesis about relative prices." Here, we mentioned Marx just to illustrate how dangerous it is to interpret and even forecast long-run dynamic economic reality, applying conclusions from the analysis upon the basis of assuming some slowly changeable variables to be fixed.

The Walrasian system or the standard economic equilibrium model (e.g., Arrow and Hahn, 1971)

The equilibrium model is a system in which maximization of households' utilities and producers' profits yields consumption components as functions of prices. The population, capital, natural resources and technology are fixed in this approach. Price dynamics are specified according to the Tâtonement. We can generally describe the system by

$$sdX/dt = F_X(X,P), \quad dP/dt = F_p(X,P), \qquad (5.4)$$

in which X and P are defined in section 2 and the parameters defined in section are taken on the following values: a = - 1, ß = 0, and t, π, E, T, ∂ ≥ 1. We neglect the "slow variables" in our expression. Setting s = 0, we get $F_X(X,P) = 0$, or X = X(P). The functional forms of F_X are determined by the functional forms of utilities and productions. Substituting X = X(P) into the price system, we have

$$dP/dt = F_p^*(P), \qquad (5.5)$$

where $F_p^*(P)$ _ $F_p(X(P),P)$. From the litearture of equilibrium approach we know that great efforts had been made to specify $F_p(P)$ by different (mainly mathematical) economists.

The Marshallian system (e.g., Samuelson, 1947)

Different from the Walrasian system, the Marshallian model assumes a relatively slow adjustment of demand and supply (in comparison to prices). The economic aspects of the model can be generally described as

$$dX/dt = F_X(X,P), \quad sdP/dt = F_p(X,P). \qquad (5.6)$$

We see that the dynamics can be expressed merely in terms of X.

Neo-classical growth theory

Another main approach to economic analysis is the so-called neo-classical growth theory (e.g., Burmeister and Dobell, 1970). This approach was popular particularly during the period from the 60s to the 70s. Different from the Malthusian analysis, this approach focuses upon capital accumulation. The model assumes that prices are relatively fast than that of capital accumulation and population growth. We may specify the dynamic system as follows

$$sdX/dt = F_X(X,P,N,K), \quad sdP/dt = F_p(X,P,N,K),$$

$$dN/dt = F_n(N,t), \quad dK/dt = F_k(N,K). \qquad (5.7)$$

As the consumption and prices are assumed to be fast variables, the dynamics appear to be given only by the motion of the population and capital. The standard model is given by

$$dK/dt = s_0F(K,N) - \partial_0 K, \quad dN/dt = nN, \qquad (5.8)$$

where s_0 is savings rate and δ_0 is fixed depreciation rate. Here, F(K;N) is assumed to be a neoclassical production function, defining the output flow attainable with given amounts of K and N. We may specify $F = K^a N^{1-a}$, where a is a positive parameter, $0 < a < 1$. In the Solow-Swan model, the population growth rate, n, is treated as a parameter. We may rewrite the above equation as

$$dk/dt = s_0 k^a - (\delta_0 + n)k, \qquad (5.9)$$

where k (= K/N) is capital per capita at time t. It is well known that the system has a unique positive equilibrium. Furthermore, it is globally stable in the region $k > 0$.

We will not further classify the economic models, such as the input-output/von-Neumann/Sraffa models, the models with endogenous institutions and technology. It must be emphasized that the above classification is not strictly held in the sense that no economists mentioned above are so narrow. No one can say that Adam Smith only cares about equilibrium prices without knowing the significance of morality for social harmony. Schumpeter obviously had much deeper knowledge about motion of monetary systems. There is no evidence that neoclassical economists have completely neglected endogenous population dynamics. For instance, although the one-sector neoclassical growth assumes a given growth rate of the population, this does not imply that the population growth is exogenously given under any circumstances. I wish that my simple classification may help the reader to recognize validity and limitations of economists' ideas, but will not cause any further misunderstanding of them.

It should be noted that the author has recently suggested a much more general dynamic framework for analyzing various social and economic issues (e.g., Zhang, 1994d). For instance, dynamic models (without spatial structures) of national economies with capital, knowledge accumulation and endogenous economic structures are examined in Zhang (1990a, 1991c, 1992a, 1993a, 1993c, 1993h, 1994c). Models (without spatial structures) of regional and international dynamic interactions are proposed in Zhang (1991a, 1991b, 1992b, 1992c, 1993b, 1993g). In Zhang (1993d, 1993e, 1993f, 1994a), models for spatial economies of isolated states are developed. In Zhang (1994b), trade models with urban structures are developed. The author is still examining various cases of the general model and extending it more broadly. When speaking about developing a theory, the author is aware of the following criterion by Kuhn (1977, p.321-22):

> First, a theory should be accurate within its domain.... Second, a theory should be consistent, not only

> internally or with itself, but also with other currently accepted theories applicable to related aspects of nature. Third, it should have broad scope: in particular, a theory's consequences should extend far beyond the particular observations, laws, or subtheories it was initially designed to explain. Fourth, and closely related, it should be simple, bringing order to phenomena that in its absence would be individually isolated and, as a set, confused. Fifth ... a theory should be fruitful of new research findings: it should, that is, disclose new phenomena or previously unnoted relationships among those already known. These five characteristics - accuracy, consistency, scope, simplicity, and fruitfulness -are all standard criteria for evaluating the adequacy of a theory.

From the author's studies which are mentioned above, it can be shown that the general framework includes some well established economic systems, such as the Arrow-Debreu equilibrium model, the Solow-Swan model, the Uzawa two-sector model, the Kaldor-Passinetti two-group model, the Oniki-Uzawa trade model, the Arrow learning by doing model, the Ricardian model by Pasinetti and Samuelson, the Alonso urban model and the Muth housing model, as special cases. That is, we can now treat various ideas in economic theory and location theory within a single theoretical framework. Indeed, the usefulness of the framework lies not only in that it unifies some theories, but mainly in that it can explain, in a compact way, many economic phenomena which cannot be explained by the traditional partial theories.

6. Concluding Remarks

> **Thus what we gain is Something, yet it is by virtue of Nothing that this can be put to use.**
>
> **- Lao Tzu**

This paper dealt with one of the most important topics in dynamic economic analysis. We argued that change speeds of social and economic variables are changeable and such changes can be explained if we extend our vision to a historical perspective. We also showed that changes in change speeds of economic variables affect the way how we analyze economic dynamics. The significance of synergetic economics lies not only in explicitly classifying social and economic variables according to change speeds, but mainly in pointing out the relationship between change speeds in reality and time scale in analysis and in providing analytical methods to effectively handle with the problems.

Both nature and society consist of complicated dynamic interactions of different subsystems with different orders of speeds of changes. It is through recognizing the difference of temporary orders of different variables of the same dynamic system that we can effectively carry out scientific analysis of actual dynamics. This study showed that through classifying economic variables in terms of changes speeds, we can sometimes reduce dynamic problems of high dimensions to lower dimensional ones.

The ideas about change speeds and time scales are, either explicitly or implicitly, recognized by authors in different fields of social sciences. The following three examples further suggests distinction between speeds of changes in reality and time scales in scientific investigation.

The great French historian Fernand Braudel applies the idea about the correspondence between change speeds in reality and time scale in analysis to interpret social and economic history. In the preface to the first edition of "The Mediterranean and the Mediterranean World in the Age of Philip II", he divides historical phenomena according to different time scales in the following way:

"The final effect then is to dissect history into various planes, or, to put it another way, to divide historical time into geographical time, social time, and individual time. Or, alternatively, to divide man into a multitude of selves. This is perhaps what I shall be least forgiven, even if I say in my defence that traditional divisions also cut across living history which is fundamentally one, even if I agree, ... that the historical narrative is not a method, or even the objective method par excellence, but quite simply a philosophy of history like any other; even if I say , and demonstrate hereafter, that these levels I have distinguished are only means of exposition, that I have felt it quite in order in the course of the book to move from one level to another."

His great book "Civilization and Capitalism" is also organized in the order of change speeds of social and economic variables over time and space. Our above discussion about the relationship between change speeds and time scales may provide a theoretical basis for his approach. Braudel's approach also suggests some of reasons for the failure of analytical economics in interpreting economic history. If one is only interested in fast economic processes (as equilibrium economists do), one may not need any deep knowledge about history and culture as the slow variables can be "effectively fixed" in a short-run analysis. But in order to deal with long-run historical and cultural problems, one cannot effectively omit fast processes. This may be the reason that history is so difficult to interpret.

Hayek (1944) mentions possible differences between long-run and short-run social effects of the law as follows:

"... there will apart from the long-run effects which cannot be predicted, also be short-run effects on particular people which may be clearly known. But with this kind of [general and permanent] laws the short-run effects are in general not (at least ought not to be) the guiding consideration. As these immediate and predictable effects become more important compared with the long-run effects, we approach the border-line where the distinction, however, clear in principle, becomes blurred in practice."

Applying Weber's idea about relationships between religion and capitalism and modern growth theory, Morishima discuss why Japan has economically succeeded in modern time. His argument provides another example of the significance of dynamics of "slow variables" in shaping history of different civilizations. Morishima (1982) states:

"Weber made it clear that, as far as Christianity was concerned, differences in the interpretation of the Bible between Catholic and Protestant produced significant differences in people's modes of worldly behavior. One of the main purposes of this book is to look for this kind of knife-edge property in the differences between the interpretations of the classics of Eastern ethical (or religious) doctrine (especially Confucianism) in China and Japan, and any consequent wide divergence in the patterns of worldly behavior of the Chinese and Japanese people and the paths of economic development which they followed. 'Ethology' makes clear that behavior patterns and economic mechanisms differ in accordance with variations in ethos, and assuming the knife-edge theorem is correct, the instability whereby minute variations in ethos can result in huge differences in daily life and the fate of a nation, is found in the correspondence relationship between ideology and economy".

The significance of nonlinear economics lies in that not only does it explicitly recognize differences of change speeds and time scales in scientific investigation, but also it explodes different analytical methods to analyze the complexity of economic evolution as a whole process.

References

Allen, P./ Sanglier, M. (1979): A Dynamic Model of a Central Place System. Geographical Analysis 11

Andersson, Å.E. (1986): The Four Logistical Revolutions. Papers of Regional Science Association 59

Arrow, K.J./ Hahn, F.H. (1971): General Competitive Analysis. Amsterdam: North-Holland

Blaug, M. (1985): Economic Theory in Retrospect. Cambridge: Cambridge University Press

Braudel, F. (1972): The Mediterranean and the Mediterranean World in the Age of Philip II. Vol. I, translated from the French by S. Reynolds. New York: Harper & Row

Burmeister, E./ Dobell, A.R. (1970): Mathematical Theories of Economic Growth. New York: Macmillan

Carr, J. (1981): Applications of Centre Manifold Theory. Berlin: Springer

Chiarella, C. (1990): The Elements of a Nonlinear Theory of Economic Dynamics. Berlin: Springer-Verlag

Chow, S.N./ Hale, J.K. (1982): Methods of Bifurcation Theory. Berlin: Springer

Dendrinos, D.S./Sonis, M. (1990): Chaos and Socio-Spatial Dynamics. New York: Springer-Verlag

Haken, H. (1977): Synergetics: An Introduction. Berlin: Springer-Verlag

Haken, H. (1983): Advanced Synergetics. Berlin: Springer-Verlag

Hayek, F.A. (1944): The Road to Serfdom. London: Routledge

Haavelmo, T. (1954): A Study in the Theory of Economic Evolution. North-Holland, Amsterdam

Kevorkian, J./Cole, J.D. (1981): Perturbation Methods in Applied Mathematics. New York: Springer

Kuhn, T.S. (1977): The Essential Tension. Chicago: University of Chicago Press

O'Mallwy, R.E. (1988): On Nonlinear Singularly Perturbed Initial Value Problems. SIAM Review 30

Morishima, M. (1982): Why Has Japan Succeeded?. Cambridge: Cambridge University Press

Morishima, M. (1989): Ricardo's Economics - A General Equilibrium Theory of Distribution and Growth. Cambridge: Cambridge University Press

Nicolis, G./Prigogine, I. (1977): Self Organization in Nonequilibrium Systems. New York: Wiley

Pliss, V.A./Sell, G.R. (1991) Perturbations of Attractors of Differential Equations. Journal od Differential Equations 92

Prigogine, I. (1980): From Being to Becoming. San Francisco: W.H. Freeman

Puu, T. (1989): Nonlinear Economic Dynamics. Berlin: Springer-Verlag

Ricardo, D. (1817): On the Principles of Political Economy and Taxation. London: Everyone's Library, 1987

Samuelson, P.A. (1947): Foundations of Economic Analysis. Cambridge, Mass.:

Harvard University Press
Schumpeter, J.A. (1954): History of Economic Analysis. New York: Oxford University Press
Solow, R. (1985): Economic History and Economics. American Economic Review, May
Rosser, J.B.Jr. (1991): From Catastrophe to Chaos: A General Theory of Economic Discontinuities, Boston: Kluwer Academic Publishers
Toffler, A. (1990): Powershift. New York: Bantam Books.
Zhang, W.B. (1990a): Economic Growth and Technological Change. International Journal of Systems Science 21
Zhang, W.B. (1990b): Economic Dynamics - Growth and Development. Heidelberg: Springer-Verlag
Zhang, W.B. (1991a): Regional Dynamics with Creativity and Knowledge Diffusion. The Annals of Regional Science 25
Zhang, W.B. (1991b): Economic Development with Creativity and Knowledge Diffusion. Socio-Spatial Dynamics 2
Zhang, W.B. (1991c): Wealth Accumulation and Endogenous Technology in a Dynamic Monetary Economy. The Indian Economic Journal 39
Zhang, W.B. (1991e): Synergetic Economics. Heidelberg: Springer-Verlag, (Trnaslated into Japanese by Yuri Aruka et al., Tyoko: the Chuo University Press, 1994)
Zhang, W.B. (1992a): A Development Model of Developing Economies with Capital and Knowledge Accumulation. Journal of Economics 55
Zhang, W.B. (1992b): Trade and World Economic Growth -Differences in Knowledge Utilization and Creativity. Economic Letters 39
Zhang, W.B. (1992c): Economic Structural Change with Endogenous Capital and Knowledge - Knowledge as an International Public Good. The Indian Economic Journal 40
Zhang, W.B. (1993a): An Extension of the Ricardian System with Endogenous Knowledge and Infrastructure, in Structure and Change in the Space-Economy, edited by T.R. Lakshmanan and P. Nijkamp. Berlin: Springer-Verlag
Zhang, W.B. (1993b): Trade, Knowledge and Government Research Policy. International Review of Economics and Finance 2
Zhang, W.B. (1993c): Knowledge, Economic Structure and Growth, Technological Forecasting and Social Change 43
Zhang, W.B. (1993d): Location Choice and Land Use in an Isolated State - Endogenous Capital and Knowledge Accumulation. The Annals of Regional Science 27
Zhang, W.B. (1993e): An Urban Pattern Dynamics with Capital and Knowledge Accumulation, Environment and Planning A, 25
Zhang, W.B. (1993f): Knowledge, Economic Geography and Growth in a Two-Group Island-Economy. Technological Forecasting and Social Change 44
Zhang, W.B. (1993g): A Multi-Country Free Trade Model With Capital Accumulation. International Economic Journal 8

Zhang, W.B. (1993h): Woman's Labor Participation and Economic Growth - Creativity, Knowledge Utilization and Family Preference, Economics Letters 42

Zhang, W.B. (1994a): Capital, Population and Urban Pattern in an Isolated State. Regional Science and Urban Economics 24

Zhang, W.B. (1994b): The Dynamics of the J-island Economy - The Complexity of Economic Geography. Chaos, Solitons and Fractals 4

Zhang, W.B. (1994c): Wealth Distribution and Unemployment -Endogenous Capital and Knowledge in a Two-Group Growth Model. Umeå Economic Studies No. 350, University of Umeå.

Zhang, W.B. (1994d): Knowledge, Growth and Patterns of Trade, Annals of Regional Science 28

A Dynamic Model and Numerical Experiment on the Evolution of Macroeconomics*

Li Honggang and Fang Fukang

Institute of Non-equilibrium Systems,
Beijing Normal University, Beijing 100875, China

Abstract. An overall dynamic model on macroeconomics is presented. The model gives a comprehensive consideration on behavior of the products market, money market, and labor market, and explores growth and fluctuation of economic aggregate amount. Owing to emphasizing on the entirety and dynamic on the model, its numerical experiments exhibit the complexity of economic evolution.

Key words. Macroeconomics, Evolution

1 Introduction

Macroeconomics is the study of the behavior of the economy as a whole (David (1981)). It explores how the Gross National Output (GNP) and the gross expenditures of resource are determined, moreover, how these aggregate amounts evolve at specific time horizon. It does try to answer the important question about the economy such as questions on the scale and growth rate GNP, the scale of employment and the rate of unemployment, the price level and the rate of inflation, the rate of interest and so on. It is the behavior of economy as a whole that contains the complexity of economic systems.

First of all, building an *overall* macroeconomics model in the theoretical level is essential. It is to say that the model should include and must answer all the preceding macroeconomics question. Furthermore, the model should be a dynamic one and it can describe the behavior of economic evolution. However, although macroeconomics theories have made great progress since the *General Theory* (Keynes (1936)) was published, the majority of theoretical models on macroeconomics are confined to being local and/or static ones, and the overall models on macroeconomics have almost not be seen. In view of such circumstances, this paper will present an overall dynamic model on macroeconomics, and make a study on economic growth and fluctuation with the model. The model gives a comprehensive consideration on the behavior of the products market, money market, and labor market, among which the products market and money market are regarded as leading markets, and the labor market is

* Supported by College Doctoral Project Funds of China.

in the position of a dependency. It makes a detailed study of the key variables such as GNP, employment and unemployment, price level and inflation, wage, money supply and son on. In this sense, it is an overall and dynamic model, which explores growth and fluctuation of economic aggregate amount.

The second, an analytical method is always effective for a model, but it will face great difficulty when a more complex macroeconomic model is discussed. So another way should be sought. It is lucky to see that the methods of numerical experiment and simulation have an advantage in these circumstances. So this paper tries to adopt numerical experiment method in System Dynamics and wish to grasp the basic characteristics of economic evolution by simulation technique. In our work, the applied software *Ithink* for System Dynamics is employed.

2 The Model

The basic framework of the model is exhibited as follows: the rate of interest is determined through money market. Combining with the expected rate of profit which results in situation of products market, it determines this term investment. The investment brings about two effects: one is to increase this term effective demand, the other is to promote next term latent supply capacity. Both of the effective demand and this term latent supply capacity jointly determine this term gross output, and gross output determines this term employment. As can be seen, there are two special assumptions in the model:

The first, the output is determined by the effective demand and the latent supply capacity. Especially, the output equals to the minimum of the effective demand and latent supply capacity (see equation 2.5). Obviously, this view fails to agree with either Keynesian school, which holds that the output is controlled only by effective demand, or supply side school, which holds that supply capability controls output (Thomas (1972)). In our view, this model presents a better framework. If different output-determining mechanisms of keynesian school and supply side school are considered to act in different cases which can exist in economic evolution, this framework can contain the views of either keynesian school or supply side school.

The second, the investment-decision in this model is expressed as a function on the difference of expected average rate of profit and expected rate of interest (see equation 2.7). Meanwhile, the investment equation is a dynamic adjustment equation. In particular, when the expected average rate of profit equals to the rate of interest, the investment increase at a speed of *natural growth rate*. Comparing with the majority of macroeconomics models, although the average rate of profit in this model is not in accordance with marginal rate of profit in *General Theory*, this model is nearer to Keynes's thought.

For convenience, a table of essential variables is given as follows:

K: capital stock

D: depreciation of capital
pL: output per labor
Lp: total available labor
M: money stock
p: price level
kc: reciprocal of the velocity of circulation
u: the rate of unemployment
gy: the growth rate of GNP
ipo: last term rate of inflation ip_{t-1}
gw: the growth rate of wage
C: gross consumption
Ys: latent supply capacity
Ro: last term average rate of profit R_{t-1}
ro: last term rate of interest r_{t-1}
I: capital investment
dc: the rate of depreciation
gpl: the growth rate of output per labor
glp: the growth rate of labor
gm: the real growth rate of money stock
h: the ratio of gross tax to GNP
L: real employment
Y: real GNP
ip: the rate of inflation
w: wage
b_K: the ratio of capital to output
Yd: effective demand
R: average rate of profit
r: the rate of interest
Yo: last term real GNP
s: the ratio of savings

The main equations of this model are presented.

$$dK/dt = I - d_c K \tag{2.1}$$

$$Y_s = Y_s(K, L) = \min(b_K K, Lp \times L) = b_K K \tag{2.2}$$

$$dpL/dt = gpl \times pL \tag{2.3}$$

$$Y_d = C + I \tag{2.4}$$

$$Y = \min(Y_s, Y_d) \tag{2.5}$$

$$C_t = (1-s)[(1-h)Y_{t-1} + dM/p] + hY_{t-1} \tag{2.6}$$

$$I = I(R^*, r^*) = I(R_{t-1}, r_{t-1}) = (dc + glp)\exp[a(R_{t-1} - r_{t-1})] \tag{2.7}$$

$$dLp/dt = glp \times Lp \tag{2.8}$$

$$R = (Y - wL/p)/K \tag{2.9}$$

$$r = l_0 /[M/(k_c pY) - 1] \tag{2.10}$$

$$dp/pdt = ip = j_1 ip^* + j_2(Y_d - Y_s)/Y_s = j_1 ip_{t-1} + j_2(Y_d - Y_s)/Y_s \tag{2.11}$$

$$L = Y/pL \tag{2.12}$$

$$u = 1 - L/Lp \tag{2.13}$$

$$gw = ip^* - j_3(u - u_0) + gpl = ip_{t-1} - j_3(u - u_0) + gpl \tag{2.14}$$

$$dM/dt = gm \times M \tag{2.15}$$

a, j_1, j_2, j_3 are parameters.

Notes:

1. The expression of production function in equation 2.1 depends on the assumption that available labor is unlimited in comparison with available capital equipment.
2. A variable with star * means expected value of the variable. For simplicity, the expected value of a variable in this model is assumed to equal to the last term value of the variable.
3. The equation 2.10 is deduced from $M = k_c pY + L_2(r) = k_c pY(1 + l_0/r)$ and l_0 is a parameter indicated liquidity preference.
4. The equation 2.14 is one kind of expression of Phillips Curve (Frisch(1983)).

Fig.A.1 in appendix is a System Dynamics Structure Diagram of this model.

3 Numerical Experiment

By selecting some parameters and initial condition, numerical experiments on this model proceed. The evolving behavior of variables, which are divided into two groups such as *Y, P, L, I* and *gy, ip, u, Ro,* is exhibited. As an example, Fig.3.1 and Fig.3.2 present one evolving result of the eight variables. On the figures, abscissa denotes evolving time.

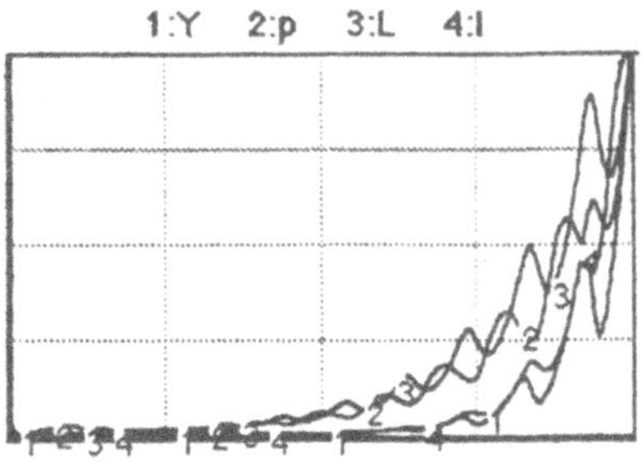

Fig. 3.1. Time series of *Y, P, L, I*

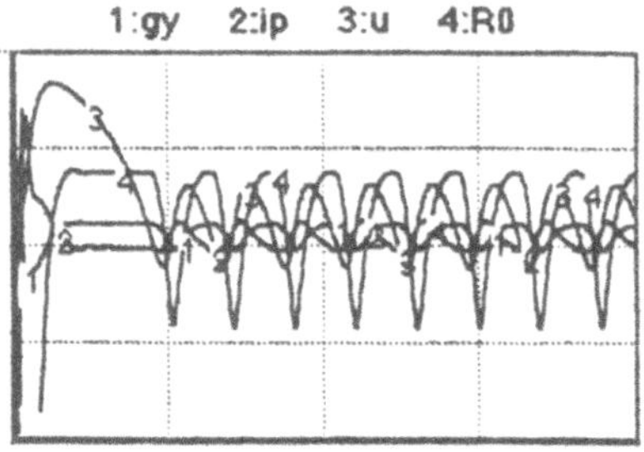

Fig. 3.2. Time series of *gy, ip, u, Ro*

Ignoring temporary process, some basic characteristics of economic evolution is obtained as follows by the experiments.

(1) Growth and fluctuation are united in economic evolution. For example, curve *Y* shaped as *steps by steps*, which indicates a step-like growth in real economy, and the curve of growth rate *gy* exhibits fluctuation. The evolution of other variables such as *ip, u, Ro* also exhibits fluctuation and usually has same period as *gy*. Obviously, the fluctuations in this model are not caused by external shocks, and they are just endogenous behaviors of evolving systems.

(2) As some parameters are given, business cycle can either explode or decline to zero. But at a wide range of given parameters, the explosion and decline are not apparent. This is different from cycle behaviors in the accelerator and multiplier model (Gabisch / Lorenz (1987)). It means that the cycle behavior in this model is more robust for some parametric changes.

(3) Business cycle varies as parameters change. Especially, given some parameters, the period of cycle tends to the infinite. This means disappearance of business cycle in a specific sense. So cycle behavior can be regard as normal characteristics of economic evolution, and non-cycle phenomena just correspond to a long-period cycle behavior which may be disturbed repeatedly. Furthermore, the parameters are evolving themselves in real economy. So the ordinary business cycle does make up of a series of different business cycle, and it usually exhibits irregular wavy curve.

(4) There exists diversified wavy curve. For example, *para-square wavy curve* and *para-sawtoothed wavy curve* can be obtained. The former denotes one case in which long term boom is accompanied by short term depression, the later denotes another case in which the period of upswing and recession are asymmetrical.

Certainly, more results on macroeconomic evolution can be obtained from this model. Owing to the limitation of space, this paper does not cite them any more. Then, some parametric analysis is presented on the model. The main parameters which have an effect on the economic evolution are divided into three groups: the first are responding parameters (or named adjusting parameters), and the *a* in investment equation 2.7 is an example; the second are state parameters, and the growth rate of output per labor *gpl* is an example; the third are policy parameters, and the real growth rate of money supply *gm* is an example. Then, taking *a*, *gpl*, *gm* as representatives of the proceeding three group parameters, parametric effects on economic evolution are exhibited as follows:

(1)When responding parameter *a* increases, the periods of wavy curve such as *gy*, *ip*, *u*, *Ro* shorten, and it makes it clear that a promotion for responding ability of economic system will cause economic fluctuation more frequently. As for the amplitude of the business cycle, it shows a non-monotonous variations: When *a* increases at a lower level, the amplitude decreases, which indicates that improvement of responding intensity can absorb the fluctuations; however, when *a* increases at a higher level, the amplitude increases too, which indicates that improvement of responding intensity just aggravates the fluctuation. Moreover, the effect of alteration of *a* on the GNP level also depends on the *a* level, and there exists different *a* region in which *a* has a positive or negative effect on GNP level. This represents that responding parametric effect on economic growth is nonmonotonous, and it shows that a suitable responding intensity is necessary for an economy. Neither the lack of response nor over-response does benefit to economic growth.

(2)The state parameter *gpl* not only has a positive effect on the level of economic growth, but also has effect on the period of the business cycle. For instance, when *gpl* increases, the periods of the cycle lengthen and the amplitude of the fluctuation decrease. It represents that speeding-up promotion of technology can absorb the economic fluctuation. This conclusion is not direct but of significance.

(3)The policy parameter *gm* also has an effect on business cycle. With *gm* increasing, the periods of the cycle lengthen. The amplitudes of the cycle have a nonmonotonous variations: when *gm* increases at a lower level, the amplitudes of *gy*, *ip*, *u*, *Ro* curve all decrease; when *gm* increases at a higher lever, the amplitudes increases. Except for *u*, the average values of the proceeding variables have same altering direction with their amplitudes. It shows that effect of the growth rate of money supply on economic evolution is complex. Therefore, when the growth rate of money supply is utilized to adjust business cycle, a suitable value is very important. Similarly, the other paramtric analysis can be presented although they are not included in this paper.

4 Conclusion

To sum up, owing to emphasizing on the entirety and dynamic of the model, the numerical experiment results on the economic growth and fluctuation exhibit the *complexity* of economic evolution. In particular, the results are not usually direct. It is to say that they show the characteristics of *non-intuition*. Moreover, some results are unexpected, this means the characteristics as *anti-intuition*. A key source of these characteristics is the nonmonotonous relationship between the results of economic evolution and the economic variables (including parameters),this represents a *nonlinear causal relation*, which does not agree to a *linear thinking* which is developed from simple systems.

Of course, this model has a long way to exhibit the real complexity of real economic system (Anderson/Arrow/Pines (1988)), and some further work can advance on the way. Some instances are given as follows:

(1) This paper just gives a simple consideration about expectation. However, expectation is complex, and exists widely, which has important effect in real economy. In addition, this paper has no consideration about the uncertainty, which is also a main source of complexity of economic system.

(2) In this model, the parameters are viewed as constant. However, economy is an evolving system, the parameters may change themselves. Therefore, it gives rise to a question on a time robust of the parameters. So we must take note of comprehension on the results.

(3) The model does not involve a real particular economy, so its results are detached. If a real particular economy is discussed, some variation for the model is necessary, and more results with individuality of the real particular economy will be obtained.

References

Anderson, P./Arrow, K./Pines, D. (eds. 1988): *The Economy as an Evolving Complex System*. Redwood City:Addison-Wesley

David, W. (1981): *Dictionary of Modern Economics*. London: The Macmillan

Frisch, H. (1983): *Theories of Inflation*. London: Cambridge University Press

Gabisch, G. /Lorenz, H. (1987): *Business Cycle Theory*. Berlin: Springer-Verlag

Keynes, J.M.(1936): *The General Theory of Employment Interest and Money*. London: the Macmillan

Thomas, S.(1972): *Say's law; An Historical Analysis*. Princeton: Princeton University Press

Appendix

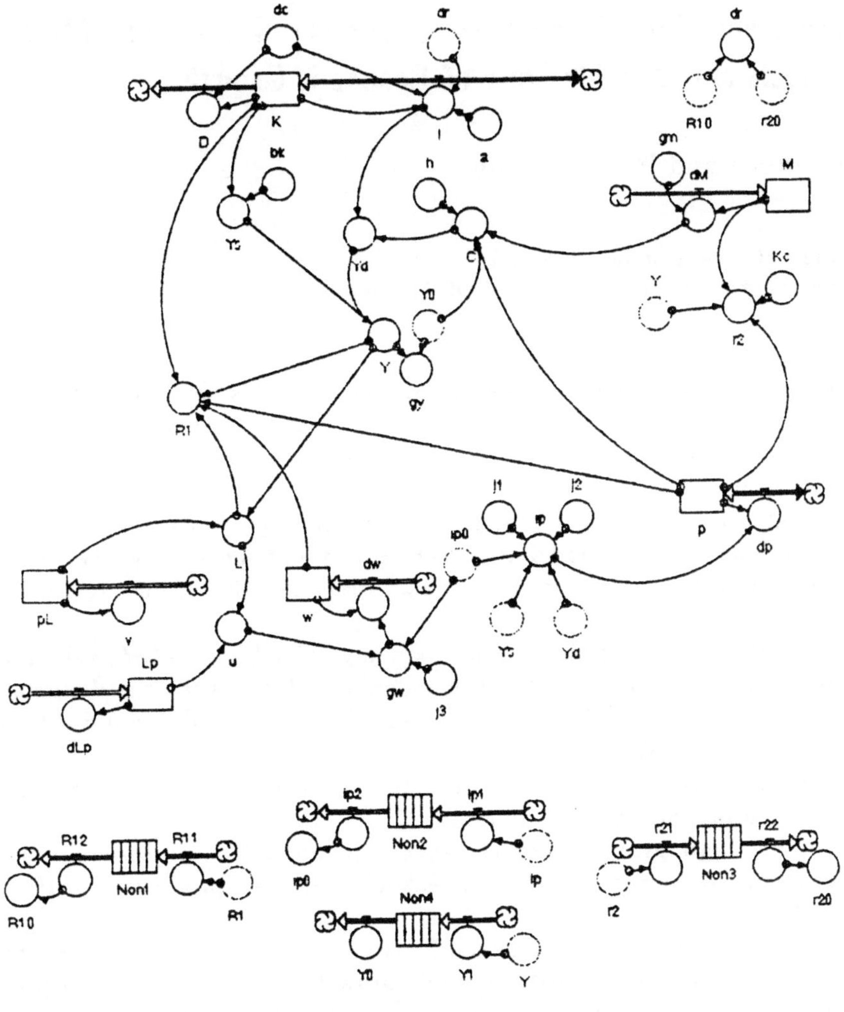

Fig. A.1. System Dynamics Structure Diagram of the model

Investment for Technology Progress, Increasing Marginal Products and Bistable State of Economic Growth

Di Zengru and Fang Fukang

Institute of Nonequilibrium Systems,
Beijing Normal University, Beijing, 100875, China

Abstract. For an open developing economy, besides the effect of R & D, an important way of technology progress is to get the advanced technology by certain investment. But only when the investment reaches a certain amount, can the level of technology be raised obviously. So there is a large set up cost in the importation of technology and equipment. A S-curve is used in the model to describe this nonlinear property. By the static equilibrium and dynamic analysis, the following results are obtained:

1. Such a small open developing economy (SODE) is *locked in* the initial state which is in the lower level of technolgy. Only when the disturbance (investment for technology import) exceeds a critical value could it lead to the *take—off* of SODE.
2. In the period of economic take off, the economic growth can reach a high speed in a short time interval.
3. This high growth rate is caused by the effect of self-reinforcing mechanism arising from the increasing marginal products (IMP) of capital.

IMP is a important cause of nonlinear interaction in economic system. On the basis of neoclassical economic growth theory, it has been proved by singularity theory that when there is IMP in the economy, there will be bistable state of economic growth. Exceeding a certain economic barrier is the basic condition of economic take — off. The influence of capital accumulation and population growth on the economic development is discussed.

1 **Introduction**

With the development of the research on the properties of nonlinear systems, the important effect of nonlinearity on the evolution of economic system is recognized gradually. There are many reasons that lead to the nonlinear interaction in economic system, such as nonlinear acceleration mechanism (Goodwin (1951)), effect of pollution (Day (1982)), economic externalities (Boldrin (1992)) and so on. The nonlinearity will cause the complexity of economic evolution, such as multi-equilibria and chaos. B. Arthur discussed the self-reinforcing mechanism in economic system and its influence on economic evolution (Arthur (1988)). He pointed out that a large set up or fixed cost is an important reason of increasing returns. We will discuss a small open developing economy (SODE) in the following. The SODE can get the advanced technology by certain amount of investment, and this will lead to the development of the economy.

Technology progress is an important factor of economic growth. Recently, the theory of endogenous macroeconomic growth provides a new description of the relationship between growth and technology. Romer has taken the view that technology progress is created by the sector of R & D in the economic system, and the changing rate of technology is determined by the investment of human capital and the stock of knowledge (Romer 1986). Lucas has discussed the influence of the accumulation of human capital on technology progress and growth (Lucas 1988). Their theories have changed the focus toward explanations of sustained long-run growth. But it is only the case of developed economy. For an open developing economy, besides the effect of R & D, the main source of technology progress is to import the advanced technology. Especially for a small open developing economy (SODE), the investment for import technology basically determines the rise of its technology level.

In fact, the raise of technology level is not in proportion to the investment. There is a large amount of set up costs, and this determines the nonlinear relationship between investment and technology progress. This is the basic idea of following research. A small open economy (SOE) is an interesting object for economic research. South Korea and Taiwan are the examples of SOE. The special economic zones and some other relatively independent economic regions of China can also be treated as SOE. Of course they have different economic features. They are small open developing economy (SODE). Grossman, Helpman and K.-y. M. Fung have discussed economic growth of SOE based on the endogenous economic growth theory. The importation of technology and the development of SODE are discussed under the same framework in the following.

Section 2 describes the basic model and the results of equilibrium and dynamic analysis. Some interesting results are obtained in the model.

I. There are two kinds of equilibria: a low-level initial equilibrium and a high-level equilibrium. The SODE is *locked in* the initial state which is in the lower level of technology. Only when the disturbance (investment for technology import) exceeds a critical value could it lead to the *take-off* of SODE.

Ⅱ. In the period of economic take-off, the economic growth can reach a high speed in a short time interval.

Ⅲ. This high growth rate is caused by the effect of self-reinforcing mechanism arising from the increasing marginal products (IMP) of capital.

Section 3 describes the neoclassical economic growth model under the assumption of IMP. IMP is the basic source of nonlinearity in economic system. It makes SODE have bistable state of economic growth. Exceeding a certain economic barrier is the basic condition of economic take-off. The influence of capital accumulation and population growth on the economic development is discussed.

2 Investment for technology import and increasing marginal products of capital

We examine a SODE with one sector. It use two primary factors [labor (L) and capital (K)] to produce product Y under certain technology level A. It has following features:

Ⅰ. SODE has a large economic background. The changing of its economy can not influence the whole economic system;

Ⅱ. SODE has access to the world capital market at an exogenously given world interest rate r. There is capital flow between SODE and its environment.

Ⅲ. Its technology progress is determined by the investment for advanced technology importation.

Y is produced under Cobb-Douglas production function with Harrod neutral technology A:

$$Y = b(AL)^{a}K_{1}^{1-a} \tag{1}$$

Assume that labor L is constant in SODE. The rise in technology A is determined by the investment K_2. If $K_2 = 0$, that is, there is no investment for importation of advanced technology, then $A=A_0$. With the increasing of K_2, $A=F(K_2)$ has the form of S-curve (Fig. 1). Figure 2 is the curve of dA/dK_2. A most important property of $A=F(K_2)$ is that the rise in A is not in proportion to K_2. Only when K_2 reaches a certain amout, can the level of technology A be raised obviously.

For initial state, $K_2=0$, $A=A_0$, the equilibrium capital stock satisfy:

$$\partial Y/\partial K_1|_0 = r \tag{2}$$

where the subscript 0 represents the initial state.

When there is investment for importation of advanced technology, the

The equilibrium point 2 is stable. It is the final state of economic development. The equilibrium point 1 is unstable. It forms the economic barrier of development. If the initial investment for technology progress ΔK_2 is less than K_{21}, it could not lead to the qualitative change of SODE. But when $\Delta K_2 > K_{21}$, the marginal product of capital (including K_1 and K_2) will be greater than the interest rate r. So SODE will attract further investment from the world economy. And with the increasing of capital stock, its marginal product has a stage of increasing. Increasing marginal product (IMP) forms the self-reinforcing mechanism of economic growth. It leads to the take—off of SODE, and finally the economy will stabilize in equilibrium 2. The existence of critical point K_{21} is the result of nonlinear relationship between investment and technology progress. It will change with the variation of interest rate r (Fig. 4). The bigger r is ,the larger the initial set up capital K_{21} is and the higher the economic barrier will be. Also we can discuss the effect of the changing of other parameters on critical point K_{21}.

Investigation of the evolution of SODE could give us a deeper understanding of the system. The change of capital is based on the difference of its marginal product. Assume it follows the equations:

$$dK_1/dt = m(\partial Y/\partial K_1 - r)$$

$$dK_2/dt = \begin{cases} 0 & \partial Y/\partial A \cdot dA/dK_2 \leq r \\ m(\partial Y/\partial A \cdot dA/dK_2 - r) & \partial Y/\partial A \cdot dA/dK_2 > r \end{cases} \quad (7)$$

The corresponding change of product is:

$$dY/dt = \partial Y/\partial K \cdot dK_1/dt + \partial Y/\partial A \cdot dA/dK_2 \cdot dK_2/dt \quad (8)$$

In the following numerical simulations, the relation of A and K_2 is given by:

$$A = A_0 + B(1 - e^{-K_2^2/2\lambda}) \quad (9)$$

thus:

$$dA/dK_2 = \frac{BK_2}{\lambda} e^{-K_2^2/2\lambda} \quad (10)$$

The value of parameters are: $a=1/3$, $b=0.3$, $r=0.1$, $A_0=1.0$, $B=1.5$, $\lambda=1.0$, $m=2.5$. The initial state is $K_{20}=0$, $A=A_0$, and from equation (2):

$$K_{10} = \left[\frac{(1-a)b}{r}\right]^{1/a} A_0 \quad (11)$$

Under the influence of investment ΔK_2 for importing advanced technology, we get following results:

Ⅰ. The initial investment ΔK_2 has a critical value ΔK_{2c}. When $\Delta K_2 < \Delta K_{2c}$, althought it could raise the technology A and lead some growth of product, the economy has no qualitative change in final. When $\Delta K_2 > \Delta K_{2c}$, SODE will exceed economic barrier and take off from the initial state. These are the same as the results of equilibrium analysis.

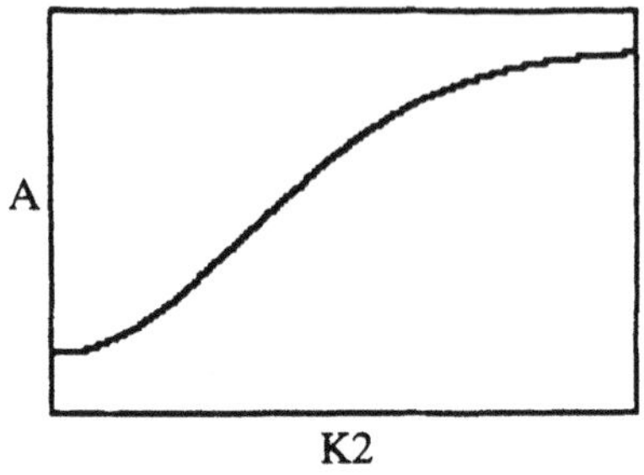

Fig. 1 $A=F(K_2)$

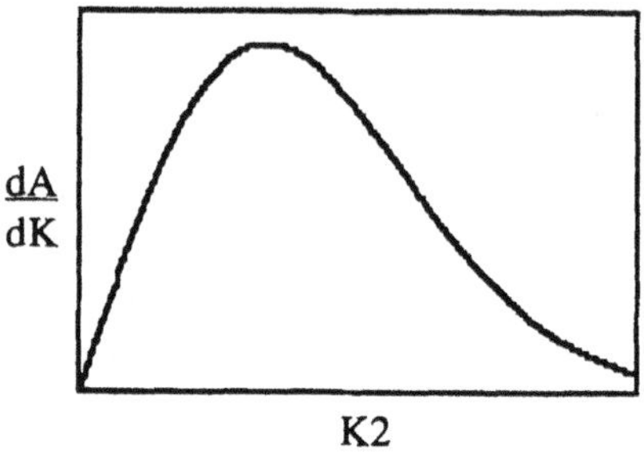

Fig. 2 Curve of dA/dK_2

marginal product of capital K_1 will increase with the progress of A. So there will be capital flow between SODE and the world economy. The new equilibrium points are determined by following equations:

$$\partial Y/\partial K_1 = \partial Y/\partial K_2 = \partial Y/\partial A \cdot dA/dK_2 = r \tag{3}$$

From equations (1) and (3), we obtain:

$$\alpha K_1 \cdot dA/dK_2 = (1-\alpha)A \tag{4}$$

$$A = K_1\left(\frac{r}{b(1-\alpha)}\right)^{1/\alpha} \tag{5}$$

Thus, the fundamental equation that determines the equilibrium points is:

$$dA/dK_2 = \frac{1-\alpha}{\alpha}\left(\frac{r}{b(1-\alpha)}\right)^{1/\alpha} \tag{6}$$

According to the properties of dA/dK_2, the equation (6) has two solutions in general. That is, there will be two equilibrium points. The corresponding investments are K_{21} and K_{22} (Fig. 3).

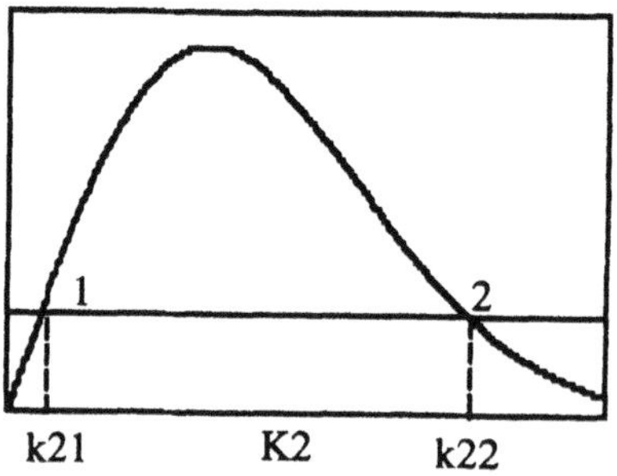

Fig. 3 The equilibrium points

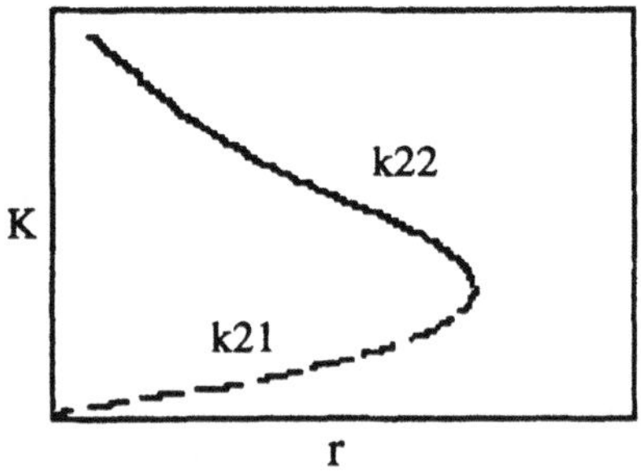

Fig. 4 The changing of K_{21}, K_{22}

$$dk/dt = sf(k) - gk \qquad (12)$$

where s is average propensity to save, g is constant growth rate of labor, $k=K/L$ is capital stock per capita, $f(k)$ is production function. In general, the following assumptions are imposed:

$$f(k) > 0 \qquad f'(k) > 0 \qquad f''(k) < 0$$
$$f(0) = 0$$
$$f'(0) = \infty \qquad f'(\infty) = 0 \qquad 0 < s \leqslant 1 \qquad (13)$$

But for SODE, we suppose that $f(k)$ has following properties:

$$f(k) > 0 \qquad f'(k) > 0$$
$$f''(k) \begin{cases} > 0 & 0 < k < \mu \\ = 0 & k = \mu \\ < 0 & k > \mu \end{cases} \qquad f'''(\mu) < 0 \qquad (14)$$
$$f'(0) = 0 \qquad f'(\infty) = 0 \qquad f(0) = p$$

The key point of these assumptions is increasing marginal product (IMP) of capital. Under the assumptions(14), $f'(k)$have a unique maximum at $k = \mu$. Let$f'(\mu) = M$. With the parameters p and $\lambda = g/s$, the qualitative properties of (12) is determined by the function

$$G(k,\lambda,p) = f(k,p) - \lambda k \qquad (15)$$

Under the assumptions(14), the following theorem can easily be proved:

Theorem 1. For any $\mu > 0, M > 0$, in the space $\Omega\{k,\lambda,p\}$, there exists a unique point $Z_0 = (\mu, M, p_0)$, such that the $G(k,\lambda,p)$has the properties:

$$G(\mu,M,p_0) = \frac{\partial}{\partial k}G(k,M,p_0)\,|_{k=\mu} = (\frac{\partial}{\partial k})^2 G(k,M,p_0)\,|_{k=\mu} = 0$$

$$(\frac{\partial}{\partial k})^3 G(k,M,p_0)\,|_{k=\mu} < 0 \qquad (\frac{\partial}{\partial \lambda})G(\mu,\lambda,p_0)\,|_{\lambda=M} < 0$$

From the recognition propositions of singularity theory the following result can be achieved:

Theorem 2. For any $\mu > 0$, $M > 0$, there exists a unique point $Z_0 = (\mu, M, p_0) \in \Omega$, such that $G(k, \lambda, p_0)$ is equivalent to the hysteresis in a neighborhood of (μ, M)

In the point Z_0, $G(k,\lambda,p)$ satisfies:

$$G_\lambda = -\mu \qquad G_{\lambda k} = -1$$
$$G_p = 1 \qquad G_{pk} = 0$$

and

$$det\begin{Bmatrix} G_\lambda & G_{\lambda k} \\ G_p & G_{pk} \end{Bmatrix} = det\begin{Bmatrix} -\mu & -1 \\ 1 & 0 \end{Bmatrix} = 1$$

According to the propositions of universal unfolding. we can get the following theorem:

Theorem 3. The one-parameter unfolding $G(k,\lambda,p)$ in theorem 2 is a universal unfolding of $G(k,\lambda,p_0)$ near (μ,M).

From the above theorems, the singularities of $G(k,\lambda,p_0)$ are described in Fig. 8. In a certain regions of parameter space, the economy described by production function (14) has a bistable state of economic growth (Fig.

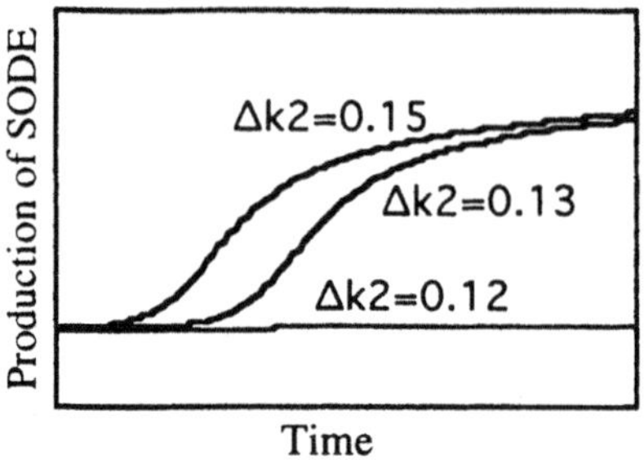

Fig. 5 The development of SODE

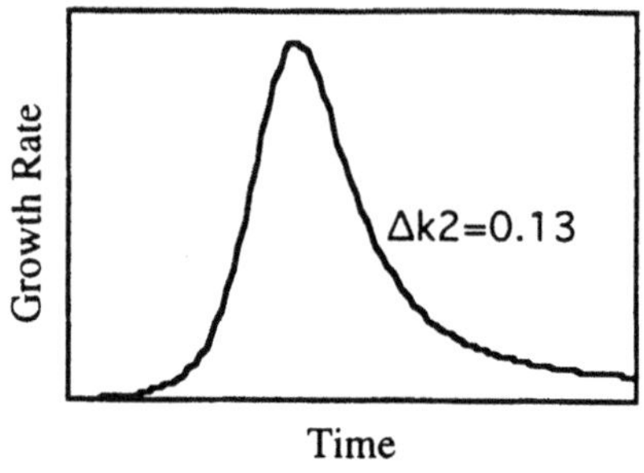

Fig. 6 The growth rate

Ⅱ. When $\Delta K_2 > \Delta K_{2c}$, the economic development can be divided into two stages: gradual growth and sudden change. The larger ΔK_2 is, the earlier the sudden change occur (Fig. 5).

(3)In the sudden change stage, the economic growth can get a relatively high speed (Fig. 6).

(4)The marginal product of total capital of SODE $(K_1 + K_2)$ has a stage of increasing (Fig. 7). The property of increasing marginal product (IMP) is very important for the rescarch of economic development. In the following section we will discuss its effect on economic growth in the basis of neoclassical theory.

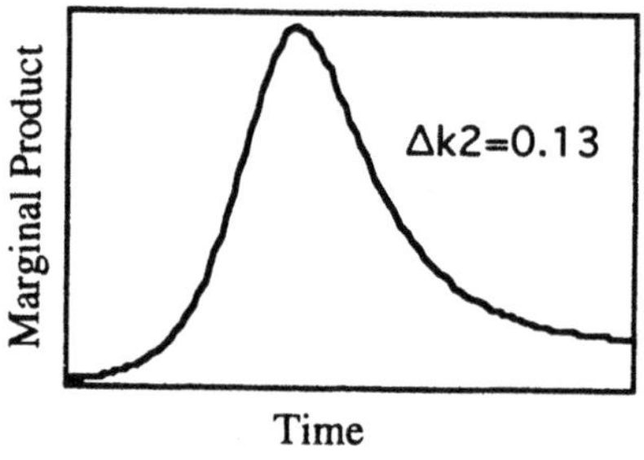

Fig. 7 The marginal product

3 IMP and the Bistable State of Economic Growth

According to the neoclassical economic growth theory, under the condition of constant return to scale, economic growth is determined by equation:

8(c), Fig. 9.) When $\lambda=g/s$ is large or small enough the system has only one steady state. There exist λ_{c1} and λ_{c2} when $\lambda_{c2}<\lambda<\lambda_{c1}$, there will be three steady states. One of them is unstable. Because $\lambda=g/s$, so we can discuss the effect of labor growth and capital accumulation on economic growth.

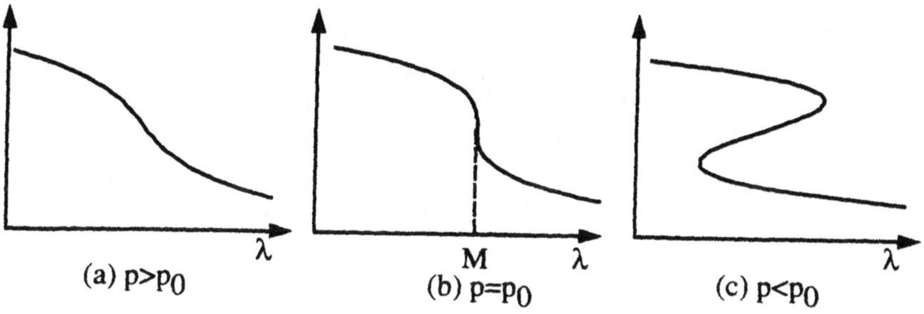

Fig. 8 The singulacities of G(k,λ,p)

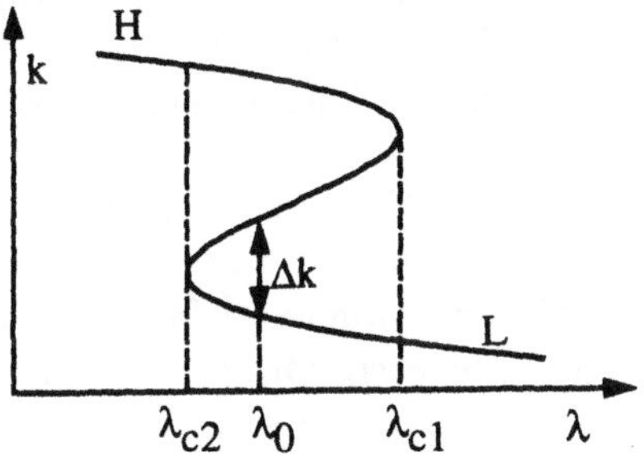

Fig. 9 The bistable state

Fig. 10 A description of economic development

For a given saving propensity s, if labor growth rate g makes $\lambda>\lambda_{c1}$ although the economic growth can get a higher rate through the expansion of inputs, the capital per capita and the product per capita will be in the lower branch L. With the diminishing of g, when $\lambda<\lambda_{c1}$, there will be a higher stable branch H. But because the branch L is still stable, the economy will be locked in the branch L. A small perturbation cannot cause the sudden change of the economy. Only When $\lambda<\lambda_{c2}$ can the economy take—off from the branch L, and finally stabilize in branch H.

Then so long as $\lambda < \lambda_{C1}$, the economy will be stable in higher branch H. When g is constant, by the same method we can get the effect of parameter s. A high accumulation rate s is favorable to economic take-off.

4 Concluding Remarks

Economy is an evolving complex system. The study of nonlinearities will certainly be helpful in uncovering important properties of its evolution. From the nonlinear relationship between technology progress and investment, the effects of importing advanced technology on economic development are discused above. There are several typical nonlinear phenomena, such as multi-equilibria, lock in, critical effect, sudden change and so on. The further research in section 3 has indicated that the increasing marginal return will lead to the bistable state of economic growth, and under some conditions there will be sudden change of the state. Our results are obtained from a realistic economic model, and a lot of evidence for the conclusions could be gotten from the development of some countries and regions.

W. W. Rostow introduced the concept of economic take—off in 1960 to describe the structure change and high speed growth in economic development (Rostow (1960)). In *Synergetic Economics*, W. B. Zhang indicated that economic take—off can be described by the catastrophe of nonlinear system (Zhang (1992)). Our research could be a development of above theory. From the above results, we can give a simplified description of economic development (Fig. 10). Of course, economic development especially economic take off is determined by a lot of factors including social, political, economic, cultural, environmental factors and so on. Our model is only a very simplified description of economic evolution.

Reference

Arthur, B. (1988): Self-reinforcing Mechanism Economics. P. W. Anderson, K. J. Arrow and D. Pines, eds, *The Economy as an Evolving Complex System*. New York: Addison-Wesley, 9-31.

Boldrin, M. (1992): Dynamic Externalities, Multiple Equilibria, and Growth. *Journal of Economic Theory* 58. 198-218.

Fung, K.-y. M, Ishikawa, J. (1992): Dynamic Increasing Returns, Technology and Economic Growth in a Small Open Economy. *Journal of Development Economics* 37. 63-87.

Day, R. H. (1982): Irregular Growth Circle, *American Economic Review* 72, 406-414.

Goodwin, R. M. (1951): The Nonlinear Accelerator and the Persistence of Business cycles. *Econometrica* 19. 1-17.

Grossman, G. M. and E. Helpman (1989): Growth and Welfare in a Small Open Economy. Working Paper, No. 2970 ,NBER, Cambridge, MA.

Lucas, R. E. (1988): On the Mechanics of Economic Development, *Journal of Monetary Economics* 22, 1-41.

Romer, P. M. (1986): Increasing Returns and Long Run Growth. *Journal of Political Economy* 94, 1002-1037.

Rostow, W. W. (1960): *The stages of Economic Growth.* Cambridge: Cambridge University Press.

Solow. R. (1956): A Contribution to the Theory of Growth. *Quarterly Journal of Economics* 70, 65-94.

Zhang, W. B. (1991): *Synergetic Economics-time and Change in Nonlinear Economics.* Berlin: Springer—verlag

No Limit Cycle:
Chen's Learning Competition Model Revisited

Guangzhen Sun

Centre for Management Science,
Peking University, Beijing 100871, P. R. China

Abstract. Chen's learning competition model, which was introduced to describe the nonequilibrium dynamics of social evolution and regarded as a succeesful application of Prigogine's nonequilibrium paradingm to social science, is revisited. A simple proof of the nonexistence of a limit cycle in Chen's model is given and related issues are briefly discussed.

1 Introduction

As Chen (1987) remarked correctly, the paradigm of nonequilibrium, which was due to the revolutionary work by Thom, Haken and especially Prigogine (1984), has not only brought about a great advance in natural sciences such as chemistry and physics but greatly enriched our understanding of social phenomena. Chen's learning competition model (Chen ((1987)) was one of the positive results the prigogine School obtained when they attempted to shed new light upon social processes such as the origin of the division of labor, the competition behavior of different species, the process of information diffusion and so on. It seems surprising and interesting to me that Chen's learning competition model concerning two species with different degrees of sensitivity to strangeness and risk has aroused repercussions in a seminar on the arms race sponsored by the military of the United States(Chen(1993)).

2 Main Results

For convenience of discussion, we recite Chen's learning competition model *for two species with different cultures* as follows:

$$\frac{\partial n_1}{\partial t} = s_1 n_1 (M_1 - n_1 - \beta_{12} n_2) \tag{1}$$

$$\frac{\partial n_2}{\partial t} = s_2 n_2 (M_2 - n_2 - \beta_{21} n_1) \tag{2}$$

where n_i is the number of knowers in species i, M_i, s_i and β_{ij} are the effective carrying capacity of resources, effective growth rate and effecticve competition coefficient respectively. And i, j is 1 or 2.

As Chen (1987) noted, the condition of coexistent species is

$$\beta_{ij}M_i < M_j < M_i/\beta_{ij} \tag{3}$$

We have the following theorem:

Theorem. If the condition (3) holds, then there is no limit cycle in Chen's learning competition model (1)−(2)and there exists a unique and asymptotically stable equilibrium point in the first quadrant for system (1)−(2).

Proof. from condition (3) and the criterion for the stability of equilibrium points Zhang(1987), the unique equilibrium point in the first quadrang

$$(n_1^*, n_2^*) = \left(\frac{M_1 - \beta_{12}M_2}{1 - \beta_{12}\beta_{21}}, \frac{M_2 - \beta_{21}M_1}{1 - \beta_{21}\beta_{12}}\right)$$ is asymptotically stable.

For the proof of the nonexistence of limit cycle, the deduction to absurdity is used. Suppose there exists a limit cycle $\Gamma_0: n_1 = n_1(t), n_2 = n_2(t)$, so there exists $T > 0$, $s.t.$, $n_1(0)(T) = n_1(0), n_2(T) = n_2(0)$. The index of $\Gamma_0$is found by compution (Zhang (1987)).

$$\gamma_0 = \frac{1}{T}\int_0^T \left[\frac{\partial}{\partial n_1}(s_1 n_1(M_1 - n_1 - \beta_{12}n_2)) + \frac{\partial}{\partial n_2}(s_2 n_2(M_2 - n_2 - \beta_{21}n_1))\right]dt \tag{4}$$

Rewriting Chen's model:

$$s_1(M_1 - n_1 - \beta_{12}n_2)dt = \frac{dn_1}{n_1} \tag{5}$$

$$s_2(M_2 - n_2 - \beta_{21}n_1)dt = \frac{dn_2}{n_2} \tag{6}$$

Integration of both sides of the equations above ablong Γ_0 Yields:

$$\int_0^T S_1(M_1 - n_1 - \beta_{12}n_2)dt = \int_{n_1(0)}^{n_1(T)} \frac{dn_1}{n_1}$$

$$= ln|n_1(t)|\,|_{n_1(0)}^{n_1(T)} = 0 \tag{7}$$

and

$$\int_0^T s_2(M_2 - n_2 - \beta_{21}n_1)dt = 0 \tag{8}$$

Therefore $\frac{1}{T}\int_0^T n_1(t)dt$ *and* $\frac{1}{T}\int_0^T n_2(t)dt$ satisfy:

$$s_1(M_1 - n_1 - \beta_{12}n_2) = 0 \tag{9}$$

$$s_2(M_2 - n_2 - \beta_{21}n_1) = 0 \tag{10}$$

Hence

$$\frac{1}{T}\int_0^T n_i(t)dt = n_i^*, i = 1, 2.$$

so we have:

$$\gamma_0 = \frac{1}{T}\int_0^T \Big(\frac{\partial}{\partial n_1}(s_1 n_1(M_1 - n_1 - \beta_{12}n_2)) + \frac{\partial}{\partial n_2}(s_2 n_2(M_2 - n_2 - \beta_{21}n_1))\Big)dt$$
$$= \frac{1}{T}\int_0^T [s_1(M_1 - n_1 - \beta_{12}n_2) + s_2(M_2 - n_2 - \beta_{21}n_1)]dt$$
$$- \frac{1}{T}\int_0^T (s_1 n_1(t) + s_2 n_2(t))dt$$
$$= - s_1 n_1^* - s_2 n_2^* < 0 \qquad (11)$$

so Γ_0 is stable, but the equilibriom point (n_1^*, n_2^*) which lies inside the closed orbit Γ_0 is also stable, this can't obviously be true. There fore, there must be no limit cycle in the first quadrant.

We find that the two species competing for the same resources cannot fluctuate in size periodically, provided the environment remains unchanged. In other words, either the two species coexist in the near neighbour of the equilibrium point (n_1^*, n_2^*) or eventually one species replace another. This somewhat surprising conclusion sheds some light on the differences between the learning competition model and the predator—prey model (Durand (1992)), which displays a limit cycle.

3 Concluding Remarks

The brief discussion above suggests the possibility of constructing nonlinear socioeconomic, biological and ecological models in the light of nonequilibrium paradigm, which may exhibit complicated behavior that is difficult for the intuitive idea to reach (May/Oster (1976)). The nonexistence of limit cycle in Chen's learning competition model unveils an intrinsic distinction from the classical predator — prey model. The repercussion from the American millitary circle on the learning competion model is an inspiration to further exploration into the nonlinear modelling and simulation of social phenomena.

References

Chen, P. (1987): Origin of the division of labor and a stochastic mechanism of differentiation, *European Journal of Operational Research*, 30(3), 246—250.

Prigogine, I. and Stengers, I. (1984): *Order out of Chaos: Man's New Dialogue with Nature*, Bantam Books.

Chen, P. (1993): Private communication, Oct. 17

Zhang, J. (1987): *The Geometric Theory of Ordinary Differential Equations and the Bi furcation Problems* (in chinese), Peking University Press.

Durand, J. and Durand R. (1992): Fitting and testing a *predator—prey*

model, *Journal of Mathematical Sociology*, 12(1), 51—62.
May, R. and Oster, G. F. (1976): *Bifurcation and Dynamic Complexity in Simple Ecological Models*, 110, 573—599.

Growth and Fluctuation Analysis of Chinese Economy

Zhangang Han

Institute of Non-equilibrium Systems, Beijing Normal University,
Beijing 100875, People's Republic of China

Abstract. In this paper, some indicators with data of recent years of Chinese statistics are selected and the growth and fluctuation of the economy are analyzed through exponential regression and Fourier transformation. Coefficients of the exponential regression functions are determined and business cycles with periods of 10 years, 6 years and 4.3 years are observed in the overall growth of Chinese economy.

Keywords. Growth, Fluctuation, Chinese Economy, knowledge

1 Introduction

The economic reform of China is in its teens. The Chinese economy has exhibited many phenomena such as growth, fluctuation, etc., during the past 15 years, while the economic reform led China from a planned economy system to a market economy system. It is necessary to explore and describe Chinese economy in theoretical and econometric ways.

Studies on economic growth and business cycle have attracted attention of many researchers who have done fruitful works (Gabisch/Lorenz (1989), King (1992)). Systematic formal modeling of growth was based partly on the proposition of Harrod (1939) and Domar (1946) that a steady-state rate of growth was feasible only in fortuitous circumstances. Later works on economic growth theory concentrate on investment-driven models and innovation-driven models.

Several periodic patterns have long been known when one concentrates on specific phenomena and related variables. The following are some examples (Gabisch/Lorenz (1989)). Kondratieff Cycles with a period about 40 - 60 years observed when studying British and German iron consumption. Juglar Cycles with a period between 7 and 11 years observed in an investigation of French, British and US banking figures, interest rates, and prices. Kitchin Cycles with a period between 2 and 4 years observed in a study of British and US bank clearings and wholesale prices.

The measurement of business cycles of an economy in an aggregate level is of important economic interest, but is not easy to pursue, of course. Superposition of some simple harmonic oscillations may result in a rather complex motion (Schumpeter (1939)), not to mention that business cycles in practical mode can never be strictly harmonic. So, it's difficult to distinguish each single cycle motion in an aggregate economy. What variables to choose to observe and analyze is another difficulty.

To describe the overall movement of an economy, different types of indicators were constructed, such as Harvard Barometer, NBER Indicator that is developed at the National Bureau of Economic Research in the US and indicators in Germany.

Analysis of economic time-series' data sometimes can give good results without paying much attention to the interrelationships of the variables (Nerlove/Grether et. al. (1979)).

In this paper, the author selects some indicators of Chinese statistics in section 2 and analyzes the growth and fluctuation of the economy through exponential regression and Fourier transformation in section 3 and 4. Coefficients of the exponential regression functions are determined and business cycles with periods of 10 years, 6 years, and 4.3 years are found existing in the overall growth of Chinese economy. These works can be referred to as "measurement without theory" (Koopman (1947)). Koopman distinguished between what he called the "Kepler stage" and the "Newton stage". We are in the "Kepler stage" now. In the conclusion section, works on finding empirical laws, or functional dependencies automatically in both the statistical field and the Artificial Intelligence (AI) field are introduced.

2 Selection of Indicators

Sargent (1979) (Zhang (1991)) proposed 7 indicators to reflect the US economy. The indicators are real GNP, real output per man-hour, unemployment rate, Baa bond rate (interest rate), the percentage rate of change in the real money supply, inflation rate in the GNP deflator, an estimate of the strait time real wage. Not all of them, however, are proper to describe the movement of Chinese economy. Unemployment rate, for example, which is a very important indicator to most economies, is not a good indicator to Chinese economy in the present for political, economical and statistical reasons in the Chinese history, even though there really exist apparent or hidden unemployment.

Consider statistical conveniences and as a preliminary step, real GNP index, overall price index, total value of imports and exports, deposit and loan interest rates are selected. The statistical data of real GNP index (1978 = 100), growth rate of GNP, total value of imports and exports in US dollars, rate of change of total value of imports and exports, overall retail price index (1950 = 100), inflation rate in the rate of change of overall retail prices, deposit and loan interest rates are listed in table 2.1 and table 2.2 with the start point of time for interest rates being 1979, and for others, 1978 (Statistical Year Book of China (1993), Banking Year Book of China (1994)). Figure 2.1, figure 2.2, figure 2.3, and figure 2.4 give an easy view of the indicators selected above. The specific interest rates, that is,

Table 2.1. List of data of real GNP index (1978 = 100), growth rate of GNP, total value of imports and exports in US dollars, rate of change of total value of imports and exports, overall retail price index (1950 = 100), inflation rate in the rate of change of overall retail prices.

Time	GNP Index	GNP Growth Rate	Tot. Val. of Imp. & Exp. ($)	Growth Rate of Tot. Val. of I. & E.	Overall Retail Price Index	Inflation in O.R.P.I.
1978	100.0	11.7	20.64	39.46	135.9	0.7
1979	107.6	7.6	29.33	42.10	138.6	2.0
1980	116.0	7.9	38.14	30.04	146.9	6.0
1981	121.2	4.4	44.03	15.44	150.4	2.4
1982	131.8	8.8	41.61	-5.50	153.3	1.9
1983	145.5	10.4	43.62	4.83	155.6	1.5
1984	166.9	14.7	53.55	22.76	160.0	2.8
1985	188.2	12.8	69.60	29.97	174.1	8.8
1986	203.5	8.1	73.85	6.11	184.5	6.0
1987	225.7	10.9	82.65	11.92	198.0	7.3
1988	251.2	11.3	102.79	24.37	234.6	18.5
1989	262.1	4.4	111.68	8.65	276.4	17.8
1990	272.7	4.1	115.44	3.37	282.2	2.1
1991	295.0	8.2	135.63	17.49	290.4	2.9
1992	333.4	13.0	165.61	22.10	306.1	5.4
1993	---	---	---	---	347.1	13.4

Table 2.2. List of data of three-year interest rate in deposit and three to five-year interest rate in loan

Time	Deposit Rate	Loan Rate
01/79		4.23
04/79	4.5	
04/80	6.12	
01/82		5.04
04/82	6.84	
01/83		7.2
12/83	6.84	
04/85	7.92	7.92
08/85	8.28	9.36
09/88	9.72	10.08
02/89	13.14	14.4
03/90		11.52
04/90	11.88	
08/90	10.08	10.8
04/91	8.28	9.54
05/93	10.8	12.06
07/93	12.24	13.86

three-year interest rate in deposit and three to five-year interest rate in loan, are selected after scrutiny because they are regarded roughly reflecting the overall motions of interest rates of the economy.

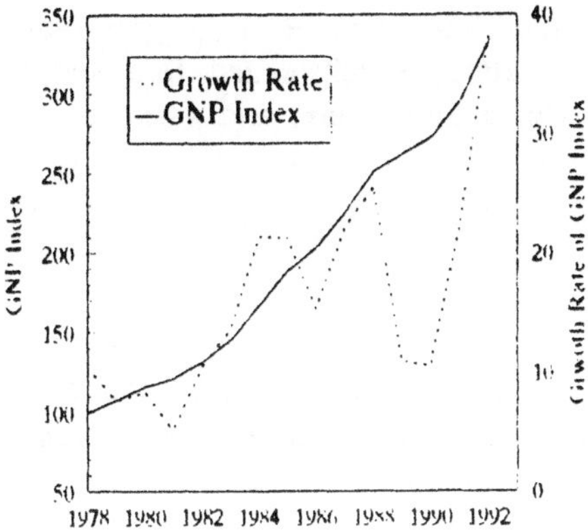

Fig. 2.1. Real GNP index (1978 = 100) and the growth rate of real GNP

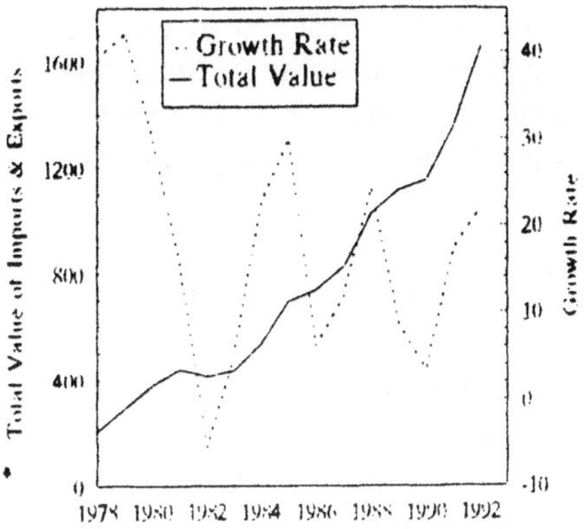

Fig. 2.2. Total value of imports and exports in US dollars, rate of change of total value of imports and exports

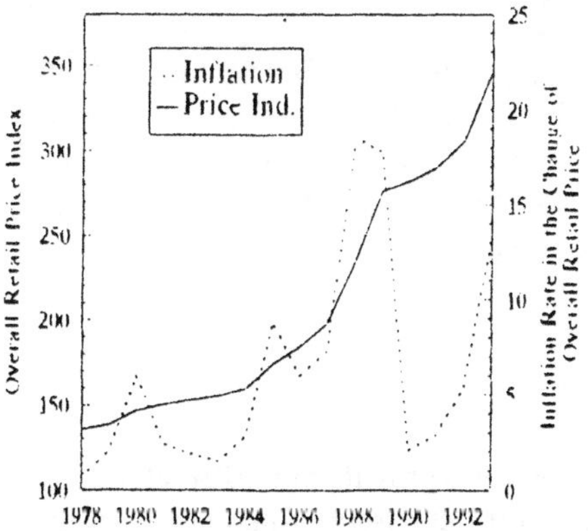

Fig. 2.3. Overall retail price index (1950 = 100), inflation rate in the rate of change of overall retail prices

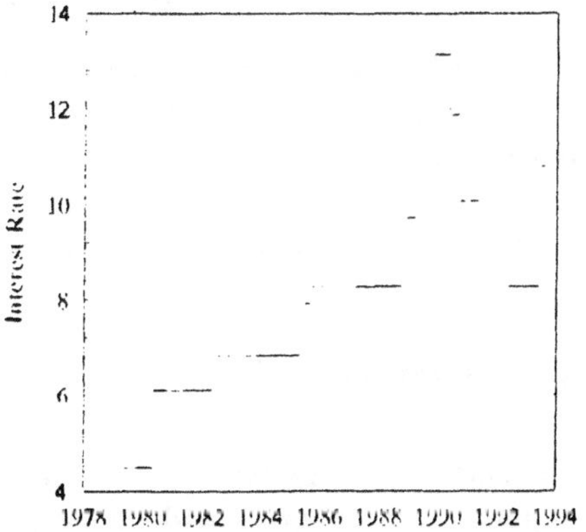

Fig. 2.4. Three-year interest rate in deposit

The larger values of the growth rate of GNP at 1984, 1988, and 1992 give an implication of higher speed growths of the overall economy that correspond to the economic leaps of China, and the troughs at 1981, 1986, and 1990 correspond to the recessions that are referred to as "The Adjustment Periods". It is directly perspective from the curve of the variables that there exist approximately three to four cycles in the period concerned. The growth rate of GNP increased rapidly in 1984, 1988, and 1992. The inflation rate was high in the year 1985, 1988, and 1992. The interest rates rose to local maximums in Feb., 1989 and Jul., 1993. These finally resulted in the declining of growth rate of GNP in the year 1986, 1990. The changing of these three variables is almost synchronized. In a general expression way, it is a chasing behavior with a time delay, and variables are divided into leaders, laggers and coinciders.

3 Exponential Analysis

From Figure 2.1, Figure2.2, and Figure 2.3, we can get the conclusion that GNP index, overall retail price index, total value of imports and exports increase monotonously. An exponential form can be employed to describe such an appearance of curves.

$$Y = ae^{bt} \tag{3.1}$$

and its logarithmic form

$$\ln Y = \ln a + bt \ . \tag{3.2}$$

For GNP index $\ln a = 4.48901$, $b = 0.088753$, correlation coefficient $r = 0.996$. For total value of imports & exports $\ln a = 5.39529$, $b=0.133349$, $r = 0.988$. For price index $\ln a = 4.74597$, $b = 0.0632906$, $r = 0.964$. The correlation coefficients reflect how well the equation form fits the statistical data. Obviously, the motion of GNP index is more likely an exponential growth.

4 Fourier Transformation Analysis

The curve of the growth rate of GNP, inflation rate, growth rate of total value of imports and exports, and interest rates show apparent fluctuating motion characters. Fourier transformation is a tool that transforms data in time domain to frequency domain. We can find from most fundamental college mathematical courses or mathematical handbooks the Fourier transformation form of a function f(t).

$$f(\omega) = \int_{-\infty}^{\infty} f(t) e^{-i\omega t} dt = |f(\omega)| e^{i\theta(\omega)} \tag{4.1}$$

where |f(w)| is the amplitude, θ(w) is the phase, $i = \sqrt{-1}$, and discrete Fourier transformation (DFT) form

$$f(m\Delta\omega) = \sum_{n=0}^{N-1} f(n\Delta t) e^{im\Delta\omega\Delta t} \tag{4.2}$$

where N is the number of sampling data.

By applying DFT to the growth rate of GNP, inflation rate, growth rate of total value of imports and exports, and interest rates we get the amplitudes of the harmonic waves with different periods (frequencies) that the actual motions of the variables are composed of. We find that harmonic waves with the periods of 10 years, 6 years and 4.3 years have larger amplitudes which means that these harmonic waves dominate. So, we conclude that business cycles with periods of 10 years, 6 years and 4.3 years exist in the overall growth of Chinese economy. These business cycles may be explained as corresponding to the 5-year plan system of China.

Harmonic waves with periods of 30 years and 15 years also have larger amplitudes. For the number of sampling data is limited by the number of sampling years, however, business cycles with long periods as 30 years and 15 years do not have enough evidence to prove their existence.

5 Conclusion

With the above treatment to the data accepted, forecast can be made easily. Here we do not concentrate on this matter.

At least three reasons can be listed to explain why the business cycles which are got above may be or may not be in conformity with any theoretical results or in keeping with any other observations concerning other economies.

The first is that small number of sampling data can not give convincing evidences to the existence of long period business cycles and the increasing of the number of sampling data may slightly adjust the periods.

The second is that the same set of variables may behave differently in different economies.

The third is that even the same set of variables in the same economy may have different motions in different periods of time .

Finally, we briefly introduce the works in empirical law discovery. Everyone would hope that such a question has a positive answer as whether the "Kepler" stage as mentioned above can be done automatically. GMDH which stands for Group Method of Data Handling is a statistical way to manipulate data with the assistance of computer to find empirical laws (Ivakhnenko (1968), Farlow (1984), Han/Fang (1992)). The famous BACON system in the field of Scientific Discovery in Artificial Intelligence has rediscovered Kepler's third law, ideal gas equations, etc. (Langley/Zytkow et. al. (1986)). There are other systems in AI also which find functional dependencies implicated in the data concerned (Zembowicz/Zytkow (1992), Wu/Wang (1989)). Dz̃eroski, S and Todorovski, L (1993) presented LAGRANGE, a system that constructs a set of differential and/or algebraic equations that describe an observed behavior of a dynamic system. Discovery of functional dependencies of variables in temporal data bases by using domain dependent and domain independent heuristics is an interesting task. The author hope that further works will make it realistic.

References

Banking Year Book of China, (1994), Editorial Department of Banking Year Book of China.

Domar, E.D. (1947): Expansion and Employment, *American Economic Review 37.*

Dz̃eroski, S. / Todorovski, L. (1993): Discovering dynamics, *Proc. of Tenth Internationsl Conference on Machine Learning, pp. 97 - 103*, Morgan Kaufmann, San Mateo, CA.

Farlow, S.J., ed. (1984): Self-Organizing Methods in Modeling: GMDH Type Algorithms, N.Y., Marcel Dekker Inc.

Gabisch, Günter / Lorenz, Hans-Walter ed. (1989): Business Cycle Theory, A Survey of Methods and Concepts, 2nd ed. Springer-Verlag.

Han, Zhangang / Fang, Fukang (1992): Non-equilibrium Systems Theory and Manpower Planning, *Proc. of First Academic Annual Meeting of Youths, China Association for Science and Technology, Volume of Interdisciplinary Science*, 4, 1992, Beijing.

Harrod, R.F. (1939): An Essay in Dynamic Theory, *Economic Journal 49.*

Ivakhnenko, A.G. (1968): The Group Method of Data Handling: A Rival of the Method of Stochastic Approximation. *Soviet Automatic Control (Avtomatika), 1968(3).*

King, Mervyn, (1992): Growth Theory: Recent Development in Historical Perspective, Growth and Distribution, *European Economic Review 36 (1992) 585 - 592*, North-Holland.

Koopman, T.C. (1947): Measurement without Theory, The Review of Economic Statistics, 29, In: *Readings in Business cycle Theory, 1966*, American Economic Association Series, London: Allen and Unwin.

Langley, Pat / Zytkow, J.M., etc. (1986): The Search for Regularity: Four Aspects of Scientific Discovery, In: Ryszard, S. M., ed. *Machine Learning, An Artificial Intelligence Approach, Vol. II,* MORGAN KAUFMANN Publ., Inc., 1986.

Nerlove, M. / Grether, D.M., etc. (1979): Analysis of Economic Time Series, A Synthesis, New York: Academic Press.

Sargent, T.J., (1979): Macroeconomic Theory, Academic Press.

Schumpeter, J.A., (1939): Business Cycles, Volume 1, McGraw-Hill.

Statistical Year Book of China, (1993): The State Statistical Bureau, Statistics Pub. of China.

Wu, Y. / Wang, S. (1989): Discovering Knowledge from Observational Data, In: Piatetsky-Shapiro, G., ed., *Knowledge Discovery in Databases, IJCAI-89 Workshop Proceedings,* Detroit, MI, 369-377.

Zembowicz, Robert / Zytkow, J.M. (1992): Discovery of Equations: Experimental Evaluation of Convergence, *Proc. of Tenth National Conference on Artificial Intelligence, AAAI-92, California, 70-75.*

Zhang, Wei-Bin (1991): Synergetic Economics, Time and Change in Nonlinear Economics, Springer-Verlag.

III. Microeconomics: Technological change, market structure and regional economics

EVOLUTIONARY COMPLEX SYSTEMS: THE SELF-ORGANIZATION OF COMMUNITIES

Peter M. Allen
International Ecotechnology Research Centre
Cranfield University
Bedford, MK43 OAL
ENGLAND

Abstract. Any mathematical models of human systems that consist of deterministic, mechanical equations are only temporary representations of the structure and organisation present in the system at a particular time. In fact, the structure and organization of the system in question changes qualitatively over time, as the components and interaction mechanisms emerge and change through time. This paper addresses the mathematical modelling of the over-arching process which leads to the emergence and evolution of "ecologies" of interacting entities that make up socio-economic systems. It describes the underlying processes that change the taxonomy of a system, and through which new behaviours and challenges emerge in the system. These changes are essentially unpredictable, as is the expected time of stability of any existing structure and taxonomy. Sustainability and wisdom are therefore shown to lie in the maintenance of the capacity for adaptation and change, rather than in the efficiency of any particular temporarily fixed system. Several applications of these ideas are discussed.

EVOLUTION AND MECHANICS

If we examine a region, and consider the remains of populations and artifacts that litter the landscape, then after dating and classifying them, an evolutionary tree of some kind emerges, possibly with discontinuities suggesting disaster and invasion, but nevertheless suggesting a changing "cast of characters" and of behaviours, over time.

On the left of Figure (1) we have "reality". It is drawn as a cloud, since we can say little about it other than that it includes all detail of everything, everywhere, as well as all perceptions and all points of view. However, if we simply list what we see then it includes a landscape with people of many kinds performing a variety of tasks, businesses, factories, homes, vehicles, and also fossils, disused mines and factories, closed railways, buried cities and evidence of much that has disappeared. By constructing a series of taxonomic rules concerning the differences and similarities of the objects, together with their dates, we can construct an "evolutionary tree", showing that species, behaviours, forms, or artifacts emerged and evolved over time.

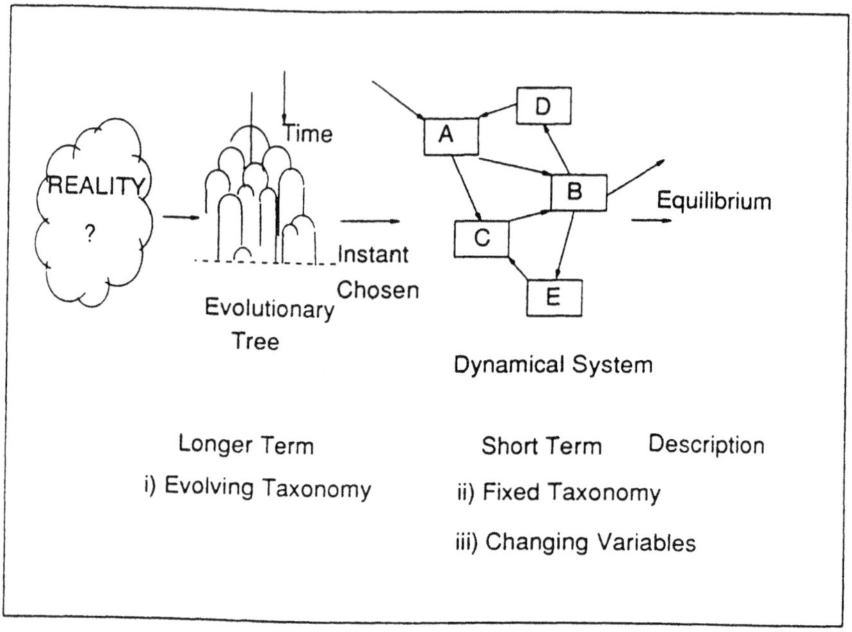

Figure (1). Data and classification of populations and artifacts leads to the picture of an evolutionary tree of some kind. Mathematical models have concentrated on the causal relations at a given time.

This is really subjective however, since the differences that we choose to recognize reflects already our vision of what is "coherent" in a social and economic system. The rules of classification that we use result from previous experience about such systems and what matters in them. Are there socio-economic "types"? Do firms of the same sector and size behave similarly? What is a sector? Is there as much variation within a group as between groups? Whatever the precise arguments advanced, in order to "understand" a situation, and its possible outcomes, we do classify the system into components, and attempt to build mathematical models that capture the processes that are increasing or decreasing these different components.

At any particular moment therefore, we identify the different objects or organisms that are present, and attempt to write down some "population dynamics" describing the increase and decrease of each type. We apply the traditional approach of physics, which is to identify the components of a system, and the interactions operating on these, both to and from the outside world and between the different populations of the system. In ecology, this will consist of birth and death processes, where populations give birth at an average rate if there is enough food, and eat each other according to the average rates of encounter, capture and digestion. In economics, the macroscopic behaviour of the economy is assumed to result from the aggregate effects of producers attempting to maximise their profits, and of customers attempting to maximise their utility. This assumes that they know the outcome of what they have not yet tried and also that transactions, production, and consumption occur at average rates, changing the GNP, unemployment and other macroscopic indicators. These ideas are all based on the "mechanical paradigm" of Newtonian physics, and assume that all individuals, producers, and consumers of a given type are taken to be identical and equal to the average type. Such a model expresses the behaviour or functioning of the system at that time as a result of the causal relationships that are present. This gives the illusion that we have a mechanical representation of the system which can be run on a computer, to give predictions.

However, as we see clearly from our broader picture of the "evolutionary tree", the predictions that such a model can give can only be correct for as long as the taxonomy of the system remains unchanged. The mechanical model of deterministic equations that we can construct at any given time has no way of producing "new" types of objects, new variables, and so the "predictions" that it generates will only be true until some moment, unpredictable within the model, when there is an adaptation or innovation, and new behaviour emerges.

In terms of figure (1), the basis of scientific understanding has traditionally been the mechanical model (Prigogine & Stengers,1987; Allen,1988) constructed from the causal relations that exist between the components of the system at a particular time. These are used to construct a pseudo-mechanical representation of the system which can be run forward to provide predictions, and whose component variables reflect the taxonomy of the system. In many cases a further assumption is introduced that the system is also supposed to have run itself to equilibrium, so that the correspondence between the real object and that model is made through equilibrium relations of balance between the variables.

In economic geography, and models of transportation and land-use, the models that are used operationally today are still based on equilibrium assumptions. Locations of jobs and residences, land values, traffic flows etc. are all assumed to reach their equilibrium configurations within say, five years, following some policy or planning action. Such as approach fails to take into account the possibility of any "run-away" processes where growth encourages growth, decline leads to further decline and so on, and where actions simply affect which evolutionary trajectory the regional system may be on, an evolutionary trajectory that does not stop after any particular delay. Similarly, the equilibrium approach supposes that urban form and hierarchy express some maximised utility for the actors, where consumers had minimised distance of travel for goods and services and producers had maximised profits. This approach assumes that all the actors know what they want, know, know how to get it, and are doing what they would wish - given the choices open to them. Such ideas gave rise in reality to a purely descriptive approach to problems, tracing, in a kind of post hoc calibration process the changes that occurred.

In fact, those wishing to use equilibrium methods should have to accept the burden of proof, since it is they who make the assumptions. It should be necessary to prove that the relaxation times of the processes involved in the system are short with respect to any time of interest, and therefore that the methods are justified. In reality, such evidence has never been presented, and non-equilibrium methods have simply been ignored. The real justification for equilibrium methods was expediency - the computing power was not available to make a proper attempt at understanding such complex systems. But as computers became more powerful, the need for such strong and unrealistic assumptions gradually disappeared. System Dynamics and simulation were thought to offer a path to the prediction of system behaviour, and because of this to offer a basis for rational policy and decision making in complex systems.

Obviously, however, if we look at figure (1), we see that however interesting a system dynamics model might be, it cannot anticipate the changes that may still occur in the evolutionary tree from which the "moment" studied is taken. The taxonomy of the system will change over time, and therefore the mathematical model of causal relations will be incorrect. It might be good for some time, while the taxonomy is stable and no new classes or types have appeared. But, this will only be revealed when the model is shown to be incorrect, and in need of re-formulation.

Despite this, however, system dynamic models of problems have been developed, and much attention has rightly been given to the interesting behaviours of non-linear dynamical systems. Such systems are characterized by dynamical equations of the type:
where G is a function which have non-linear terms, leading to changes in x which are not simply proportional to its size. Also, these functions are made up of terms which involve the variable x and also parameters expressing the functional dependence on these. These parameters reflect two fundamentally different factors in the working of the system:

- the values of external factors, which are not modelled as variables in the system. These reflect the "environment" of the system, and of course may be dependent on spatial coordinates. Temperature, climate, soils, world prices, interest rates are possible examples of such factors.

- the values corresponding to the "performance" of the entities underlying x , due to their internal characteristics like technology, level of knowledge or strategies.

These two entirely different aspects have not been separated out in much of the previous work concerning non-linear systems, and so the whole issue of the evolution of the populations involved in the system has not been addressed clearly. Equations of the type shown above display a rich spectrum of possible behaviours in different regions of both parameter space and initial conditions. They range from a simple approach to a homogeneous steady state, characterized by a point attractor, through that of sustained oscillation of a cyclic attractor, to the well known chaotic behaviour characteristic of a strange attractor. These can either be homogeneous, or can involve spatial structure as well. This possibility of rich behaviours has proved to be of great significance for many fields of science.

However, in this paper, we are concerned with evolution, and that concerns modelling systems in which adaptive and structural change can occur. The internal characteristics of the participating actors change endogenously and new variables and new mechanisms of interaction can appear spontaneously from within the system itself, leading to a changing taxonomy. The model that we shall describe will discuss not only the evolution of improved techniques for producing a given good, but also the diversification and growth of markets into new areas.

Let us first consider the assumptions that are made in deriving system dynamics equation such as in (1). In the complex systems that underlie something like the "economy", there is a fundamental level which involves individuals and discrete events, like making a widget, buying a washing machine, driving to work etc. However, instead of attempting to "model" all this detail, these are treated in an average way, and as has been shown elsewhere (Allen, 1990), in order to derive deterministic, mechanical equations to describe the dynamics of a system, two assumptions are required:

- events occur at their average rate (Assumption 1)
- all individuals of a given type, x say, are identical and of average type (Assumption 2)

The errors introduced by the first assumption can be addressed by using a deeper, probabilistic dynamics, called the "Master Equation" which essentially assumes that all individuals are identical and equal to an average type, but that events of different probabilities can and do occur. So, sequences of events which correspond to successive runs of good or bad "luck" are included, with their relevant probabilities. As has been shown elsewhere (Allen, 1988) for systems with non-linear interactions between individuals, what this does is to destroy the idea of a trajectory. The evolution is described by a probability distribution for an ensemble of systems that gradually changes its shape from being sharply peaked and centred on the initial value to spreading and splitting into a multimodal distribution with peaks that correspond to the different "attractors" of the dynamics. These may be point, cyclic or chaotic attractors, but clearly, if there are different possibilities then the idea of a trajectory for any single system breaks down. The fact is that unpredictable runs of good and bad luck can occur, and that as a result the system can spontaneously change its pattern of behaviour as it "jumps" into some new dynamical attractor, for some time.

However, in thinking about the problem of technological change and evolution, it is more important to discuss the other hypothesis that leads to the mechanical equations, that is that all individuals are identical and equal to the average type. Obviously, the first and most important fact about two individuals is that they cannot be at the same place at the same time, and so spatial structure is one of the underlying issues that has been treated inadequately by population dynamics of the usual kind. In the next section we show the result of correcting non-linear equations in order to take the effects of microscopic diversity into account.

In physics and chemistry the predictive models which work so well rely on the fact that the individual elements that make up the system must obey fixed laws which govern their behaviour. The mechanisms are fixed, and the molecules never learn.

But, living systems cannot be described by such deterministic laws. To see why, let us imagine a very simple human situation, for example, of traffic moving along a highway or of pedestrians milling around a shopping centre. Clearly, movements cannot be predicted using Newton's laws of motion because acceleration, change of direction, braking and stopping occur at the whim of each driver or pedestrian. Newton's laws, the laws of physics are obeyed at all times by each part of the system, but, despite this, they are not of help in predicting what will happen because the decision to coast, turn, accelerate or brake lies with the human being. Planets, billiard balls, and point particles are helpless slaves to the force fields in which they move, but people are not! People can switch sources of energy on or off and can respond, react, learn and change according to their individual experience and personality. They can see the potential usefulness for some modification in their timing, technique or tools, and they can tinker and experiment perhaps to find ways to overcome a problem, or a new way to achieve some desired result. This is where innovation comes from, and so, the diversity of the experiments performed or ideas tried out will reflect the diversity of the people concerned, and the ability of these experiments to be translated into improved and new production and business will reflect the encouragement or discouragement experienced by innovative individuals, and the information flows and scanning that organizations are doing to gather and evaluate such initiatives.

Because of this uncertainty in the longer term, we cannot know what actions are best now. Even if an individual knows exactly what he would like to achieve, then because he cannot know with certainty how everyone else will respond, he can never calculate exactly what the outcome will be. He must make his decision, and see what happens, being ready to take corrective actions, if necessary. Since, in business, on the road and in the shopping centre we are all making these kinds of decisions, simultaneously, all the time, it is not surprising that occasionally there are accidents, or that such systems run in a "non-mechanical" way. An important point to remember here of course, is that human beings have evolved within such a world and therefore that the capacity to live with such permanent uncertainty is quite natural to us. It may even be what characterises the living. However, it also implies that much of
what we do may be inexplicable in rational terms.
The "mechanical" approach is softened but not fundamentally changed by statistical models of decision processes where the probability of making a particular choice is proportional to the expected utility derived. This gives rise to probabilistic behaviour for individuals and deterministic behaviour for sufficiently large populations. However, this simple approach ignores the fact that decisions made by individuals are not really independent of each other, and that there is an effect of the communication between individuals. Fashions, styles and risk minimising strategies affect collective behaviour considerably, and mean that it cannot be derived necessarily as the sum of independent, individual responses.

EVOLUTIONARY DRIVE

As we have seen above, in deriving kinetic equations in order to model the system that exists at a given time, it has been necessary to derive a reduced description of reality. This is made in terms of typical elements of the system, stereotypes, according to the classification scheme that we have decided to apply. Underneath the "model" there will always be the greater particularity and diversity of reality.

In the mechanical view, predictions can be made by simply running the equations forward in time, and studying where they lead. Is there a unique "attractor", into which all initial states eventually fall, or are there many possible final end points? Does the system continue in a series of eternal cycles? Or, does it display chaotic behaviour, as the trajectory wraps itself around a "strange attractor"? Despite the interest of these questions, we should remember they are only of any significance if the equations and the fixed mechanisms within them remain a good description of the system, and explanation can be obtained in terms of the internal functioning of the system. But, from the picture of the evolutionary tree in fig.(1) that we know really characterizes complex systems, the taxonomy of the system, the variables present and the mechanisms which link them actually change over time. Because of this, the dynamical system that we are running as a model of the system will only be a good description for as long as there is no evolutionary change, and no new variables or mechanisms appear. In other words, the predictions of the dynamical system model will only be correct for as long as the model itself is a correct description of the system, and this is only for some unpredictable length of time.

Figure (1) offers us a conceptual framework within which we can understand technological evolution, and this has been described elsewhere (Allen P.M. 1994). In order to describe evolutionary change, we must try to suppress assumption 2 discussed above and put back the effects of innovators. Nelson and Winter (1982) have set out a seminal framework for economics in which internal variabilities and the differential survival of firms are explicitly taken into account as they compete in the production of a particular good. The evolution concerns returns on investment and techniques of production, and been the basis for many later studies Goodwin et al, 1984; Anderson et al, 1988; Silverberg et al, 1988; Lorents, 1989 and Saviotti and Metcalfe(1991). Clark and Juma (1988) have also set out the essential points concerning the difference between the long and short term view of economic systems, and how this leads to an evolutionary view.

Returning to the general conceptual framework of figure(1), we see that in order for us to understand and model a system that can change its taxonomy endogenously we must "put back" what assumptions 1 and 2 took out in order to get to the deterministic description of non-linear dynamics. Clearly, the future of any system will be due to two kinds of terms: changes brought about by the deterministic action of the typical behaviour of its average components, and structural qualitative changes brought about by the presence of non-average components and conditions within the system.

We really have a dialogue between the "average dynamics" of the chosen description (a process that results in what we may call selection) and the exploratory, unpredictable "non-average" perturbations around this that results from the inevitable occurrence of non-average events and components -a search or exploration process that generates information about the "pay offs" for other behaviours. This leads to the new concept of Evolutionary Drive. (Allen & McGlade, 1988, Allen & Lesser, 1993)

In order to explore the behaviour of systems with endogenously generated innovations and selection we define a "possibility space", a space representing the range of different techniques and behaviours that could potentially arise. In practice, of course, this is a multi-dimensional space of which we would only be able to anticipate a few of the principle dimensions. This "possibility space" will be explored by individuals and groups who explore the pay-offs of new behaviour. In biology, genetic mechanism ensures that different possibilities are explored, and off-spring, off-spring of off-spring and so on, spread out over time from any pure condition. In human systems the imperfections and subjectivity of existence mean that techniques and behaviours are never passed on exactly, and therefore that exploration and innovation are always present as a result of the individuality and contextual nature of experience. Local conditions, materials and needs differ and therefore any "pure" technique or behaviour that migrates into a locality will rapidly diverge in its nature and intent. The diversity of existence itself generates complexity, and hence complexity feeds on itself.

Physical constraints mean that some behaviours do better than others, and so imitation and growth lead to the increase of some behaviours and the decline of others. If possibility space is seen as a kind of "evolutionary landscape", with hills representing behaviours of high performance, then our simulations lead to the amplification of populations which are higher on the hill, and the suppression of those which are lower down.

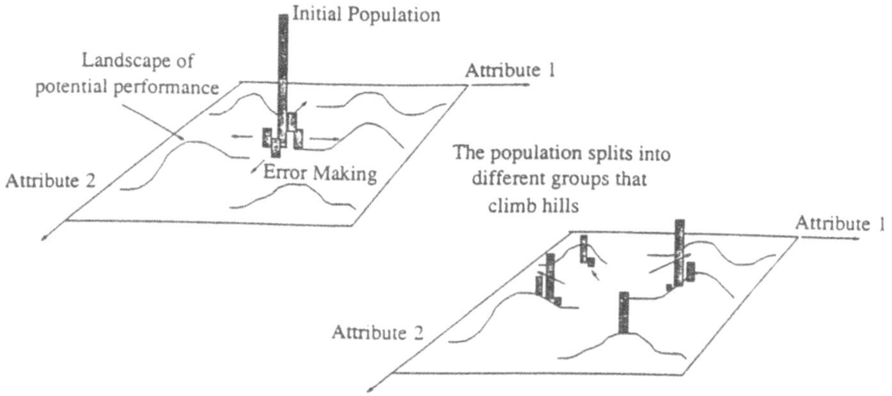

Figure (2) In "possibility space", an initially pure behaviour will diffuse outwards as a result of imperfect imitation, learning and details of the local context. Differential success provides "selection".

By considering dynamic equations in which their is a "diffusion" outwards in character space from any behaviour that is present, we can see how such a system would evolve. If there are types of behaviour with higher and lower pay-offs, then the diffusion "up-hill" is gradually amplified, that "down-hill" is suppressed, and the "average" for the whole population moves higher up the slope. This is the mechanism by which adaptation takes place. This demonstrates the vital part played by exploratory, non-average behaviour, and showed that, in the long term, evolution selects for populations with the ability to learn, rather than for populations with optimal, but fixed, behaviour.

The self-organizing geographic models developed previously are a simple particular case of these general ideas. Instead of some "behaviour" space, what we have is real, geographic space. Individuals of any particular type, X, all differ from one another by being located at different points in space. By using distributions of choice and behaviour around an average, the microscopic diversity of individuals is taken into account, and this allows the "exploration" of seemingly unpopular, irrational and non-average decisions. In this way, changes in the "pay-offs" for novel behaviour can be detected in the system, and innovations can take off. In this case, it concerns "spatial" innovations, such as the spontaneous emergence of new centres of employment, or of peripheral shopping centres, of industrial satellites and so on. Because of the presence of positive feedback loops, there were many possible final states to which the system can tend, depending on the precise position and timing of non-average events. Information can only come from the paths that were actually taken, not from those that were not and because of this, patterns of change feed upon themselves, and self-reinforcement of growth and decline are the result. Instead of an objective rationality expressing genuine comparative advantages, the beliefs and the structures co-evolve (Allen and Lesser, 1991).

THE EVOLUTION OF "COMMUNITIES"

In this section we shall take the evolutionary models a stage further and examine the mutual co-evolution of different populations. Instead of considering the evolution of techniques and behaviours in a fixed landscape expressing higher/lower pay-offs, we shall allow for the fact that the "pay-offs", the adaptive landscapes, are really generated by the interactions of a population with the other populations in the system. In the space of "possibilities" closely similar behaviours are considered to be most in competition with each other, since they require similar resources, and must find a similar niche in the system. However, we assume that in this particular dimension there is some "distance" in character space, some level of dissimilarity, at which two behaviours do not compete.

Initially, a single population is placed at the centre of possibility space, and since it has adequate resources, it grows. However, error making in the transmission through time of the "rules" underlying any specific behaviour or technique, means that there is a constant tendency for divergent behaviours to appear, and this operates just like a diffusion process, only instead of spreading outwards into geographical space, the diffusion represents the population behaviour spreading outwards to new behaviours and types.

During the initial phase of an experiment in which we start off with a single population in an "empty" resource space, resources are plentiful, the centre of the distribution, the average type, grows better than the eccentrics at the edge. The population forms a sharp spike, with the diffusing eccentrics suppressed by their unsuccessful competition with the average type. However, any single behaviour can only grow until it reaches the limits set by its input requirements, or in the case of an economic activity, by the market limit for any particular product. After this, it is the "eccentrics", the "error-makers" that grow more successfully than the "average type", and the population identity becomes unstable. The single sharply spiked distribution spreads, and splits into new populations that climb the evolutionary landscape that has been created, leading away from the ancestral type. The new populations move away from each other, and grow until in their turn they reach the limits of their new normality, whereupon they also split into new behaviours, gradually filling the resource spectrum.

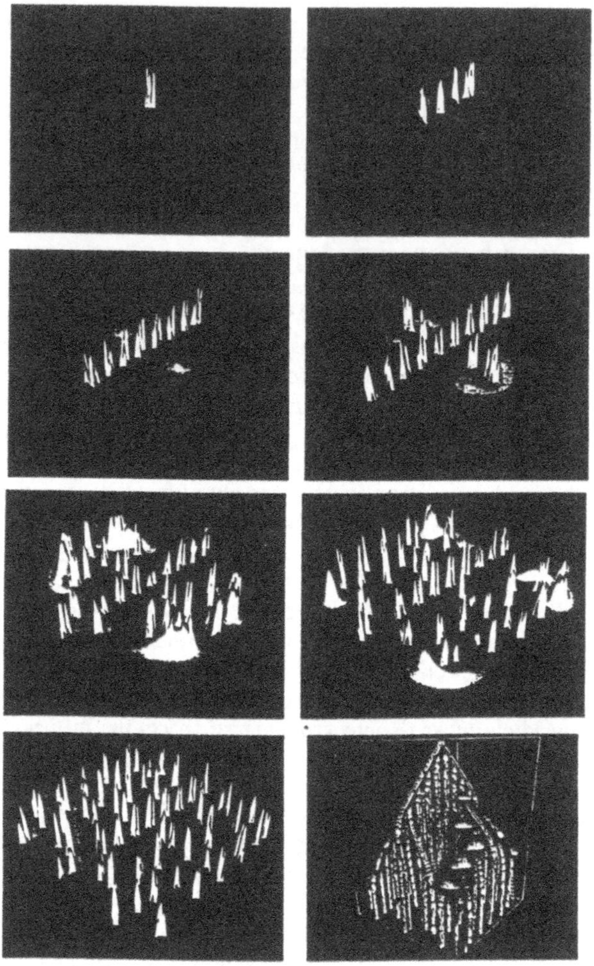

Figure (3). In this case the landscape explored by the emergent behaviours is shaped by them. Periods of stuctural stability are separated by periods of change, depending on whether the system can control its own error-making or not.

In this way, instead of simply evolving towards the peaks of a fixed evolutionary landscape, through their interactions populations really create the landscape upon which they move, and by moving across it, change it. So the different behaviours present grow, split off, and gradually fill the possibility space with an "ecology" of activities, each identity and role being formed by the mutual interaction and identities of the others.

While the "error-making" and inventive capacity of the system in our simulation is a constant fraction of the activity present at any time, the system evolves in discontinuous steps of instability, separated by periods of taxonomic stability. In other words, there are times when the system structure can suppress the incipient instabilities caused by innovative exploration of its inhabitants, and there are other times when it cannot suppress them, and a new population emerges. In figure (3) we see the changing qualitative structure of the system over time, in some two-dimensional possibility space.

In order to understand this more clearly, let us consider in detail a simple, one dimensional character space, in which competition for underlying resources exists, but so also do other possible interactions. For example, for any two particular populations i, and j, practising their characteristic behaviours, there may be an effect of one on the other. This could be positive, in that side-effects of the activity of j might in fact provide conditions or effects that help i. Of course, the effect might equally well be antagonistic, or of course neutral. Similarly, i may have a positive, negative or neutral effect on j. If we therefore initially choose values randomly for all the possible interactions between all i and j, then, these effects will come into play if the populations concerned are in fact present. If they are not there, then obviously, there can be no positive or negative effects experienced. For example, to be precise, let us consider 20 points, and between each of them a random number is used to choose a value for the potential interaction on i from j.
where random(j,i) is a random number between 0 and 1, and fr is the strength of the interaction.
Each population that is present will experience the net effect that results from all of the other populations that are also present. Similarly, it will affect those populations by its presence.
The sum is over j including i, and so we are looking at behaviours that in addition to interacting with each other, also feed back on themselves. There will also always be a competition for underlying resources, which we shall represent by:
At any time, then, we can draw the landscape of synergy and antagonism that is generated and experienced by the populations present in the system. We can therefore write down the equation for the change in population of each of the xi. It will contain the positive and negative effects of the influence of the other populations present, as well as the competition for resources that will always be a factor, and also the error making diffusion through which populations from i create small numbers of off-spring in i+1 and i-1.

Where f is the fidelity of reproduction (.99).

The simulation starts with a single population of 5 individuals placed at 10. In other words, x(10) = 5 initially. The only population initially present is 10, and therefore the evolutionary landscape in which it sits is in fact that which it creates itself. No other population are present yet to contribute to the overall landscape.

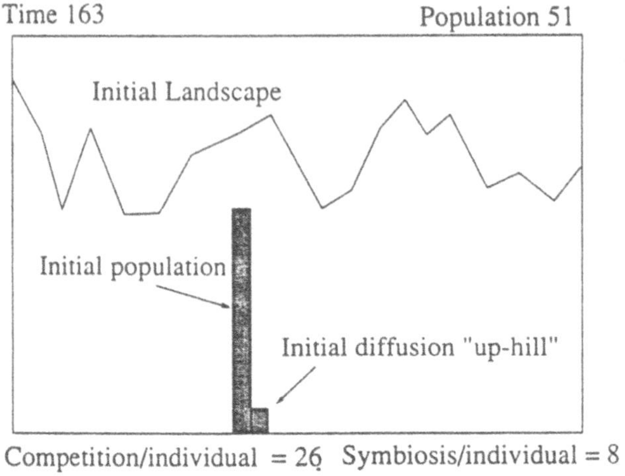

Figure (4) The initial population and evolutionary landscape of our simulation.(Time 163)

What matters then, is how the population 10 affects itself. This may have positive or negative effects depending on the random selection made at the start of the simulation. However, in general the population 10 will grow and begin to "diffuse" into the types 9 and 11. Gradually, the landscape will reflect the effects that 9, 10 and 11 have on each other, and the diffusion will continue into the other possible populations. Hills in the landscape will be climbed by the populations, but as they climb, they change their behaviour, and change the landscape for themselves and the others. The figures (4) to (6) show this process taking place over time.

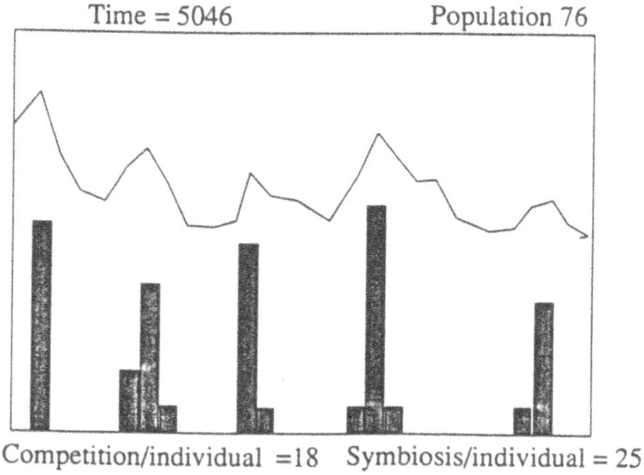

Figure (5) After 5046 time steps the system has found a stable structure with a high degree of synergy. Single, pair and triplet step hypercycles have emerged.

Although, competition helps to "drive" the exploration process, what is observed is that a system with "error making" explorations of behaviour evolves towards structures which express synergetic complementarities. In other words, evolution although driven to explore by error making and competition, evolves cooperative structures. The synergy can be expressed either through "self-symbiotic" terms, where the consequences of a behaviour in addition to consuming resources is favourable to itself, or through interactions involving pairs, triplets, and so on. This corresponds to the emergence of "hypercycles" (Eigen and Schuster, 1979).

Several important points can now be made. Firstly, a successful and sustainable evolutionary system will clearly be one in which there is freedom for imagination and creativity to explore at the individual level, and to seek out complementarities and loops of positive feedback which will generate a stable community of actors. Secondly, the self-organization of our system leads to a highly cooperative system, where the competition per individual is low, but where loops of positive feedback and synergy are high. In other words, the free evolution of the different populations, each seeking its own growth, leads to a system which is more cooperative than competitive. The vision of a modern, free market economy leading to, and requiring a cut-throat society where selfish competitivity dominates, is shown to be false, at least in this simple case.

From our example, the discovery of cooperativities, and the formation of communities of players with a shared interest in each others success, is the outcome of the evolutionary process. The third important point, particularly for scientists, is that it would be impossible to discern the "correct" model equations even for our simple 20 population problem, from observing the population dynamics of the system. Because any single behaviour could be playing a positive, or negative role in a self, or pair or triplet etc. interaction, it would be impossible to "untangle" its interactions and write down its the equations simply by noting the population's growth or decline. The system itself, through the error-making search process can find stable arrangements of multiple actors, and can self-organize a balance between the actors in play, and the interactions that they bring with them, but this does not mean that we can deduce what the web of interactions really is. This certainly poses problems for the rational analysis of situations, since this must rely on an understanding of the consequences of the different interactions that are believed to be present. Clearly, if we cannot really know how the circles of influence are formed by looking at the data, the only choice would be to ask the actors involved, in the case of a human system. And this in turn would raise the question of whether people really understand the roots of their own situation, and the influences of the functional, emotional and historical links that build, maintain and cast down organizations and institutions. The loops of positive feedback that build structure introduce a truly collective aspect to any profound understanding of their nature, and this will be beyond any simple rational analysis, used in a goal-seeking local context.

COMPLEX SYSTEM EVOLUTION - APPLICATIONS

1. SPATIAL EVOLUTION OF COMPLEX SYSTEMS - REGIONAL AND URBAN CHANGE

The first applications of these ideas to human systems (Allen & Sanglier, 1979,1981) the question of self-organisation in geographical space was examined. A non-linear dynamical system of equations underlying the patterns of supply and demand of different goods and services evolved as a result of the random occurrence of entrepreneurs at different points and times in the system. Consumer demand was assumed to reflect relative prices. The creative interplay of random exploration and rational selection resulted in the gradual emergence of self-consistent market structures and patterns of settlement as economic functions either prospered or declined at their locations.

Regional structure emerged as a result of the interplay of positive and negative feedbacks:
- positive due to the urban multiplier, economies of scale and externalities.
- negative through spatial competition both for producers and for residential space.

Studies showed that many futures are possible initially, but gradually systems may "lock in" to a somewhat unsatisfactory market structure, as a result of a particular history. These simulations show us that a very large number of possible stable structures could potentially result, involving different numbers of centres in different locations, and necessarily not offering the same level of cost, utility, or efficiency. In some ways they show rather clearly that a "free market" system does not necessarily run to an "optimal" solution, but just to one of many possible solutions. The "invisible hand" of Adam Smith therefore, although ensuring that incompatible entities do not cohabit the space, can lead to a great number of possible structures - each with its own mixture of good and bad qualities. Real choices exist, but we can only successfully make these strategic choices if we can understand the qualitative evolution of the system over the long term, using this kind of model.

These models show many important principles: many final states are possible, precise prediction in the early stages is impossible, approximate rules appear (centre separations etc.) but always with considerable deviation and local individuality present. The results are affected by the particularities of the transportation system, as well as by information flows affecting the mental maps of consumers (Gould & White, 1978). This approach leads, therefore, to the first integrated land-use/transportation models -and showed how the strategic evolution of structure as a result of changing technology, transportation, resource availability etc. could be explored, as the changing patterns of demand and supply affect each other in a complex dynamic spatial process.

The fundamental basis for these models are the decisions of the different types of individual actors, which reflect their values and functional requirements. Although these are represented by very simple rules for each type of actor, when distributed among average and non-average individuals, they give rise to very complex patterns of structure and flow, and to a structural emergence and evolution at the collective level. In turn, the macrostructures that emerge constrain the choices of individuals, and fashion their experience, so that without the knowledge afforded by such models, there may not be any simple relation between the goals of actors, and what really happens to them. Each actor is co-evolving with the structures resulting from the behaviour of all the others, and surprise and uncertainty are part of the result.

The "selection" process on the other hand results simply from the success or failure of enterprises in the competitive and cooperative dynamical game that is running. Models were developed showing the evolution of cities and regions as a result of these evolutionary processes. For example, the generic interaction scheme of figure (6) was shown to successfully generate the emergence and evolution of the spatial structure of the city of Brussels.

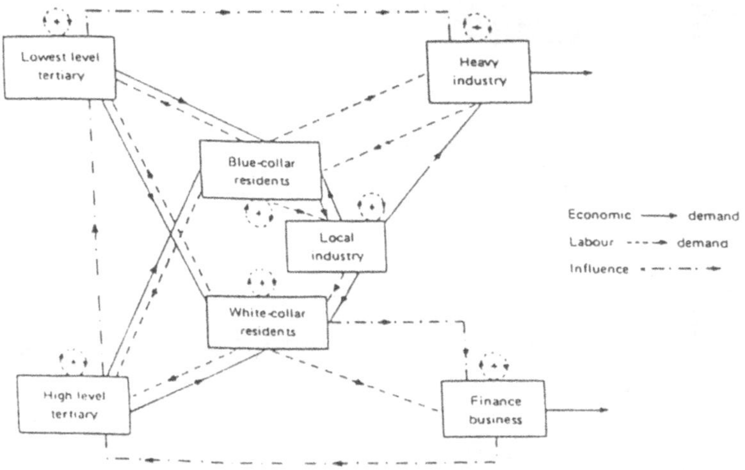

Figure (6). The intra-urban interaction scheme which leads to the development of urban structure.

In this model, the decisions of individual actors of different types is simulated as each of them changes the conditions which affect the others. As the city grows, so the demand for space changes the price of available land, and the different abilities of actors to pay, affects their responses. These differences reflect the particular spatial requirements of economic activities, where for example, manufacturing industry may require twenty times the surface area as an insurance office, for the same "value added". Also, different actors will have different requirements concerning their location, such as either being very central for communication and contacts, or needing transportation infrastructure such as a port, rail and road access for the import of raw materials and the export of finished products. Residents too will have different locational needs depending on where they work, and on their age, family composition and socio-economic group. Through the spatial interaction of all these decisions, running over time, the city structures and generates business and administrative districts, industrial satellites, retailing centres, and areas of high and low quality residential housing. All the spatial choices of the different actors are made according to the networks of private and public transportation, which will themselves be changed according to the intensity of demand and congestion that occurs. The models therefore constitute a unique "intelligence" about the possible evolution of a city, providing a basis for investment decision for housing, retail, office or industrial developments.

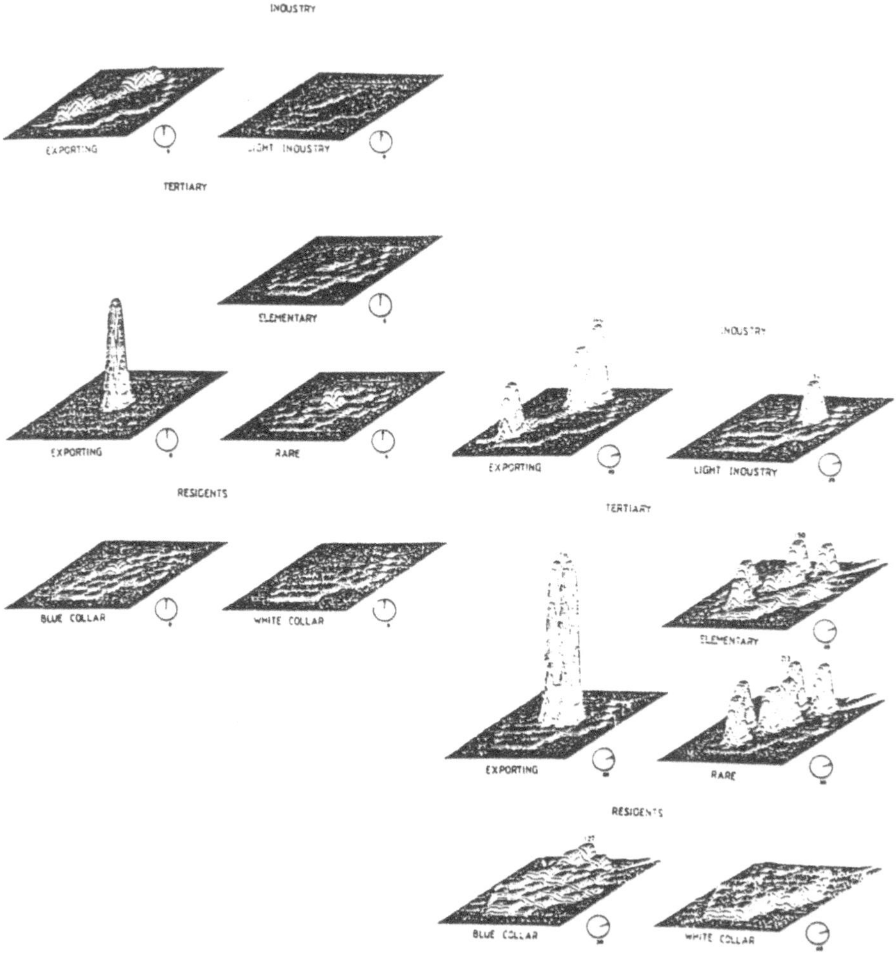

Figure (7). Over 20 units of time, a complex spatial pattern of jobs and residences, resembling that of Brussels, emerges from a simpler initial distribution.

Such models therefore are the basis of "intelligent" systems which can be used for decision support for a whole range of investment and policy matters.

Similarly, regional models were developed which showed how the urban centres within the system interacted. This mutual interaction was both influenced by, and in its turn influenced the flows of investment and of migrants. From this an evolutionary model of Belgium, for example, was developed and has been described in detail elsewhere (Sanglier & Allen 1989) The overall effectiveness of a city is conditioned by the costs and benefits that result from its location within the national framework, and also from its internal structure. So, cities that suffer high levels of congestion, have poor infrastructure, dissatisfied residents with poor educational and training levels, environmental problems and high taxes, for example, will not be characterized by the same parameters of "functioning" as they would be if they had better internal structures and facilities. Because of this, the particularities of the internal structure, and the success or failure of urban centres with respect to their inhabitants, penetrates upwards to affect their capacity to attract investment and migrants, and hence their long term growth.

The spatial models of urban and regional evolution therefore demonstrate the fact that what emerges are ecologies of populations, clustered into mutually consistent locations and activities, expressing a mixture of competition and symbiosis. This nested hierarchy of structure is the result of evolution. It is not "optimal" in any particular way, because there are a multiplicity of subjectivities and intentions, fed by a web of imperfect information.

The total pattern emerges as a result of the interaction of imperfect patterns of behaviour for each type actor, and what this really means is that there is an intrinsic element of unpredictability in the system. Creativity, and adaptive response are therefore powered by the degree of heterogeneity of the population, and their microscopic diversity. Applications of these ideas have been made in the USA, Belgium, Holland, Senegal and France, as well as in understanding intra-urban evolution in cities of Belgium and France. Such models provide an "intelligent" basis for decision support and policy exploration since they can show the complex, creative responses of a system, and not simply the directly imposed effects.

2. MANAGEMENT OF NATURAL RESOURCES

This evolutionary approach was also used to develop intelligent decision support models for the management of natural resources. This work has been discussed elsewhere in detail (Allen & McGlade,1987), but it is worth mentioning briefly some of the main conclusions. One essential and very general point that emerged was that success in fishing, requires two almost contradictory facets of behaviour. First, the ability to organize one's behaviour so as to exploit the information available concerning "net benefits" (to be rational) which we have called "Cartesian" behaviour. More surprisingly, however, a second ability is required, that is to be able to ignore present information and to "explore" beyond present knowledge. We have called these kinds of fishermen "Stochasts". The first makes good use of information, but the second generates it! At the root of creativity is always this second type.

In the short term it is always true that the more "rational" actor must outperform the less, and therefore that for example taking steps to maximise present profits must, by that yardstick, be better than not doing so. Nevertheless, over a longer period the best performance does not come from the most rational but instead from behaviour which is some complex compromise. For example, a fleet of Cartesians which goes where available information indicates highest profits will in fact lock into zones for much too long, remaining in ignorance of the existence of other, more profitable zones simply because there is no information available concerning them. This underlines the important point that:

"You don't know what it is you don't know".

New information can only come from boats which have "chosen" not to fish in the "best" zones, or who do not share the consensus values, technology or behaviour, and hence who generate information. They behave like risk takers, but may or may not see themselves as such. They may act as they do through ignorance, or through a belief in some myth or legend. Whatever the reason, or lack of it, they are vital to the success of the fishing endeavour as a whole. It is their exploration that probes the value of the existing pattern of fishing effort, and lays the foundations for a new one.

As information is generated concerning the existence of new, rich fishing grounds, so the value of this starts to fall as the news spreads, and exploitation rates increase there. We see a cyclic pattern in the discovery of value in a zone, the spread of information and with it the saturation or exhaustion of the discovery, calling for fresh explorations.

The model can either be used as a simulator, for the overall management of the fishery, or for the benefit of any particular fleet wishing to improve its performance. The parameter values which appear in the mechanisms governing the decision making of fishing boats are calibrated so as to give realistic behaviour. It is also possible to make a model which will run competing strategies against each other, and eventually discover for itself robust and successful sets of strategies - again generating an "ecology" of fishing strategies. (Allen, 1991). This kind of model can also be used for the management of grazing, or of forests or other natural resources.

3. DECISION SUPPORT IN ECONOMIC AND FINANCIAL MARKETS

The idea that economics should be thought of in "biological" terms occurred to authors as far back as Marshall (1927) and of course before that Darwin himself was inspired partially by the ideas of Adam Smith. However, for various reasons, economics borrowed the inappropriate "equilibrium" perspective of classical physics. Economists such as Schumpeter, 1934 and later, Goodwin 1951, who attempted to introduce dynamical considerations and non-linear effects were not followed by the mainstream. Nelson and Winter set out an evolutionary perspective, of competing firms subject to "mutation". This has helped to inspire much of the research that is going on concerning the evolution of technology, and of technical change (Dosi et al. 1988). A particularly interesting perspective was developed by Clark and Juma, 1990 who clearly separated out the short term picture of an economic system from the long term processes that govern its evolution.

Self-organising simulation models similar to the regional, urban and natural resource management models described above have been built. These allow an exploration of the possible consequences of different product and pricing strategies in a changing market. Instead of considering only geographic space the arena of evolution may be multidimensional, concerning all the different possible qualities that the product could have. The customer characteristics are also diverse, and the model requires an analysis of how the products of one particular company will attract potential clients, compared to competing products. Sales strategies are realistically represented, with their costs and so the simulation proceeds and the market changes as it matures. Clients which have just bought a product cease to be potential clients for some length of time. Clients are seeking the qualities important to them, at the lowest price, and so the relative competitivities of different companies leads to changing market shares, and this in turn to different economies of scale, and profits. As well as providing decision support for company strategy, the system shows how a market of possible products will self-organise, leading to an evolving pattern of supply and demand.

Models of this kind are under development for the testing of different possible strategies in several industries, such as banking and telecommunications. Although everyone recognizes the use of a flight simulator for pilots, the need for a "business simulator" for companies was not previously understood.

Another area of applications concerns the development of trading and portfolio management systems. In conventional economics general equilibrium theory and the "efficient market" hypothesis portray changes in the market as being due to external factors represented as a random walk (Osborne 1964, Muth 1961, Fama 1970). The subsequent realisation that equilibrium forms only a partial view and indications of the existence of instability through market crashes has motivated the search for alternative paradigms. Nonlinear dynamics, in particular chaos theory, has been the focus of much recent research (Blank, 1991; Chen, 1988; Day, 1983; Grandmont & Malgrange, 1986; Hsieh, 1991, Kesley, 1988; Larrain, 1991; Peters, 1991a; 1989; Savit, 1988; 1989; Scheinkman & LeBaron, 1989). Of course the value of such research would be to demonstrate the persistence of a particular chaotic attractor for some time, during which it could be used to trade successfully. However, this does not get around the problem that as soon as this "persistence time" became known, then it, and the chaotic attractor, would change!

Clearly, if any trend or knowledge becomes apparent, traders react to it, and by their actions change what subsequently will occur in reality(Soros, 1988). This implies that markets will always drive themselves to the "edge" of predictability and that it might be easier to learn how to survive uncertainty, rather than trying to predict the dynamics of future prices. In order to do this, an intelligent model has been developed which uses parallel strategies and an internal selection to choose behaviour which is sufficiently good to survive, despite the fact that we cannot know "the" future. Intelligence in trading depends on maintaining a whole range of strategies in play, and in switching to those that are working well at any given time.

As a basis for our strategies, we have used the moving average method. It is one of the most simple, yet versatile and widely used of all technical indicators (Murphy, 1986). It does not pretend to anticipate events, but only to respond to them. Successful trading depends on which moving average is chosen. Too short, and the system trades too often, losing money each time. Too long, and it comes in too late, and stays in too long so that money is lost while waiting for the signal. In addition, however, if the price produces a "spike", cutting the moving average curve and then immediately cutting it in the opposite direction, then losses occur. A bandwidth can be added to the moving average method to act as a precaution against unnecessary trades.

Evolutionary intelligence then consists in comparing the performance of different strategies over a recent period, and using the best for some time. As the other players change their games, and as players enter and leave the market, so the price time series are affected, and our system adapts the parameters of its strategy in response. Our "possibility space" for strategies has four dimensions: over what length of time to test the performance; how often to re-adapt, what moving average and band-width to use.

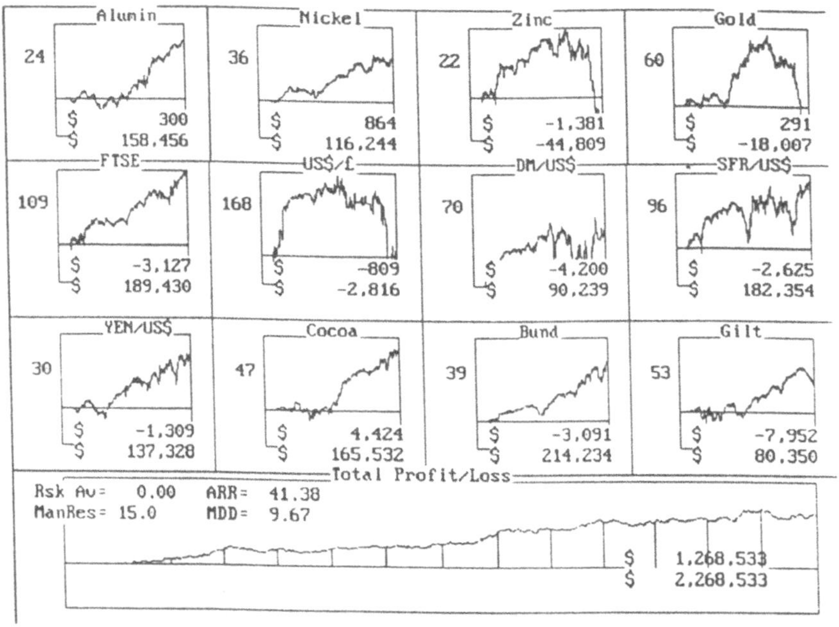

Figure (8). The final screen after 615 days trading of 12 futures contracts. An initial $1,000,000 becomes $2,268,533 trading 10% of the fund, excluding interest on the 90% and management fees. This is a 41% annual rate of return.

The trading model includes things like commission charges incurred in executing trades, fluctuations in exchange rates as well as slippage costs when transactions were not carried out at the expected price as a result of delays in communicating trades to the trading floor. These factors bring a sense of reality to the simulation results obtained.

The system has been developed at present to trade in the futures markets of various commodities, currencies and financial instruments(Allen and Phang, 1993). The trading in different commodities and currencies has been combined in a "self-adapting" portfolio system. In this, the recent success of trading in different commodities affects the number of lots that are traded. This trading can be either long (buying what you don't have) or short (selling what you don't have), and the trading success encountered affects the weighting of the commodity within the portfolio. There is a parameter which the user is free to choose, which determines the "strength" of the portfolio management. If it is set to zero, then whatever the trading has been like, there is an even spread of investment right across the portfolio, while if it is set high, then on the contrary the fund reacts strongly to the success for different contracts. Similarly, there is a parameter which concerns "risk aversion", and this affects the fraction of the total fund that is traded. The system described here represents the performance of an ungeared fund, with only 10% being traded. In figure (8) we show the result for 12 contracts over the two years, with an annual rate of return of 41% with a maximum drawdown of 10%, excluding management fees and the interest earned on the 90% of the fund.

DISCUSSION

The idea that evolution leads to a community of interlocking behaviours is an important result. The history of a successful society within a region, is largely a tale of increasing cooperation and complementarity, not competition. If competition dominated it would "spread things out", rather than building dense concentrations of people and activities. An economy is a "complex" of different activities that to some extent "fit together" and need each other. Competition for customers, space, or for natural resources is only one aspect of reality. Others are of familiar suppliers and markets, local skill development and specialization, co-evolution of activities to each other, networks of information flows and solidarities, that lead to a collective generation and shaping of exchanges and discourse within the system.

These ideas also throw new light on the origins of coherence in human systems. A first point is of course that in classical physics, the smooth behaviour of macrovariables such as temperature and pressure, arises from the incoherent, random behaviour of the molecules. It is statistical averaging that leads to smooth behaviour. In self-organizing systems, however, the individual elements really are behaving coherently, either as the result of an external parameter that affects each individual separately, or as the result of co-evolution. For example, the day/night cycle affects everyone separately, and leads to the coherent behaviour of people going to work and coming home. However, the interlocking of activities in such a way that food flows from the fields, through various processing and wrapping stages, and arrives on the supermarket shelves in time for the saturday shopping rush, has demanded an enormous amount of skill and organization, resulting from a long learning process. The working of a modern economy certainly displays great coherence, but the ideas discussed here show us that the range of coherence, the spatial and hierarchical structures that evolve are the result these processes of self-organization, and that structure can change and reorganize over time as well. What is important is to have models capable of anticipating such changes and of exploring the different possible types of coherent structure that might emerge. This is really what policy exploration should be about.

The evolution of a society is not about a single type of behaviour "winning", through its superior performance, since as we see evolution is characterised more by increasing variety and complexity than the opposite. Instead, it is about the emergence of self-consistent "sets" of activities, with mutually helpful effects on each other. Potential "supply" and "demand" are not given independently of one another. People cannot experience what is not made available, but can only be affected by what is produced. Their lifestyle, demands and preferences are shaped by the supply that really occurs, and so a "learning" dialogue shapes the patterns of consumption that develop in the system. These patterns emerge, and the chance details of the process of emergence alter what is finally "revealed". Supply affects demand, and vice versa, and cultural structures are formed by the effects of positive and negative feedbacks - imitation, economies of scale, learning by doing, etc. are positive, and competition for attention, market and for resources are negative.

This brings to the important question of speculation and beliefs in human systems. Clearly, the expected return on an investment is what drives investment, but this must depend on what other people believe about the system. What people believe affects what happens, and what happens affects what people believe! This is a positive feedback loop which can be understood on the basis of the kind of models which we are developing. It severely affects the outcome of "free markets", as we have seen repeatedly in commodity cycles, land speculation, the prices of almost anything of which there is a limited supply. Instead of free markets leading to a sensible, and effective allocation of investment and resources, we find that prices, although they are "numbers", are still driven by peoples' beliefs, and these feed on each other resulting in peaks and troughs, and often in massive misallocations of resources and waste. Clearly, the fact that "trend creates trend" offers a considerable opportunity for instability and chaos, and this is only rendered manageable by the diversity of perceptions and motivations of human actors. Models can and are being developed to "learn" robust mutually consistent strategies, and also how to encourage diversity in the face of the mass media, and instantaneous shared information.

Diversity is absolutely vital to the functioning of the system. Social interaction and mutually advantageous exchange can only occur if two actors are different. If they are both identical and "average", then there can be no useful interchange. The evolution of a society and of the urban or regional landscape therefore reflects the specificities of individuals who have different aims, different information and different resources. Imperfect knowledge, and plain ignorance all play a role in smoothing the responses of a population to a given situation and as decisions are made by some individuals, so they change the conditions and constraints on others provoking successive responses and adjustments to the evolving circumstances.

The idea that we can solve our problems by simply releasing the forces of the "free market" is an illusion. The real complexity of the world involves the fact of collective structure, which is not amenable to any simplistic solution, be it central planning, or free markets. The goals and strategies, the ethics and the understanding of individuals, fashion the collective structure that emerges, and give it complex properties, which act on each individual uniquely, and which cannot easily be resumed in a few criteria. Similarly, the collective structure that emerges enriches and constrains the experiences and choices that are open to individuals, and so one is dealing with the dialogue between individual freedom and beliefs, and the social, cultural, technological and physical realities in which they are embedded, and which they shape.

This discussion of self-organization in complex systems hopefully teaches us humility. Science has revealed its own limitations, and this too is an achievement. Knowing that we cannot know is an important step on the road to wisdom. If we are to learn from the way that the natural world copes with its inability to predict the future, then we see that parallelism, microdiversity and local freedom are key factors in its ability to deal with whatever happens. We must attempt to find a system that while evolving enough coherence to function, retains enough individual freedom and microscopic diversity to provide a pool of adaptability and innovation so that it can constantly evolve and restructure in the face of change. In other words, we seek to create a "learning" society, since this, in effect, is the basis of a sustainable future.

ACKNOWLEDGEMENT

The urban and regional models were developed with the collaboration of Michele Sanglier, Guy Engelen and Francoise Boon. The financial trading and portfolio models were developed with Hoon Khing Phang and Mark Strathern. This work was partially supported by Toppan Moore Systems Limited (Japan), by the Open Society Fund of New York, and by Futures Management Ltd, London. The 3-D visualization was made by Jack Corliss and M.Lesser at the Goddard Space Flight Center, NASA.

REFERENCES

Allen P.M. 1984, Self-Organization and Evolution in Urban Systems in Cities and Regions as Non-linear Decision Systems, AAAS Selected Symposiua, 77, Ed. R. Crosby. Westview Press, Boulder Colorado.

Allen P.M., 1988 Evolution: Why the Whole is greater than the sum of its parts, in Ecodynamics, Eds Wolff, Soeder & Drepper Springer Verlag, Berlin.

Allen P.M. 1991, Fisheries: Models of learning and Uncertainty, in Pecheries Ouest Africaines, Variabilité, Instabilité et Changement, Eds Ph. Cury & Cl.Roy ORSTOM, Paris

Allen P.M. 1994 Evolution, Sustainability and Industrial Metabolism, in Industrial Metabolism, Eds R. Ayer and U.E. Simonis, United nations University Press, Tokyo

Allen P.M. and Lesser M., 1991, Evolutionary Human Systems: Learning, Ignorance and Subjectivity, in Evolutionary Theories of Economic and Technological Change, Eds P.Saviotti and S.Metcalfe, Harwood, Chur. Harwood, Chur, Switzerland

Allen P.M. and McGlade J., 197, The Modelling of Human Systems: A Fisheries Example, European Journal of Operational Research, June 1987

Allen P.M. and M.Sanglier, 1979, Dynamic Model of growth in a Central Place System, Geographical Analysis, Vol 11, No 3.

Allen P.M. and M.Sanglier, 1981, Urban Evolution, Self-Organization and Decision Making, Environment and Planning A.

Allen P.M. and J.M.McGlade, 1987, Evolutionary Drive: The Effect of Microscopic Diversity, Error Making and Noise, Foundations of Physics, Vol.17, No.7, July. p723-728

Anderson P.W. Arrow K.J. and Pines D. 1988, Eds. The Economy as a Complex Evolving System, Reading, Addison-Wesley

Blank, S.C., 1991, Chaos in Futures Markets ? A Nonlinear Dynamical Analysis, Journal of Futures Markets, 11:p711-728.

Chen, P., 1988, Empirical and Theoretical Evidence of Economic Chaos, System Dynamics Review 4.

Clark N. and Juma C. 1987, Long-run Economics - An Evolutionary Approach to Economic Change, London, Pinter Publishers, Limited

Day, R., 1983, The Emergence of Chaos from Classical Economic Growth, Quarterly Journal of Economics, 98:201-213.

Dosi G, Freeman C. Nelson R. Silverberg G. and Soete L. Eds , 1988, Technical Change and Economic Theory, Pinter, London.

Eigen M. and Schuster P., 1979, The Hypercycle, Springer, Berlin.

Fama, E.F., 1979, Efficient Capital Markets: A Review of Theory and Empirical Work, Journal of Finance, 25:p383-423.

Goodwin R.M., 1951, The Non-Linear Accelerator and the persistence of Business Cycles, Econometrica, Vol.19.

Goodwin R.M. Kruger M. & Vercelli,A. 1984, Nonlinear Models of Fluctuating Growth, Lecture Notes in Economics and Mathematical Systems, Vol.228, Berlin-Heidelberg-New York-Tokyo, Springer-Verlag.

Grandmont, J.; Malgrange, P., 1986, Nonlinear Economic Dynamics : Introduction, Journal of Economic Theory 40.

Haken H. 1977, Synergetics, in the Synergetics Series, Springer Verlag, Heidelberg.

Hsieh, D.A., 1991, Chaos and Nonlinear Dynamics : Application to Financial Markets, The Journal of Finance, 66:p1639-1877.

Kesley, D., 1988, The Economics of Chaos or the Chaos of Economics, Oxford Economic Papers 40.

Larrain, M., 1991, Empirical Tests of Chaotic Behaviour in a Nonlinear Interest Rate Model, Financial Analysts Journal, Sept-Oct, p51-62.

Lorenz H.W. 1989, Non-Linear Dynamical Economics and Chaotic Motion, Lecture Notes in Economics and Mathematical Systems, Vol.228, Berlin-Heidelberg-New York-Tokyo, Springer-Verlag.

Marshall A., (1890/1927), Principles of Economics, 8th Edition, Macmillan, London.

Murphy, John J., 1986, Techncial Analysis of the Futures Market, New York Institute of Finance, New York.

Muth, J.F., 1961, Rational Expectations and the Theory of Price Movements, Econometrica, 29:p315-335.

Nelson R.R and Winter S. G. 1982, An Evolutionary Theory of Economic Change, Cambridge, The Belknap Press of Harvard University press.

Osborne, M.F.M., 1964, Brownian Motion in the Stock Market in P. Cootner, (ed.), "The Random Character of Stock Market Prices", Cambridge, MA:M.I.T. Press. (Originally published in 1959)

Peters, E., 1991a, A Chaotic Attractor for the S & P 500, Financial Analysts Journal.

Peters, E., 1989, Fractal Structure in the Capital Markets, Financial Analysts Journal.

Peters, E., 1991b, R/S Analysis using Logarithmic Returns : A Technical Note, Financial Analysts Journal

Prigogine I. and I.Stengers, 1987, Order out of Chaos, Bantam Books, New York

Sanglier M. and P.M.Allen, 1989, Evolutionary Models of Urban Systems: an Application to the Belgian Provinces, Environment and Planning, A, Vol.21.p477-498.

Saviotti P. 1991, The role of variety in economic and technological development, in Evolutionary Theories of Economic and Technological Change, Eds P.Saviotti and S.Metcalfe, Harwood, Chur.

Saviotti P and Metcalfe J., 1991 Present developments and trends in Evolutionary Economics, in Evolutionary Theories of Economic and Technological Change, Eds P.Saviotti and S.Metcalfe, Harwood, Chur.

Savit, R., 1988, When Random is Not Random : An Introduction to Chaos in Market Prices, The Journal of Futures Markets, 8:p271-289.

Savit, R., 1989, Nonlinearities and Chaotic Effects in Options Prices, The Journal of Futures Markets, 9:p507-518.

Scheinkman, J.; LeBaron, B., 1989, Nonlinear Dynamics and Stock Returns, Journal of Business, 62:p311-337.

Schumpeter J.,1934, The Theory of Economic Development, Harvard University Press, Cambridge, Massachusetts.

Silverberg G., Dosi G. and Orsenigo L., Innovation, Diversity and Diffusion: A Self-Organization Model, The Economic Journal, Vol 98 p1032-1054

Soros, George, 1988, The Alchemy of Finance, Weidenfeld and Nicolson, London.

About a Dynamic Model of High Technology Industry : Impact of Investments on the Competitiveness of the Products

M. Sanglier, E. Maillet
Instituts Internationaux de Physique et de Chimie fondés par E. Solvay, Campus Plaine CP231, B. 1050- Bruxelles.

Abstract. The research described in this paper aims at developing an integrated dynamic model for the micro-electronic domain. The model mainly focus on the competition among the four most important geostrategic zones (namely US, Japan, Europe and South East Asia). It takes into account the dynamics of investment, the dynamics of the production, the product life cycle and the strategic choice in term of alliance and conmpetition. Three levels of the microelectronic activity have been considered in the model: the semiconductors producers, the industries of electronic equipments and the final demand of each geographical zones. The first economic field which has been investigated by means of our generic model is the highly strategic DRAM market. The simulations performed so far have given very encouraging results. Our model fits nicely sampling taken from Dataquest data and estimations on the evolution of the DRAM production capacity.

1 Introduction

The empirical evidences (Dauvin, 1990; J. Lesourne, R. Leban, K. Oshima, T. Yakushiji, 1989) show that the growth process of the microelectronic market is cyclic and polarized in four zones highly connected and competitive. In such a framework, the actors must adapt and react very rapidly. This industry is also characterized by rapid technological changes. The acceleration of the birth of new products induces an increase of the rate of substitution of new products as well as the coexistence and competition between several generations.

The complexity of the highly dynamic and interactive market has led us to adopt an *'original'* multidisciplinary approach including psychological and geostrategic factors and the physics of non-linear complex systems, based on the concept emerging from the study of 'Dissipative Structure' (Nicolis and Prigogine, 1977). The economical and technological interdependency between the market of semiconductors and those of electronic equipment has led us to consider explicitly these two industrial levels and their interactions. The heart of the model is the dynamics of investment, which is related to the capacity of production of the successive generations of products. This process is included at the level of semiconductor industries as well as the electronic equipment industries.

2. Characteristics of the model

The model is characterized by an integrated multidimensionnal approach which links in a dynamic non-linear framework the economical, technological, geostrategical and behavioral dimensions. The model is constructed on a modular structure, each module representing a category of industry in one zone .

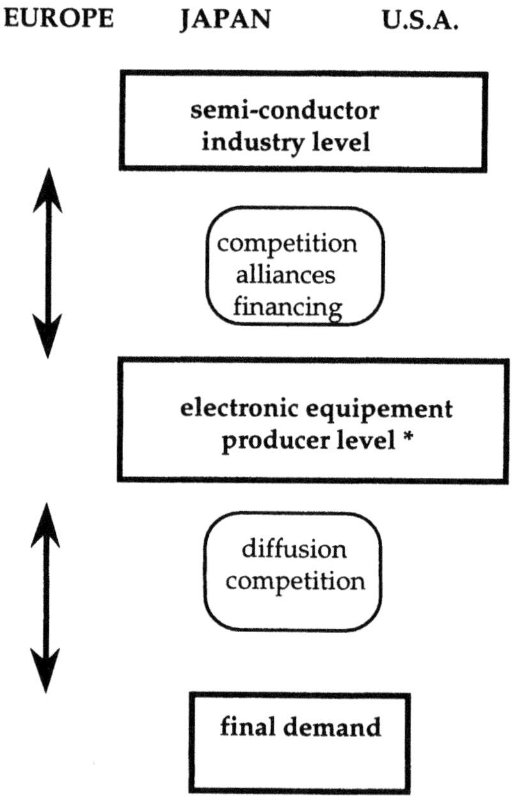

* telecommunications, informatic, automobile, electronic consumer, defense and spatial

Fig. 1 : General scheme of the different levels of the microelectronic activity considered in the model.

The two categories of industries considered here are the semiconductors industry and the electronic equipment industry. At last, the relation with the consumers is established through the final demand of the goods of this sector (figure 1).

The interactions between the different levels of the microelectronic activity is accounted by an attribution function that considers economical variables (like prices and delivery delays) as well as vertical integration and agreements between the different zones.

3 Description of the model

1° Economic interactions between the two levels

In order to understand the behavior of this complex system (figure 2), let consider first one zone and start with the final demand. The evolution of the demand of the electronic equipment goods is described by an equation similar to the diffusion of an technological innovation, taking into account the fashion and the imitation effect.

The evolution of the final demand of one zone is given by (Mahajan and Peterson ,1985) :

$$\frac{d\, \mathbf{m}_l^{\mathbf{ee}}(t)}{dt} = \left(\omega_l + \zeta_l\, \mathbf{m}_l^{\mathbf{ee}}(t) \right) \left(\mathbf{m}_l^{*\mathbf{ee}}(t) - \mathbf{m}_l^{\mathbf{ee}}(t) \right) \qquad (1)$$

for l = 1,nz nz: number of zone

$\mathbf{m}^*{}_l^{\mathbf{eu}}(t)$ is the potential final demand of the zone l. The coefficients ω_l and ζ_l are related respectively to the fashion and the imitation effects.

This demand evolves according to a potential demand of the zone $\mathbf{m}_l^{*\mathbf{ee}}(t)$ which is stimulated by the generation of new products.

The demand coming from one zone is addressed at the level of the producers of electronic equipments of all the zones according to the relative attractiveness of one zone with respect to the others. This relative attractiveness of one zone is represent by an attribution function $\mathbf{f}_{jl}^{\mathbf{ee}}(t)$ and allows to calculate the market share of the electronic equipments industry j coming from the final demand of the zones (l) $\mathbf{n}_j^{\mathbf{ee}}(t)$.

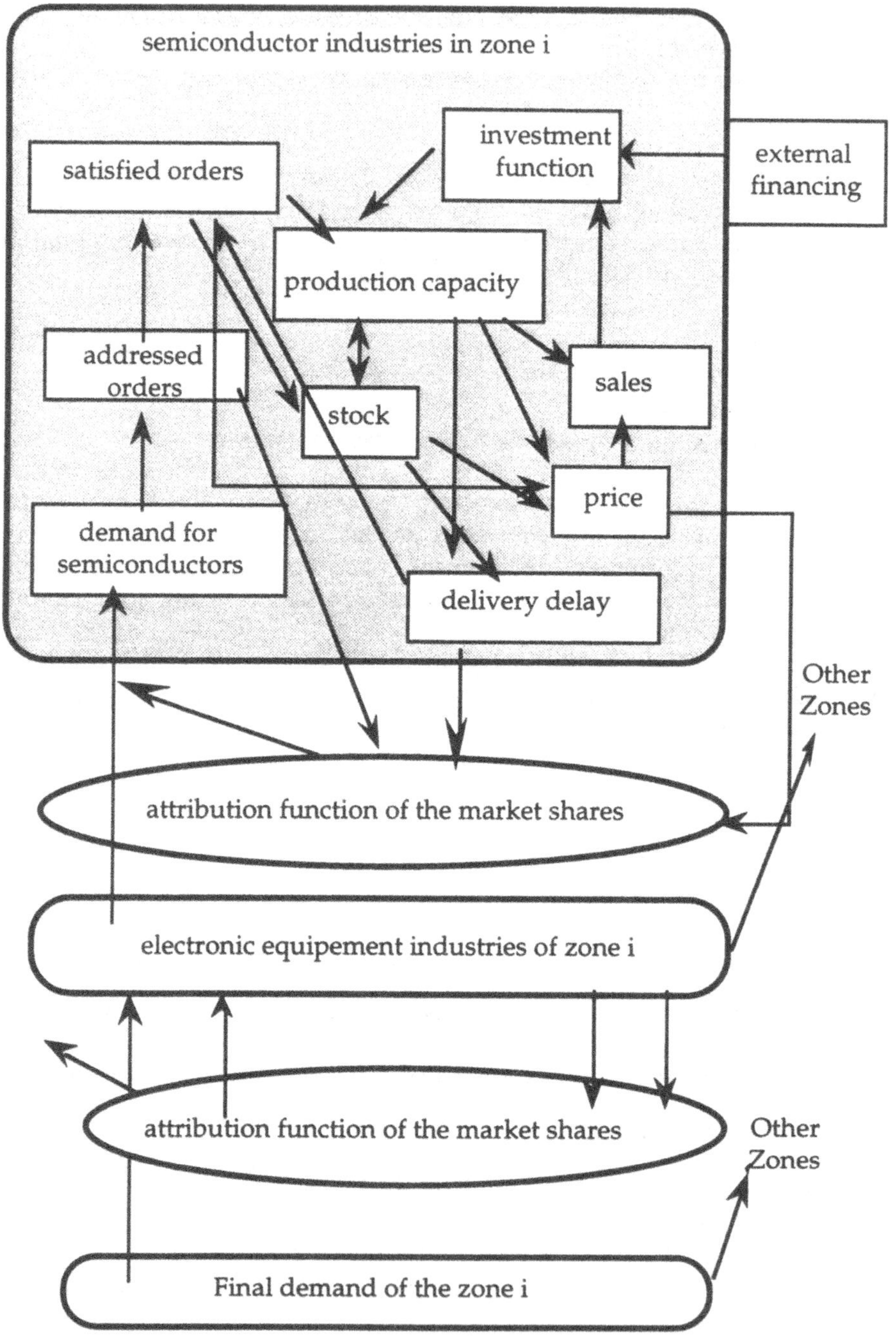

Fig. 2 : Detail scheme of the mechanisms occurring in one zone

$$n_j^{ee}(t) = \sum_{l=1}^{4} m_l^{ee}(t)\, f_{jl}^{ee}(t) \qquad \text{for i=1,nz and j=1,nz} \tag{2}$$

$$f_{ij}^{ee}(t)=\frac{a_j\left(1-\dfrac{p_{ij}^{ee}(t)}{\sum\limits_{i'=1}^{nz} p_{i'j}^{ee}(t)}\right)+b_j\left(1-\dfrac{d_{ij}^{ee}(t)}{\sum\limits_{i'=1}^{nz} d_{i'j}^{ee}(t)}\right)+c_j\dfrac{x_i^{ee}(t)}{\sum\limits_{i'=1}^{nz} x_{i'}^{ee}(t)}+g^{\circ}{}_{ij}^{ee}}{\sum\limits_{j'=1}^{nz}\left(a_{j'}\left(1-\dfrac{p_{ij'}^{ee}(t)}{\sum\limits_{i'=1}^{nz} p_{i'j'}^{ee}(t)}\right)+b_{j'}\left(1-\dfrac{d_{ij'}^{ee}(t)}{\sum\limits_{i'=1}^{nz} d_{i'j'}^{ee}(t)}\right)+c_{j'}\dfrac{x_{j'}^{ee}(t)}{\sum\limits_{j^*=1}^{nz} x_{j^*}^{ee}(t)}+g^{\circ}{}_{ij'}^{ee}\right)}$$

for i=1,nz and j=1,nz (3)

where :

$p_{ij}^{ee}(t)$ is the sale price in the currency of the producer,

$d_{ij}^{ee}(t)$ is delivery delays

$x_i^{ee}(t)$ is the cumulate orders addressed to the producer of electronic equipments i by the final demand j.

$g^{\circ}{}_{ij}^{ee}$ is the agreement between the producer in the zone i and the demand coming from the zone j (if i=j that could correspond to the intensity of vertical integration).

This function accounts for the impact of the price, the delivery delay, the previous commercial relations and the agreements. These indicators are weighted according to the relative sensitivity of the 'actors' to this criteria. They allow to simulate a variety of behaviors which could even include cultural aspects. The coefficients a_j , b_j , c_j, represent the different sensitivity of the actor j to the price, the delivery delay and the previous commercial relations.

This final demand of products generate to orders at the level of producers of electronic equipments. If these orders lead his monthly production to increase, the producer will adjust this production according to the degree of adaptability depending on his capacity investment. However an adjustment will be feasible provided the required inner components (importance of the delivery delay of the SC) are of a sufficient quantity.

This price will influence the sale price of the final products. This will induce orders to the producers of semiconductors according to an attractiveness function. These orders will affect the capacity of production of the semiconductor producer in the related zone.

The prices evolve according to the laws of supply and demand modulated by a factor of economy of scale and by a competition effect. The price of the product cannot go below a minimum price related to a break even point.

$$\frac{d\, p_j^{ee}(t)}{dt} = e_j \left(y_j^{ee}(t) - s_j^{ee}(t) + \beta_j \left(1 - \frac{c_j^{ee}(t)}{c_j^{ee*}(t)} \right) - \eta_j \frac{c_j^{ee}(t)}{c_j^{ee*}(t)} \right) * \left(1 - \frac{p_{j\,Min}^{ee}(t)}{p_j^{ee}(t)} \right) + \psi_j * \frac{d}{dt} \sum_{i=1}^{4} f_{ij}^{sc}(t)\, p_{ij}^{sc}(t) \tag{4}$$

for i=1,nz and j=1,nz

$p_i^{ee}(t)$: sale price in the currency of the producer;

$p_{Min\,i}^{ee}(t)$: minimum sale price related to a break even point;

$s_i^{ee}(t)$: number of units in the stock;

$c_i^{ee}(t)$: capacity of production;

c_i^{ee*} : maximal capacity of production that correspond to an utilization rate of 1.

The delivery delays are function of the transports, stocks and the production capacities of each semiconductor producer. The production capacity of one module reacts to an increase of the demand following its own technological and economical limits.

$$\frac{d\, c_j^{ee}(t)}{dt} = \left(y_j^{ee}(t) - s_j^{ee}(t) \right) \varphi_j^{ee}(t) \left(1 - \frac{c_j^{ee}(t)}{c_j^{ee*}(t)} \right) \qquad \text{for } j=1,nz \tag{5}$$

where the function $\varphi_j^{ee}(t)$ relies the capacity of production of the electronic equipment to the investment module.

The evolution of the stock is given by this balance equation where $r_j^{ee}(t)$ represent the possibility to have negative stock.

$$\frac{d\, s_j^{ee}(t)}{dt} = c_j^{ee}(t) - y_j^{ee}(t) + r_j^{ee}(t) \qquad \text{for } j=1,nz \tag{6}$$

$$r_j^{ee}(t) = \frac{1}{2}\left(y_j^{ee}(t) - s_j^{ee}(t) - c_j^{ee}(t) + \left| \, y_j^{ee}(t) - s_j^{ee}(t) - c_j^{ee}(t) \, \right| \right) \tag{7}$$

for j=1,nz

The adressed orders $y_j^{ee}(t)$ results from the sum of the demand term $n_j^{ee}(t)$ and the rest to be delivered $r_j^{ee}(t)$.

All these mechanisms represented in figure 2 show the importance of the relationship between the electronic equipment industry and the semiconductor one in terms of price, delivery delays and agreements.

2° Investment and generation of new products

In this economical sector, the technological innovation is highly strategic and depend on investment granted. In this model the dynamic of investment is endogenous and directly related to the successive generations of products what are simulated in the following way. Each 36 months, a new product appears in one zone provided the investments for its generation exceed than a minimal threshold. However, since this new product enters in competition with the old ones, its survival probability will be function of the price, sales and investments of the older ones. The investments come from the profits of the sales and external financing and directly influence the production capacities, (more precisely the rate of adaptation).

The generation of products is modelled by a function $\theta_k^j(t)$ (the indices j is related to the zone and k to the generation). This term is defined by the product of the creation of the new product $\sigma_k^j(t)$ and the competition with the older ones $v_k^j(t)$:

$$\theta_k^j(t) = \sigma_k^j(t)\, v_k^j(t) \tag{8}$$

with : $\sum_{k=1}^{n} \left(\theta_k^j(t) \right) = 1$

for j=1,nz and k=1, ng ng : number of generation

The appearance of a new generation is modeled by a sigmoïdal form like :

$$\sigma_k^j(t) = \frac{1}{1 + \exp^{(k\, \varepsilon_k^j(t) - t - \tau)}} \qquad \text{for } j=1,nz \text{ and } k=1,\ ng \qquad (9)$$

with $\varepsilon_k^j(t)$ given by:

$$\varepsilon_k^j(t) = \tau * \left(1 - \frac{\frac{1}{2}\left(\mathbf{I}_k^j(t) - \mathbf{I}_{k\,Min}^j(t) + \left| \mathbf{I}_k^j(t) - \mathbf{I}_{k\,Min}^j(t) \right| \right)}{\sum_{j=1}^{4} \left(\mathbf{I}_k^j(t) - \mathbf{I}_{k\,Min}^j(t) \right)} \right) \qquad (10)$$

for j=1,nz and k=1, ng

where $\mathbf{I}_{k\,Min}^j(t)$ is the minimum investment for the generation k and τ the average time life of a generation.

The new generation appears as soon as its investments exceed the minimum one for a given generation. The investment for a generation k is calculated according to the share of the profits of the sales of the previous generations and to the external financing $(\mathbf{I}_k^{j\,ext})$. This particular form has been chosen to take into account more explicitly the competition effects.

$$\mathbf{I}_k^j(t) = (1 - \sigma_k^j(t)) * \int_{t_0}^{t} dt' \sum_{l=1}^{k-1} \theta_l^j(t')\, \mathbf{y}_j(t') \left(\mathbf{p}_j(t') - \mathbf{p}_{Min}^j(t') \right) - \mathbf{I}_l^j(t') + \mathbf{I}_k^{j\,ext}$$

for j=1, nz , k=1, ng and l=1, k-1 (11)

The competition of a generation k is given by :

$$v_k^j(t) = \frac{k * I_k^j(t)}{\sum_{k=1}^{n} \left(k * I_k^j(t) * \sigma_k^j(t) \right)} \qquad \text{for j=1,nz and k=1, ng} \quad (12)$$

This relation relies on two assumptions : first the new product has a better quality than the previous one, secondly, the technological level is a growing function of the investments .

We calculate the cumulated investments for the generation k:

$$IC_k^j(t) = \int_{t_0}^{t} dt' \, I_k^j(t') \qquad \text{for j=1,nz and k=1, ng} \quad (13)$$

The function $\varphi_i(t)$ expresses the competition with the other producers, and

$$\varphi_i(t) = \frac{\sum_{k=1}^{n} I_k^j(t) \; * \theta_k^j(t)}{\sum_{j=1}^{4} \sum_{k=1}^{n} I_k^j(t) * \theta_k^j(t)} \qquad \text{for j=1,nz and k=1, ng} \quad (14)$$

gives rise to the rate of reaction of the capacity of production of the producer i (see eq. 5) . This mechanism of new products generation operates simultaneously at the level of semiconductors and electronic equipments industries.

4 Results of the simulations

These first simulations have been performed relying on real data available in Dataquest concerning the production of DRAMS in the various zones. We present also some implications in term of investments.

The model allows to simulate the evolution of the capacity for the different generations of products. At that level, we observe a some qualitative and quantitative agreement between the results of the simulation and the data for the evolution of the successive generations of DRAMs in Europe (cf. fig. 3and fig. 4) and in the World (cf. fig. 5 and fig. 6).

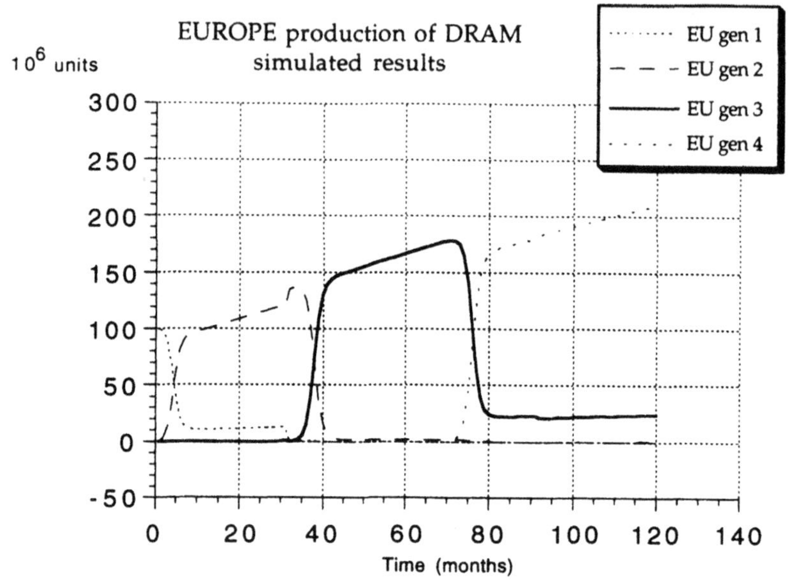

Fig. 3 : Evolution of the production of successive generations of DRAM in Europe, results of the simulation (units : million of units, t_0 =1986, t_f =1996).

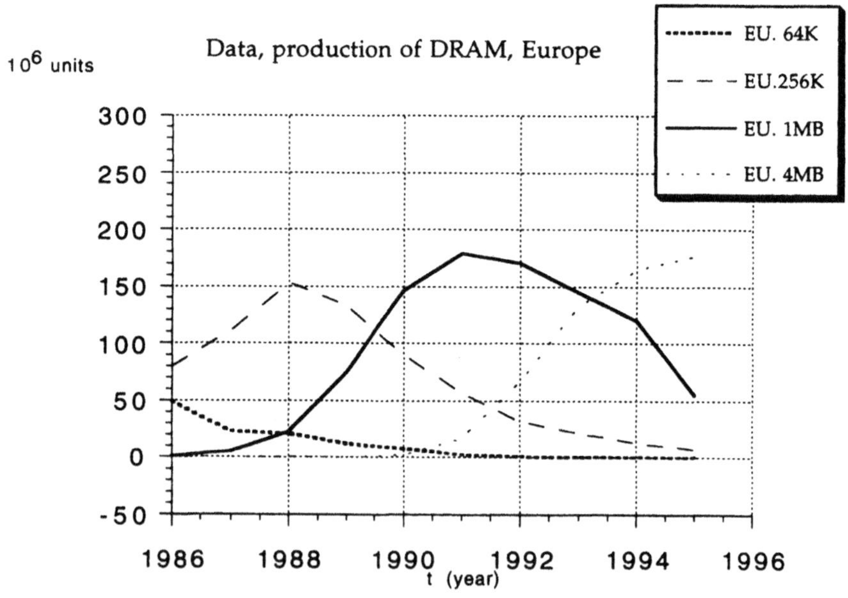

Fig.4 : Evolution of the production of successive generations of DRAM in Europe, data, source : Dataquest (units : million of units)

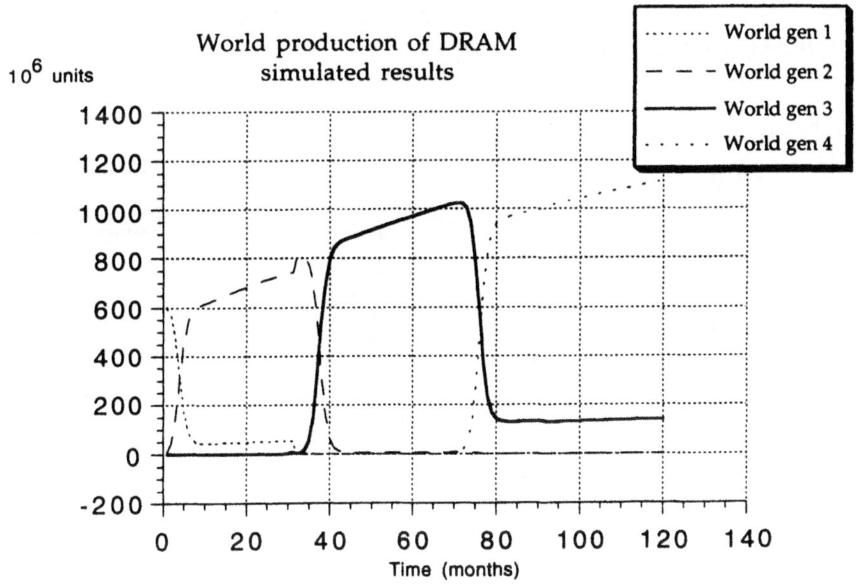

Fig. 5 : Evolution of the production of successive generations of DRAM in the world, results of the simulation (units : million of units, t_0 = 1986)

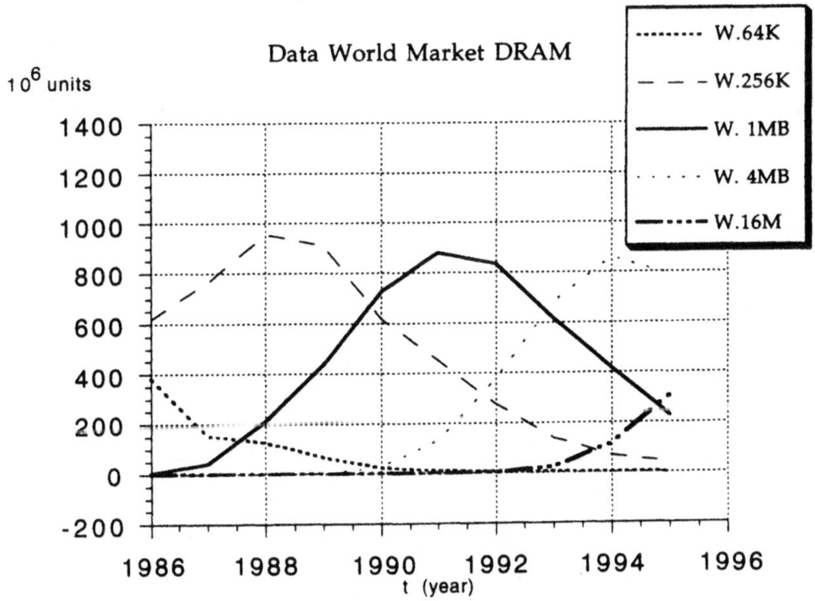

Fig. 6: Evolution of the production of successive generations of DRAM in the world, data, source : Dataquest (units : million of units)

The evolution of the simulated production of DRAMS for Japan and US are presented in the following graphs.

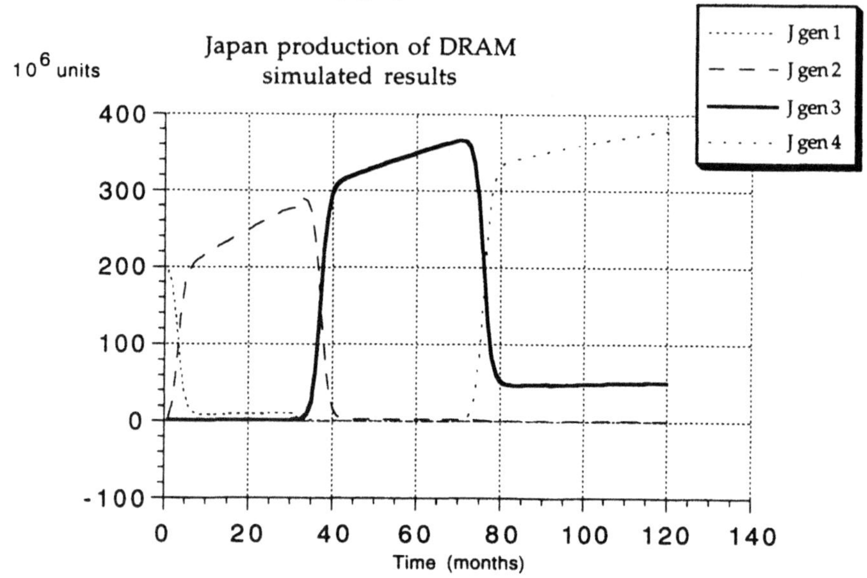

Fig.7: Evolution of the production of successive generations of DRAM in Japan, results of the simulation (units : million of units, t_0 =1986).

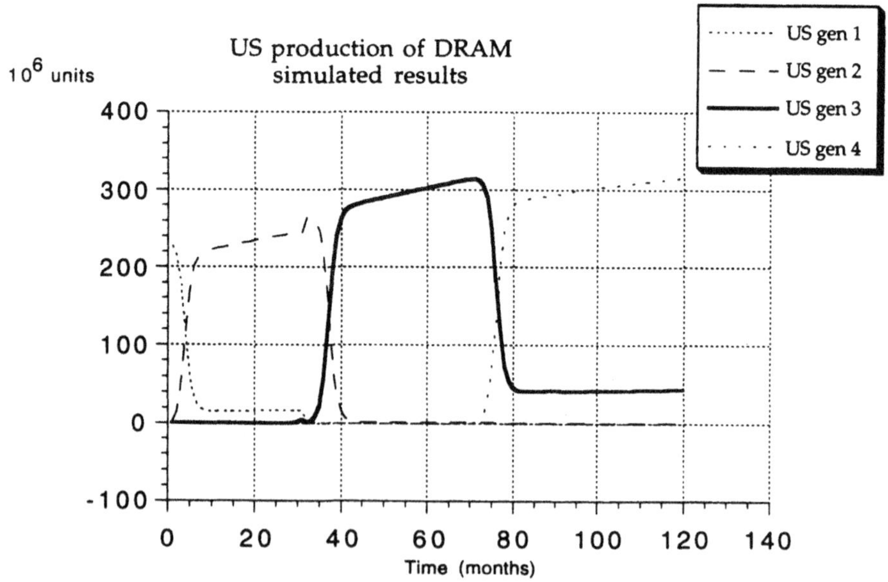

Fig. 8: Evolution of the production of successive generations of DRAM in US, results of the simulation (units : million of units, t_0 =1986).

We can analyze also the production of the different generation of products of the electronic equipment industry (for that level we have only consider three different generations of product) (fig. 9). This has not been calibrated on data, because this level must be disaggregated according to the different type of industries and even different specific lines of products having each own characteristics.

The figure (fig. 10) shows clearly the different behaviors of the geostrategic actors in terms of rate of reaction of the capacity of production and their ability to apply the 'just in time' as it seams to be the case for Japan since 1990 (according to the simulation). This scenario correspond to a situation where the demand exceed the supply.

The results given by the monthly investments underline the growing of the minimal cost of investment (fig. 11) of the new generations as in the real data. As early mentioned about the capacity of production we observe the great difference in the monthly investments for a given generation (fig.12).

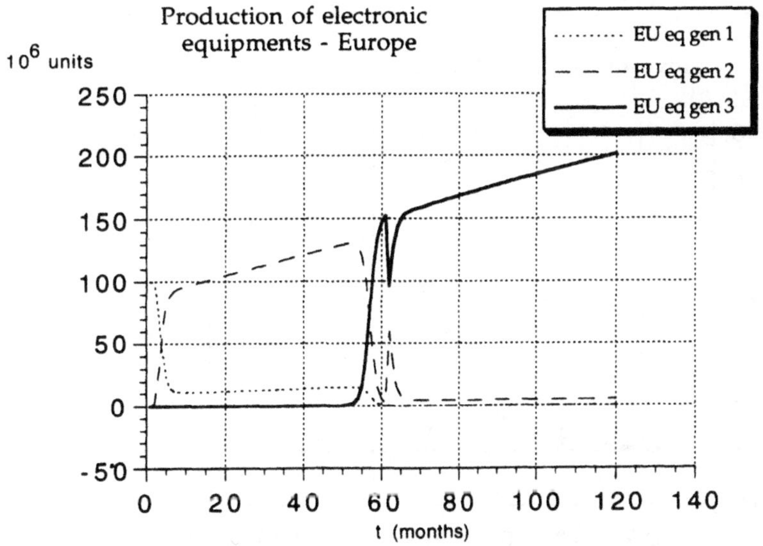

Fig. 9: Evolution of the production of successive generations of electronic equipment goods in Europe, reference simulation.

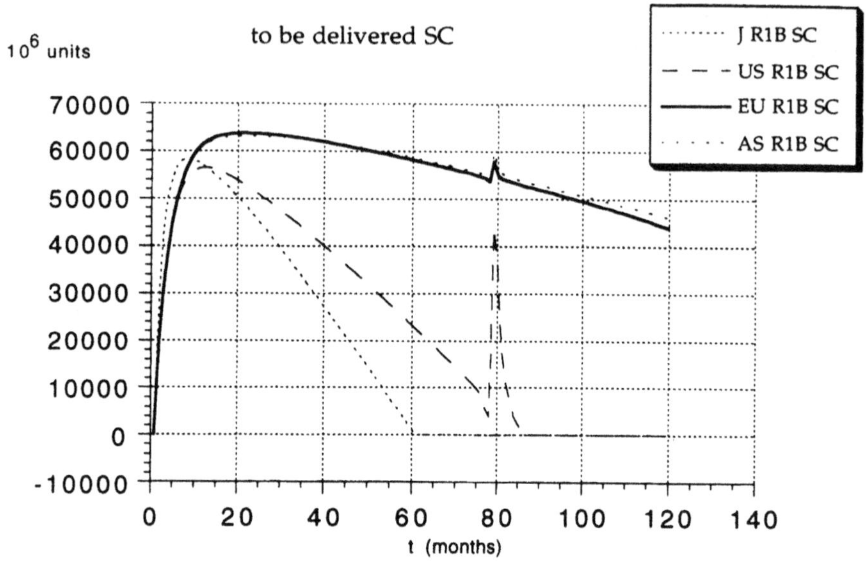

Fig. 10: Evolution of the rest to be delivered for the different actors

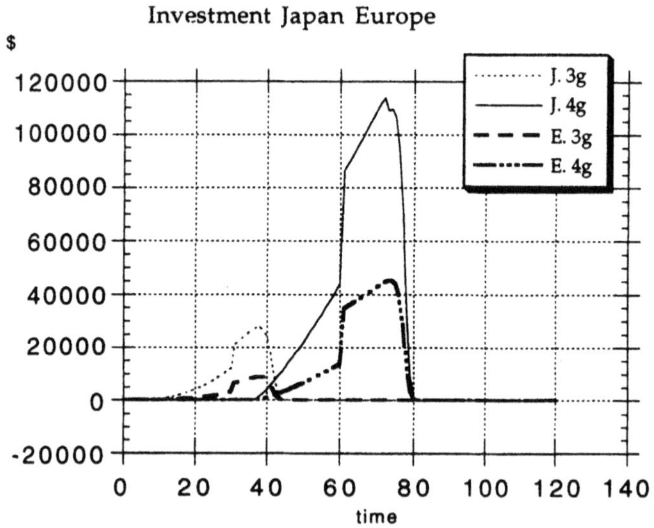

Fig. 11 : Evolution of the monthly investment of the third and fourth generations of SC for Japan and Europe (units : 10^4\$).

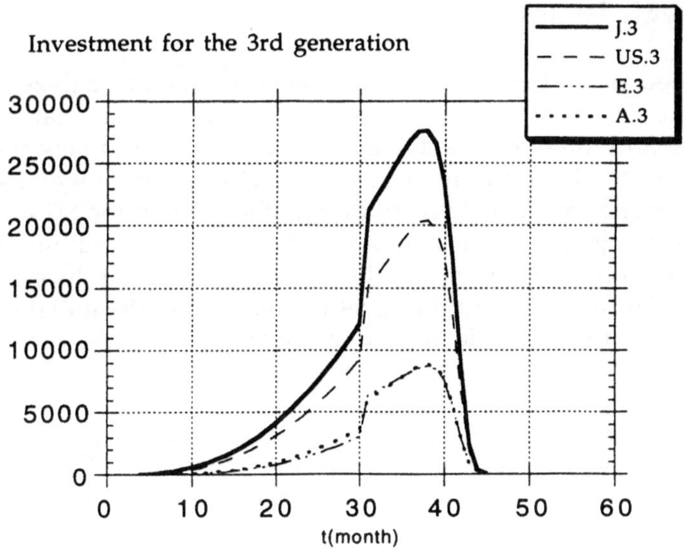

Fig.12 : Evolution of the monthly investment of the third generation of SC for the different zones (units : 10^4\$).

The following table shows the percentage of external investment compare to the total investment. Of course, these results are coming from a possible scenario and have not been calibrated on real data. A rather interesting behavior appear by comparing the results for Europe to Asia, the dependance from external financing is very high for Europe, in opposition Asia keep a rather low level of external financing even for the fourth generation. Note that this differentiate behavior does not appear in the production and price variables.

	3rd generation	4th generation
Japan	29%	79%
US	24%	75%
Europe	34%	88%
East Asia	23%	25%

Table 1 : Percentage of the external investment compare to the total one.

All the variables could also be analyze at the level of the electronic equipment industries.

5 Geostrategic issues

The integrated multidimensionnal approach allows to analyze some geostrategic issues. Empirical data show the highly dynamic character of the polarized and interconnected market. The relationship between the level of the semiconductor industry and the electronic equipment one has a strategic importance. The delivery delays, the price of the SC and the profile of the successive generation of products have a crucial influence. Delays of several months in the supply of SC could prevent the entrance on a market. Since the largest part profit is realized in the initial phase, this could have an irreversible impact on the evolution of the concerned industry.

The analyze of the structural changes of the industrial sector shows the crucial impact of the dynamic of investment in term of successive generation of products. The complexity and the growing cost of the minimal investment of the new generation of DRAM increase the competition between the present and the future generations. These factors as well as the acceleration of the announcement of the new products show that an investment policy based on a single generation cannot be sustainable. The investment policy must take the form of a series of investment corresponding to the successive generation of products. But moreover, the growing of the minimal cost of investment of the new generations shows that the financial management can no more be sustained by a single producer. So vertical integration and agreements could be analyze not only at the level of the market but mainly in terms of R&D and capacity investments.

6 Outlook

The proposed methodology is unique in that it combines the complementary strengths of two leading-edge qualitative and quantitative approaches to produce an integrated multidisciplinary instrument which can be fruitfully applied to company and industry levels. The resulting methodology will help strategy-makers to identify and validate strategic interventions in target markets. It provides ways for companies to assess and determine the competitiveness of alliances, partnership and mergers which may follow promising results from R&D investment, and consequent adaptation of internal strategies to new marketing goals.

This model presented here is the first step of the elaboration of a tool for analyzing within a multidimensional network, the strategic factors of the dynamic of investment and the correlated economic variables. Various problematic could be apprehended by this approach such as :

- impacts of strategy of price, delivery delays or management of stock at the level of one actor;
- influence of vertical integration or special agreement between two zones;
- various profiles of the final demand;
- strategic importance of the link between semiconductor producers and electronic equipment industries in term of production constraints as well as financing policy;
- investment strategy in term of the need or not of 'external financing' to overcome the financial threshold of new generations.

Acknowledgements

This research has been made possible by a funding from DGXIII of the European Community Commission and this work is supported by the Solvay Institute for Physics and Chemistry. We would like to thank Joël Le Quément for its constant interest and support. We are also very grateful to Mr Solvay, Luc Soete, Rolando Guzzi and Driss Elkorchi for their fruitful and stimulating comments.

References

Dauvin J.Ph., (1990), *"Les Semi-conducteurs"* Economica .

Lesourne J., Leban R., Oshima K., Yakushiji T., (1989), *'Europe and Japan Facing High Technologies'*, Economica.

Mahajan and Peterson (1985), *'Models for Innovative Diffusion'*, Saje University, Paper series on quantitative applications in the social sciences (n° 07-048), Beverly Hills and London Sage Publications.

Nicolis G. and Prigogine I., (1977), *'Self-Organization in Non-Equilibrium Systems'* , Wiley, New York.

A MODEL FOR CORPORATE PRODUCTIVITY

J. Solvay and M. Sanglier

Instituts Internationaux de Physique et de Chimie fondés par Ernest Solvay
Campus Plaine CP 231
B - 1050 Bruxelles

1. Introduction

1.1. Purpose of the study

There is an emerging school of thought that presumes the existence within a corporate structure of a cognitive microeconomy (P. Bourgine, 1992). Its dynamics obeys predictable rules (A. Newell, 1990) that can be quantified. Our purpose here is to verify the existence of such a behaviour by checking the validity of a model for the rate of growth of productive capacity per individual of a corporation and to consider the consequences of such a relation.

1.2. Accepted principles

There is first a general principle that in the fifties was expressed by Robert Solow (1957) when he said that the permanent rate of productivity growth per person depends entirely on the rate of technological progress in the broadest sense. Productivity is usually expressed as a number of units per person, and the fact that the growth is permanent implies a steady non cyclical growth of the economy.

A second principle is the experience relationship between the growth of value added and accumulated experience. It also dates back to the early sixties, is applicable in a permanent steady state economy and was generalized by the Boston Consulting Group (BCG).

There is a third principle which is the innovation effect which states that the relative creativity performance of the agent is proportionnal to the cumulative R+D effort (R. Foster, 1986).

Taken together, the steady state growth of an agent's productivity expressed as the growth of his value added depends entirely on the manner in which he draws on the technical experience and knowledge acquired by all agents through the life time of the project he is associated with.

In the real economy, the agent has to live through business cycles whose ups and downs are of a magnitude such that they affect considerably the judgement of what could be the underlying steady state growth.

The model uses value added per agent, year as the productivity unit for corporations. The data, published by Compuserve, are extracted from annual reports and summarized according to 10-K's prescriptions for stocks quoted on the NYSE.

The value added obtained from annual reports that is introduced in the model represents the total cash income per agent It is equal to :
- (total sales - inputs) / number of total personnel or
- (total wages + EBITD) / number of total personnel.

The model assumes for the permanent rate of growth a deflated constant price structure in monetary units, using the official price index. It does not normally take into account structural evolution of prices.

The increase in the agent's productivity through technological means (experience and innovation effects) leads to improvements in value added which allow for increases of salaries and or of individual EBITD.

The global market evolution defines the number of participating agents and the firm's market share defines its number of personnel with the assumption that the firm's market share is equal to its personnel share.

In our model, in order to account for the business cycle we have had to consider productivity equal to the product of capacity per agent times its rate of utilization. We have assumed a production capacity subject to steady state growth and a rate of utilization subject to cyclical variations as defined below.

2. Development of the model

2.1. Production activity : MA

A = capacity of the production structure in value added/person year,expressed in constant monetary units

M= utilization rate in % of value added
In the steady state structure referred to by Solow (1988) M is kept constant.
When duplicating corporate data M2 is a variable.
When the production structure is shared between a number of employees as in a plant, A is the proportional share per agent of the total production and sales structure.

The cash generated by the operation of the agent's share of the structure is invested to increase his productive capacity by an amount that results from the difference between receipts at actual rate of operation minus break even receipts. We then have :

$$\frac{dA}{dt} = ka * A(Ma - Mastar) \qquad (1)$$

with ka = the prevailing Capital / Output ratio

Mastar = breakeven rate of utilization in the agent's plant operation (receipts - expenditures = 0).

Mastar is a function of A. If the plant operates under constant technological conditions and if Al is the maximum achievable capacity per agent under those technological conditions, (Al is then a constant,) one can write :

Lim A —> Al	when	Mastar —> 1
Lim A —> 0	when	Mastar —> 0

We have therefore assumed a linear relationship between Mastar and A of the form

$$Mastar = \frac{A}{Al} \qquad (2)$$

In practice, Al is the growing function of technology referred to by Solow under his "permanent conditions".

A follows the growth of Al. In our model, we have introduced the experience relationship (f BCG) and the innovation effect (fRD) as the technological factors responsible for the growth of Al.

The experience effect can be expressed by

$$\frac{dAl}{Al} = kSNA*\left(\frac{pNA}{\sum pNA}\right) \qquad (3)$$

where pN= number of people employed

Each time accumulated production doubles, the production of the agent's value added increases by 20 - 30% (cfr BCG)

$$\text{and} \quad \frac{dAl}{Al} = kSRD*kp\sum RD \qquad (4)$$

Growth due to the innovation effect is proportional to accumulated R+D

The evolution of the maximum potential capacity is then given by

$$\frac{dAl}{dt} = Al\left(kSNA * \frac{pNA}{\sum pNA} + kSRD * kp * \sum RD \right) \quad (5)$$

Difference between A and Al

Under constant technological conditions, but cyclical demand Al is a constant. The evolution of A depends only on the evolution of demand, as it influences the rate of capacity utilization M2. This is expressed by equation 1.

Under Solow's permanent conditions, M is a constant and A depends only on the technological evolution which takes into account both scientific and technological factors as they affect capital investment. It also takes into account organization factors.

The information system which could be available to the average agent includes some of the latest progress in technology. However, according to the principle of bounded rationality, the agent's potential capacity Al as defined in equation 2 is smaller than the Al that could be deduced from available information. This results from the limitations of the average agent's production ability which depends on motivation, education, training and corporate culture. A corporate culture is the emergence of a "collective self" which defines the admissible individual strategies and models. The integration of those strategies and models leads to the evolving maximum potential production capacity per agent Al.

Equation (1) represents, under permanent conditions, the differential of the capacity of value added per agent. It is also equal to the cash flow necessary for the investments to increase the agent's capacity through improved technology. An increase in Al leads to decreasing values for the break even rate.

We have to consider for equation (1) the investment in R+D, which is also a decision to allocate funds, of the same nature as capital for expansion of capacity. We have also included in equation (1) a parameter kpr which represents a systematic annual change in the price of value added. It is a direct structural component of cash flow, used when the strategy is not to maintain market share but to eliminate a competitor or to accumulate cash flow through a dominant position. One then has :

$$\frac{dA}{dt} = ka * A\left(M - \frac{A}{Al} + kRD * RD + kpr \right) \quad (6)$$

2.2. The market MNA

N= total number of people employed in the market. This presumes that the value added per agent in competing corporations is approximately the same

If D =Demand =NA

We assume that during the initial phase of a product's development it follows a logistic expansion :

$$\frac{dD}{dt} = kNA * D * \left(1 - \frac{D}{Dl}\right) \qquad (7)$$

Later, when its market has become mature, its growth rate is exponential For most mature or diversified firms D/Dl is close or equal to one.

$$\frac{dDl}{dt} = knal * Dl \qquad (8)$$

knal defines the growth rate of the mature market.

For most sufficiently diversified companies, one can represent sufficiently accurately their steady, permanent growth with an exponential, even if this means diversification into different products.

Equation (1) represents the evolution of value added capacity per individual

Equation (7) represents the growth of the market. Once the market's expansion has been defined, the evolution of the corporation's total value added VA depends on its market share p and on its rate of capacity utilization M so that

$$VA = MpNA \qquad (9)$$

Equation (9) includes the personnel pN necessary to satisfy the firm's share of that market. Equating production with demand determines the number of people employed : pN.

2.3. The problem of prices

Under cyclical conditions, the six above equations relate the growth of value added per agent with the quality of the management and technology employed and with the rate of utilization of the capacity. The existence of an additional variable; price, not accounted for in the general principles governing the model, but among the factors that determine the data employed is a complicating factor.

We have envisaged the impact of various mechanisms on the effect of prices.

2.3.1. Competition

The model calculates (through equation 1) the cash flow necessary to realize the planned capacity expansion without taking into account the price structure which is assumed to follow the price index.

The producer, with best technological performance, will have the highest productivity which in turn will give him an advantage in cash flow. If simultaneously, he has the largest market share, he could be in a dominant position.

If he decides to allow the number 2 producer to maintain his market share, he will have a cash flow superior to that needed to maintain his own position. That additionnal cash has to be accounted for by kpr in equation (6). He can use that cash flow to diversify.

2.3.2. Cases where the model remains valid

a. The long term growth of necessary investment imposed by demand, is assured by the available EBITD (earning before interest taxes and depreciation) included in the growth of individual value added (see equation (6)) multiplied by the necessary number of agents (ref. to (9)).

b. In the cyclical real economy, prices together with the utilization rate are subject to cyclical variations above and below the long term trend, so that ultimately they even out for the determination of the permanent growth of productivity. The variation of M2, calculated by the model, includes this effect.

c. The long term trend of prices is such that their evolution is parallel to costs. According to the Boston Consulting Group, this is true in 60 % of the cases in the United States and is generally true in Japan.

2.3.3. Cases where the model is affected by price policies

a. Growth of prices > growth of costs over a number of years

This can be a deliberatly sustained policy when a patent has been obtained on a substantial technological improvement. It could also conceivably be the result of a monopoly. It usually affects only a fraction of the sales of most quoted corporations.

b. Growth of prices < growth of costs

This can happen when a company with a strong technological position reduces prices in order to eliminate a competitor.

These two latter cases, patent or the elimination of a competitor, are essentially temporary even though they can last for a number of years. We have introduced the possibility of a deliberated long term price policy through kpr in equation (6). An understanding of the company's performance would allow one to take this into account during modelization.

We believe that in most cases the model will be sufficiently valid to allow extrapolations and the introduction of scenarios.

3. Setting the model up

Essentially, for each corporation, one has a set of value added data over a period of minimum 10 years, each of which results from a different rate of capacity utilisation M2. The problem is to determine the permanent capacity evolution (at constant M) and the rates of utilisation M2 corresponding to the data employed.

In order to fit the parameters of the above six equations to the evolution of a specific corporation agent's productivity, one has to distinguish between its long term trend for which the parameters have to be determined by trial and error and its cyclical evolution for which data are available. This is done by interconnecting two identical models :

1. a long term trend model with structural value added MA
2. a cyclical model with cyclical value added M2A2

which both operate simultaneously.
As one calibrates the parameters in the trend model, the identical cyclical model delivers an estimate of the cyclical value added M2A2 corresponding to the original data. One also obtains the simultaneous rates of utilization M2 that have to be applied to the cyclical model's value added capacity A2 in order to reproduce the original data.

3.1. Range of applications

For commodities, the use of the learning effect to characterise productivity growth is often sufficient. We have found that for a division of Solvay Corp. such as Alcali where units produced can be identified and quantified, the learning effect model is satisfactory over a period of over 100 years. Equally, if the enterprise is a conglomerate, engaged in a simultaneous production of different commodities, we have found that the consolidation of value added for commodities leads to an overall structure where the experience effect is dominant. The linear relationship between $\log A_1$ and logSpNA that results from the expression of the learning effect in equation (3) remains therefore verified.

For pharmaceutical corporations, the introduction of the innovation effect using published R+D expenditures in % leads to a better fit with original data. The same was done with electronic firms such as Intel or Motorola. The model is also applicable for services such as distribution and banking. The fit between calculated values of M2A2 and published data depends on the evolution of the rate of value added capacity utilization M2. In fact in a cyclical economy, value added varies because of cyclical changes in rates of operation and because of cyclical price changes. The values of M2 produced by the model represent not only operating rates but include additionnally price variations. We believe M2 is representative of the economic environment as it affects demand.

3.2. M2 is the interface with environment

It is interesting to compare the index of economic activity of the Belgian National Bank with the rate of capacity utilization M2 of the Solvay corporation between 1975-1995. The correlation is remarkable. The Belgian level of activity is very close to Europe's level, because of the importance of Belgian exports. Solvay's activity is similarily dependent on the continent because it is over 70 % located in various countries of Europe.

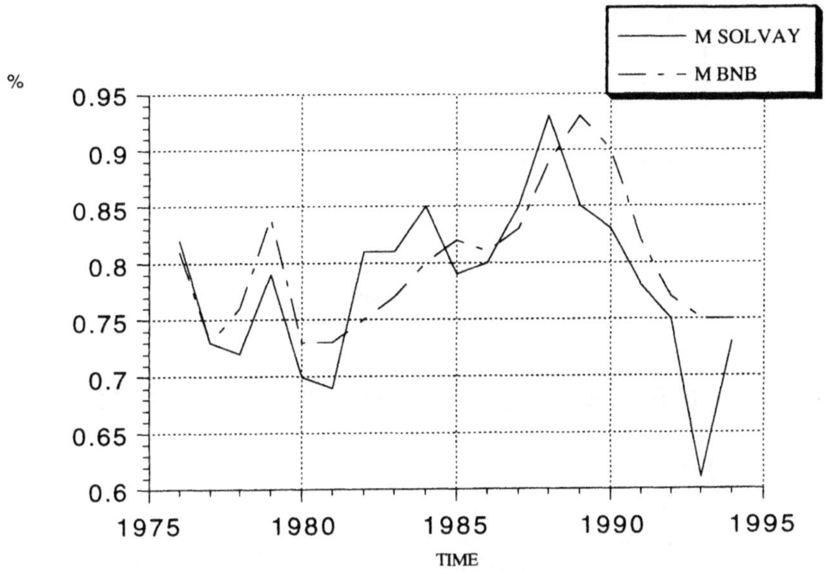

Fig. 1 : Comparison of the Index of the Belgian economy with the simulated utilization rate of a company

It is instructive when applying the model to a firm, to verify the interface with the environment by comparing M2 of the firm with that of other firms competing in the same environment. We have attempted to do so in six distinct cases of very different economic environments. Apart from the firm's peculiarities, there appears to be a clear common trend in each market for the perception of the firm's interface with its environment. This is illustrated by the following six diagrams where M2 is a measure of cyclicality in terms of rates of operation and prices.

Chemical

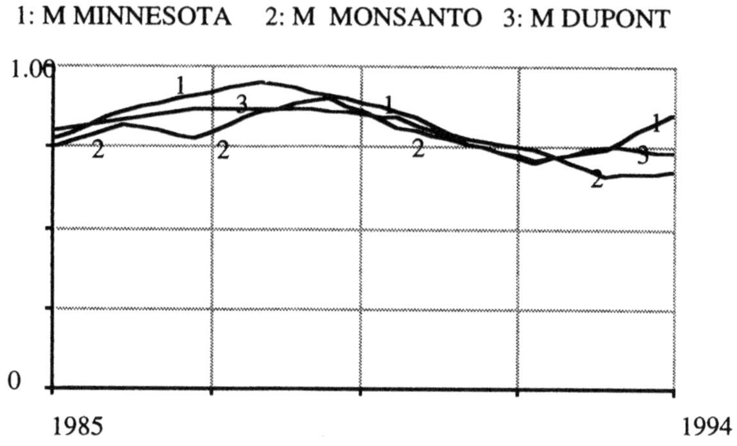

Petroleum

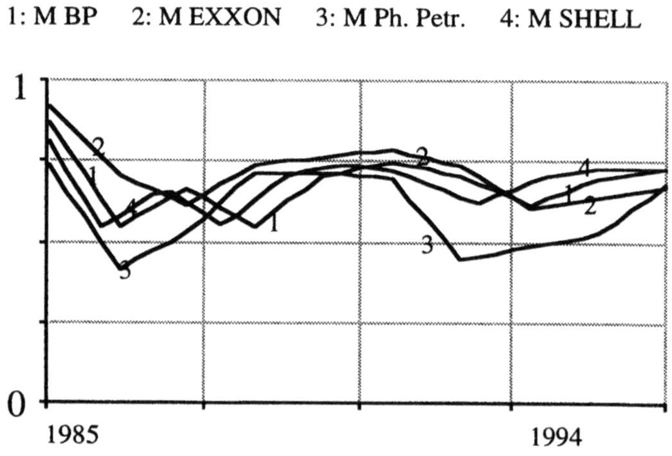

Distribution

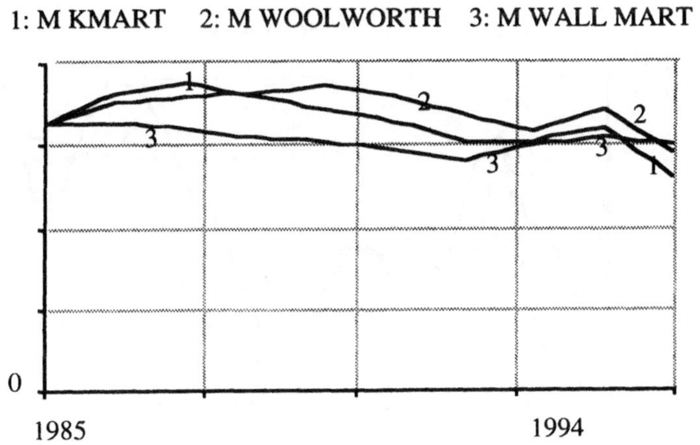

Pharma

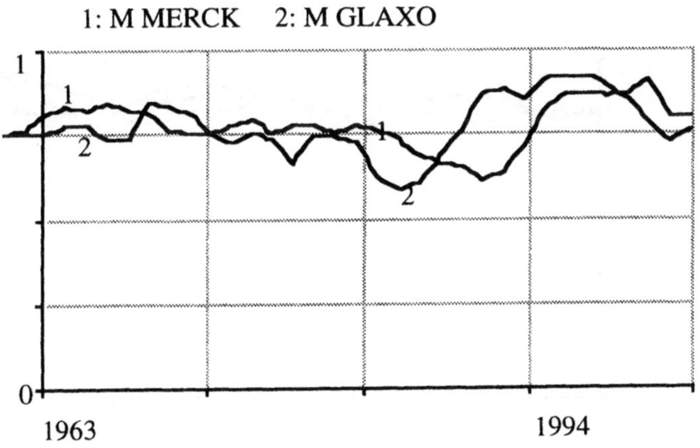

Electronics

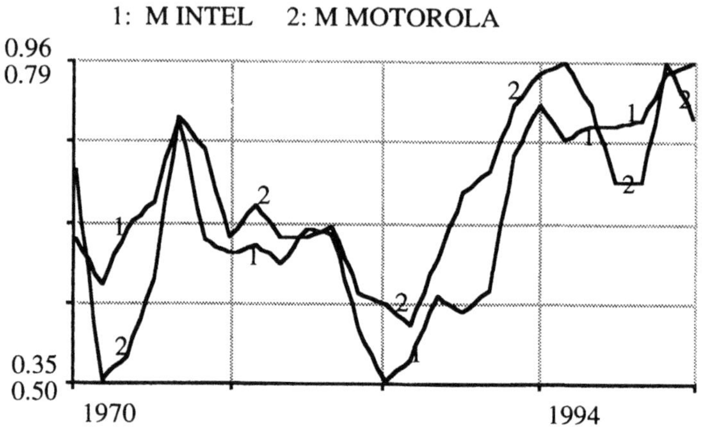

Belgian Banks

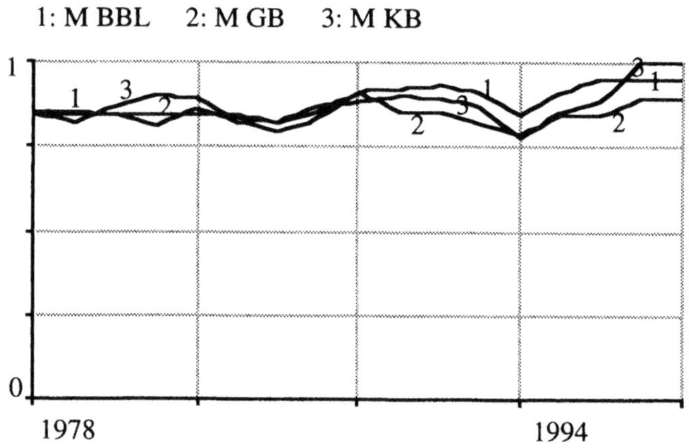

Fig. 2 : Comparison of M2 for differents firms

3.3. Taxonomy

It is possible to characterize the behaviour of a firm in its market by the growth of two variables taken from the permanent steady state model.
These two variables are :

- the growth of value added capacity A per individual which depends on its technological performance
- the growth of total personnel pN which depends on its marketing performance.

We have chosen to analyse three corporations which typify three possible well-managed performances. Each one of these firms presents an excellent growth record of its EBITD/share, but they follow radically different developments strategies.

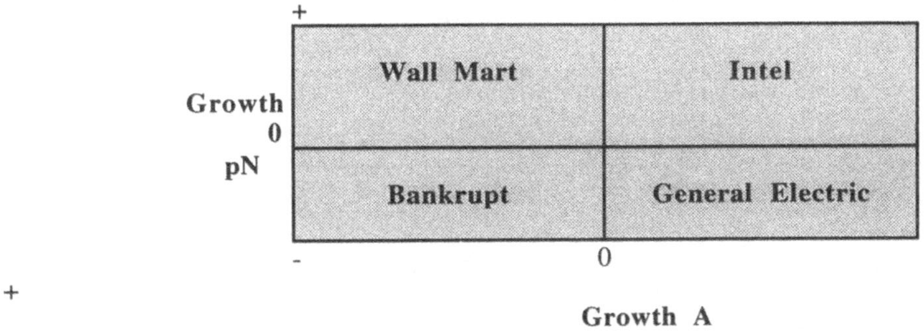

Fig. 3 : Taxonomy based on the growth of personnel and the growth of value added

MA= Value added/person

curve 1 = MA cst = data extracted from annual reports
curve 2 = MA = permanent value added per person
curve 3 = MA2 = actual value added per person, calculated

WALL MART

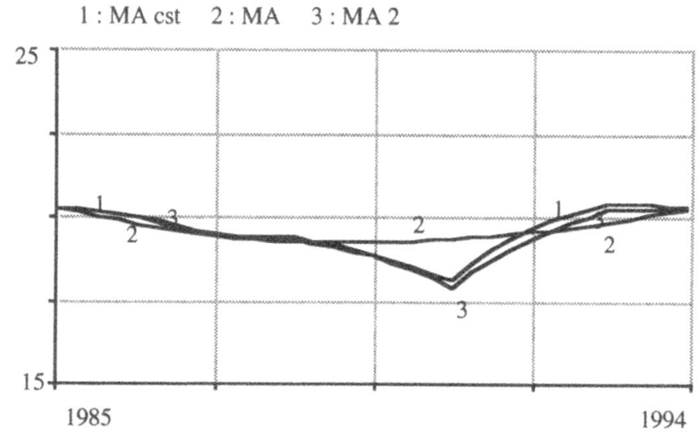

INTEL

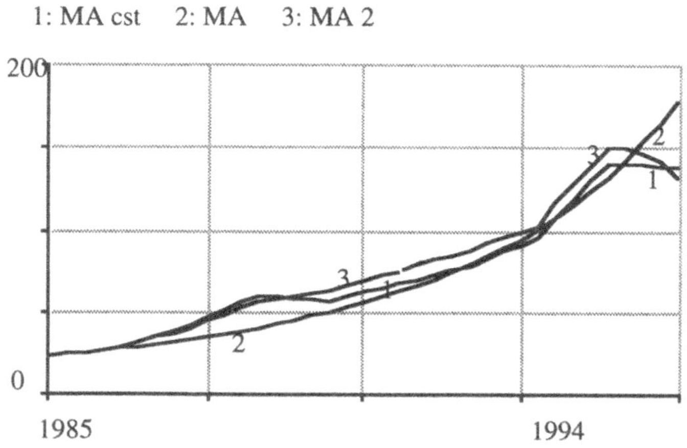

GENERAL ELECTRIC

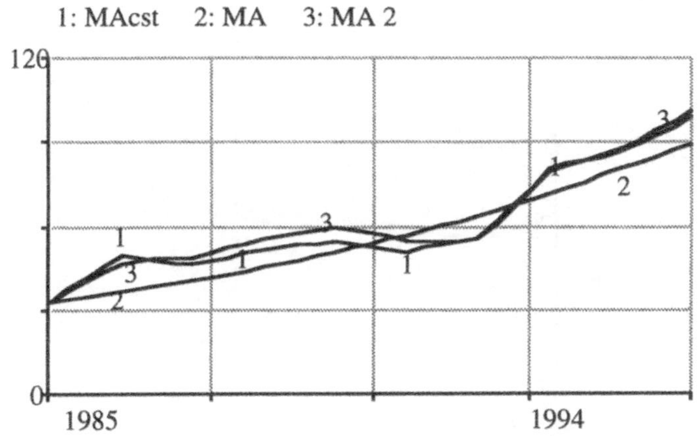

pN= personnel

curve 1= pNdat = data extracted from annual reports
curve 2 = pN = permanent evolution of n° of employees
curve 3 = pN2 = actual personnel, calculated

WALL MART

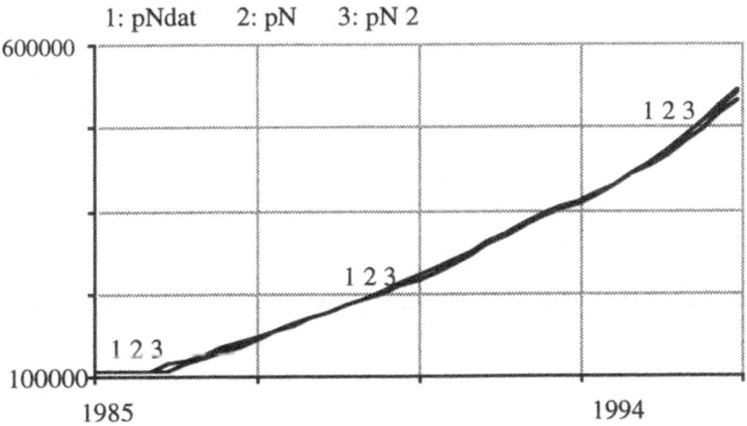

INTEL

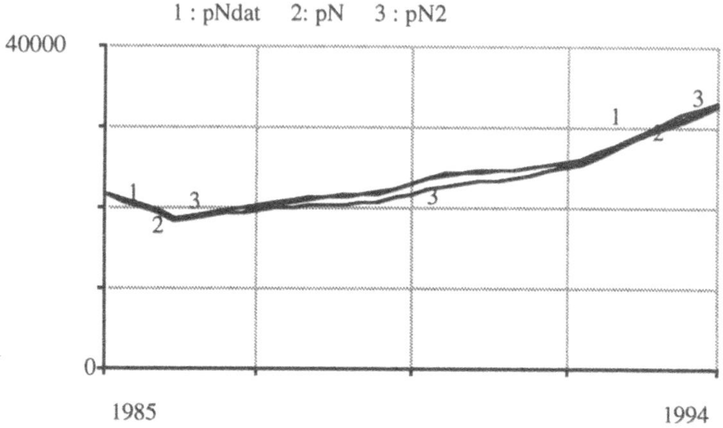

GENERAL ELECTRIC

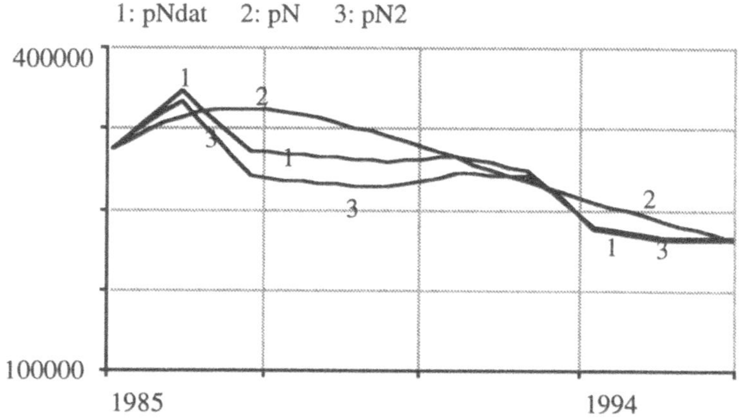

Fig. 4 : Calibration of value added/person and personnel for different firms

Discussion

The values given to parameters lead to a fit of calculated value added or total personnel with annual report data of less than +/- 5% relative error.

General Electric

The (2) curves in the GE graphs above, show the steady permanent growth of value added and the reduction of personnel. In order to express the evolution of consolidated values, we have assumed a consolidated market for all divisions growing at a 4% rate of which GE supplies 15%. Considering the permanent productivity growth of 11% achieved by MA necessarily the number of people employed has to decrease. Most corporations, by a large margin, conform to this case. There is then no need to introduce a systematic price effect parameter in order to duplicate cyclical behaviour.

Intel

This is an exceptional case where there appears simultaneously an unusually high productivity growth of 21 to 26 % together with an appreciable personnel increase which means a growing market share in a rapidly expanding market (at a 8.5 % average rate). This could only be duplicated by the model by introducing in the evolution of value added a systematic value added price increace resulting from the attribution to kpr a value of 20% in equation (6) until 1992. This is indicative of a dominant position in technology and in the market.

Wallmart

The combination of a slightly negative value added growth of -3 to +1 % with an extremely rapid increase of market share and of personnel by a factor of five times could only be duplicated by the model through the introduction of a systematic value added price reduction obtained by giving kpr a value of minus 15 % . This implies that there must be a technological value added growth of at least the importance of the price reduction.

3.4. Extrapolations and scenarios

Once the parameters in the equations have been determined through existing data, extrapolations can be used in order to appraise different strategies. If one wants an indication of performance in a steady permanent state under generally constant price conditions one assumes a constant value of M.

We have taken the GE model discussed above and extrapolated it by six years while considering three scenarios :

- at constant price and market share.
- with a yearly increase in market share leading progressively to an overall improvement of 15% by the year 2000. This can imply a corresponding price reduction in order to obtain customer preference.
- with a yearly decrease of market share leading to minus 15% by the year 2000. We have not, here, taken into account the eventuality of a price increase.

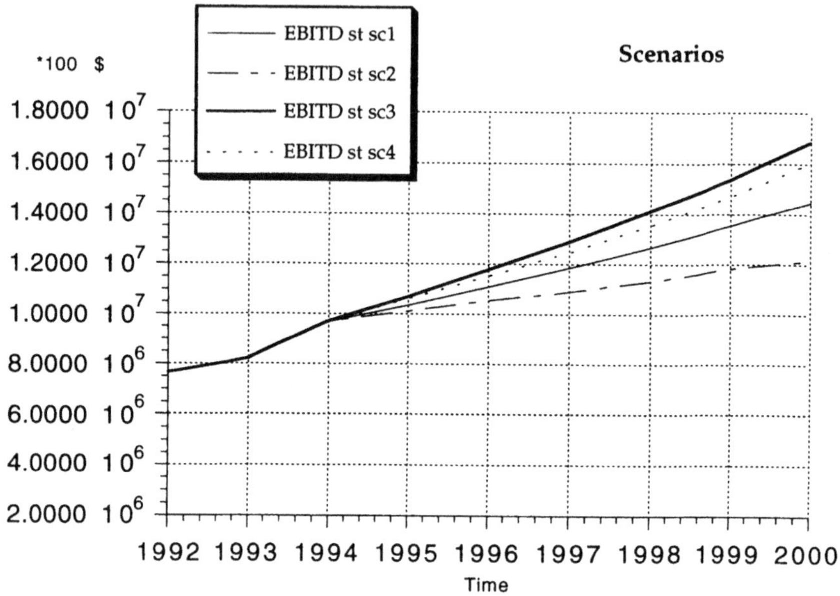

Fig. 5 : Evolution of the permanent EBITD under different scenarios

In the graph above :

- curve (1) represents the permanent evolution of total earnings before interest taxes and amortization that corresponds to the cash flow necessary for the expansion of capacity at the constant previous rate of market share.
- curve (3) depicts the EBITD that allows the financing of an additional 15% market share expansion ,over six years, without price concessions.
- curve (4) results from the introduction of a kpr value of -5% which leads after six years to a price reduction of 6.4%.
  The difference between (3) and (4) is the additional financial cost, or loss of EBITD, due to the price reduction. However curve (4) does not correspond to the evolution of the cash flow for expansion
- curve (2) is the evolution of the lesser EBITD necessary for an expansion of 15% below that of curve (1).

The evolution of the market, the behaviour of competition, a merger or the disposal of a division are not events that can be foreseen by the model. They may however, in some cases, be introduced in the model. A merger is a change in market share plus a change in personnel. Its successfull implementation will depend on the compatibility of corporate cultures. A change in market growth can also be introduced in the model. Such scenarios or extrapolations can be useful too for a firm in order to get a quick apraisal of a range of possible strategies.

The growth of most product markets when mature slows to eventually approach the rate of the whole economy's expansion. In order to maintain a sufficient level of motivation and remunerations, it may become appropriate to diversify into new and faster growing activities. This can be either through research and marketing efforts or it can be through the acquisition of new areas of activities with which there may be a synergy. The strategy to be followed can be roughly evaluated with the help of the model. It will indicate the best productivity improvements to be expected depending on corporate culture.

4. Conclusion

The model quantifies Solow's relationship between the individual's productivity growth and the evolution of the firm's technology as determined by its corporate culture. The technological expression of growth in a mathematical form is applied through time to the average agent's productive capacity. Most of the firm's creative ideas come from the average agent. The learning and the innovation effects depend on a total quality management policy that is intimately related to corporate culture which top management must influence but cannot change authoritarily.

Just as the US defense department in 1940-45 was able to use the experience effect to negociate price reductions from its suppliers, a similar approach could be used by a firm's management. It would concentrate on a capacity for productivity improvements in a division of the firm through an optimization of the parameters that are imbedded in the firm's formula. Understanding and progress need communication which in turn needs words. A formula, calculated by the model would become part of the language used by the corporate culture. It would improve understanding and motivation.

References

P. Bourgine, B. Walliser, (1992), '*Towards a practice of autonomous system*', F. Varela and P. Bourgine (ed) MIT Press, Bradford books. pp3-10.

R. N. Foster, (1986), *'Innovation: The Attacker's Advantage'*, Summit Books (a division of Simon & Schuster,Inc.).

Bruce D. Henderson, (1980), *'The experience curve revisited'*, Boston Consulting Group, ' Perspective n°229.

Boston Consulting Group, (1971), *'Perspectives Expérience et Stratégie'*, Boston Consulting Group, .

A. Newell, (1990), *'Unified Theories of cognition'*, Harvard University Press.

R.M. Solow, (1957), *'Technical change and the aggregate production function'*, Review of economic and statistics, vol. 39, p. 312-330.

R.M. Solow, (1988), *'Growth Theory : An Exposition'*, Oxford University Press.

COGNITIVE MICROECONOMY IN A SOCIETY OF AUTOTEACHING AND SPECULAR HEDONISTIC AGENTS

Paul Bourgine
CREA, Ecole Polytechnique 1 rue Descartes, 75005 Paris, France
Tel : 33 1 46343623, Fax : 33 1 43252944
email : paul.bourgine@poly.polytechnique.fr

Abstract. Because humanity enters the era of knowledge, it becomes important to understand the role of immaterial investments in knowledge. That explains the importance of an macroeconomy of knowledge. As a first step in this direction, this paper proposes a cognitive microeconomy in human society. Humans are considered as specular, autoteaching and hedonistic agents.
The cognitive microeconomy has for object to study the bounded rationality of specular and autoteaching agents in changing their hedonistic strategies in a society of such agents. One main question is how the compromise between exploration of new strategies and exploitation of better known old strategies can be managed by agents despite their bounded cognitive capacities and their limited experience capacities.

INTRODUCTION

Mankind is entering the knowledge era. More and more evolutionist processes in human society, such as the technological and scientific ones and even the cultural and social ones, acquire a global dimension at the world level. All these processes are of lamarkian type and based on the transmission of knowledge between agents and generations : that grounds the very importance of an macroeconomy of knowledge in human society. As a first step in this direction, this paper proposes a cognitive microeconomy in human society. Humans are considered as specular, autoteaching and hedonistic agents.

In order to sketch such an economy, we have first to choose which cognitive paradigm we are going to use to modelize autoteaching hedonistic agents. The proposed model takes place in the cognitive approach which can be named constructivism according to Piaget or enactivism according to Varela. The most important ideas can be summerized as followed. The mind is no longer a pure mind. It is embodied. The agent enacts the pertinent distinctions and categorizations for its viability and pleasure during the history of its coupling with its environment. It acquired the abductive capacity to guess viable and hedonistic actions in various and changing environments. Cognition is the emergence of a world of meanings and strategies which comes from experience through autoteaching metadynamics. Knowledge is neither purely objective nor purely subjective, but both objective and subjective.

In this constructivist point of view, the hedonistic agent can be modelized as a family of alternative jobs at different scales of time recursively constructed above a basic family of sensorimotor jobs. Two very big cognitive difficulties happen for the hedonistic agent (i) a computational difficulty to choose among a huge number of jobs and to autoteach from experience (ii) the difficulty due to a dramatic lack of experiences. The cognitive microeconomy has for object to treat these two difficulties.

The computational difficulties are treated in the framework of the theory of bandit processes. This theory allows to define the perfect hedonistic agent with his perfect strategy - an index strategy - and his perfect autoteaching metadynamics - bayesian revision of his knowledge -. But the cognitive and computational difficulties of a perfect hedonistic agent lead to consider hedonistic agents with bounded rationality : they have to use near optimal but more tractable index evaluations and autoteaching metadynamics.

But the most important bottleneck for autoteaching hedonistic agent is their lack of experience. We have to search for a specific property of human to accumulate knowledge despite their lack of experience. This specific property is specularity which refers to the common knowledge that everyone acts and reasons in a situation by thinking at the same time how the others act and reason in the same situation. Humans are the only typical specular animals. This property is very important for human collective intelligence because it affects all the aspects of the human autoteaching metadynamics. Then specularity allows humans to acquire a big amount of plausible knowledge despite their bounded experience and cognitive capacities.

There is another and equivalent way to present a cognitive microeconomy. The question is how to deal with the compromise between exploration of new bad known strategies and exploitation of old better known strategies can be managed at the individual level in a society of specular and autoteaching agents. This cognitive microeconomy has to be completed by a macroeconomy of knowledge which has to deal with the same compromise at the collective level. Both constitute together the economy of knowledge.

THE AUTOTEACHING AGENT AND ITS BOUNDED RATIONALITY

There are many reasons to adopt the hedonistic paradigm in the present attempt to found an cognitive microeconomy. Without a pleasure principle, anything has to be learned, which is impossible. Another essential idea is that an economy of cognition is far above of the classical microeconomy which suppose monetary exchanges. Autoteaching concerns all the instants of life and is more often concern by an economy of reciprocal gift based on reciprocal pleasure than by the classical economy.

Thus the framework of the utilitarist economy is a little too restrictive for the present attempt. Thus we enlarge the utilitarism framework inside the hedonism one. In this movement we remain faithful to the founders of utilitarism who grounded precisely utilitarism on hedonism.

1. THE PARADIGM OF THE AUTOTEACHING HEDONISTIC AGENT

But what is an autoteaching hedonistic agent ? Such agent is a sensorimotor system with a cognitive system embodied inside a sensorimotor apparatus. The dynamics of the cognitive system provides viable actions from perceptions. Viability supposes the abductive capacity at each time to eliminate a huge number of actions in order to choose the one which will be submitted to experience. And the metadynamics provide autoteaching to acquire a better abductive capacity to perform viable and hedonistic actions (cf fig 1).

Let us consider first the dynamics. The perceptions of the agent are of three kinds : the proprioception of what it is doing ; the exteroception of what its sees in its environment ; and the interoception of what its perceives inside itself. All its perceptions cause a certain level of immediate pleasure/pain, which is an internal reward also perceived. All its perceptions are internal, not only the proprioception and the interoception but even the exteroception and the immediate reward. And the dynamics provides reactively, in an abductive way, new actions from these internal perceptions.

The first important fact is that everything happens inside the same cognitive system. No principle of correspondence between what is perceived and what happens "really" in the outside world is needed. No representationist hypothesis is necessary. The only useful hypothesis is : what is perceived inside can be correlated together.

The second important fact is the recurrent nature of the sensorimotor system which can be observed in the neural network. Such recurrent network can remember not only the immediate perception but also a few past ones. And correlation between what has just happen and what will just happen becomes possible.

Based on these two facts, a metadynamics for anticipations in the close future from the perception of the close past is thus possible to obtain better abductive capacities.

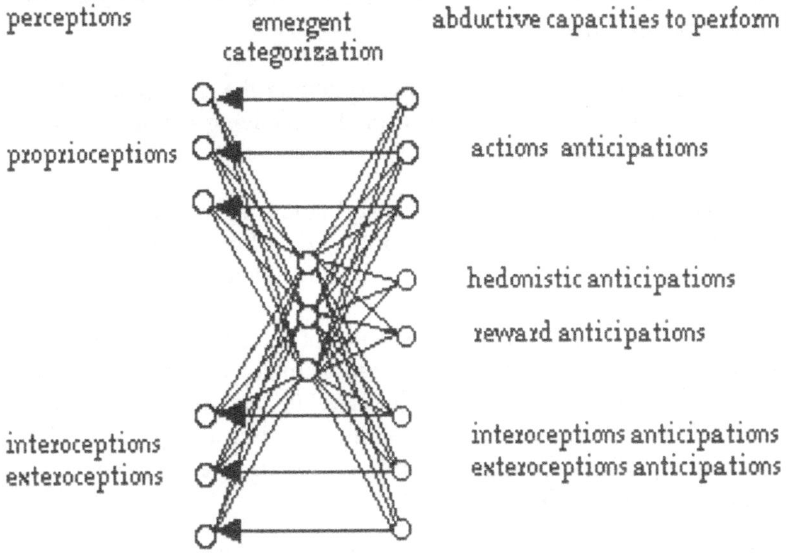

fig 1 : the autoteaching hedonistic agent has a cognitive system which acquires abductive capacities to perform viable anticipations from its perceptions. The cognitive system is a recurrent network (the back arrows) whose the dynamics provides the anticipations and whose the metadynamics allows to learn from all its internal events, i.e. autoteaching. All the autoteaching process supposes that the system acquires emergent categorization which is adequate and pertinent for its useful anticipations : that is the role symbolized by the hidden intermediate layer(s).

There are four important metadynamics. The first one autoteaches anticipations of the hedonistic value of its sensorimotor state, i.e. the discounted sum of the internal rewards for a short term future. The second one autoteaches anticipations of the next action which is excellent in respect to this short term hedonistic anticipations. The third one autoteaches anticipations of the next sensorial state by correcting its errors of anticipation with what is effectively perceived. Together the second and the third ones represent a global abductive capacity to anticipate the sensorimotor state.

But such anticipations can not be performed by directly correlating each piece of perception with what will occur inside. Intermediate categorization of the perception is absolutary necessary to obtain perceptive invariants and to facilitate the anticipations. Through the history of the coupling with its environment, the agent enacts the categories which allow useful distinctions for his anticipations. Through his own activity of categorization, the agent enacts an internal world of significations for pragmatic anticipations. The fourth metadynamics concerns precisely this emergent categorization and recategorization [Edelman, 92].

We can summerize this discussion by expliciting the deep potential property of all sensorimotor agents. All we need for the following is not a representationist hypothesis but the following property.

> **Property** : every hedonistic sensorimotor agent has potentially the possibility to enact useful categories to perform anticipations of (i) the hedonistic value of its sensorimotor state (ii) its next sensorimotor state.

There is another fundamental consequence of categorization. A huge number of sensorimotor patterns emerge. For each sensorimotor pattern there is the need to anticipate the next sensorimotor state and its hedonistic value as described above. And a cognitive history is nothing else but a long chain of successive sensorimotor patterns. Because of their huge number the choice between them is a new and fantastic complex question.

But the question is even more complex. When a family of sensorimotor patterns has been trained during a long time, the strategies become both very good and reactive, i.e. abductive because of the autoteaching metadynamics. Thus at a higher scale of time, the hedonistic agent can construct a more integrated activity pattern by using a subfamily of sensorimotor patterns. When at this higher scale the activity patterns have become abductive by autoteaching, the process can continue to create new activity patterns at a more higher level....

Such process is very close to the constructivism of Jean Piaget. We summerize the previous discussion in the following modelizing hypothesis for an hedonistic agent at a particular moment of his development.

> **Hypothesis 1** (the hedonistic agent as a FAAP)
>
> The hedonistic agent is defined by his Family of Alternative Activity Patterns (FAAP) such as (i) an arborescence of precedence constraints between activity patterns can exist in the family (ii) new activity patterns can appear (iii) each activity pattern can be a FAAP at a smaller scale of time (iv) this recursive operation can be reproduced until the scale of time of sensorimotor cycles is reached.

2. MODELIZING A FAMILY OF ACTIVITY PATTERNS AS A FABS

A family of alternative bandit superprocesses (FABS) is a family of alternative semi-Markov decision processes among which only one is active at each time [Gittins, 89]. The correspondence with a family of alternative activity patterns is thus convenient if a sensorimotor pattern can be modelized by a semi-Markov decision process.

As described above, an activity pattern can be thought as a Markov decision process : At each decision time, an action has to be chosen in a finite set $A(x)$ depending on the perception state x. The resulting state is x' with a probability $p(x' \mid x,a)$, the mean reward is $r(x,a)$[1] and the decision problem is to find a strategy $a=g(x)$ to maximize the expected total reward. But a semi-Markov decision process is more general than a Markov one because the next decision time is not a priori fixed as in an Markov decision process. In a semi-Markov process it is randomly distributed with a distribution $f(\Delta t \mid x, a, x')$. Thus we have a more general framework to modelize a sensorimotor pattern as usually thought.

> Theorem (semi-Markov decision process D) : If the semi-Markov decision process D satisfies condition A and B, there is a unique optimal strategy $g(x)$ which is deterministic, stationary and Markov and maximizes the expected total discounted reward :
>
> $$E \sum_{i=0}^{\infty} \alpha^{t_i} r(x_i, a_i) \text{ where } \alpha \text{ is the discount rate}$$

The condition A means that the distribution of the random variable $t_i - t_{i-1}$ is not concentrated at time 0. The condition B means that the truncated sum after time t tends uniformly to 0 if t tends to infinity. Under these conditions we obtain a unique optimal strategy which is deterministic, not depending on the time and on the previous state.

But what we have at each time is not a unique decision process for time until infinity but a family of such alternative processes. At each time only one is active and the others are frozen. The general idea is to search an *index* for each decision process which allows to choose the best one up to an optimal stopping time. As proposed by Gittins a very intuitive index is the *equivalent constant reward rate* up to an optimal stopping time. This equivalent constant reward is the expected total discounted reward by unit of expected discounted time until the *stopping time* τ :

$$v(D, x_0) = \mathbf{Max}_{g,\tau} \frac{E \sum_{0 \le t_i < \tau} \alpha^{t_i} r(x_i, g(x_i))}{E\left(\int_0^{\tau} \alpha^t dt\right)}$$

Theorem (semi-Markov decision process) : If the semi-Markov decision process satisfies the condition A, there is an optimal deterministic stationary Markov policy g and an optimal stopping time τ which maximize the equivalent constant reward. The stopping set corresponding to the stopping time τ can be chosen as :

$$\{ x : v(x) < v(x_0) \}$$

There is a probability equal to one that applying the optimal strategy the index remains superior to its initial value before the stopping set and thus the stopping time were reached.

Now we come back to a family of alternative semi-Markov decision process. Thus because at each time only one is active and the others frozen, we have to add to each action set the frozen action. Each semi-Markov decision process with a frozen action is named a bandit superprocess. What we obtain is a Family of Alternative Bandit Superprocesses (FABS). And we have now to find when a bandit process becomes active and when it gets frozen again, i.e. what is the optimal policy for the FABS.

Theorem: If the Family of Alternative Bandit Superprocesses **F** satisfy the condition D, then the optimal policy consist to choose the superprocess which has the best index :

$$v(\mathbf{F}) = \mathrm{Max}_i \; v(D_i, x_i)$$

Before defining the condition D, we have to comment this result. The optimal policy is an *index policy* which consists to choose at each time the bandit with the best index. Such an index policy is a *forwards induction policy,* that is a policy which uses a iterative construction forwards in time, Such a policy is in contrast to the familiar backwards induction policy of the programming dynamics which uses the familiar iterative construction backwards in time. A more general formulation of the above theorem sets that the optimal index policies, the forwards induction policies and the optimal policies are the same.

Simple bandit processes are semi-Markov decision processes with two possible different actions : one freezes the process in the sense that it does not bring any reward and the process does not change ; the second action is the continuation action. For a Family of Alternative Bandit Processes (FABP) the previous theorem is always true without the condition D. The simplest bandit process is the *standard bandit process with the index* v Indeed, when it is active, it provides continuously in time the reward v and its index is effectively v. Now the condition D means simply that the own strategy of the superprocess is not affected by the presence of a standard bandit process which is less good.

Let us return to the hedonistic agent by reformulating the hypothesis of §1.1. In this reformulation we replace *activity pattern* not by *bandit superprocess* but by *job*. The definition of a job is slighly less general than a bandit process. A job is a bandit superprocess whose reward is essentially received at a random completion time of the job. Its meaning is more intuitive and corresponds better to the hypothesis 1 as we will see.

> Hypothesis 2 (the perfect hedonistic agent) : let us consider an hedonistic agent defined by his family of alternative jobs (FAJ) such as (i) an arborescence of precedence constraints between jobs can exist in the family (ii) new jobs can appear at completion time (iii) each job can be continued by FAJ at a smaller scale of time and that recursively until the scale of time of sensorimotor cycles. The perfect hedonistic agent chooses at each completion time the next possible job which has the best index.

It is proved for such a FAJ that the optimal strategy is this index policy [Gittins, 89]. Thus the perfect hedonistic agent exists theoretically. What we have to examine now is the cognitive difficulty to be perfect or, more precisely, to become perfect by autoteaching. By this movement our next hypothesis will be the autoteaching hedonistic agent with his bounded rationality.

3. THE DIFFICULT EXPLORATION/EXPLOITATION COMPROMIZE AND THE BOUNDED RATIONALITY OF THE AUTOTEACHING AGENT

Through the modelization of an hedonistic agent as a family of alternative jobs, it is implicitly all the know-how of the autoteaching agent which is modelized. In order to understand not only how his know-how is structured but how this know-how changes with experience, we have to come back to the autoteaching metadynamics.

One of the most important difficulty behind these metadynamics concerns the compromise between exploration of new actions and exploitation of the acquired know-how. That is a crucial question : all the cognitive economy of an autoteaching hedonistic agent lies behind this compromise. Does he have to continue exploration before exploiting what he has experimented ?

At first what we have to understand is the nature and theory of this compromise. Such theory is necessary before proposing and comparing autoteaching metadynamics. This theory can be also found in the best index rule for family of alternative bandit superprocesses, even if it was until here not obvious.

Let us consider the simple example of the family of two alternative bandit processes {S(v), S'(1/2)}. The bandit S' provides the mean known reward of 1/2. In contrast the bandit S(v) provides 1 with the unknown probability v and 0 with the probability 1-v . Suppose your discount rate is such that the length of the repeated game will be a few dozen of playing. Probably you avoid the strategy of always playing the known bandit S'. Only what you know at first is the uniform distribution on [0,1] for the unknown probability. You will try the unknow one in the hope of a better index. Suppose after a few playing that your estimation of v is a little less than 1/2. Intuitively it is clear than even if the estimation of v is a little less than 1/2 we feel the necessity to continue to experiment until the difference is sufficiently certain. But if you continue exploring the unknown bandit, when do you stop to play definitely either S or S' ?

In the bayesian framework - i.e. if the initial a priori distribution is known, here the uniform distribution on [0,1] - this problem of stopping or continuing to play the unknown bandit has a rigorous solution which is given by the following theorem.

Theorem (The One-arm bandit process) : let us consider the FABP {S(q), S'(v)} where S et S' are Bernouilly processes. S' has a known index v. But only the hyperstate q of S is known, i.e. the distribution of the unknown probability θ to receive either 0 or 1 unit.

(i) V(q,M) obeys to the following dynamic programming equation :

$$V(q,M) = \mathbf{Max}\{M; \int_0^1 q(d\theta)[\theta+\beta[\theta V(S(q),M)+(1-\theta)V(F(q),M)]]\}$$

$$\text{with } S(q)(d\theta)=\theta q(d\theta) / \int_0^1 \theta q(d\theta)$$

$$\text{and } F(q)(d\theta)=(1-\theta)q(d\theta) / \int_0^1 (1-\theta)q(d\theta)$$

(ii) The Gittins index of the machine is given by :

$$\gamma(q)=\inf\{M(1-\beta) : V(q,M)=M\} = \sup\{M(1-\beta) : V(q,M)>M\}$$

and the stopping time of S is given by :

$$\tau = \inf\{t \geq 1 : \gamma(q_t) \leq \gamma(q)\}$$

The most important fact is that this bayesian adaptative control problem can be expressed as a dynamical programming problem, even if it a very sophisticated one. The discounted value of the FABP is at least superior to the value of the known bandit and is written classically as the average of the immediate reward added to the value of the new hyperstate. Depending on the fact of that last reward is 1 or 0, the Bayes rule modifies the a priori distribution q into the a posteriori S(q) or F(q) respectively. Thus the value of the distribution q becomes respectively V(S(q), ν) and V(F(q), ν).

The second important fact is the paradigmatic nature of this problem. It provides a new interpretation of the meaning of the index : the index of a bandit superprocess is the parameter of a standard bandit process which is equivalent to the superprocess. The previous theorem is in correspondence with the condition D. And in fact this theorem can be generalized to a large class of superprocesses.

What we have understood now is the optimal cognitive strategy in the bayesian framework to achieve the compromise between exploration and exploitation in a family of alternative bandit processes. This cognitive strategy takes into account both the effective reward and the gain of knowledge. Its corresponding metadynamics is the bayesian revision.

Despite the deep character of the above theory, the computational cost of calculating indexes is cumbersome. There is a need for approximated strategies and metadynamics if they are more tractable. For example the least failure rule in a family of Bernouilly bandits is proved to be very close - at the beginning - to the index rule : the least failure rule consists to choose at every time the arm with the least failure.

But the most important example to discuss is the choice of Boltzmann law by the connexionist community of reinforcement learning. The topics of reinforcement is exactly the same as here. And the compromise between exploration and exploitation is thought through the Boltzmann law : the actions are chosen at random proportionally to the exponential of their expected value. More work has to be done to verify how the non deterministic strategy of Boltzmann law approximates the index rule.

The most important role of the neural network is to perform parallel distributed processing. What is more important is probably not an exact evaluation of the index but a large scanning between a huge number of activity patterns. Thus specific indexes and metadynamics have to be thought in relation with neurosciences. Let us summerize the above discussion.

> Hypothesis 2 (the autoteaching hedonistic agent and its bounded rationality) : the autoteaching hedonistic agent has continuously to manage inside its family of alternative jobs the compromise between exploration and exploitation by finding (i) nearly optimal but easily tractable indexes (ii) nearly optimal but more tractable metadynamics to revise his knowledge

In this direction of research the paradigmatic framework of bandit superprocesses and jobs can be very useful. Indeed it becomes possible to evaluate the consequence on the hedonistic level of a lot of metachoices of an autoteaching agent : the choices of indexes, of strategies of exploration, and of metadynamics for the revision of knowledge. A microeconomy of empiric knowledge can be grounded with this approach. It is not only a theory of perfect rationality as played by the bandit superprocesses. In the same movement a theory of bounded rationality for the acquisition of empiric knowledge was proposed by taking into account the computational difficulties.

SPECULAR AGENTS AND THE COGNITIVE MICRO-ECONOMY

The great capacity of an embodied mind to choose between activity patterns would be nothing without the capacity of experiment. An autoteaching agent can perform by itself only very limited experiences. The most important bottleneck for it is its dramatic lack of experience.

The fundamental question is how to deal when there is a lack of experience. The simplest answer is that the agent can observe the behavior of the others and think that it is better to try the most frequent behavior than to experiment by itself. An implicit presupposition for that is the specularity hypothesis which affects all the fundamental cognitive metadynamics of an autoteaching agent.

1. SPECULAR AGENTS IN HUMAN SOCIETY

Specularity [Vullierme, 89] refers to the common knowledge that everyone acts and reasons in a situation by thinking at the same time how the others act and reason in the same situation. Humans are the only specular animals. This property is very important for human collective intelligence because it concerns the four above autoteaching metadynamics (cf §1.1).

First no human language would have happened without this property. No common categorization would have occured. No categorization about categorization, which is one of the main roles of language, would have developed. For the emergence of symbols, each human has to postulate that the other understands this symbol like himself. But at the same time, he has to think that the meaning of symbols and combinations of symbols for the others is also different. Netherthelesss the road is open for a collective meaning of symbols and for communicating a symbolic description of activity patterns. One of the most important difficulty in individual autoteaching is thus bypassed. Everyone can then acquire a new activity pattern in a direct way.

Second no human tradition would have happened without specularity. What is the value of tradition ? Believing the tradition is grounded on the idea that it was experienced by a lot of people like us during a lot of generations. But at the same time we know that people of the same generation have different interpretations from the previous ones : what happens is the classical opposition between ancient and modernity ; and the tradition has to evolve in the present time through this opposition. Wathever the issue of such opposition, the question for an individual to choose between several alternative activity patterns becomes easier with specularity and tradition. In the absence of individual exploration everyone has to be confident with the activity patterns selected by tradition as an openended process. A second big difficulty in the choice of activity patterns, their combinations and their scheduling in time is thus bypassed.

Third no human science would have been possible without specularity. The object of science is to extract regularities from human observations. An implicit hypothesis of each researcher is that another human at the same place as himself would do the same observation. And because it is also common knowledge that the other people are different, we need to be very careful in our observation protocols. What emerges from observation protocols is not truth and reality but a specular reality and truth, which receive the consensus of a scientific community. Even if the scientific knowledge is continously changing, non scientific people have interest to be confident in the models proposed by the scientific community. This is very helpful in the individual activity of modelization which corresponds to perceptive anticipation.

We have seen that specularity affects all autoteaching metadynamics. But autoteaching doesn't disappear with specularity for two reasons. The first reason is the idea that personal direct exploration is tranformed in another form of autoteaching and exploration : to explore how other people perform their tasks and the activity patterns they use for that. The second reason is that people have a particular history and have to experiment by oneself his own activity patterns. That is a general fact, especially in their own domains of competence.

By this new experiencing, new activity patterns emerge in the human society. They can disappear if they are less good than concurrent activity patterns. They can also percolate significantly in some concerned population.

2. REVISITING THE COMPROMISE EXPLORATION/EXPLOITATION

Let us come back to the N-armed bandit problem but in its non-bayesian version. As we will see the non-bayesian version is well adapted to the social level.

Thus we don't presuppose now that an a priori distribution law is known. And we don't look for a short term strategy as in the bayesian version which presents a discount rate. The problem is now to find a strategy which maximizes the very long term reward. We are even the most demanding because we want almost surely the best possible value, i.e. the probability of the best arm :

$$\lim_{T \to \infty} \frac{1}{T} \sum_{t=1}^{T} r_t = \max_{n=1}^{N} \theta_n \quad \text{almost surely}$$

Surprisingly there is not only one strategy but an infinity as showed by the following theorem :

> Theorem (Non bayesian N-armed bandit problem) : The following family of strategy converge almost surely to the best average reward : let play always the best known arm except for any increasing sequence $\{t_i\}$ of times reserved to experiment the N arms which satisfies :

$$\lim_{T \to \infty} \frac{(\text{number of } t_i \leq T)}{T} = 0$$

Indeed there is an infinity of such infinite sequences and thus an infinity of optimal strategy. It is thus possible to search which kind of sequences minimizes the loss due to exploration, i.e. is nearly optimal for the bayesian N-armed bandit problem. More work has to be done on this question.

The very simplicity of the rule (use the best known arm and a relatively small number of experiences) of the non-bayesian version of the N-armed bandit problem contrasts with the complex strategy of the bayesian one. This simplicity comes from the fact that a huge number of experiments simplifies the strategies of learning. A small number of experiments makes the learning much more complicated. And a huge number of experiment is much easier at the social level than at the individual level. That is the reason why the non bayesian version is well adapted to the social and cultural level.

3. THE COGNITIVE MICROECONOMY

Through the huge number of experiments in a society and the cultural transmission from generation to generation, a huge number of successful behaviors have been selected. In animal society the selected behaviors can diffuse by mimetism. But in the human society the diffusion is not only mimetic. Under the specularity hypothesis everyone can think explicitly that not only the behaviors he observes but also a huge number of behavior he does not observe have been effectively experienced. And everyone can be very confident in using the most frequent activity patterns he observes.

The specularity mechanisms allow everyone to access quite rapidly to commonsense knowledge, to good categorizations, to the novice level in many domain and to well established scientific theories. This acquisition of empirical and theoretical knowledge is obtained through very few individual experiments without comparison with the collective effort of experimentation to enact this knowledge. The role of communication through the language is fundamental in the symbolic transmission of empirical and theoretical knowledge.

But the specularity mechanism also leads everyone to enact their particular expertise inside their personal, social and professionnal life. The experience of others is here much less important. Everyone has to perform their own experience. That is a necessity in all domain of life. The case of the expert is paradigmatic. He has to accumulate a huge number of experiments. But it is very difficult for him to provide a symbolic communication of his empirical knowledge.

All the previous discussions are now summerized into a proposition to consider the cognitive microeconomy as a new field. The agents considered in this microeconomy are specular, autoteaching and hedonistic. The only existing agents which have this property are humans. But in the spirit of cybernetics this cognitive microeconomy can be used for designing in some unknown future artificial agents which can share the same property with us.

Proposition (The cognitive microeconomy)

> The cognitive microeconomy has for object to study the bounded rationality of specular and autoteaching agents in changing their hedonistic strategies in a society of such agents. One main question is how the compromise between exploration of new bad known strategies and exploitation of old better known strategies can be managed despite the bounded cognitive capacities and the dramatic lack of experiences.

A possible standard model for a cognitive microeconomy is the following coupling between a huge number of specular hedonistic agents.

a) each agent is defined at a given time of his history by two family of jobs (i) the first family of jobs consists to autoteach during the coupling with the others to become a good novice in all domains which are useful for his second family of jobs (ii) the second family of jobs concerns his personal, professional and social life where he has to enact his own expertise by autoteaching his own strategies from a lot of experiences. Because of his bounded rationality, he uses nearly optimal but tractable index evaluations and autoteaching metadynamics.

b) during the coupling with others directly or through media, each agent observes the strategies they use to perform their jobs. He adds the job with the associated observed strategy if it has a good index (or a better index than the alternative job he disposes already).

But much more work has to be done to better specify and study the dynamical properties in a network of specular and autoteaching agents. For example it would be important to see under which conditions some strategies or knowledge emerge, diffuse and even invade most of the society.

Let us remark that there is not formally a very big difference between an isolated autoteaching agent and a specular autoteaching agent. Both are autoteaching from his own experience. There is only one difference but of very great consequence : the experience of the specular agent consists in his observation of the strategies of the others and thus inheritate from the whole experience of the others. And the transmission of very sophisticated jobs is facilited because specularity facilitates all the autoteaching metadynamics. The communication through all type of media is specially important for the specular and autoteaching mecanisms. Despite the emergence of new kind of media, the communication of knowledge through the language remains the most important mecanism.

CONCLUSION : FROM THE COGNITIVE MICROECONOMY TOWARDS A MACROECONOMY OF KNOWLEDGE

What was developed above is essentially a cognitive microeconomy between specular and autoteaching hedonistic agents. Because of his specularity he can autoteach quickly to become good novice in several domains by trusting the most frequent abductive strategies he observes. But also by specularity he has to enact his own role and expertise in his personal, professional and social life by autoteaching his own strategies. In all this mecanisms the role of technological, scientific and cultural knowledge is essential.

Because humanity enters the era of knowledge, it becomes important to understand at least globally and approximatly what the social cost and benefice of the immaterial investment in knowledge are. The above cognitive microeconomy provides some useful categories to sketch a macroeconomy of knowledge :

(i) commonsense knowledge, novice specialized knowledge and well established scientific knowledge are acquired with a little amount of experiments. This kind of knowledge coevolves slowly. The social cost is the effort of education or formation. The social benefit is the possibility for everyone to acquire a huge number of empirical and theoretical knowledge which is useful for (ii)

(ii) personal knowledge, expert knowledge and new scientific knowledge have to be acquired with a big amount of experiments. This kind of knowledge evolves rapidly by coevolution. The social cost is the activity of exploration of individual agents. The social benefit is first productivity gain, new products and services and second useful knowledge to (i).

If we thought the cognitive microeconomy as how to deal with the compromise between exploration/exploitation at the individual level in a society of specular and autoteaching agents, we can think the macroeconomy of knowledge as how to deal with the same compromise at the collective level.

REFERENCES

1. Bourgine P. (1989), *Homo oeconomicus is also homo cogitans, homo cogitans is also homo oeconomicus*, Theory and Decision, july 89, Reidel.
2. Bourgine P., F. Varela (1992), *Towards a practice of autonomous system.* Towards a practice of autonomous system, F.Varela & P.Bourgine (ed). MIT Press/Bradford Books.pp 3-10.
3. Bourgine P. , B. Walliser (1992), *Economics and cognitive science,* Pergamon Press.
4. Dupuy J.P. (1989), *Common knowledge, common sense* in :P.Bourgine (ed), Economic Reasoning and Artificial Intelligence, Theory and Decision 27, 37-62.
5. Gärdenfors Peter, (1988), _*Knowledge in flux* , M.I.T. / Bradford Books, Cambridge, MA.
6. Gittins J.C. (1989), *Multi-armed Bandit, Allocation Indices,* John Wiley & Sons
7. Holland J.H., 1975. *Adaptation in natural and artificial systems.* Ann Arbor : the University of Michigan Press.
8. Edelman G. (1992), *Bright Air, Brillant Fire : On the Matter of Mind,* Basic Books.
9. Feistel R ., Ebeling W. (1989), *Evolution of Complex System,* Kluwer Academic.

10. Nicolis G., Prigogine I. (1989), *Exploring Complexity: An Introduction,* R.Piper GmbH & Co. KG Verlag.
11. McClelland J. L., Rumelhart D. E. (1986), *Parallel Distributed Processing : Exploration in the Microstructure of Cognition.* MIT/Bradford Book, Cambridge, MA.
12. Simon H.A. (1976) *From subtantive to procedural rationality.* Method and Appraisal in Economics, Latsis S.J.(ed.), p. 129-148. Cambridge University Press, Cambridge.
13. Vapnik V.N. et Y. Chervonenkis (1981),*On the uniform convergence of relative frequencies of events to their probabilities.* In Theory of probability and its applications, XXVI, pp 532-553.
14. Varela F. (1986), *Trends in Cognitive Science and Technology*.in:J.LRoos (ed.), Economics and Artificial Intelligence, Pergamon Press, Oxford, pp. 1-8.
15. F.Varela F., Thompson E., Rosch E. (1991),*The Embodied Mind,* MIT Press.
16. Varela F., Bourgine P. (1992), *Towards a practice of autonomous system,* MIT Press/Bradford Books.
17. Vullierme J.-L. (1989), *Le concept de système politique,* PUF.
18. Walliser Bernard (1989), *Instrumental rationality and cognitive rationality,* in :P.Bourgine (ed), Economic Reasoning and Artificial Intelligence, Theory and Decision 27, pp. 7-36.
19. Walliser B. (1993), *A spectrum of cognitive processes in game theory,* in Second European Congress on System Science, Prague, oct 93.
20. Watkins C. (1989), *Learning with Delayed Reward,* PhD, Cambridge University Psychology Department.

---

[1] The mean reward don't depend from x' because $r(x, a) = \sum p(x' \mid x, a)\, r'(x, a, x')$

A Dynamic Analysis of Regional Inequality in China's Economic Development

Kong Shuhong[1] and Zhou Meng[2]

[1]Department of Social Science, Shantou University, Shantou 515063, P. R. China
[2]Department of Mathematics, Beijing University of Aeronautics and Astronautics, Beijing 100083, P. R. China

Abstract. In this paper we analyse the economic regional inequality with dynamic point and study its causes and tendency. In the first part of this paper the three regions dividing is given. In the second part we introduce the inverted-U theory of regional economic differential. The third part is devoted to analysing historical regional economic differential and its causes. In the last part we give a forecast and analysis of the differential by means of establishing a mathematical model.

Keywords: Regional Inequality, Economic Differential, Regional Differential Indicator.

1 Introduction

There are large differences in economic development among regions of China. There exists a regional inequality in economic development for a long time . In recent years the east economy grows rapidly with our country's reforming and opening. This also makes a growing economic differential between east region and centre region, west region. We are going to analyse the economic regional inequality with dynamic point and study its causes and tendency. We divide China into three economic regions of east, centre and west . We put 19 economic indications and choose the data of 1990, obtain the three regions dividing by Hierachical Cluster Analysis . The east region includes 11 provinces: Beijing, Tianjin, Hebei, Liaoning , Shanghai, Jiangsu, Zhejiang, Fujian, Shandong, Guangdong, Hainan . The centre region includes 9 provinces: Neimong, Shanxi, Jilin, Heilongjiang, Anhui, Jiangxi, Henan, Hubei, Hunan. The west region includes 10 provinces: Sichuan, Guizhou, Yunnan, Xizang, Shaanxi, Gansu, Qinghai, Ningxia, Xinjiang, Guangxi.

2 On the Inverted — U Theory of Regional Economic Differential

The inverted-U hypothesis was given first by American economist Kuznets at his speaking to E. A. A. in 1955 . He said,[1] in the process of economic development the long tendency of income inequality is that the inequality grows rapidly in the early period of economic growth from pre-industrial civilization to industrial civilization, then the inequality would steady shortly and in the latter period of economic growth it would reduce slowly. In 1965, American economist Willoamson[2] used the inverted-U theory to the study of regional economics and concluded that there is an inverted-U moving tendency of regional economic differential related to economic development . He showed that at the early stage of economic developing , for a country, the regional economic differential will increase, then stop at some level with the growth of economy and will decrease when economic development arrives at higher stage. This is decided by the developing of social productive force. In the early stage of economic developing some regions which have better investment climate and larger investment profits than others would get priority to develop. These regions therefore become so-called "developing poles "or"growing points". This effect comes from the following: facilities for getting raw materials and technique; excellent capital construction such as communication, energy sources, city management, etc; low cost of labour, lands, transportation, information , etc. So these regions would attract large amounts of investment and manpower and form strong "pole effect"which makes increasing differential from other regions. Then the regional inequality grows. But when economic development arrives at higher stage, these"developing poles"would produce many"expansion diseases"such as traffic jam, population boom, shortage of lands, poor resources, overload of basic facilities, surplus of capital, etc. Then in those developed regions productive cost increases, economic effect decreases, new investment yields little profits. Economic growth would slow down in developed regions. In this condition capital, technique and labour would be transfered from developed regions to other developing regions and form so-called "spread effect". Thus economic growth of developing regions speeds up and this causes decreasing of the regional economic differential . This is the inverted-U rule related economic growth to regional inequality. See Figure 2. 1.

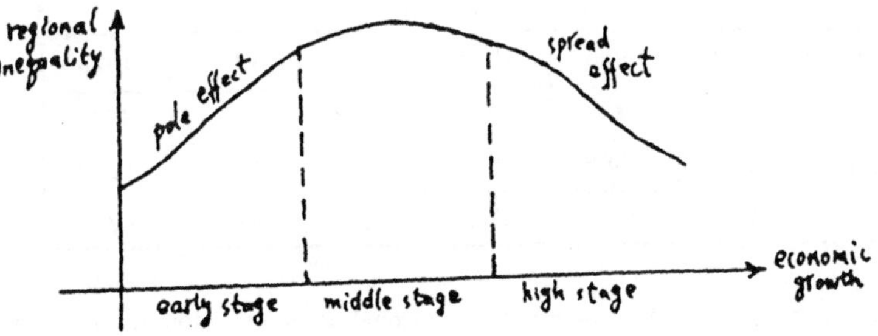

Fig. 2. 1. The inverted—U curve

3 A Dynamic Anlysis of Economic Differential Among china's Three Regions in the Time 1950—1990

In the process of country's economic developing, regional income differential indicates the regional inequality in economic development. We are going to analyse this inequality with differential indicator which is the ratio of SD (Standard Deviation) in three regions' national income to arithmetic average of three regions' national income. The yearly data of three regions' national income is the following. [3]

Table 3. 1 National income of three regions. unit: hundred million Yuan

years regions	east	centre	west
1952	282. 65	179. 10	106. 09
1958	545. 22	363. 67	209. 86
1964	556. 86	377. 64	232. 92
1970	908. 49	639. 52	376. 24
1974	1227. 45	760. 67	463. 59
1978	1474. 47	947. 72	569. 44
1982	2196. 84	1331. 32	741. 37
1986	4084. 76	2488. 3	1425. 55
1990	7712. 72	4334. 6	2691. 99

Tabble 3. 2 Economic differential indicators of three regions %

years	1952	1955	1957	1966	1973	1978
C_v	37. 6	34. 7	33. 1	31. 4	33. 3	37. 9
years	1980	1982	1985	1987	1989	1990
C_v	40. 7	41. 8	42. 1	42. 3	42. 8	42. 5

Explaination: $C_v = (S/\bar{Y}) \times 100\%$, where C_v is regional economic differential indicator, if the value of C_v is large then differential is large. S is SD in three regions' national income. $\bar{Y}$ is arithmetic average of three regions' national income.

According to Table 3. 1, 3. 2 we draw Figure 3. 1 and 3. 2.

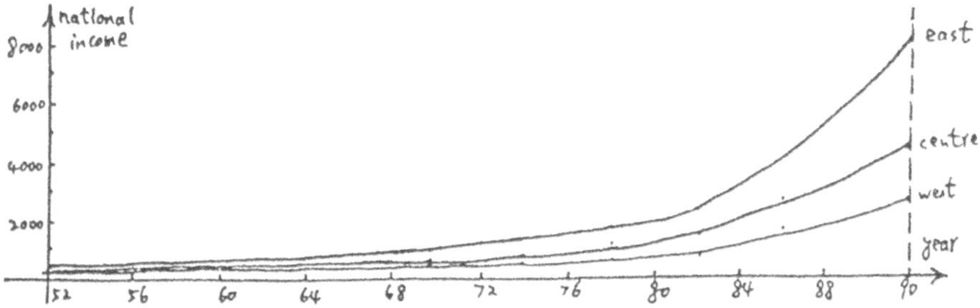

Fig. 3. 1. National income of three regions

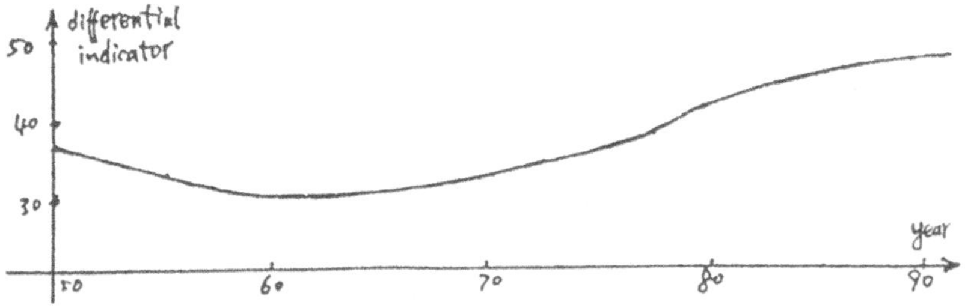

Fig. 3. 2. Economic differential indicators curve

We can divide the period of 1952—1990 into two stages. One is of 1952—1978 in which economy is dominated by highly centralized planing system. Another is of 1978—1990 in which economy is dominated by dual system of combining plan with market.

From observation of Fig. 3. 1, 3. 2, in the first stage (1952—1978) the change of regional absolute differential wasn't large and the differential indicator changed in U—form. This was caused by that, for equilibrium in regional developing, country invested largely in direction of centre and west regions and developed many new industrial base in these regions. In stage of "the first five year plan" capital construction investment ratio of east, centre and west was 36. 9 : 28. 8 : 18, and national income ratio was 47. 8 : 32. 6 : 19. 6. In "the second five" stage, capital construction investment ratio was 38. 4 : 34 : 22 and national income ratio was 50. 07 : 31. 84 : 18. 09. In "three year adjustment" stage, capital construction investment ratio was 34. 9 : 32. 9 : 25. 6 and national income ratio was 47. 27 : 32. 3 : 20. 43. In "the third five" stage, capital construction investment ratio was 26. 9 : 29. 8 : 34. 9 and national income ratio was 47. 3 : 33. 37 : 19. 3. We see that country's investment was largely in direction of centre and west regions, regional differential decreased slowly and the differential indicator descended to the lowest point in "the third five" stage. But effect in centre and west regions wasn't good. In "the fourth five" stage, a little change occured. Capital construction investment ratio was 35. 3 : 29. 9 : 24. 5 and national income ratio was 48. 24 : 32. 24 : 19. 52 in that stage. The differential indicator started to rise. In "the fifth five" stage, capital construction investment ratio was 42. 2 : 30. 1 : 19. 9 and national income ratio was 50. 35 : 31. 45 : 18. 22. The differential indicator continued to rise. Summarily, in the period of 1952—1978 the regional differential indicator curve was a U-form, first decreased and then rose. This is because that our country took equilibrating strategy in regional economic developing and, with highly centralized planning economic system, invested in large amounts to the centre and the west with little effect. But practically such an equilibrium failed to be obtained. It deviated from the general law of regional economic developing from inequality to equilibrium, and can only get a kind of balance in low level and never get rapid growth of country's economy.

In the second stage (1978—1990) our country started reforming and opening, production factors started to slant towards east region. Since investment has high effect in the east and it has advantage of position, many special economic zones and open cities were established and economy of east region growed rapidly. In "the sixth five" stage, apart from foreign capital, country's investment ratio of east, centre ane west regions was 47. 7 : 29. 3 : 17. 2 and national income ratio was 51. 44 : 31. 14 : 17. 42. In "the seventh five" stage, the investment ratio was 53. 17 : 25. 04 : 16. 12 and the income ratio was 52. 06 : 29. 97 : 17. 96. Regional absolute differential increased rapidly and the regional differential indicator rose continuously (See Fig. 3. 1 and 3. 2)

To summarize, in the period of 1950—1990 the regional economic differential indicator curve was a composition of a U-form and the former half of a inverted-U-form. In the stage associated with U-form our country's equilibrating strategy in regional economic devoloping seemed to be unsuccessful. In the stage associated with the former half of a inverted-U-form our country took inequality strategy after reforming and opening and made a rapid growth of economic development with increasing regional differential. This fit in with the inverted-U theory of regional economic differential.

4 A Forecast and Analysis to China's Regional Economic Differential

4.1 The Choice of Forecasting Model

We are going to forecast the regional differential by means of statistic method and use the regional differential indicator to obtain a quantitative forecasting result. From data and regional differential indicator curve as Table 3.2 and Fig. 3.2 we see that the indicator curve was a U-form before 1975 and an inverted-U-form after 1975. Since economy was dominated by highly centralized planing system before 1975 and our forecasting involved future condition of market system, we omit data before 1975 and take data after 1975. By the inverted-U theory of regional economic differential, regional differential increase first and decrease when economic developing arrive at high stage. So we choose the model of quadratic curve $Y = b_0 + b_1 t + b_2 t^2$. where Y is the indicator and t is time. Take $t = 0$ for the year 1975, data and figure are the following.

Table 4.1 %

year	75	76	77	78	79	80	81	82	83	85	87	89
t	0	1	2	3	4	5	6	7	8	10	12	14
Y	37.0	40.6	39.4	37.9	39.7	40.7	42.1	42	42.7	42.1	42.3	42.8

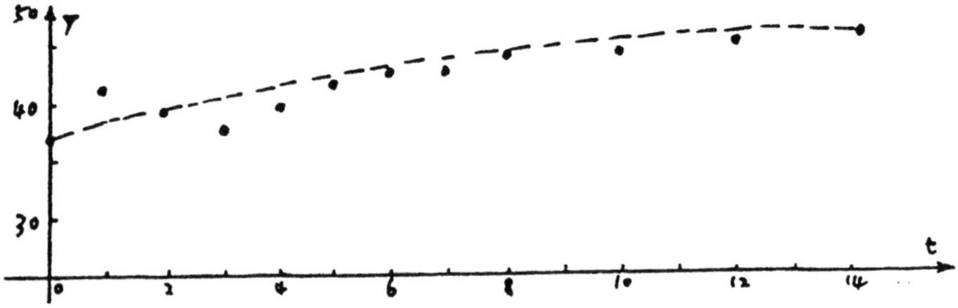

Fig. 4.1. The curve of indicator

According to above data we can decide the value of b_0, b_1, b_2 with the Method of Least Squares in Multivariate Linear Regression. Using computer we get the model $Y = 37.79 + 0.763\,t - 0.019\,t^2$.

4.2 An Analysis of the Model

The comparison between model data and actual data is the following.

Table 4.2 %

year	75	76	77	78	79	80	81	82	83	85	87	89
t	0	1	2	3	4	5	6	7	8	10	12	14
actual data $\hat{Y}$	37	40.6	39.4	37.9	39.7	40.7	42.1	42	42.7	42.1	42.3	42.8
model data Y	37.8	38.5	39.3	39.9	40.5	41.2	41.65	42.2	42.6	43.5	44.2	44.7

The Mean Propotional Error of model values and actual values is that: $MPE = \sum_{i=0}^{n} \frac{1}{n}[(Y_i - \hat{Y}_i)/Y_i] \times 100\% = 0.248\%$. The Mean Absolute Propotional Error of model values and actual values is that: $MAPE = \sum_{i=0}^{n} \frac{1}{n} |(Y_i - Y_i)/Y_i| \times 100\% = 1.97\%$. The Regression Standard Deviation of the model is that: $S = \{\sum_{i=0}^{n} [(Y_i - \hat{Y}_i)^2/(n-2)]\}^{\frac{1}{2}} = 1.126$. (Note that $n = 12$ in Table 4.2)

Usually a model is thought useful if $MPE \leqslant 2\%$ and $MAPE \leqslant 10\%$. In our model they are respectively 0.248% and 1.97%. So our model is very satisfactory. If we take Confidence Interval of 95%: $(Y \pm 2S) = (Y \pm 2.25)$, then actual values are all in the Confidence Interval. (See Table 4.2).

4.3 A Revision of the Model and Analysis of Forecasting Result

In order to apply the model to forecast the indicator Y after 2000 or longer we must consider the influence of market economy in ,90s. So we introduce a parameter y which indicates the market economy influence. We get a revision of the model:

$\bar{Y} = Y + y$

$Y = 37.79 + 0.763\,t - 0.019\,t^2$

$y = 0.1(t-15) + 0.014(t-15)^2$

Explaination: Suppose $y = \alpha(t-15) + \beta(t-15)^2$. In order to decide the value of α, β we consider the two : (1) α would influence the differentiability of function $\bar{Y}$ on point $t = 15$. If $\alpha = 0$ then $\bar{Y}$ is differentiable. So α must be taken as little as possible. But according to data of 1991—1992 $\bar{Y}$ increased certainly on point $t = 15$. So we put $\alpha = 0.1$. (2). Consider growth of market economy ,it would be mature in thirty years. So we take β such that y is largest after thirty years. Because that function $ax^2 + bx + c$ is largest on $x = -b/2a$, we get: $(0.763 + \alpha - 30\beta)/[2(0.019 - \beta)] = 45$ and then $\beta = 0.014$.

Now we apply the revised model to forecast the regional economic differential indicator from 1990 to 2050. We take Confidence Interval of 95%: $(Y \pm 2S) = (Y \pm 2.25)$. Forecasting result is the following.

Table 4.3 %

year	1990	1993	1995	1997	1999	2000	2005	2010
t	15	18	20	22	24	25	30	35
forecasting value	44.9 ±2.25	45.6 ±2.25	46.4 ±2.25	46.8 ±2.25	47.2 ±2.25	47.4 ±2.25	48.2 ±2.25	48.8 ±2.25
year	2015	2020	2025	2030	2035	2040	2045	2050
t	40	45	50	55	60	65	70	75
forecasting value	49.1 ±2.25	49.25 ±2.25	49.1 ±2.25	48.7 ±2.25	48 ±2.25	47.1 ±2.25	45.9 ±2.25	44.5 ±2.25

From the result ,in 1990—2000, the regional economic differential indicator values are in 44.75—49.65. After 2000 it will continue to increase and arrive at the largest point in 2020. Then it will decrease slowly . See Figure 4.2.

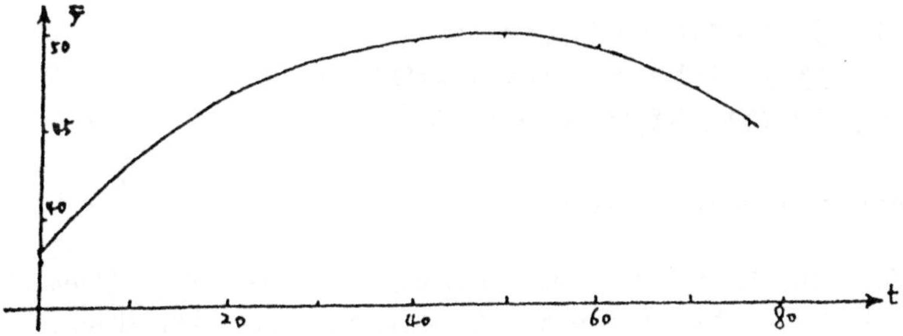

Fig. 4. 2. Forecasting curve of the indicator

With analyses as above we can make the conclusion: In order to develop economy of total country we should develop first some regions such as east and coastal regions. Although this would cause increasing regional economic differential ,this is necessary for the maturation of economy and industrialization of country . And a great disparity of regional economic developing would be avoided. So taking regional inequality developing strategy in economy of China is a realizable and scientific choice.

References

[1]Kuznets (1955): Economic Growth and Income Inequality. *American Economic Review*. Vol. 45

[2]Willoamson(1965): Regional inequality in the process of national development: a description of patterna. *Economic Development and Cultural Change. Vol. No. 4*

[3]《National Income Statistic Data of 1949—1985》 and 《Yearly Data of China's Statistic》 1986—1991. *The Statistic Publ. of China.*

THE SELECTION OF BEHAVIORAL CONVENTIONS IN AN EVOLUTIONARY MODEL OF ECONOMIC DYNAMICS

Gerald Silverberg and Bart Verspagen

Maastricht Economic Research Institute on Innovation and Technology, University of Limburg, P.O. Box 616, NL-6200 MD Maastricht, The Netherlands. The research of Bart Verspagen has been made possible by a fellowship of the Royal Netherlands Academy of Arts and Sciences.

1. Introduction

Economic theory has been dominated by a description of firm-behaviour that abstracts from almost all real-life features with which managers are familiar: fundamental uncertainty, complexity, and the necessity of making decisions with limited information and calculating capacity. Actual business-practice, as many observers have pointed out, provides a rather conflicting viewpoint: firms often rely on rather simple rules of thumb or routines, rather than explicit optimization procedures. That is, they are boundedly rational in the sense of Simon (1986a,b). Or, they base their decisions on whims or impulses that defy any rational explication, that is, they display what Keynes termed animal spirits.

Implicit in the rejection of full rationality as an adequate description of economic behaviour, the notion of the 'representative firm' loses the central importance it is assigned in neoclassical theory. Rather than the single firm that a theory based on full rationality is often forced to posit, any theory based upon bounded rationality has to proceed from heterogeneity in firm behaviour, firm competences and firm performance. And observation of the 'real world' can only confirm the prominent role of diversity in human affairs.

Yet the economy can often be characterized by certain regularities, be it in terms of the use of similar behavioral rules by firms (such as price markups, investment payback periods, or target levels for inventories and R&D spending), or in terms of the outcomes of the dynamics at the sectoral or macro-level (such as the product life cycle, or prolonged periods of steady growth such as the Western world experienced after 1945). The emergence of these types of regular macro-patterns from systems that show heterogeneity and 'simple' (i.e., 'routine-based') behaviour at the micro-level, has recently become the subject of the field of 'complexity studies', which extends to such fields as 'artificial life' (Langton, 1989; Langton *et al.*, 1992), or 'artificial worlds' (Lane, 1993). The central message emerging from this literature seems to be that complex interactions between agents characterized by relatively simple behavioral rules at the micro level can give rise to 'self-organization' dynamics, yielding unexpected regularities at the macro-level.

The term artificial life is being used to illustrate the analogy to the phenomenon of biologically living systems, which appear to be organized along similar lines. However, the ideas of complexity and self-organization also seem to apply to 'socially living' systems, such as the economy (as in Arthur, 1991).

Much of the work on complexity is based on artificial intelligence and computer science, e.g., neural nets, genetic algorithms, and classifier systems. In contrast to evolutionary game theory, the complexity of the problems addressed in this approach has made analytical results difficult to come by. Whereas in the beginning most work focused on computing standard optimization problems and thus converging to a hopefully unique point, more recent efforts have been directed at using these tools open-endedly to simulate the self-organization of complex systems.

Rather than the unique steady state so familiar from neoclassical economic theory, two heuristic phenomena that have often been commented on without precise definition have emerged from this literature. The first is *emergent properties*, i.e., complex but identifiable patterns of behaviour that emerge spontaneously at some point in the history of the system and are not in any obvious way inherent in the constitution of its parts. The second is *punctuated equilibria*, periods of quasi-stable behaviour separated by usually very rapid periods of transition and disorder.

Drawing on these methods, as well as the evolutionary tradition originating with Nelson and Winter (1982), this paper seeks to investigate the ways in which macro-regularities may emerge in a dynamic economic model with boundedly rational firms interacting with each other in the marketplace. A simpler version of the model has been described in Silverberg and Verspagen (1994a,b). While those papers focused on rather general descriptions of the outcomes of the model with only one possible type of behavioral rule, this paper will more thoroughly investigate under which conditions a particular rule will be selected by firms.

The central challenge for firms in our model is to determine what proportion of their investment budget will be devoted to R&D as an operating routine.There is no obvious way in which the firms can predict the exact outcome of their actions. To provide some anecdotal evidence, we recall an interview with the director of R&D of the Japanese firm Canon published in *The Financial Times* a number of years ago. The director reported that the firm had some time before raised its R&D/turnover ratio from 11% to 11½%. This appeared to have been beneficial to firm, so that the directors were debating whether to cautiously raise it even further. There in fact did not seem to be any way to determine where an upper limit might lie, and what the optimum policy might be, short of actually trying it out, but the firm was set to continue in this direction.

The rest of the paper is organized as follows. In the next section, the salient features of the model are summarised. Section 3 describes some of the outcomes of a number of simulation experiments. Finally, section 4 summarizes the argument and outlines the main conclusions.

2. The Model

The model consists of three basic blocks. The first block describes how the artificial economy evolves with a given set of technologies and firms. This block consists of equations for the rate of capital accumulation, the diffusion of new technologies in the total capital stock of the firms, and the real wage rate. The second block describes a set of rules that is used to introduce new technologies and firms into the economy. This block takes the innovative behaviour of firms (to be explained below) as given, and then describes the probability that individual firms will make an innovation, as well as how this innovation is introduced. The third block describes how innovative behaviour changes under the influence of the evolution of the economy and firm learning. This block, in other words, describes a feedback from performance to innovative behaviour and thus a form of collective learning. The parameters of the model and the values used in the simulations are summarized in the Appendix.

2.1. The Evolution of the Artificial Economy With a Given Set of Firms and Technologies

The basic framework of the model is taken from Silverberg and Lehnert (1993), which in turn draws on Silverberg (1984) and Goodwin (1967). Let hats above variables denote proportional growth rates, w be the (real) wage rate, v the employment rate (persons employed as a fraction of the labour force), and m and n parameters (both positive). Then the wage rate is determined by the following differential equation:

$$\hat{w} = -m + nv. \tag{1}$$

It is assumed that there is a fixed number q of firms in the economy, while each of these firms has a variable number p_q of different types of capital goods that it utilizes to produce a homogeneous product. New capital arises from the accumulation of profits, a process described by the following equation:

$$\hat{k}_{ij} = (1-\gamma_{1i})r_{ij} - \frac{\gamma_{2i}}{c} + \alpha(r_{ij}-r_i) - \sigma. \tag{2}$$

The capital stock is denoted by k, r stands for the profit rate, and σ is the exogenous rate of *physical* depreciation of capital (technological obsolescence is an endogenous component of the model itself). The subscript i (1..q) denotes the firm, and j (1..p_q) the type of capital (the absence of any these indices indicates an aggregation over this particular dimension). Eq. (2) assumes that the principal source for type ij-capital accumulation is profits generated by ij-capital. This is modelled by the first term on the rhs of (2), i.e., $(1-\gamma_i)r_{ij}$. A firm-specific portion of profits (denoted by γ_{1i}) plus a firm-specific portion of total output (sales) (denoted by γ_{2i}) is used for the development of knowledge (R&D) (when $r_i<0$, γ_{1i} is set to zero).

However, profits may also be redistributed in such a way that more profitable types of capital accumulate even faster, less profitable even slower, than would otherwise be the case. The mechanism used to model this was first proposed by Soete and Turner (1984), and is represented by the second term on the rhs of eq. (2). By changing the value of α, redistribution of profits takes place faster (larger α) or slower (smaller α).

It is assumed that each type of capital is characterized by fixed technical coefficients, c and a (for capital coefficient and labour productivity, respectively). The capital coefficient is assumed to be fixed throughout the economy (and time), while labour productivity is assumed to change under the influence of technical progress. The profit rate of ij-capital is then given by $(1-w/a_{ij})/c$.

The principal variable used to describe firm dynamics is the share of the labour force employed on each capital stock. Production is assumed to be always equal to production capacity (the influence of effective demand is absent), so that the amount of labour employed by each capital stock is equal to $k_{ij}/(a_{ij}c)$. Dividing this by the labour force (assumed to grow at a fixed rate β) gives the share of labour employed, v_{ij} (called the employment share hereafter). The expression for the growth rate of this variable is

$$\hat{v}_{ij} = \hat{k}_{ij} - \beta = (1-\gamma_i)r_{ij} - \frac{\gamma_{2i}}{c} + \alpha(r_{ij} - r_i) - (\beta + \sigma). \tag{3}$$

R&D also has an employment effect. We assume that the ratio between R&D expenditures and R&D labour input is equal to a fraction δ of the economy-wide labour productivity. The employment rate v_q resulting from production is then found by summing v_{ij} over i and j. Under these assumptions, it can then be shown that the overall employment rate v is equal to $(1+\delta(\gamma_1 rc+\gamma_2))v_q$.

Eqs. (1) and (3) together create a selection mechanism in our artificial economy. Eq. (3) describes how more profitable (i.e., with above-average labour productivity) technologies tend to increase their employment share, whereas more backward (below-average) technologies tend to vanish. The real Phillips curve eq. (1) ensures that real wages tend to track labour productivity in the long run. In a situation in which new technologies are continually being introduced, this implies that all technologies, after an initial phase of market penetration and diffusion, will eventually vanish from the production system.

However, for a given set of technologies, long-run per capita growth is no longer possible once all firms converge to exclusive employment of the highest productivity technology. The next section outlines how new technologies can enter the system and thereby open up the possibility of long-run growth.

2.2. The Introduction of New Technologies and Firms Into the Economy

The main difference between this model and the ones in Silverberg (1984) and Silverberg and Lehnert (1993) is the way in which innovation is "endogenized". It is assumed that in each time period, firms devote resources (R&D) to the systematic search for new production possibilities (i.e., new types of capital). The outcome of this search process is assumed to be stochastic.

Each time an innovation occurs, the firm creates a new type of capital. The labour productivity of this type of capital is given by the following process:

$$a_{i,t}^{*} = (1+\tau)a_{i,t-1}^{*}, \tag{4}$$

where τ is the fixed proportional increase in labour productivity between innovations and $a_{i,t}^{*}$ is the firm-specific best practice labour productivity. The new type of capital is seeded with a small employment share (say 0.0001).In order to keep the total employment rate constant, this seed value is (proportionally) removed from the other types of capital of the innovating firm. The number of technologies employed by any given firm may vary in time.

As real wages rise over time, every technology will generate negative profits at some stage (because of its fixed labour productivity). It is assumed that these losses are financed by an equivalent decrease of the capital stock. In other words, losses imply that capital will be scrapped, and scrapped capital can be "consumed" to cover the losses. Note that for individual capital stocks, the point at which scrapping occurs lies *prior* to the point where profits are negative, due to the α-related diffusion term in eq. (2). When a technology's employment share falls below a specified (very small) value E, it is scrapped completely.

A firm's R&D activities as well as possibly those of its rivals enter an innovation potential function T_i. This in turn determines the firm's probability of making an innovation according to a Poisson process with arrival rate ρ_i. The simplest relation is simply linear:

$$\rho_i = AT_i + \rho_{min}, \tag{5}$$

where ρ_{min} is the (small) autonomous probability of making a fortuitous innovation without doing formal R&D, and A is the innovation function slope. One can also posit a nonlinear relationship with both increasing and decreasing returns to R&D, such as a logistic:

$$\rho_i = \frac{\rho_{min}\rho_{max}}{\rho_{min} + (\rho_{max} - \rho_{min})\, e^{-AT_i}}. \tag{6}$$

This logistic function has intercept ρ_{min} and (asymptotic) saturation level ρ_{max}. In this case, the parameter A determines the speed at which the saturation level is approached.

T_i, the innovation potential, is determined both by the firm's own R&D level (h_i, to be defined below) and its ability to profit from other firms' R&D (technological spillovers):

$$T_i = h_i + \phi_1 h + \phi_2 h h_i. \tag{7}$$

These spillovers can take two forms. First, there is a term related to the economy-wide value of h (written without subscript). The economy-wide R&D level h is defined to be the market share weighted average of firm-specific R&D levels. Second, there is a term related to the product of the economy-wide and the firm-specific value h_i. This latter term takes into account the argument that in order to assimilate spillovers, a firm has to have some technology-generating proficiency itself (see Cohen and Levinthal 1989, Nelson 1990). The parameters ϕ_1 and ϕ_2 determine the importance of each spillover mode[1].

The firm-specific R&D level h_i is defined to be the ratio of a moving average of firm R&D investment to its total physical capital stock. A ratio is used to normalize for firm size, since otherwise such a strong positive feedback between R&D and firm growth exists that monopoly becomes inevitable. While *a priori* it is by no means clear why the size of individual R&D effort should not directly relate to innovative success, a pure scale effect must be ruled out by the continuing existence of competition and the ability of small countries to remain or even advance in the technology race. The exponential moving average RD_i on R&D for a lag of L (or a depreciation rate of $1/L$) is given by the following differential equation:

$$\frac{d}{dt}RD_i = ((\gamma_1 r_i + \gamma_2 / c) k_i - RD_i)/L. \tag{8}$$

Hence the firm-specific R&D level is

$$h_i = RD_i / k_i. \tag{9}$$

An innovation can be defined in a narrow or a wide sense. In the wide sense, the adoption of any technology not yet employed by a firm (or a country) is an innovation to that unit. In the narrow sense, only technologies that have never been employed before anywhere are considered innovations at their time of introduction. If firms innovate according to the above Poisson arrival rates in the narrow sense, however, a very considerable intertemporal externality is created, because firms' innovations always build on each other. Thus there can be no duplication of effort and, as long as firms maintain a minimal level of R&D, no cumulative falling behind. On the other hand, once an innovation has been introduced somewhere into the economy, it should be progressively easier for other firms to imitate or duplicate it; it should not be necessary to reinvent the wheel. We capture this by

[1] Spillovers will not be dealt with in this paper. They are examined within the context of one-parameter strategies in Silverberg and Verspagen (1994a,b).

introducing a catching-up effect. Let the labour productivity of the economy-wide best practice technology be a^*, and the best practice technology of firm i a^*_i. Then firm i's innovation potential T_i will be augmented by a measure of its distance from the best practice frontier:

$$T_i' = T_i(1 + \kappa \ln(a^*/a_i^*)). \tag{10}$$

Thus, adopting an old innovation is facilitated for backward firms, but they are still required to invest in their technological capacity to reap these catchup benefits. Here, however, R&D efforts should be interpreted in the larger sense of technological training and licensing, reverse engineering, or even industrial espionage (all costly activities, if not as costly as doing state-of-the-art R&D).

We have also experimented with innovations in the narrow sense, but the results on strategic selection are rather ambiguous. This is not surprising, since the import of the intertemporal externality is indeed quite large. We consider the Ansatz in eq. 10 therefore to be a justifiable first formulation, since technology adoption decisions are never passive, but rather require technological efforts of the adopting firm. However, it does place too much of the burden of catching up onto R&D.

In the artificial economy modelled here, entry of a new firm occurs only as a result of exit of an incumbent firm. Exit occurs whenever a firm's employment share (excluding its R&D employment) falls below a fixed level E. While exit of incumbent firms is completely endogenous, entry only occurs in case of exit, so that the total number of firms is constant. Naturally, this feature of the model is not very realistic, as in reality entry may be independent of exit and the total population of firms may vary. However, it is not the aim of this model to describe the phenomena of entry and exit as such. Instead, the main function of entry and exit is to maintain potential variety in the population of firms while providing for firm elimination.

Whenever entry occurs, the entrant is assigned a single technology with an amount of capital corresponding to an employment share of $2E$ (the remaining employment is proportionally removed from other firms so that total employment remains constant). The labour productivity of this technology is drawn uniformly from the range $[(1-b)A,(1+b)A]$, where A is the unweighted mean value of labour productivity of all the firms in the economy, and b is a parameter. The values for h and γ are (uniformly) drawn from the range existing in the economy at the time of entry.

2.3. Firm-Strategies for Innovation

In Sections (a) and (b) we have outlined the system whereby innovating firms generate technical change and undergo selection in a closed economy model as a function of their R&D strategy parameters γ. Learning now enters the picture in the form of two "genetic" operators: mutation and imitation. With probability Π each decision period, which is set exogenously and equal for all firms, a firm will draw from a normal distribution and alter one or both of its strategy-parameters γ within the admissible range [0,1] (mutation). Given that mutation occurs, each possibility (change either one or both parameters) occurs with equal probability:

$$\begin{aligned} \gamma_{1it} &= Min(1, Max(\gamma_{1it-1}+\varepsilon, 0)), \quad \varepsilon \sim N(0,s), \ or \\ \gamma_{2it} &= Min(1, Max(\gamma_{2it-1}+\varepsilon, 0)), \quad \varepsilon \sim N(0,s), \ or \\ \gamma_{lit} &= Min(1, Max(\gamma_{lit-1}+\varepsilon_l, 0)), \quad \varepsilon_l \sim N(0,s), \quad l=1,2. \end{aligned} \tag{11}$$

With variable probability Π^c_i the firm simply imitates the strategy of another firm. Again, given that imitation occurs, each possibility (imitate either one or both parameters) occurs with equal probability:

$$\begin{aligned} \gamma_{1it} &= \gamma_{1jt-1}, \ j(\neq i) \in [1..q]_i, \ or \\ \gamma_{2it} &= \gamma_{2jt-1}, \ j(\neq i) \in [1..q]_i, \ or \\ \gamma_{lit} &= \gamma_{ljt-1}, \ j(\neq i) \in [1..q]_i, \ l=1,2. \end{aligned} \tag{12}$$

The imitation probability is partly endogenous to reflect satisficing behaviour. Only firms with unsatisfactory rates of profit with respect to economy leaders will choose or be forced (for example by their stockholders or by hostile takeovers) to adopt the strategy of a competitor:

$$\Pi_i^c = \mu\left(1 - \frac{y_i - y_{min}}{y_{max} - y_{min}}\right). \tag{13}$$

y_i is the firm's rate of expansion of physical capital (defined as $min(r_i - \gamma_{2i}/c, (1-\gamma_i)r_i - \gamma_{2i}/c))$, y_{max} and y_{min} are the maximum and minimum values of y in the sample, and μ is the (exogenously determined) maximum imitation probability. Thus, the more profitable a firm is, the less likely it will change its strategy by imitating another firm. The most profitable firm has an imitation probability equal to zero; the least profitable the maximum probability μ. Once a firm has decided to imitate, it selects a firm to imitate randomly from the industry with weight equal to the target firm's market share in output. If neither imitation nor mutation occur, the firm simply retains its strategy from the previous period.

3. The Emergence of Stable Firm Behaviour

The model has been implemented to run on both MS DOS and Unix computers. To make the solution as time-step invariant as possible, the selection mechanism, which is basically a system of differential equations, is solved using a fixed-step, fourth-order Runge-Kutta algorithm. The innovation decisions are executed during each computational step (using Poisson arrival rates scaled by the computation time step), and when an innovation is made, the corresponding changes in initial conditions, number of equations, and coefficients are made for the next step. Mutation and imitation are only performed at fixed intervals of one "year", which may be many times the step employed in the Runge-Kutta algorithm.

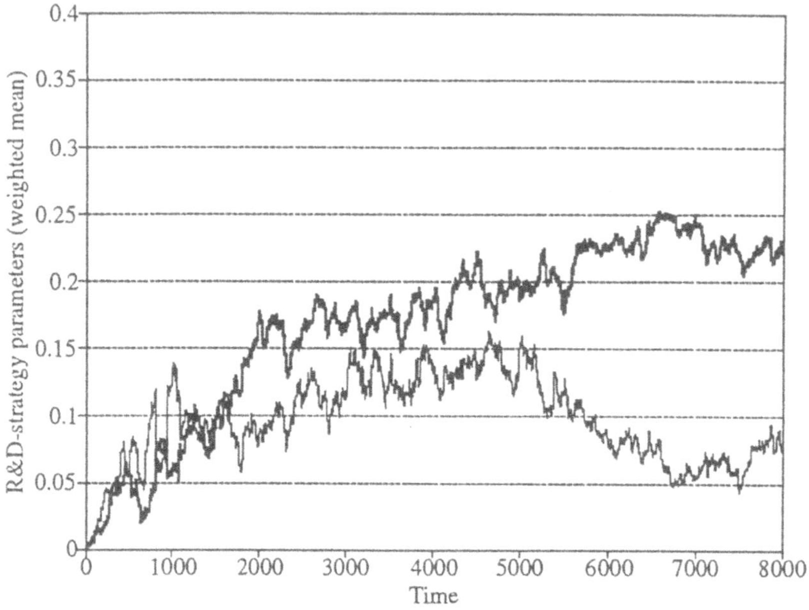

Figure 1. Time paths of market share-weighted-strategy parameters in a spontaneous generation run (50 firms, $\tau = 0.04$). The light line is γ_1, the heavy line is γ_2.

Figure 1 displays the market-share-weighted values of the two strategy parameters for a typical run over 8000 years. Starting from zero values of R&D and an economy in stasis, the firms rapidly discover R&D as a useful activity, and converge to a situation in which both R&D-strategy parameters have positive mean values. After year 5000, however, a new stage sets in, where strategy parameter 1 gradually falls towards zero, and the value of parameter 2 is increasing to a value slightly above 0.2. Figure 2 shows the time paths of the rate of technical change and the Herfindahl concentration index[2] for the same run. Viewed as a process in historical time and not just as out-of-equilibrium transient, this figure recapitulates a piece of virtual economic history. The economy starts off with no R&D and an essentially vanishing rate of technical change. Within this regime the rate of market concentration is quite high, although the identity of the near monopolist changes at almost regular intervals, as indicated by the breaks in the level of concentration. As the γ's rise with time and with them the overall rate of technical change, this market regime breaks down. It is replaced by low levels of concentration and

[2] This is defined as $H = \Sigma f_i^2$, where f_i is the market share of the ith firm. It ranges from $1/n$, for n equally sized firms, to 1, for complete monopoly.

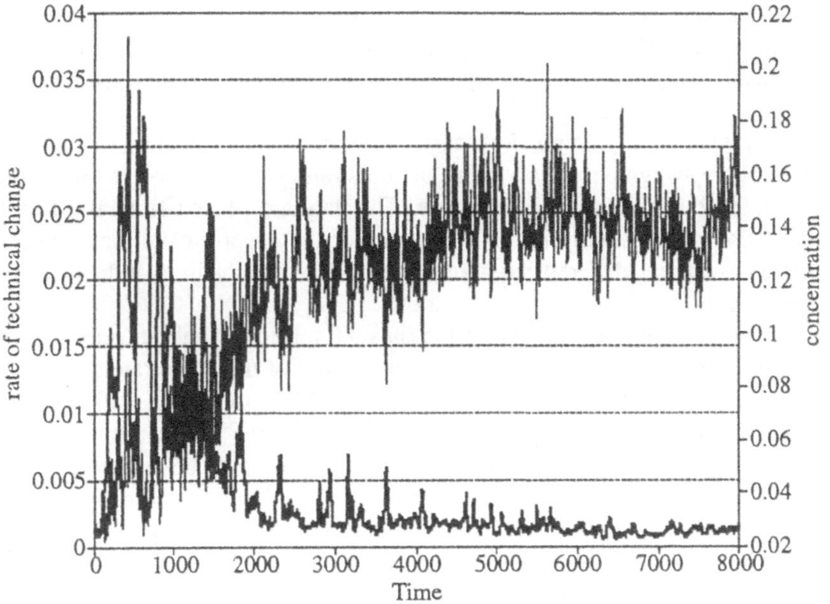

Figure 2. Time paths of rate of technical change (light line) and Herfindahl index of concentration (heavy line) for the same run as in Figure 5.

considerable market turnover.

We thus see that, despite the relatively low demands the model makes on rational behaviour of firms, endogenous growth emerges. Collective learning by the firm population leads to a situation in which both technical change and market structure evolve endogenously as a function of (average) R&D behaviour.

However, the question arises how unique the results from the single run in Figures 1 and 2 are? In order to provide a useful interpretation of economic development and growth, one would want to have a model that displays some general outcomes, rather than just random realizations of a wide spectrum of outcomes. In order to investigate the properties of the model in this respect, we have repeated the simulations many times, with different sequences of random numbers, and with different parameter constellations, and investigate whether or not some common patterns exist between runs.

The main feature of the model we will investigate with this method is the existence and nature of an 'evolutionary attractor' in the dynamics, i.e., whether a 'stable' configuration of firm R&D strategies exists to which our artificial economy will converge from particular classes of initial conditions. We have initialized the system in two ways: first in a 'grapeshot' mode we term random generation in which the initial γ's are drawn from a uniform distribution over [0,1] and [0,0.2] (respectively for γ_1 and γ_2); and second, in a 'spontaneous generation' mode in which all initial γ's are set to zero. We present the results of these experiments by means of density plots made on the basis of 3-dimensional histograms of the two γ's. On the horizontal axis we plot the experimental parameter that is being varied through different simulation runs (A or μ). The (market share weighted) mean value of the strategy parameter over the firms in each run is shown on the vertical axis. The data are pooled from the last 1000 years of five simulation runs for each value of the experimental parameter, each generated with a different random seed. Darker shading indicates higher frequencies.

In Figure 3, we plot the results for the runs initialized by random generation. The figure shows clearly that the converging behaviour of the two strategy parameters is quite different. Parameter 1 (the targeted R&D to profits ratio) does not converge very clearly, except for higher values of the innovation slope, when relatively high frequencies are found at values near zero. Parameter 2 targeting R&D to sales shows a more tight convergence, although there are still high frequencies near zero (the white band between the horizontal axis and the attractor is quite narrow). Thus, firms show a tendency to select a relatively tight range of values for parameter 2, while parameter 1 tends to drift or, if anything, go to zero. Summarizing, firms seem to display a tendency to select tightly defined strategies based upon parameter 2 and indifference to parameter 1.

Figure 4 shows corresponding results for the case of spontaneous generation, i.e., a situation in which firms have to discover R&D as an activity. In this case, the economy starts out in a stagnant phase, with no intentional technical progress. As firms explore the strategy space by mutation and imitation, they may (or may not) find R&D a useful activity. The density plots show that in this case, the evolutionary attractor is much more clearly defined. The type 1 strategy parameter remains at values near zero (in our interpretation, the positive values found are largely attributable to random 'evolutionary' noise). The type 2 strategy parameter, however, shows a well-defined peak significantly distant from zero, as indicated by the white space bordering it from below.

This behaviour of the system can be interpreted as a particular form of lock-in or path dependency. When the system is started 'clean', without any form of 'commitment' to any type of R&D-strategy, it will select a much more unambiguous evolutionary attractor than in the random generation case. This is not the case when only the type 1 strategy parameter is employed (compare Silverberg and Verspagen 1994a,b). There the asymptotic steady states of the two initializations are identical.

For a logistic innovation function (eq. 6) we obtain similar patterns from the histograms over innovation opportunity (Figure 5). In contrast to the linear case, however, the steady-state value of parameter 2 does seem to decline somewhat with increasing technological opportunity. What is also remarkable is the sudden collapse of the technological regime below values of A of about 40. The steady-state values of parameter 2, in the range 20—30%, are also higher than in the linear case.

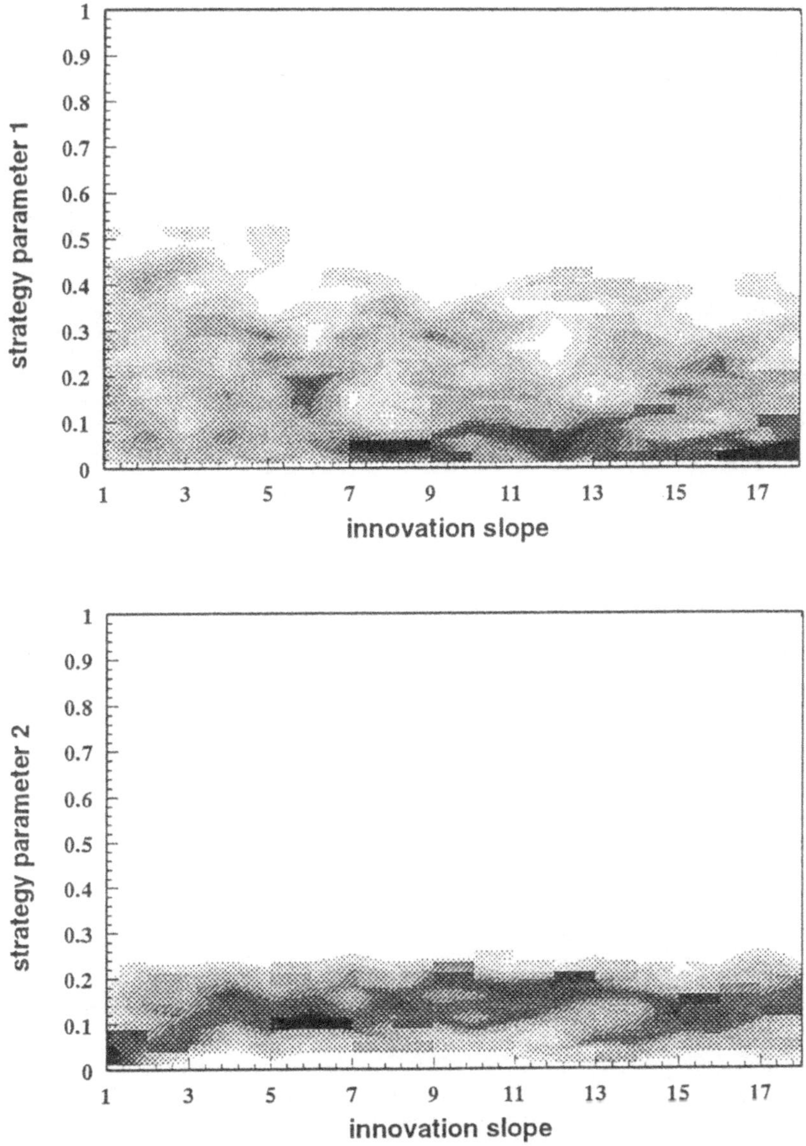

Figure 3. Histograms of strategy parameters from pooled data of five runs per value, last 1000 years of 8000 year runs (random generation), for a linear innovation function.

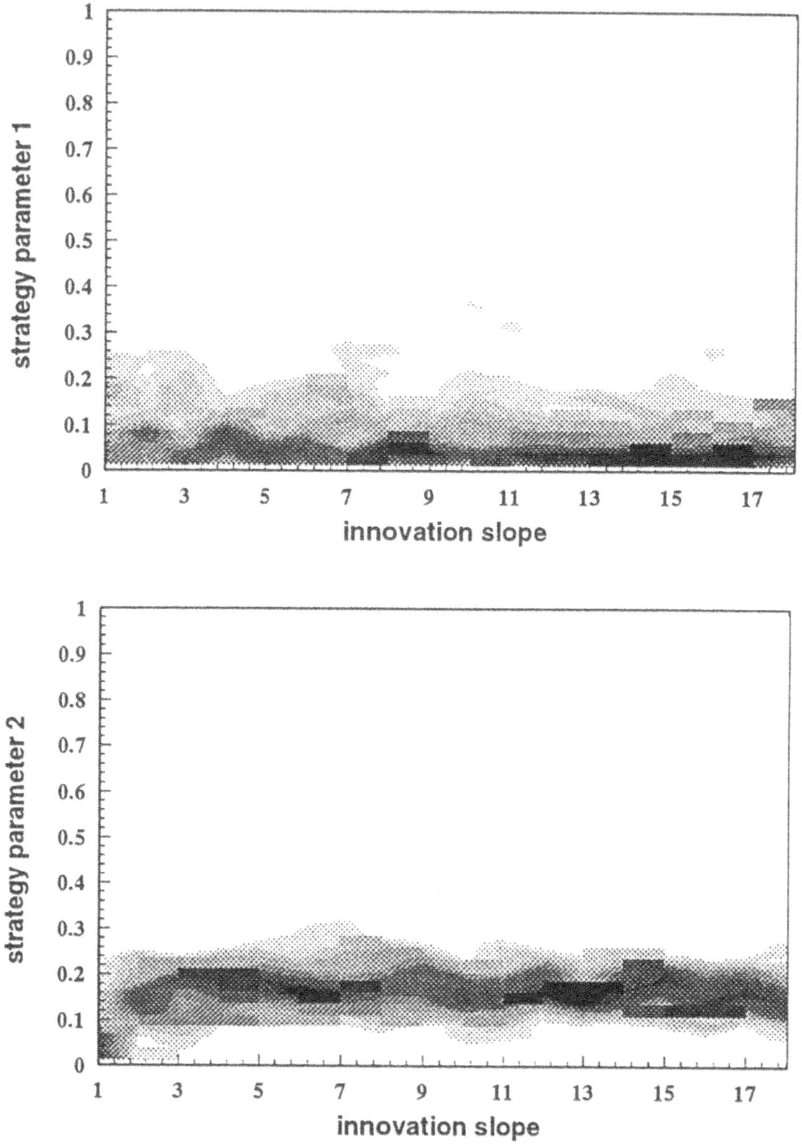

Figure 4. Histograms of strategy parameters from pooled data of five runs per value, last 1000 years of 8000 year runs (spontaneous generation), for a linear innovation function.

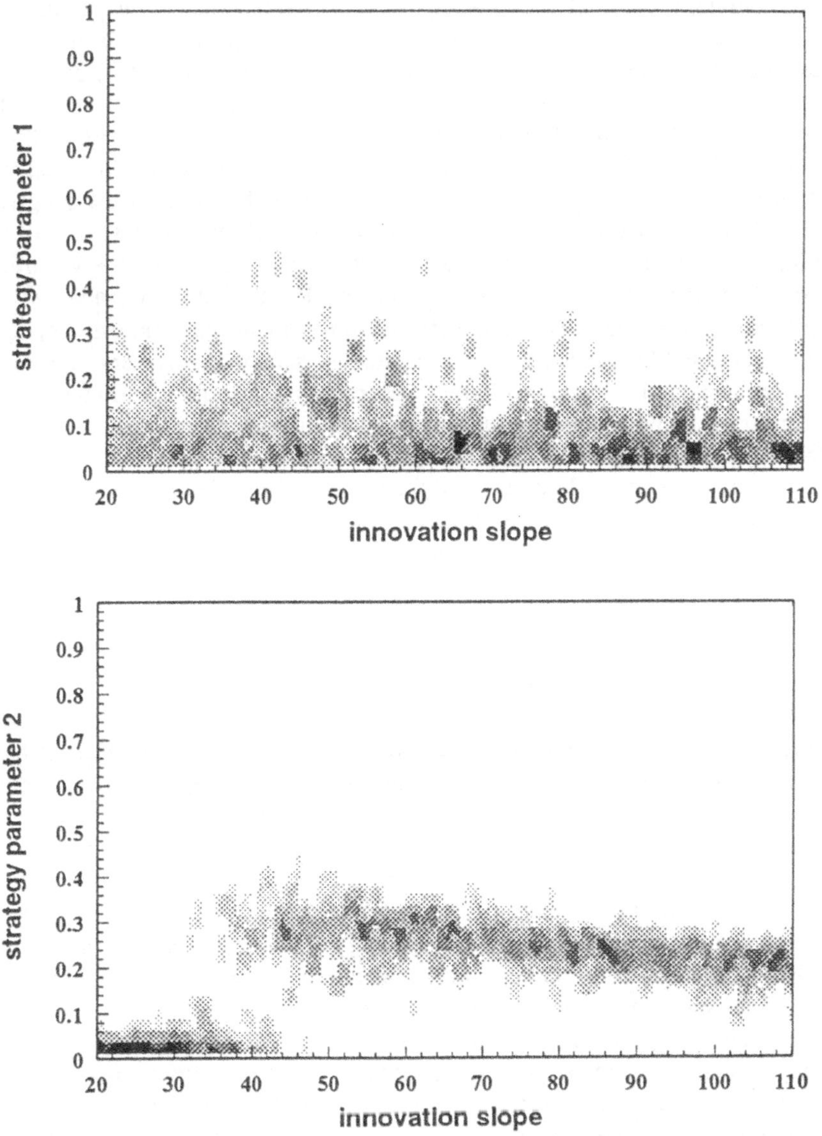

Figure 5. Histograms of strategy parameters from pooled data of five runs per value, last 1000 years of 8000 year runs (spontaneous generation), for a logistic innovation function.

Why is strategy parameter 2 subject to positive selection, while parameter 1 displays either drift or is constrained to zero? Our interpretation is that R&D comes to be regarded as a 'core' business activity in the model, for, due to the 'Goodwin' business cycles of the underlying economy, profits are more variable than sales. Thus, firms which base their R&D expenditures upon profits will have more fluctuating R&D stocks than firms which base their R&D on sales. The selection environment seems to favour the latter firms because, in the long run, their R&D behaviour provides a more reliable stream of innovations.

We have also begun to investigate how the structure of the evolutionary learning process affects the outcomes of these experiments. Recall that the variables Π and μ, representing the probability of mutation and imitation, are exogenously imposed. We have compiled histograms for the two strategy parameters by varying each of these rates separately. Figure 6 shows the results for mutation, Figure 7 for imitation, for runs with $A = 10$ and random generation initial conditions. Varying the mutation probability does not change the picture in any essential way. In contrast, increasing the ceiling on the imitation probability leads to a progressive collapse of γ_2 selection. If firms imitate each other too strongly, they become involved in an evolutionary game of musical chairs, and no nontrivial strategy is able to establish itself.

4. Summary and Conclusions

We have presented an evolutionary model in which boundedly rational firms have to compete on the marketplace by choosing an R&D strategy. Our simulation results suggest that, given the choice between two different strategies, firms tend to choose the one in which R&D does not vary with market-wide fluctuations in profitability. Instead, firms which base their R&D activities on the more constant stream of sales tend to be selected. This leads to an evolutionary stable state in which all firms adopt the same R&D strategy. However, for low innovation possibility curves, or for very high imitation rates, this evolutionary stable state breaks down, and firms tend to adopt zero R&D strategies.

These results suggest that although firms may not be able to optimize their decisions, as is assumed by mainstream economic theory, there are also clear differences in the outcomes of various 'rules of thumb'(or 'routines') applied by firms acting under bounded rationality. The selection mechanism, although modelled in a stylized way, provides an explanation of why some of these routines are more common than others, and also of why relatively stable states of the economy may occur on the macro-level. The imitation rate seems to be a crucial parameter in this evolutionary process.

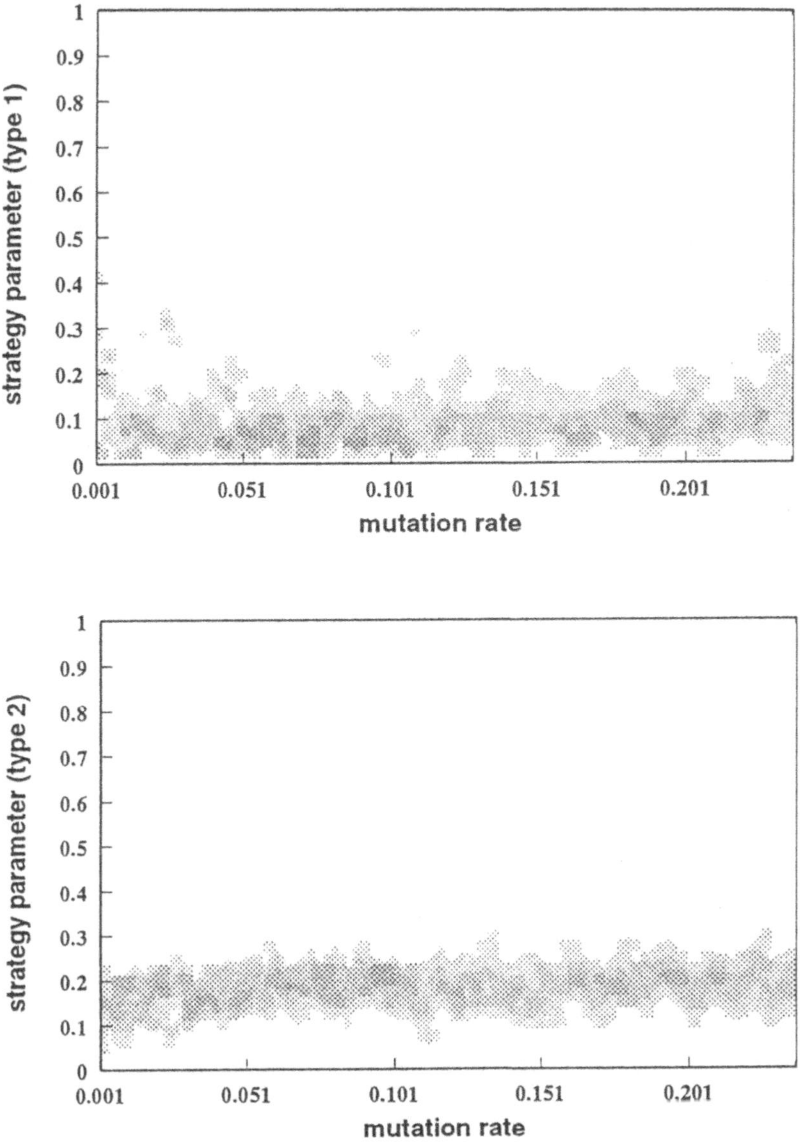

Figure 6. Histograms of strategy parameters for varying rates of the mutation probability (A = 10).

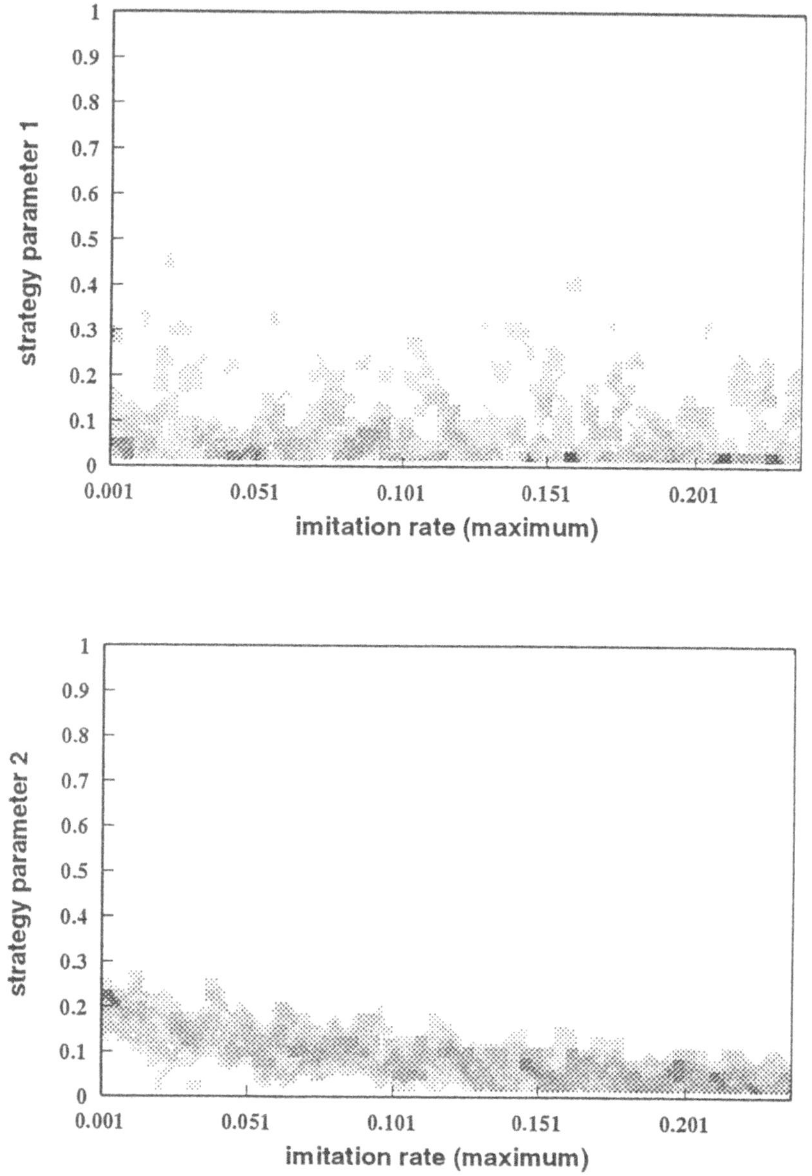

Figure 7. Histogram of strategy parameter for varying rates of the maximum imitation parameter (A = 10).

5. Appendix

A summary of the parameters and the values employed in the runs analyzed in the paper is presented below.

$q = 10$	number of firms
$m = 0.9$	parameters of the Phillips curve eq. 1
$n = 1$	
$\alpha = 1$	Soete-Turner coefficient eq. 2
γ (endogenous)	R&D/investment ratio in eq. 2
$c = 3$	capital-output ratio
$\sigma = 0$	rate of physical depreciation in eqs. 2 and 3
$\beta = 0.01$	rate of growth of labour force eq. 3
$\delta = 1$	ratio of productivity in goods and R&D sectors
$\tau = 0.06$	proportional jump in labour productivity eq. 4
A (variable)	innovation slope in eq. 5
$\rho_{min} = 0.01$	autonomous rate of innovation eq. 5
ϕ_1 (variable)	type 1 spillover coefficient in eq. 7
ϕ_2 (variable)	type 2 spillover coefficient in eq. 7
$L = 5$	lag for R&D moving average eq. 8
$\kappa = 4$	catch-up parameter eq. 10
$\Pi = 0.02$	mutation probability eq. 11
$s = 0.02$	standard deviation of mutation step size eq. 11
$\mu = 0.02$	maximum imitation probability eq. 12
$E = 0.005$	exit level in employment share
$b = 0.1$	labour productivity bandwidth for entrants

6. References

1. Aghion, P. and Howitt, P., 1992, *A Model of Growth through Creative Destruction*, Econometrica, **60:** 323-351.
2. Arthur, W.B., 1991, *Designing Economic Agents that Act Like Human Agents: A Behavioral Approach to Bounded Rationality*, American Economic Review. Papers and Proceedings, **81:** 353-359.
3. Cohen, W.M. and Levinthal, D.A., 1989, "Innovation and Learning: The Two Faces of R&D", *Economic Journal,* **99:** 569-596.
4. Goodwin, R.M., 1967, *A Growth Cycle*, in C.H. Feinstein, (ed), *Socialism, Capitalism and Economic Growth,* London: Macmillan.
5. Lane, D.A., 1993, *Artificial Worlds and Economics. Parts 1 and 2*, Journal of Evolutionary Economics, **3:** 89-108, 177-197.
6. Langton, C.G., (ed), 1989, *Artificial Life,* Redwood City, CA: Addison-Wesley.
7. Langton, C.G., Taylor, C., Farmer, J. D. and Rasmussen, S., (eds), 1992, *Artificial Life II,* Redwood City, CA: Addison-Wesley.
8. Nelson, R.R., 1990, "What is Public and What is Private about Technology?", Berkeley: CCC Working Paper No. 90-9.
9. Nelson, R.R. and Winter, S.G., 1982, *An Evolutionary Theory of Economic Change,* Cambridge MA: The Belknap Press of Harvard University Press.
11. Romer, P.M., 1990, *Endogenous Technological Change*, Journal of Political Economy, **98:** 71-102.
12. Silverberg, G., 1984, "Embodied Technical Progress in a Dynamic Economic Model: the Self-Organization Paradigm", in *Nonlinear Models of Fluctuating Growth*, ed. R. Goodwin, M. Krüger, and A. Vercelli, Berlin, Heidelberg, New York: Springer Verlag.
13. Silverberg, G. and Lehnert, D., 1993, "Long Waves and 'Evolutionary Chaos' in a Simple Schumpeterian Model of Embodied Technical Change", *Structural Change and Economic Dynamics,* **4**: 9-37.
14. Silverberg, G. and Verspagen, B., 1994a, "Learning, Innovation and Economic Growth: A Long-Run Model of Industrial Dynamics", *Industrial and Corporate Change,* **3**: 199-223.
15. Silverberg, G. and Verspagen, B., 1994b, "Collective Learning, Innovation and Growth in a Boundedly Rational, Evolutionary World", *Journal of Evolutionary Economics,* **4**: 207-226.
14. Simon, H.A., 1986a, *Rationality in Psychology and Economics*, in Hogarth, R.M. and Reder, M.W. (eds), *The Behavioral Foundations of Economic Theory,* special issue of *The Journal of Economics*, **59**: 209-224.
15. Simon, H.A., 1986b, *On the Behavioral and Rational Foundations of Economic Dynamics*, in R.H. Day and G. Eliasson (eds), *The Dynamics of Market Economies*, Amsterdam: North Holland.
16. Soete, L. and Turner, R., 1984, *Technology Diffusion and the Rate of Technical Change*, Economic Journal, **94**: 612-623.

Improving Foreign Investment Structureto Promote Industrial Structure Optimization

Wan Dan and Hui Xiaofeng

School of Management, Harbin Institute of Technology, Harbin 150001,China

Abstract. The adjustment of industrial structure is the key in transforming domestic-oriented economy to export-oriented economy and consequently the key in the national economic development. Improving foreign investment structure can help optimize a country's industrial structure. Having described the important role and pointing out existing problems in foreign investment in our national economy, this paper analyzes the possible reasons affecting the rationalization of foreign investment and goes further to propose some feasible measures to improve foreign investment structure so as to optimize our industrial structure.

1 Introduction

Since opening to the outside world in 1978, China has made great achievements in acquiring direct foreign in vestment which has given impetus to the adjustment of our industrial structure. But meanwhile, we are in a blind and passive position in that we have not combined foreign investment with optimization of industrial structure, and many foreign investment projects are not in line with the adjustment of our industrial structure. We shall probe into foreign investment and the rationalization of industrial structure in this paper.

2 The Industrial Structure and Foreign Investment

The industrial structure refers to a certain proportion of all economic resources including labor and material labor distributed among and inside of various departments of the national economy. It is a major in indicator of economic development of a country and reflects the focal points of the country's economic development, the division patterns of labor in society as well as the distribution of all productive factors among industries. Facts show that economic development in various countries has experienced transition in industrial structures. The adjustment of industrial structure is the key to changing domestic-oriented economy to export-oriented economy. China is at present undergoing the adjustment of industrial structure. Acquiring foreign investment will be one of the important methods in the adjustment.

For years, foreign investment in China has played an important role in our industrial structure.

A. The investment of foreign capital in such strategically important departments as energy, transportation and agriculture, in light industrial departments, textiles, foodstuffs and pharmaceutics as well as in high-techrelated industries as metallurgical machinery, electronics and chemical industry has helped promote the renewal of products in these industries and has enlarged production capacity of new products.

B. Some production projects with foreign capital, especially those capital-intensive and technology-intensive projects, have given impetus to the establishment of some new industries, thus making our industrial structure tend toward completion.

C. The investment in the third industry by foreigners has promoted the development of service industry such as tourist hotels, ect. It has played an important role in improving investment environment.

3 Irrationality in Foreign Investment Structure and The Reasons

3.1 Irrationality in Foreign Investment Structure

A. Less investment in the national critical industries as energy, communications and agriculture than in manufacturing industries as light industry, textiles, pharmaceutics, electronics and mechanics. According to statistics, from 1985 to 1990, foreign investment in construction materials, metallurgy, power, chemical industry and oil was less than one fourth in total investment. Too much foreign investment in manufacturing industries aggravates the shortage problem of energy resources and raw materials.On the other hand, these enterprises cannot work to full capacity due to the shortage of raw materials and energy resources.

B. Too much foreign investment in the third industry. According to statistics, from 1985-1990, in the total contract amount of foreign investment, investment in the first and second industries only amounted to 45 percent, where as the third industry received 55 percent Enterprises with foreign capital in the third industry can neither acquire advanced manufacturing technology nor enlarge export to get foreign exchange although it is beneficial to our development of tourism and improvement in investment environment.

C. Little investment in enterprises with advanced technology producing export products and substituting imports. This situation provides export-oriented economic department with insufficient investments, which makes their technology slow in development.

D. Dispersed investment and small scale production makes it impossible to make use of economy of scale. The success of some newly industrialized countries in acquiring foreign capital lies in their creation of corresponding policies in different development phases to direct foreign investment and made it in line with local development. But the foreign investment acquired in our light industries, foodstuffs, drinks and plastic products occupies a great proportion, whereas the rest of investment disperses in more than ten industries. It is disadvantageous to make the most of foreign investment to enhance technical levels in our backward departments and industries. Besides, small-scale production cannot get economy of scale. Thus, it is impossible to lower production costs, improve productivity or play the role of labor and resources.

3.2 Reasons of Affecting Irrationality of Foreign Investment

A. Contrary goals of investment from Chinese and foreign sides. As far as markets are concerned, the goal of acquiring foreign investment for the Chinese side is to increase product competitiveness and launch them into the world market. On the contrary, the goal of foreign investors is to enter into the Chinese market. As to technology transfer, the Chinese side wants to get advanced technology and capital-intensive as well as technology-intensive projects. But for the purpose of maintaining their technical advantages and control of the market, foreign investors are reluctant to invest advanced technology. As a result, foreign investment mainly goes to labor-intensive industries. Additionally, we wish that foreign investment went to weak links in our national economy as well as some advanced industrial projects so as to rationalize the whole industrial structure, whereas foreign investors prefer those projects with little investment and quick return on investment.

B. Influence of investment environment. In recent years, our government has done plenty of work to improve investment environment for foreigners. But there are still many defects restricting the rationalization of foreign investment, for instance, financial support, energy supply, etc. Besides, our lack of managerial and technical talents as well as low quality of labor all become obstacles for foreign investment going to capital and technology intensive industries. Additionally, the horizontal conveyance system in related industries is not complete and cannot effectively be combined with capital and labor intensive projects with foreign investment.

C. Unfavorable macroscopic control policies. Our policies of acquiring foreign investment are favorable to cities along the seaside rather than to capital and technology intensive industries Besides, our price system is not rational in that prices of raw materials and energy resources are rather low which makes foreign investors unwilling to invest in these industries with low profits, large input and long ROI. Furthermore, we have not actually made a program for attracting foreign direct investment. It is not beneficial to adjust and optimize industrial structures.

4 Measures of Improving Foreign Investment Structure

A. Foreign investment should be guided in accordance with our national industrial policies so as to hasten the development and construction of such infrastructure and basic industries as communications and transportation, energy resources, raw materials and water conservancy facilities. Mechanics, electronics, oil and chemical industry, automobile manufacturing and civil engineering and those industries that we should pay special attention to. Technical transformation in enterprises should be quickened, and investment fields should be enlarged to include finance and insurance, accounting, commerce and transportation. Foreign investment in projects with large investment scale and high technical levels should be encouraged and given favorable terms. The stress of attracting foreign investment should gradually move from capital funds to advanced technical equipment and high-tech products.

B. Working out preferential policies to different industries so as to direct foreign investment to some weak links as well as some mainstay and newly developed industries as communications, transportation and telecommunications.

In our preferential policies, export orientation and area preference are taken into consideration; technology is also given favorable terms. However, in actual practice, export proportion is generally taken as a main factor of approval, thus making basic industries, infrastructure and high-tech industries which are in urgent need of construction cannot not get more preferential treatment due to difficulties in exporting their products and temporary unbalance of foreign exchange. Therefore, we should emphasize the development of interior mainstay industries and give even more preferential treatment to projects in major national industries in interior areas. A series of preferential treatments should be given to foreign investment projects which are in accordance with our focal points of acquiring foreign investment as well as being beneficial to the adjustment of industrial structure. The stress of policies should gradually transfer from area preference to industry preference.

C. Strengthening Macroscopic Management and Improving Investment Environment

To improve foreign investment structure, we should not only explicitly stipulate the focal points of acquiring foreign investment and revise corresponding policies, but also bring the industrial plan and program of acquiring foreign investment into the national and local economic development so as to strengthen project management and enhance the quality of utilizing foreign investment.

As far as investment environment is concerned, we should continue to improve investment environment and conditions from aspects of infrastructure construction, management and service for the purpose of creating a comfortable environment for foreign investors to carry out production and management according to international standards and practice.

Furthermore, at the time of acquiring foreign investment and improving investment structure, we should also endeavor to acquire investment form multiple sources. Apart from developing cooperation with HongKong, Singapore, ROK, Taiwan and Southeast Asia, we should also make greater efforts in developing cooperation with USA, Japan, Canada, Australia, Western Europe as well as the third world countries. In sum, strengthening macroscopic management of foreign investment, restricting investment in non-productive manufacturing projects and avoiding repeated importation is in accordance with the requirements of optimizing industrial structure.

References

Yangzhi (1985): *Introduction to Industrial Economics*, China People's University press

Liuxing and Gu Yuansheng (1994): On the Influence of Utilizing Foreign Investment to Our Technical Progress, *International Trade Journal*

Daqiang (1993): New Measures for Reforms of China's Planned Investment System, *Export-Oriented Economy*

Shi Dongming (1994): Utilizing Foreign Investment and Optimizing Industrial Structure, *Intertrade*, 4

Guangdong's Financial Policy in Transformation to a Matured Market Economy

Huang Qiang

Finance Department, Jinan University
Shipai, Guangzhou 510632, P.R.China

Abstract. Guangdong is the first province to call for a market economy and engage in the price reform. While China is shifting from a planned economy to a market economy, Guangdong is already a market economy at large. However, Guangdong's goal is to catch up with the Four Little Dragons (Hongkong, Singapore, Taiwan & South Korea) in Asia, thus Guangdong plans to improve the market economy.

What is a matured market economy? A matured market economy requires a sound market mechanism with four conditions; (1) the enterprise has a hard budgeting restraint; (2) the economy has some idle resources; (3) there are updated transportation and communication networks for production factors to move liberally; (4) there is only one price for one commodity or service and the price reflects its value in relationship to supply and demand. A matured market economy also requires a complete market system with many uniform liberal and coexistent diversified markets.

The difficult points for Guangdong to transform into a matured market economy lie in: (1)the sluggishly developed financial market shown in the interbank loans, foreign exchange transactions and securities transactions; (2)backward transportation and communication facilities in terms of the present demand for their quantity and quality; (3)state enterprises with soft budgeting restraint.

The financial policies that Guangdong should pursue are: (1)to ease the credit quota restraint or to allocate separate credit quotas for Guangdong like Shanghai and Shenzhen; (2)to establish the Southern China financial center engaging in funds settlement, foreign exchange transactions, securities transactions and offshore deposits and loans; (3)to retain the rights to adjust interest rates to a certain extent like Shenzhen and Wenzhou.

In a word, Guangdong has a lot to do to catch up with the four Little Dragons. To accomplish this there needs more liberal thought and more flexible policies.

1 The Financial Policy Adaptable to a Matured Market Economy

Financial Liberalization. There are many examples of this, such as: removal of interest rate ceilings, cancellation of credit quotas and the break up of the distinction in range of business. In America, the Act of Deregulation on Depository institutions and Monetary Control in 1980 and the Ann-Saint Germaine Act in 1982 brought forth a financial revolution, when the interest rate ceilings were removed and the range of business was broadened. In 1992, the Japanese Congress passed an act of financial reforms which terminated the segregation between short-term finance and long-term finance and the segregation between securities industry and banking industry. In GATT's Uraguay Round, a multi-party agreement on service trade was reached, which required more liberalization and openness in a country's banking and insurance industry.

Asset Securitization. About 90% of Chinese banks' assets are bank loans, which enhance the risks and hinder the steps to meet with international standards. Contrary to this, many western banks' assets take the form of securities.

Business Diversification and Globazation. At present, there is a trend to increase off-sheet business such as trust, leasing, guarantee and consultation and to promote activities abroad. Up to 50% of profits of American large banks come from oversees business.

Legislation in Financial Management. A sound financial management of banks can be realized frequently by abiding by a complete set of laws and regulations. For example, the Basle Agreement in 1988 has largely reduced the credit risks for banks.

2 Characteristics of Guangdong's Present Economy and Finance

Investment Pull. Much of the growth is caused by increase of fixed asset investment (with the yearly increase of 76.6% and 66% in the last respective two years). The proportion of heavy industry increase in industrial out put increase in 1993 has increased 2 percentage points from the previous year.

Structural Bottleneck. While industrial output increased 30% last year, electricity output and cargo transportation increased 18% and 5 respectively, which fell far behind their demands. A lot of important materials like steel and coal cannot be brought in and their prices remain high. In order to realize modernization, in 20 years the funds to be put in basic facilities amount to 8 trillion yuan, in which 3.8 trillion must be raised from the financial market.

Openness of the Economy. The export proportion in Guangdong's GDP (42.8% in 1991 and 49% in 1993) is over 40%, ranking first in the country, let alone the proportion of import & export in GDP. In reality, Guangdong's export contributes to 1/3 of the country's total.

Overwhelming Market Orientation. All of Guangdong's consumer goods and 98% of capital goods are subject to market readjustment. The provincial government adopts a lassez-faire policy while municipalities and counties play the major roles. It is believed that concentration of power means concentration of contradictions.

Capital Reliance on Hongkong. According to the Statistics Bureau, 1/3 of fixed asset investment in Guangdong relies on introduction of foreign capital, 2/3 of which comes from Hongkong.

Stagnant Financial Reforms. More than half of the funds for capital investment should be raised from the financial market, yet the present financial system hinders economic expansion. When specialized banks are still subject to credit quotas and interest rate control, they have to underwrite a large number of treasury bills and financial bonds of policy related banks, the excess reserve rate of deposits for them thus may decrease to below 4%. Moreover, some enterprises' inventories increase and sales income cannot be realized at once, yet they keep borrowing working capital credit for fixed asset investment. Meanwhile, banks don't conduct strict supervision and often make loans subjectively. Last year, however, business deposits fluctuated up and down, and savings deposits are half withdrawable at demand.

3 Suggested Financial Policies in the Transition Period

As to monetary policy, the central bank's branch should encourage and make use of special deposits and some of specialized bank's deposits in the central bank. If credit quotas are to be kept, Guangdong should ask for separate credit quotas like Shanghai and Shenzhen. While deregulating the rules on financial market the central bank's branch should rationalize and systemize behavior and operations of financial institutions.

As to savings and credit policies, there are several things to be done: (1) to enlarge the interest rat floating range and set up a normal interest rat level; (2)to create more liquid financial instruments and absorb savings as much as possible; (3) to forbid time deposits to be withdrawn without notice at the cost of giving up time deposits interest; (4) to promote securitization of bank assets and carry out ratio management of assets and liabilities; (5)to separate long-term finance from short-term finance to ensure safety and order; (6)to encourage banks to invest in industries and diversify their business; (7) to accelerate the settlement system reform and narrow the scope for use of cash.

As to foreign policy, the following measures can be considered: (1) to establish a foreign exchange swap center for businesses; (2) to set up an offshore financial market where foreign banks may enter liberally and operate under low income tax rates; (3) to actively realize the liberal convertibility of RMB with foreign exchange under current account; (4) to issue foreign exchange denominated bonds and depository receipts; (5) to introduce foreign capital in the form of BOT so as to introduce advance management experience and a large amounts of capital; (6) to let big companies set up foreign subsidiaries to raise more funds for domestic constructions.

Reference

China Society for Finance and Banking, *Almanac of China's Finance and Banking 1990*, Editorial Department of Almanac of China's Finance and Banking, 221-223.

Guangdong Statistics Yearbook, China Statistics Press, 385.

Guo Xiaoyu (1994): Market Economy Is the Key, *Asian Pacific Economic Times*, June 12th

Jinzhong (1994): *More Achievements of Efficient and Rapid Growth*, January, Guangdong Finance and Banking

History and Prospects of Money and Credit, March of 1994, Guangdong Finance and Banking,

Technological substitution effects with ISIS, a spatial, inter-sectoral nonlinear dynamic model

Rolando Guzzi , Michèle Sanglier,

Instituts Internationaux de Physique et de Chimie fondés par E. Solvay - U.L.B., Campus Plaine CP231, Bvd du Triomphe - Bruxelles 1050 - Belgium
rguzzi@ulb.ac.be , msanglie@ulb.ac.be

Abstract - At the microscopic level, an agent (household or firm) will order the necessary inputs according to its current production and equipment technology in order to execute a chosen production and investment, and this generates a flow of orders which will be dispatched to available suppliers according to their relative economic and spatial attractiveness. These new orders increase each agent's backlog of orders, which are subsequently decreased by its own production, itself monitored by the backlog of orders. The production capacity, a multiple of the capital stock, is adjusted through investments according to the backlog of orders and the average sectoral profit. The price is influenced by the ratio of new orders to the capacity of production and the production technology is slowly modified according to changing relative costs of inputs and innovations in the sector. Migrations of persons are accounted for, but not migrations of capital. These microscopic behaviours and interactions have only been validated at the macroscopic level for Germany ('75-'89) with an error range of about 10% around observations. We then carried out a sensitivity analysis for the parameter controlling price elasticity of technological change concerning the labour factor. This enabled us to assess threshold levels where positive microscopic reactions from producers and negative microscopic reactions from consumers due to macroscopic losses of purchasing power start to compensate each other in response to decreases of labour intensity.

1. Introduction

Our long term goal is to provide decision makers with new tools enabling them to analyse and design socio-economic reforms, not just incremental changes on traditional policy variables. The requirements for such tools are much more demanding than those for traditional models : reliable knowledge of transition paths, reliable global accounting and aggregation procedures, validated micro-social behaviours, taking into account their interaction with the macro level. Let us examine briefly each of these requirements : non equilibrium, bounded rationality, invariance, globality, continuous time and discrete multi-layered space.

a/ Non equilibrium. - First comes the task to spot under apparent aggregate and average stabilities the sources of possible structural changes, the nonlinear dynamics and feedbacks that operate at the more disaggregated levels, which is what structural reforms are intended for. On the one hand, many empirical studies have shown evidence for non stationarity and for nonlinearity[1] among major economic time series, and on the other hand, the research carried out at our Institutes by Prigogine and Nicolis has strongly established our belief that human society is evolving as a non equilibrium system[2]. In that perspective, we have undertaken the phenomenological[3] modelling of economic evolutions by taking into account interactions between many levels of aggregation, in order to provide behavioural interpretations of the non stationarities observed at the very aggregated levels. Among the many social phenomena witnessing non equilibrium reactions, our ISIS model integrates mathematical representations of the following nonlinearities :

- dynamics of bounded variables, like expenses and purchases which are subject to budget constraints, or spatial or temporal constraints (like purchase mappings restricted to a territory because of protectionism, or to a short time horizon because of prohibitive inflation), or like strict positivity constraints;
- nonlinear coupling of variables because of ratio-like comparisons or competition of effects, or multiplicative co-occurrence and cooperation of effects, like supply and demand interaction about prices, or predation for market resources, or inter-regional and inter-sectoral interdependencies;

---

[1] see for example Hamilton (1989) or Stock (1989)

[2] see Prigogine (1996)

[3] without considering psychological and physiological causes of human behaviour, and thus assuming that each phenomenon is acting on other phenomena as a complete, distinct entity

• birth and decay processes, like innovations and obsolescence in investments;

• perception thresholds, like indifference and over-reactions in investments, migrations;

• imitations, choices and diffusion mechanisms, all highlight the impact of the spatial dimension on the inertia of evolutions, and thus, the importance of the disaggregation problem.

b/ *Bounded rationality.* - As one opens up the modelling of structural change with nonlinear dynamics, one loses the theoretical rationality constraint to have both actions and expectations of all social actors focused on one single target : a stable node or stable focus. We may assume that no one can posses all the necessary information, that everyone has a personal bias or interpretation of the available information, and that our simplified society is in a very remote state from its (current) possible asymptotic states. Now, actors can still be "rational" over a short period by making some reasonable extrapolations (maybe linear, maybe not) and conforming their actions with those, but the attractor of the whole system may be much more complex in its geometry as well as its stability characteristics than a single point, so that people might not be able to perceive fully its characteristics nor its remoteness nor even its existence[4]...

c/ *Invariance.* - The model needs to reach a high level of genericity or invariance across time and space, i.e. it needs to contain very few parameters and these and the equations need to be independent from the variety of structures and situations that ought to be explained with them. For example, one is free to introduce specific, different fiscal policy functions for different regions only if one is not trying to explain and generate fiscal behaviour and patterns with the model. To be more concrete, this kind of validation will happen as our model becomes successfully calibrated to more countries and with increasing disaggregation details.

d/ *Globality.* - This obviously requires that the model be almost entirely endogenous in order to avoid any dependence on non controllable and non reproducible contexts. This is the case with ISIS (all endogenous variables except imports and exports when not used as a world model). The model features six

---

4 even if we assumed that the data corresponding to, say, the middle of our period, would support expectations of convergence to a stationary state, we assume that, because of permanent human intervention, the true system (which we are trying to model) would be transformed in the meantime and so much for its asymptotic states; on these issues, consult Ruelle (1991) , pp 80 - 91

basic differential equations, each of them being multiplied by the number of sectors and spatial points, but only ten behavioural parameters need to be estimated out of dynamic behaviours, and the other structural parameters can be introduced out of generally available statistics concerning the structure of the economy and the land use. The endogenous character of this model is also what enables us to research the stationary states and attractors for the social dynamic under study, and, from there, to draft some probabilities to follow certain transitory paths between initial conditions and attractors.

e/ Continuous time and discrete multi-layered space - If our macro-meso (sectors and regions) validation suggests that a completely disaggregated version of the model might be empirically tested, we nevertheless need to carry out deep field work at the microscopic level under the most extreme situations in order to verify our assumptions about the nonlinear behaviours of agents and their aggregations with density functions. A discrete network of points has been preferred to partial difference equations with respect to space treated as a continuous variable because it would have implicitly ruled out the introduction of preferential agreements among different agents (economic proximity being sometimes more relevant than geographic proximity). Also, a truly dynamic model requires that the variables be integrated over their characteristic time steps, which should be tested a-priori as smaller than the periodicity with which the system is perturbed by exogenous shocks and increased slowly to its upper limit where bahaviours start to diverge. This is the case with ISIS, where we adopted a continuous time dynamic which enables us to research empirically the characteristic times. A usual mistake of dynamic macroeconomic models is to assume a discrete time dynamic, to equate it with the time step of data availability and thus with the time step of the perturbation of the dynamic by exogenous shocks : the dynamic is thus given no time to converge towards its real, asymptotic behaviour, and no scenario analysis obtained from there is therefore totally reliable.

2. The model

In the upcoming calibration exercise of section 4, we have adopted a sectoral aggregation of economic activities in 12 sectors, but any other aggregation is valid as long as it closes the economic circuit by including work and property revenues.

1 MM = metallic manufacturing	7 CH = chemical industry
2 CO = construction	8 OM = other manufacturing
3 AP = active population	9 TR = transportation
4 AG = agriculture	10 MS = market services
5 EN = energy	11 NM = non-market services
6 BA = metallic & other minerals	12 DP = distributed profits

The first two sectors (MM & CO) are the only equipment goods producers, and two non traditional sectors have been added (AP & DP). Sector 3, AP, represents the value in millions of 1975 DM (Deutsche Mark) at constant prices (the standard unit in our model) of working services being offered by the active population, that is, their wages). The active population adapts its size to employment opportunities, as will be seen later. But since we have not yet introduced public spending and taxation, the only revenues accounted for in this model are the ones collected by occupied workers and the ones collected by capital owners. And since we did not consider different economic behaviours for different social categories, the unoccupied active persons will not receive any allocations, since these would have been extracted from workers and owners earnings anyway. Sector 12, DP, represents the distributed profits, under the hypothesis that no reserved profits are kept beyond the strict auto-financing of current investment needs and that no transaction costs nor risk premiums interfere with the allocation of the distributed profits.

In the present formal presentation of the model, we are dealing with a closed global economy divided in *ns* sectors and *nz* regions, but in section 4, we will have to open the economy by introducing imports and exports, since we will then be dealing with a single country, Germany, instead of the whole world.

There are three stock variables[5] :

* Resident "z" in region "k" : $\mathbf{g}_{kz}(t)$ (units : 10^6 persons)
* Capital stock of agent "z" in region "k" and sector "j" : $\mathbf{k}_{kjz}(t)$ (10^6 cstt DM)
* Backlog of orders of agent "kjz" : $\mathbf{b}_{kjz}(t)$ (10^6 cstt DM)

... three flow variables :

* Production of agent "kjz" : $\mathbf{o}_{kjz}(t)$ (10^6 cstt DM/rut)

---

5 time subscripts will be omitted but variables will be recognisable by Latin letters, whereas constant parameters will be designated by Greek letters. On subscripted coordinates of variables, the region appears first with letters k or l, then the sector with letters j or i, and then the individual agent with letters z or x.

* Exports, Imports in region “k”, sector “j” : $\mathbf{ex}_{kj}(t)$, $\mathbf{im}_{kj}(t)$ (10^6 cstt DM/rut)

... and three ratio variables :

* Relative attractiveness of a supplier “x” of sector “i” in region “l” as seen by a potential customer of sector “j” in region “k”: $\mathbf{a}_{kj\text{->}lix}(t)$ (dimensionless)
* Price of agent “kjz” : $\mathbf{p}_{kjz}(t)$ (units : currt DM/cstt DM => dimensionless)
* Technical coefficient : $\mathbf{w}_{kjz}(t)$ (dimensionless because w converts the value of inputs in constant DM from branch “i” into the value of output in constant DM from branch “j” in region “k”)

Let us now have a first glance at the microscopic assumptions and behaviours : each actor (household or firm) $z = 1..N_{kj}$, from sector of activity $j = 1..ns$ and region $k = 1..nz$, is supposed to be monitoring its order books through production, its capacity of production through investment, its technology of production, its choice of suppliers, and its selling price or wage, as follows :

1) in order to execute a chosen production level (o_{kjz}) and investment level (dk_{kjz}/dt), the agent will order the necessary inputs i ($w_{kij}\ o_{kjz} + \phi_{ij}\ dk_{kjz}/dt$) according to its current production technology (w_{kij}) and equipment technology (ϕ_{ij}), and this generates a flow of orders which will be dispatched to the different suppliers “lix” according to their relative attractiveness ($a_{kj\text{->}lix}$);

2) according to its spatial and economic characteristics that influence its relative attractiveness ($a_{li\text{->}kjz}$) among competitors, the agent “z” receives new orders ($a_{li\text{->}kjz}\ (w_{lji}\ o_{li} + \phi_{ji}\ dk_{li}/dt)$) that increase its backlog of orders (b_{kjz}), which is subsequently decreased by its own production (o_{kjz});

3) the production process (o_{kjz}) transforms accumulated orders into deliveries and its level is monitored by he backlog of orders (b_{kjz});

4) the production capacity, a multiple of the capital stock (k_{kjz}), is adjusted through investments according to the backlog of orders and the average sectoral profit;

5) the price is influenced by the ratio of demand (the new orders) and supply (the capacity of production);

6) the <u>production technology</u> (w_{kij}) is slowly adapted to changing relative costs of inputs and to innovations in the sector, it is assumed to be identical among all actors of a given sector and region, or to express a mean value for them.

Inasmuch as stock variables and some ratios (p(t) and w(t)) are state variables, flow variables, instead, express in many ways the speeds of change of the state variables, since flows are inevitably defined for a period of time. Since we are using a continuous time dynamic and since we are trying to grasp some microscopic behaviours within a macroscopic framework, we would like to avoid dealing with a "national accounts" style of equations[6], where decisions are deemed to obey a causality based on expected a-posteriori annual accounts. If one has to revise continuously these annual values because of the dynamic, their very existence as valid informational tools may become meaningless and even totally dangerous or useless for dynamic modelling. We will thus use instead, as a rule, an adaptive procedure based on observations available at any time, that is, stock variables and their speeds of change. Other kinds of expectational schemes might be added but they would need to be consistent with the dynamic itself. As a result, our flows will be explicitly defined as action targets related to the stock variables, for a period of time commensurate with the time step of linearity of our system, that is, for reasonably small multiples of the infinitesimal subdivision (dt)[7] of the reference unit of time (r.u.t.). And the r.u.t. borrows its meaning from the values of the speed parameters, that is, from the relationships between differentials of stock variables and their levels. As action targets, the flows monitored by the dynamic are never realised as such but they provide the r.u.t., the time frame of operations. For the realisation of flows one needs to take their average value over a reasonable time period. We have decided to equate in this model the r.u.t. with the dt, so as to ensure that plans and expectations are commensurate with the time span of relative stability in the system.

It appeared in numerical integrations that our differential system did not gain much more precision when the r.u.t. = dt was inferior to one twelfth of a year. Would things have been different, we would have had to introduce expectations and plans for longer time spans (for which the system would have been less

---

[6] most macro-economic models use a-posteriori quarterly or annual realisations of flows as decision variables in their behavioural equations; unless they use opinion surveys, in which case their relationships with basic reasoning behind economic decisions should be sought on much smaller time scales anyway.

[7] the dt is searched empirically as the largest subdivision of a r.u.t. such that all smaller subdivisions yield the same solution as this largest value does.

linearly predictable for our agents), and thus learning mechanisms would have had to be added. The reference unit of time for the flow variables in this model will thus be of one month; all reasoning, expectations and accounting will be calibrated for one month. The pace at which things change however, especially at the aggregate level, is much higher in reality, and such will be the subdivision of the year used by the numerical integration of the system. In order to obtain comparisons with official annual data, one has to integrate the "infinitesimal flows" over a whole year.

2.1 Differential equation 1 : Backlog of orders

$$\frac{db_{kjz}}{dt} = \sum_{l}^{nz} \sum_{i}^{ns} a_{li \to kjz} \left(\sum_{x}^{Nli} w_{lji}\, o_{lix} + \phi_{ji} \left(\delta\, k_{lix} + dk_{lix}/dt \right) \right) - o_{kjz}$$

This is a balance equation that accumulates the instantaneous difference between new orders and deliveries into b_{kjz}, the backlog of orders net of the stock of finished products. We assume that production corresponds to deliveries. The new orders received by producer "kjz" are formed by the sum over all regions and sectors of probable orders directed to it emanating either from the production needs ($w_{lji}\, o_{li}$) or from the investment needs (ϕ_{ji} ($\delta\, k_{li} + dk_{li}/dt$)), multiplied by its attractiveness (a_{likjz}) seen by these clients "li". These investment orders are formed by a replacement expense $\delta\, k_{li}$ and a desired variation of capital dk_{li}/dt, both multiplied by a technical coefficient (ϕ_{ji}) converting investment expenses from agents of sector "i" into orders of equipment goods for agents of sector "j". If the dk_{li}/dt is < 0, it is obvious that the replacement expense must only be partially spent inasmuch as it exceeds the decided reduction of capital, and if ($\delta\, k_{li} + dk_{li}/dt$) < 0, then we have to account for a reduction of equipment sales due to capital goods resales.

The backlog of orders is absolutely necessary in order to preserve all values through time. Without it, we would be computing production functions with inconsistent meaning through time : one day a given production level would be achieved and sold while having received and used all the necessary inputs, and another day, it could achieve the same output with only 80% of the required inputs without any consequence. This backlog is necessary in order to cope with delays of reactions between plans of production. We assume that each producer has minimal stocks of inputs at its disposal so that its production does not become disrupted, and that it keeps them furnished by re-ordering immediately any consumed inputs, so that, in the end, the stock adjustments are always transferred to the suppliers. There is no need to distinguish the origin of demand by individual client "x" since the attractiveness of an individual supplier does not take into account any characteristics of individual customers (see below).

The attractiveness[8] ($a_{kj->liz}$) is a distribution function that gives the probability for any agent "z" from category "kj" to choose a supplier "x" of product "i" in region "l". As a distribution function, its total mass over the complete domain (the whole geographical map of our theoretical closed global economy) must of course be equal to 1, which is guaranteed by the normalisation operation at the denominator.

$$a_{kj \to lix} = \frac{w_{kij}\, \kappa\, k_{lix} - \psi_{ij}\theta_{kl}\, p_{lix}\, \frac{k_{lix}}{k_{li}}}{\sum_{l'=1}^{nz} \sum_{z=1}^{Nl'i} w_{kij}\, \kappa\, k_{l'iz} - \psi_{ij}\theta_{l'k}\, p_{l'iz}\, \frac{k_{l'iz}}{k_{l'i}}} \qquad \text{but } a_{kj \to l\, ns\, x} = \begin{cases} 0 \text{ if } l \neq k \\ 1 \text{ if } l = k \end{cases}$$

with $\psi_{33} < 0$ and $w_{k33} = 10^{-10}$, so that workers (sector 3) might be attracted by high wages on other job markets, but be indifferent to the size of the active population.

Since we are trying to keep our model as endogenous as possible, the only factors playing a role in these probabilities are variables from the model, namely : the size (k_{lix}, an attracting factor) and, the magnitude of the technical dependence between customer and supplier (w_{lji}, the greater the dependency, the more size matters), price (p_{lix}, a repelling factor) from suppliers and the distance (a repellent). Parameters θ_{kl} and ψij give, respectively, the average distance between two regions (k & l), using the appropriate communications network, and the sensitivity to distance of the customer from sector "j", for that particular purchase in sector "i". Since θ is a relative distance between zones and can only be changed through infrastructure programs, we see that the higher the sensitivity ψ, the more local events might have long range, global restructuring effects. Now, the repelling effect due to the price is weighted by the relative importance of the supplier's capacity (k_{lix}/k_{li}) inside its local market "li" in order to impose the necessary macro—>micro feedback upon the individual so as to avoid free riders (rent seekers) : the more you supply, the more your price tag becomes visible and

---

8 this concept has been borrowed from Allen & Sanglier (1985) and adapted to our problem.

influences the general attractiveness of your surroundings, from which you benefit indirectly, anyway, through the reduction of your price penalty by division of your weight by the global mass of the supply in your area (k_{li}).

This way, the individual attractivenesses can be aggregated by simple summation over all agents pertaining to a functional group. Here, we need an aggregation over a single region (x = 1..Nli), so as to yield macroscopic variables which are compatible with statistical data in order to calibrate the model, but it should be noted that the choice of group boundaries is very significant for an eventual verification of these microscopic behaviours, and thus needs to embrace all relevant interdependencies of an individual actor.

$$a_{kj\to li} = \sum_{x}^{Nli} a_{kj\to lix} = \frac{w_{kij}\,\kappa\left(\sum_{x}^{Nli} k_{lix}\right) - \psi_{ij}\theta_{kl}\sum_{x}^{Nli} p_{lix}\frac{k_{lix}}{k_{li}}}{\sum_{l'=1}^{nz}\sum_{z=1}^{Nl'i} w_{kij}\,\kappa\, k_{l'iz} - \psi_{ij}\theta_{l'k}\, p_{l'iz}\frac{k_{l'iz}}{k_{l'i}}} = \frac{w_{kij}\,\kappa\, k_{li} - \psi_{ij}\theta_{kl}\, p_{li}}{\sum_{l'}^{nz} w_{kij}\,\kappa\, k_{l'i} - \psi_{ij}\theta_{l'k}\, p_{l'i}}$$

This final expression is obtained by using the following definition for the aggregate sectoral values of buffer stocks, the production, capital stock and price :

$$b_{kj} = \sum_{z=1}^{Nkj} b_{kjz}\ ;\ o_{kj} = \sum_{z=1}^{Nkj} o_{kjz}\ ;\ k_{kj} = \sum_{z=1}^{Nkj} k_{kjz}\ ;\ p_{kj} = \sum_{z=1}^{Nkj} p_{kjz}\frac{k_{kjz}}{k_{kj}}$$

The aggregate sectoral price is a weighted average of individual prices, where weights are relative capital sizes. Buffer stocks can now be aggregated in a similar way, by simple summation over the Nkj agents of sector "j" in region "k" :

$$\frac{db_{kj}}{dt} = \sum_{l}^{nz}\sum_{i}^{ns} a_{li\to kj}\left(w_{lji}\, o_{li} + \phi_{ji}\,\left(\delta\, k_{li} + dk_{li}/dt\right)\right) - o_{kj}$$

2.2 Differential equation 2 : Production

$$\frac{do_{kjz}}{dt} = \gamma\ o_{kjz}\left(\frac{POT1_{kjz}}{\sum_{x=1}^{Nkj}\beta\, b_{kjx}}\right)\left(1 - \frac{o_{kjz}}{POT1_{kjz} = \beta\, b_{kjz} + \sum_{\substack{x=1\\ x\neq z}}^{Nkj}\left(\beta\, b_{kjx} - o_{kjx}\right)}\right)$$

$$\text{or,}\quad \frac{do_{kjz}}{dt} = \left(\gamma\,\frac{POT1_{kjz}}{\beta\, b_{kj}}\right)\frac{o_{kjz}}{POT1_{kjz}}\left(POT1_{kjz} - o_{kjz}\right)$$

Each agent will work out a production plan for a whole r.u.t. after having evaluated its growth potential POT1 as a fixed proportion β of its backlog of orders (β stands for delivery delay), plus a perception of unfulfilled orders of others placed upon competitors in the surrounding market (here, the region), as if the agent could capture them, and as a perception of global turning points. Here, we assume perfect knowledge of unfulfilled orders, but some bias should be introduced. Everything else than o_{kjz} held constant, this corresponds to a logistic process with potential POT1 and with a speed parameter γ POT1/(β b) which is γ-proportional to the share of the microscopic potential POT1 in the macroscopic one (β b). This logistic nonlinearity is introduced in order to reflect the fact that producers tend to accelerate their production schedules with much less concern for competition when they are still far from perceiving the limits of the new demand, when saturation signals have not yet arisen, than when they are closer to the stagnating or regressing level of orders. This plan of production might not be realised completely if sudden changes happen before the completion of the r.u.t., but since we adopted a r.u.t. = dt, there are few chances that it might happen. And even in the case of partial fulfilment and rut > dt, the integration/averaging of results over periods of time equal to r.u.t. would give us the realised productions. Nevertheless, production schedules need some time to react to new levels of order books, because these changes need to be perceived as durable ones and also because of organisational inertias. This justifies the use of production as a state variable.

Now, with some simple algebraic operations, one can easily obtain the aggregate differential equation, as a simple sum over individual ones :

$$\frac{do_{kj}}{dt} = \gamma\ o_{kj} \left(1 - \frac{o_{kj}}{\beta\ b_{kj}}\right)$$

But for sector DP (i.e., j = ns), things are different, because ok.ns is not a state variable but a mere public accounting variable, existing only at some aggregate level. Here, we account for revenues from capital and savings on wages. This is done by subtracting input costs from sales at current prices, and by deflating the result by a global inflation index. It can be easily be demonstrated that if we assume $o_{kjz}/(\kappa\ k_{kjz}) = o_{kj}/(\kappa\ k_{kj})$, for all k, j, z, that is, capacity utilisation is quite homogeneous inside a sector, then

$$o_{k.ns} = \frac{ns - 1}{\sum_{h}^{ns-1} p_{kh}} \sum_{j=1}^{ns-1} \sum_{z=1}^{Nkj} \left[p_{kjz}\, o_{kjz} - \sum_{l=1}^{nz} \sum_{i=1}^{ns-1} \sum_{x=1}^{Nli} p_{lix}\, a_{kjlix} \left(w_{kij}\, o_{kj} + \phi_{ij} \left(\delta k_{kj} + \dot{k}_{kj} \right) \right) \right]$$

<=>

$$o_{k.ns} = \frac{ns - 1}{\sum_{h}^{ns-1} p_{kh}} \sum_{j}^{ns-1} \left[p_{kj}\, o_{kj} - \sum_{l}^{nz} \sum_{i}^{ns-1} p_{li}\, a_{kj \to li} \left(w_{kij}\, o_{kj} + \phi_{ij} \left(\delta\, k_{kj} + dk_{kj}/dt \right) \right) \right]$$

Although, in reality, investments are financed by competitive bids for capital through borrowing or equity, thus re-claiming (at a cost) some of the already distributed profits, here we assume it is not the case, since our only concern is to obtain an approximation of what share of the profits go back into investments and what share goes into consumption (the remainder going necessarily to foreign trade surplus and public deficit financing). Thus, we decided to ignore the costs of financial transactions (since most of them are already embedded in the commercial services sector, through the I-O proportionalities), and to consider as distributed profits only what remains after current investment needs have been auto-financed. These revenues will generate demand in equation 1 exactly as does the labour "sector". This equation also accounts for the gain or loss in purchasing power for the population (since all revenues are assumed to be evenly distributed with respect to consumption and savings) after the effects of relative prices changes have been applied to all "volume" transactions. Deflation by consumption prices or an average price is absolutely necessary in order to make this variable compatible with the other ones, which are all in constant prices.

2.3 Differential equation 3 : Capital stock

The capital stock is not accounted properly in this version of ISIS because we have not yet developed a model for its physical mobility, financial evaluation and technical efficiency. Thus a stable relation between its "volume" (i.e. value at constant prices across time and space) and its "services" (i.e. capacity of production) is assumed here and any investment will modify directly the production capacity in the same proportion $\kappa = o/k = 1/COR$. Thus, we will just neglect the revenues from fixed capital resales in the financing of new investments, thereby producing a non trivial error in our accounting of assets and savings. A lot more research would be needed in order to obtain some macroeconomic indicators of such transactions. Thus, the question here is reduced to knowing where should an anonymous capital be invested or disinvested.

With exactly the same reasoning used for production, the capital stock is adjusted to a potential POT2, evaluated by every agent as a "structurally unrealised profitable capacity". This amounts to subtract the market fixed capital base from the sum of order books on the market multiplied by the delivery delay parameter b and a function of the market marginal profit, and divided by the reference utilisation rate υ and the inverted capital to output ratio κ (1/COR).

$$\frac{dk_{kjz}}{dt} = \eta\ k_{kjz} \left(\frac{POT2_{kjz}}{\sum_{x=1}^{Nkj} \frac{\beta\, b_{kjx}}{\upsilon\,\kappa} e^{\mu\ profit}} \right) \left(1 - \frac{k_{kjz}}{POT2_{kjz} = \frac{\beta\, b_{kj}}{\upsilon\,\kappa} e^{\mu\ profit} - \sum_{\substack{x=1\\ x\neq z}}^{Nkj} k_{kjx}} \right)$$

which can be aggregated at the market level (region "k") by a simple summation over all its members

$$\frac{dk_{kj}}{dt} = \eta\ k_{kj} \left(1 - \frac{k_{kj}}{\frac{\beta\, b_{kj}}{\upsilon\,\kappa} e^{\mu (p_{kj} - \sum_{l}^{nz} \sum_{i}^{ns-1} p_{li}\, w_{kij}\, a_{kj\to li})}} \right)$$

2.4 Differential equation 4 : Price

$$\frac{dp_{kjz}}{dt} = \pi \left(\frac{Demand_{kjz}}{Supply_{kjz}} - 1 \right) \iff \frac{dp_{kjz}}{dt} = \pi \left(\frac{db_{kjz}/dt + o_{kjz}}{\upsilon\,\kappa\, k_{kjz}} - 1 \right)$$

so that, with $p_{kj} = \sum_{z=1}^{Nkj} p_{kjz} \frac{\upsilon\,\kappa\, k_{kjz}}{\upsilon\,\kappa\, k_{kj}}$, we may calculate the aggregate market price for the region "k" :

$$\frac{dp_{kj}}{dt} = \left(\sum_{z=1}^{Nkj} \frac{dp_{kjz}}{dt} \frac{\upsilon\,\kappa\, k_{kjz}}{\upsilon\,\kappa\, k_{kj}} + p_{kjz} \frac{\dot{k}_{kjz}}{k_{kjz}} - \dot{k}_{kj}\, p_{kjz} \frac{k_{kjz}}{k_{kj}} \right) = \pi \left(\frac{db_{kj}/dt + o_{kj}}{k_{kj}} - 1 \right),$$

if we assume $\frac{\dot{k}_{kjz}}{k_{kjz}} = \frac{\dot{k}_{kj}}{k_{kj}}$, i.e. that each agent "z" is investing in its capital stock at the same *rate* as the regional market. Reflecting market dynamics, prices vary proportionately to the discrepancy between supply and demand. The demand used here is able to react to prices through the attractiveness (spatial strategy) and through technological change dw/dt (technological strategy, see next equation). The supply, on the other hand, is able to react to prices through adjustment of capacity because of profitability considerations (see previous equation). Nevertheless, by no means can demand or supply functions be explicited (in the sense of a Cartesian graph of equally admissible couples of quantities and prices), unless the whole system of equations is solved analytically. No short-term "equilibrium tâtonnement process" is used here, because our prices are not assumed to vary fast enough[9], relatively to the other variables, so that the hypothesis of independence between prices and supply and demand functions can be maintained.

2.5 Differential equation 5 : Technical change

$$\frac{dw_{kij}}{dt} = \sum_{i'=1}^{ns} w_{kij}\, w_{ki'j} \left[\omega_{ij}\, e\left(\sum_{1}^{nz} \alpha_{i'}\, p_{li'}\, a_{kjli'} - \alpha_i\, p_{li}\, a_{kjli} \right) - \omega_{i'j}\, e\left(\sum_{1}^{nz} \alpha_i\, p_{li}\, a_{kjli} - \alpha_{i'}\, p_{li'}\, a_{kjli'} \right) \right]$$

i, j = 1... ns , but when i or i' = ns, $p_{l.i \text{ or } i'}$ is replaced by p_{kj} but by p_{k3} when j = ns

This equation is assumed to hold for a whole sector in a given region, as an average representative value of individual technologies, since our attractiveness cannot be differentiated for different members of a buying sector, say "kj". It has the property of having no effect at all upon the sum over i of the w_{ij} (vertical sum of a column from the IO table = 1). It provides us with a conservative "migration" mechanism of the input components of a given product from agents "kj", where these are allowed to compare the utility of shifting some dependence on a given input, say "i", onto another one (i') and vice versa :

$$\frac{dw_{kij}}{dt} = \sum_{i'=1}^{ns} w_{kij}\, w_{ki'j} \left[u_{kj}^{i' \to i}(p, \omega, \alpha) - u_{kj}^{i \to i'}(p, \omega, \alpha) \right]$$

where the utility $u_{kj}^{i' \to i}$ depends upon relative prices, technological trends (ω_{ij}) and some kind of price elasticity ($\alpha_{i'}$) of the input structure. We can see in this equation that the higher the $\alpha_{i'}$, the strongest the movement away from input i' for any increase of price $p_{i'}$. We see also (by putting all α's to zero, i.e. by ignoring price effects) that the higher $\omega_{i'j}$ is above the average of the ω_{ij}, the stronger the shift in favour of input i' (this corresponds to technological innovation trends). Pre-multiplication of the utility differential by the two IO coefficients involved in a given transfer is needed in order to maintain somehow their relative weights, that is, to avoid equalisation

---

[9] mainly because our "prices" are inflationary trends rather than short term terms of trade

after some time. This also prevents any coefficient from becoming null or negative.

This equation is thus responsible for relating the disembodied technical change to relative prices. The relative short term rigidity ("clay-ness") of the production function rests on the parameters α and on the stability of the price structure. Additionally, thanks to the inclusion of the output price (replacing p_{ns}) in the competition for technical change, when many input prices p_{li} increase too much above the output price p_{kj} (that comparison amounts to evaluating the purchasing power of sector kj), they create a pressure in favour of an expansion of the role of "input ns", that is, a generalised cost-cutting initiative on all other inputs. But when the production technology under consideration happens to be the consumption technology of property revenues (sector ns), the output price entering the comparison is then p_{k3}, the average wage in the region. This mechanism can be understood as a way to preserve a form of permanent or long term revenue. A more detailed analysis of this equation will naturally take place under section 4, when we analyse the impacts of a parameter change.

2.6 Differential equation 6 : Population

$$\frac{dg_k}{dt} = \nu \sum_{z=1}^{Nk} g_{kz} + \sum_{l}^{nz} \sum_{z=1}^{Nl} g_{lz}\, \chi_l\, a_{l3\to k3z} - \sum_{x=1}^{Nk} g_{kx}\, \chi_k\, a_{k3\to l3x}$$

$$= \nu\, g_k + \sum_{l}^{nz} g_l\, \chi_l\, a_{l3\to k3} - g_k\, \chi_k\, a_{k3\to l3}$$

since $g_{lz} = g_{kx} = 1$ person.

The population in a given area varies according to the sum of natural effects and net migrational effects, that is, the balance of the mobile population from other areas willing to move to the given area minus the mobile population from the given area willing to move to other areas. And χ expresses a fixed probability for an individual from zone "l" to be willing to move to other areas. Here again, the choices of the new residential area by individuals are summarised by the attractiveness function $a_{l.3\to k.3}$. Because of ($\psi_{33} < 0$, $w_{33} = 10^{-10}$) , the main factor playing on residential attractiveness will be the comparative wage. Of course, the natural growth of population synthesised through ν would require a model by itself, but we decided not to put the emphasis on it in this study.

The results of our aggregations of behaviours yield the following macroscopic set of equations :

$$
\left\{
\begin{array}{l}
\dfrac{db_{kj}}{dt} = \sum\limits_{l}^{nz} \sum\limits_{i}^{ns} a_{li \to kj} \Big(w_{lji}\, o_{li} + \phi_{ji} \, \big(\delta\, k_{li} + dk_{li}/dt \big) \Big) - o_{kj} \\[2ex]
\dfrac{do_{kj}}{dt} = \gamma\, o_{kj} \left(1 - \dfrac{o_{kj}}{\beta\, b_{kj}} \right) \\[2ex]
\dfrac{dk_{kj}}{dt} = \eta\, k_{kj} \left(1 - \dfrac{k_{kj}}{\dfrac{\beta\, b_{kj}}{\upsilon\, \kappa}\, e^{\mu \left(p_{kj} - \sum\limits_{l}^{nz} \sum\limits_{i}^{ns-1} p_{li}\, w_{kij}\, a_{kj \to li} \right)}} \right) \\[2ex]
\dfrac{dp_{kj}}{dt} = \pi \left(\dfrac{db_{kj}/dt + o_{kj}}{\upsilon\, \kappa\, k_{kj}} - 1 \right) \\[2ex]
\dfrac{dw_{kij}}{dt} = \sum\limits_{i'=1}^{ns} w_{kij}\, w_{ki'j} \left[\begin{array}{l} \omega_{ij}\, \mathbf{e}^{\left(\sum\limits_{l}^{nz} \alpha_{i'}\, p_{li'}\, a_{kjli'} - \alpha_i\, p_{li}\, a_{kjli} \right)} \\ - \omega_{i'j}\, \mathbf{e}^{\left(\sum\limits_{l}^{nz} \alpha_i\, p_{li}\, a_{kjli} - \alpha_{i'}\, p_{li'}\, a_{kjli'} \right)} \end{array} \right] \\[2ex]
i, j = 1 \ldots ns \text{, but when } i \text{ or } i' = ns,\ p_{l.i \text{ or } i'} \text{ is replaced by } p_{kj} \text{ but by } p_{k3} \text{ when } j = ns \\[2ex]
\dfrac{dg_k}{dt} = \nu\, g_k + \sum\limits_{l}^{nz} g_l\, \chi_l\, a_{l3 \to k3} - g_k\, \chi_k\, a_{k3 \to l3} \\[2ex]
a_{kj \to li} = \dfrac{w_{kij}\, \kappa\, k_{li} - \psi_{ij} \theta_{kl}\, p_{li}}{\sum\limits_{l'}^{nz} w_{kij}\, \kappa\, k_{l'i} - \psi_{ij} \theta_{l'k}\, p_{l'i}} \text{ ; but } a_{kj \to l\, ns} = \left\{ \begin{array}{l} 0 \text{ if } l \neq k \\ 1 \text{ if } l = k \end{array} \right\} \\[2ex]
o_{k.ns} = \dfrac{ns - 1}{\sum\limits_{h}^{ns-1} p_{kh}} \sum\limits_{j}^{ns-1} p_{kj}\, o_{kj} - \sum\limits_{l}^{nz} \sum\limits_{i}^{ns-1} p_{li}\, a_{kj \to li} \Big(w_{kij}\, o_{kj} + \phi_{ij} \, \big(\delta\, k_{kj} + dk_{kj}/dt \big) \Big)
\end{array}
\right.
$$

Note that these differential equations are defined for all *nz* regions but only for the *ns-1* sectors, because sector ns only matters with respect to production o.

In the subsequent practical application to Germany, the parameters of the model could be classified in two groups : 10 behavioural paramcters (speed or elasticity) had to be estimated through a dynamical fitting of the model : γ, β, η, μ, υ, π, α, χ, ψ, ν ; and $(6 + ns^2 + (nz+nz^2)/2) = 178$ structural parameters could be fixed a-priori from other information sources : δ, κ, ϕ_{ij}, ω_{ij}, θ_{kl}

3. Innovation and growth in the model

Generally speaking, in order to compare various possible economic evolutions, we want to consider the integral of the disposable income over the period, that is (since we did not take into account government functions) the sum of aggregate private consumption C with aggregate private savings S.

Using the results from Appendix 3, where it is demonstrated that the model preserves the macro-economic balance between savings and investments $S = I + \Delta St + (X\text{-}M) + (G\text{-}T)$, we have :

$$C = \sum_{k}^{nz-1} o_{k3} \left(\sum_{i}^{ns-1} w_{ki3} \right) + o_{kns} \left(\sum_{i}^{ns-1} w_{kins} \right) = \sum_{k}^{nz-1} o_{k3} \left(1 - w_{k.ns.3} \right) + o_{kns} \left(1 - w_{k.ns.ns} \right)$$

$$S = \sum_{k}^{nz-1} \left(\sum_{j}^{ns-1} o_{kj}\, w_{kns\,j} \right) - o_{kns} \left(\sum_{i}^{ns-1} w_{kins} \right)$$

$$C + S = \sum_{k}^{nz-1} \left(o_{k3} \left(1 - w_{kns3}\right) + \sum_{j}^{ns-1} o_{kj}\, w^{k}_{ns\,j} \right) = \sum_{k}^{nz-1} \left(o_{k3} + \sum_{j=1;\, j \neq 3}^{ns-1} o_{kj}\, w_{k\,ns\,j} \right)$$

$$\Leftrightarrow C + S = \sum_{k}^{nz-1} \left(o_{k3} \left(1 - w_{kns3}\right) + o_{kns} \left(1 - \text{share of } o_{kns} \text{ due to price effects}\right) \right)$$

So, according to the selected welfare criterion, we would expect the o_{k3} and the o_{kns} to be the highest possible, and the part of o_{kns} which is due to relative price effects to be the lowest possible. Indeed:

$$\text{distributed profits due to price effects} = \sum_{k}^{nz-1} \left(o_{kns} - \sum_{j}^{ns-1} o_{kj}\, w_{kns\,j} \right),$$

since we know that : $\sum_{j}^{ns-1} o_{kj}\, w_{kns\,j} =$ added values at constant prices

The r.h.s. of the identity for C + S tells us little about the dynamic roles of C and S, but tells us how growth may be defined and observed. Now, our criterion C + S contains information about the way the whole society is being transformed through time : very schematically, consumption C contains components that more or less reproduce the population as it is, and components that transform it and give it other properties (in terms of health, education, energy, organisation...) -- but currently, national accounting is still blind with respect to this kind of analysis and we won't take it into account in this model, leaving it for further developments in complex systems analysis. On the other hand, if we re-work the expression for S as follows :

$$\Delta St_{\neq 3} + (X\text{-}M) + I = S = \sum_{k}^{nz-1} o_{kns}\, w_{k\, ns\, ns} - \sum_{k}^{nz-1} \left(o_{kns} - \sum_{j}^{ns-1} o_{kj}\, w_{kns\, j} \right)$$

we now see that aggregate savings correspond to $\Delta St_{\neq 3} + (X\text{-}M) + I$, for their material counterpart (i.e. in real terms, in volumes of transactions), and to $\sum_{k}^{nz-1} o_{kns}\, w_{k\, ns\, ns}$ - (part of o_{ns} due to relative price effects), for their accounting value in terms of revenues.

The first identity thus explains the dynamic elements contained in savings S, or the material flows resulting from an excess of production over consumption and whose property titles are held by households as savings :

1) $\Delta St_{\neq 3} = -\, db/dt$ corresponds to ill invested material production since it piles up in stocks of unsold production and its equivalent in our model : a reduction of the order books levels

2) (X-M) corresponds to the dynamic impulse given by the rest of the world; its has an impact on orders and prices

3) I contains a part that merely reproduces the equipments, like C does for the human capital, and a part that transforms it in volume and quality; it has an impact on orders and supply, and thus on prices and production

We see that for a given exogenous evolution of (X-M) (as is the case in our national and regional simulations below), the component I has the power to either decrease $\Delta St_{\neq 3}$, through its impact on db/dt in differential equation 1, or increase it if its impact on the price structure leads to a destruction of aggregate value. On the other hand, any increase of $\Delta St_{\neq 3}$ can only have a negative impact on I.

4. Labour policy scenario applied to Germany

In this application, we considered $nz = 7$ zones, which broadly correspond to the Länder :

1: Baden-Wurttemberg (BW)
2: Bayern (BA)
3: Hessen (HE)
4: Niedersachsen + Berlin (NS)
5: Noordrhein-Westfahlen (NW)
6: Rheinland-Pfalz + Saarland (RP)
7: Schleswig-Holstein+ Hamburg (SH)

We used the same set of equations as the one that has been presented under section 2, except that regions are restricted to the above mentioned 7 regions of pre-1989 FRG's hinterland, and that (exports - imports) have been added to the equations of db/dt and dp/dt, as external demands. All national sectoral time series were pre-multiplied by a regional ratio obtained as the region's share in the national added value for the given sector.

Initial conditions in 1975 and parameter values are given in Appendix 1 :

1) historical annual values for the o_j, j = 1...(ns-1), divided by 12
2) o_{kns} is calculated according to its equation
3) $p_{kj} = 1$
4) $b_{kj} = o_{kj}(\beta - .03)$, in order to initiate the investment dynamics
5) $k_{kj} = \kappa \, . \, o_{kj}$. (1 year/1 r.u.t.)
6) w_{kij} are given their values from the I/O table for Germany in 1975
7) populations g_k were initialised at their historical values

$\alpha = 0.01$	$\eta = 0.2$. (1 r.u.t./1 year)	$\chi_k = 0.0005$
$\beta = 0.2805$	$\kappa = 1$. (1 r.u.t./1 year)	$\nu = 0.0006$
$\delta = 0.04$	$\mu = 0.08$	$\theta_{lk} = (d(l,k)/d\ minim)^{0.05}$
$\phi_{1j} = 0.8$ and $\phi_{2j} = 0.2$	$\pi = 0.01$	$\psi_{ij} = 1$ but $\psi_{33} = -1$
$\gamma = 0.1$. (1 r.u.t./1 year)	$\upsilon = 0.8$	

Where the (d(l,k)/minim dist) and the ω are given in Appendix 1. The ω were calculated as solutions of a linear system where the historical coefficients w_{ij} and their velocities dw_{ij}/dt at different times were taken as parameters, so that we could reproduce almost perfectly the trends in these w_{kij}. Also δ and ϕ_{1j} could be supplied from statistical sources on investments and savings structures.

The following figure shows the fit for the aggregated sum of all 11 productions at the national level, the historical evolution being the thick line, and the simulated one, the thin line, with the percentage error just in front (see Appendix 3 for detailed results concerning each sector) :

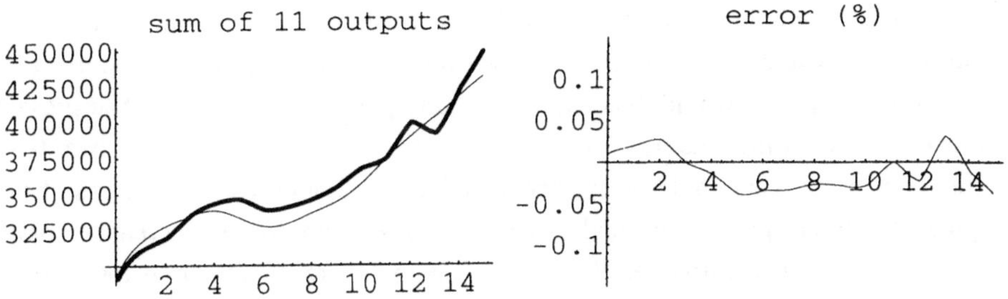

Now, we would like to concentrate on parameter α_3 in order to explore the consequences of some kind of monitoring of the labour factor. But before we turn to an examination of precise parameter variations, we would like to review here the various political contents of some of our behavioural parameters :

β : propensity to deliver "just in time", influenced by communication infrastructures and, less directly, to competition and deregulation policy

υ : utilisation rate threshold for the firing of capacity expansions, influenced by availability of reliable economic information about growth and turning points, by monetary policy and public subsidies

η : characteristic time of reaction for implementation of expansion plans, same influences as for υ , plus degree of competition, and concentration

μ : impact of the marginal profit on investments, influenced by policies stimulating R&D, venture capital, and by concentration

α_i : sensitivity of technical change to the cost of input i, influenced by fiscal and social policies, monetary and science policies

π : characteristic time of reaction of prices, influenced by monetary, fiscal, competition, price control policies and policies concerning the social bargaining process; degree of competition on the market

χ : residential mobility, influenced by cultural and unemployment policies

Suppose we were able to act exclusively on α_3 and leave the other α_i unchanged from their reference value of 0.01 . in reality, and provided our model is a fair representation of it, α_3 could be influenced by fiscal, monetary, social and science policies, all of them having undoubtedly some consequences on almost everything else in the economy. But this requires some careful thought : in order to offer meaningful parameters (constants varying exclusively through exogenous influences), the dynamic needs to capture as much as possible the indirect consequences of a parameter change, except what really pertains to the other parameters. This last remark is a pledge in favour of a modelling style where parameters would only represent discretionary decision powers of collective authorities, and that would thus appear at many places in the model. The present model does not fulfil this property, clearly, but is an intermediary step towards it, since our parameters could be further modelled as nonlinear combinations of the alleged political parameters and other variables. Suppose an increased social protection cost per employee, by increasing the share of labour in total costs, would make employers more sensitive to the direct price of labour. The same would probably happen with tightened competition rules, tightened monetary targets, increased public intervention in social disputes in favour of more flexibility of the workforce, and with increased public intervention in favour of capital substitution to labour. Suppose one of these policies is pursued and wage sensitivity can be either increased or decreased that way[10].

Now, let us reconsider the process of technical change : truly, the equations describing it are the whole model, since all our variables are only reflections of a single decision making process stemming from one decision unit (or at least a highly co-ordinated decision process among many individuals). Thus, the question becomes : to what extent can we, as modellers, distinguish relatively autonomous processes among this co-ordinated whole ? This requires very specific studies about the quantification of the coupling between variables or subsets of variables and this validation exercise is also left to further enquiry, leaving us with an a-priori partitioning in autonomous processes taken from economic theory and our own heuristic reasoning. We thus assumed that the evolutions of prices and techniques of production were sufficiently de-coupled as to allow us to model them quite separately, without thinking too much a-priori about their co-evolution, thus yielding our differential equation n° 5.

In the remainder of this section, we will simplify the notation and reasoning by considering prices and technical coefficients exclusively from their sectoral point of view : p_j and w_{ij} , since the emphasis of this scenario is more on inter-sectoral dynamics. This equation describes an average result of microscopic changes in all directions, always expressed as net balance between utility of relying more and utility of relying less on a given input :

[10] our aim is just to suggest some possible policy applications, not to discuss them in full detail

- $w_{ij}\, w_{i'j}\, \omega_{ij}\, e^{(\alpha_{i'} p_{i'} - \alpha_i p_i)}$ is the utility of having input "i" intervening for a greater proportion in output "j", by reducing the use of input i' by the same amount,
- $w_{ij}\, w_{i'j}$, always > 0 , is the smallest common multiplier between the two coefficients and gives a sort of common accounting unit for calculating transfers,
- $\omega_{ij}\, e^{(\alpha_{i'} p_{i'} - \alpha_i p_i)}$, always > 0 , is the speed factor introducing asymmetry between changes from i' to i and the opposite, without it no change would occur at all; it can also be seen as the "predatory" coefficient of input i on i' : it gives the number of transfer common units ($w_{ij}\, w_{i'j}$) that are being transferred from i' to i in one unit of time (r.u.t.),
- ω_{ij} , always > 0 , captures non-price effects of technological shift, mainly innovations as they occur by chance, or through programmed R&D, or because of imitation (spread of innovations across sectors) or social pressure (like environmental or ergonomical pressure...). But the net aggregate effect depends also on $\omega_{i'j}$, so one really has to control the ns(ns-1)/2 differences $\omega_{ij} - \omega_{i'j}$.
- α_i is at the same time the exponent of the exponential of price p_i that divides the positive contribution to the speed of transfers to input i (thus, α_i reduces the speed factor) and at the same time it is the exponent of the exponential of price p_i that multiplies the negative contribution to the speed factor (same thing).

Since all "prices" are in fact indices starting at 1 at t_0 , their value at t represents their percentage of change since t_0 and this justifies their presence in the equation of dw/dt. Indeed, as long as two price indices are different, there is, theoretically, and independently of other factors of technical change, a good reason for trying to modify the input structure in favour of the cheaper factors. This amounts to taking the structure observed at t_0 as corresponding perfectly to the price structure of t_0 (ideally, we should perform some evaluations in order to determine how far were the technologies at t_0 from their optimum, but this will only be possible when the microscopic validation tools become be ready). Also, a more fundamental critique of this equation of technical change is that it badly needs parameters restricting substitution possibilities, but, without any knowledge about these restrictions in reality, we found premature to introduce such an improvement. Now, the higher the α_i, the lower the price p_i should be, in order to avoid a general reorientation of production techniques away from input i. If that is not the case, demand for input i will decline and so will p_i , until it stabilises the technological substitution at the appropriate level. In some way, $\alpha_{i'}/\alpha_i$ gives the desired price p_i given $p_{i'}$ in order not to influence technological change through prices, e.g. : $\alpha_{i' \neq 3} = 0.01$ and $\alpha_3 = 0.03 \Rightarrow p_3$ must be 0.333 if $p_{i'} = 1$, but, as we shall see below, p_3 will decline much further if we change α_3 from 0.001 to 0.03 because that will be such a strong departure from reality (the reference scenario) that strong nonlinearities will over-amplify the reaction and generalise it to other prices, thereby prompting further decline of p_3 down to 0.1.

We decided to let α_3 vary from 0.001 to 0.03 by increments of 0.001 and to observe the change of the solution on the same short horizon we had for the reference simulation, that is, from 1975 to 1989. Below are shown the numerical derivatives of our productions aggregated at the national level with respect to α_3 , with time unfolding from 0 to 15 along the axis pointing to the front, and α_3 varying on the second horizontal axis (pointing away from the observer). After the 12 productions, only the derivatives of the first 4 prices with respect to α_3 are presented because the remaining others behave essentially the same way as the first one. Note that this should only be seen as an example of the reasoning allowed by our modelling approach, since validation of the model has not yet been performed for other parameter values : here, extreme and unrealistic values appear just for the sake of illustration of nonlinear phenomena.

Metallic Manufactures :

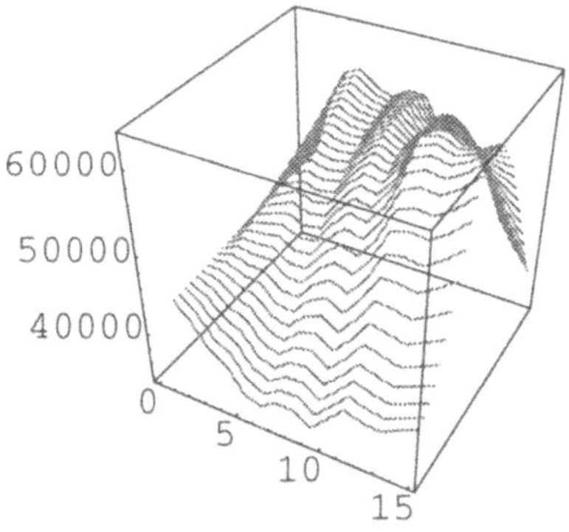

Construction :

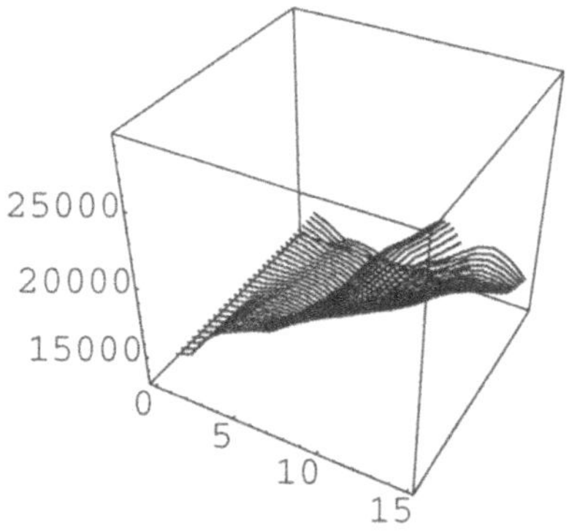

Active Population :

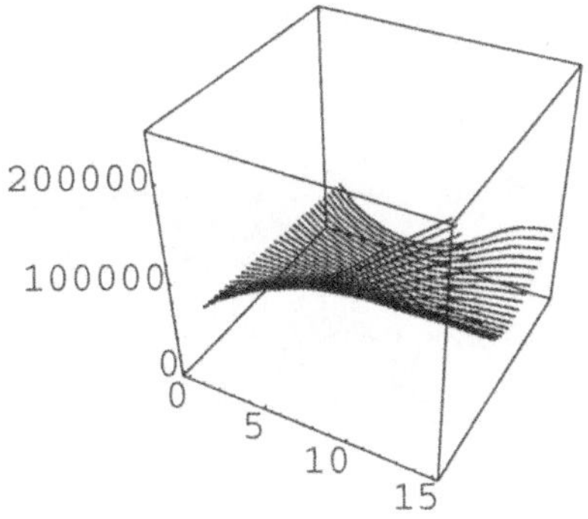

Agriculture :

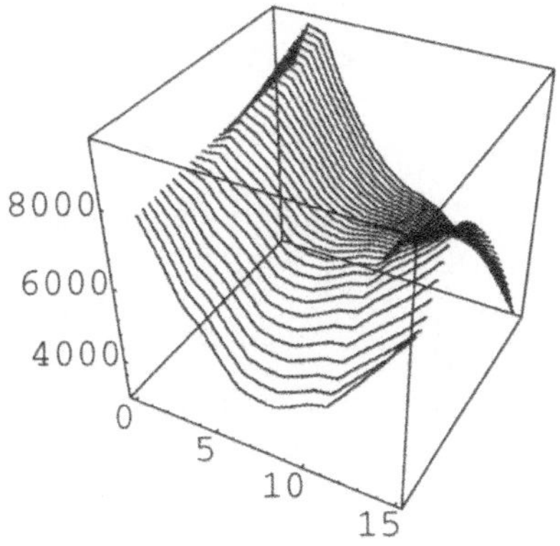

Energy :

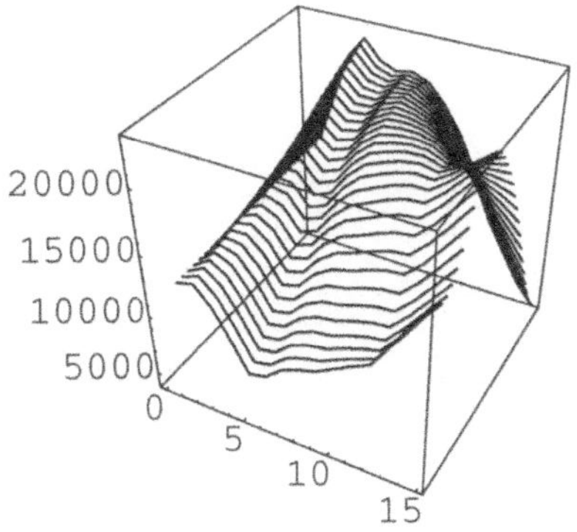

Basic industries:

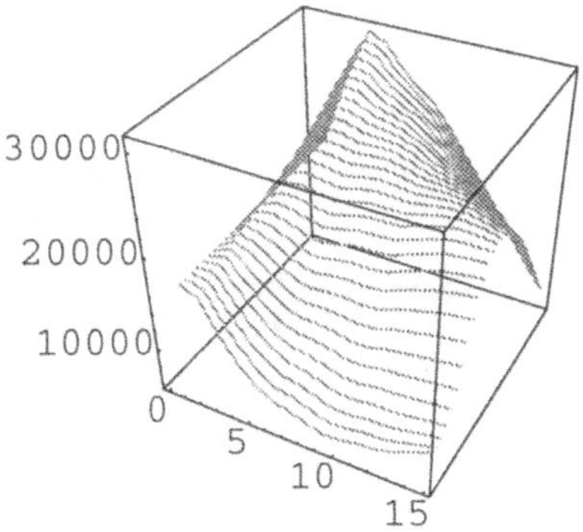

Chemical :

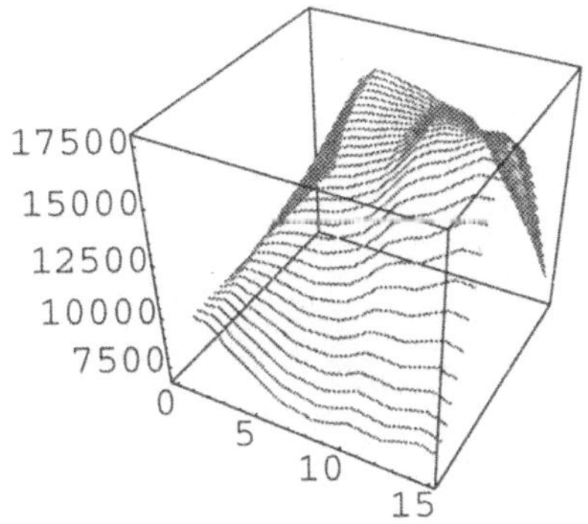

Other manufactured :

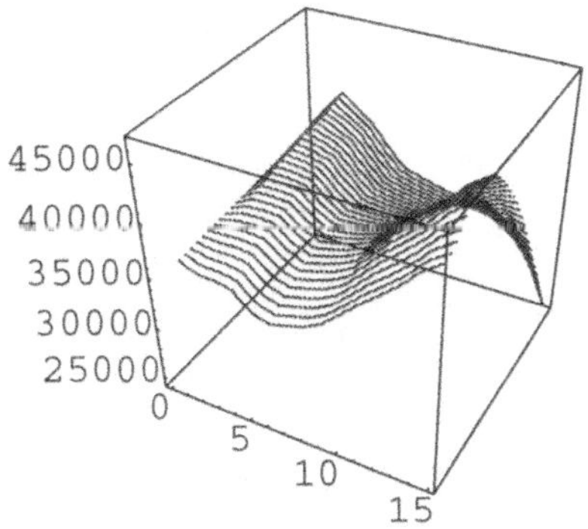

Transportation :

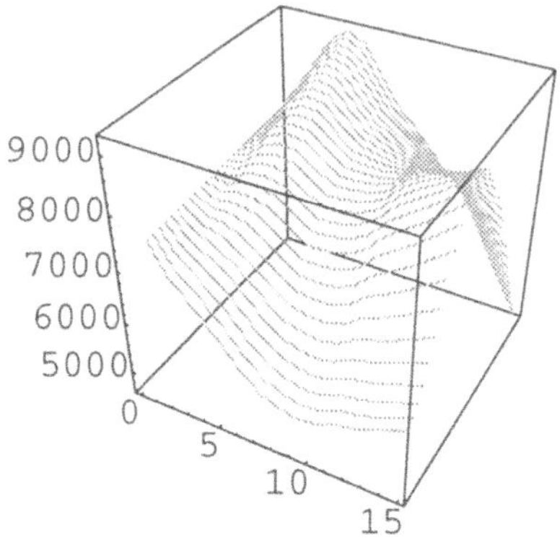

Market Services :

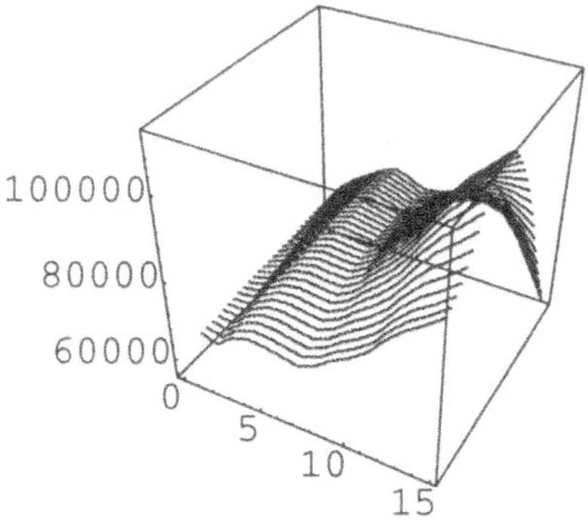

Non market services :

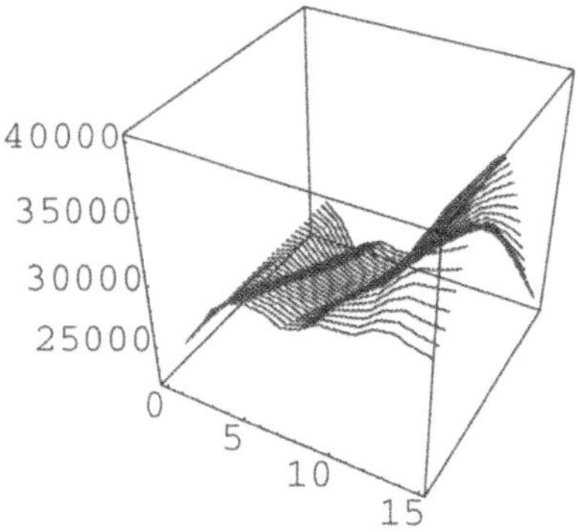

Distributed profits :

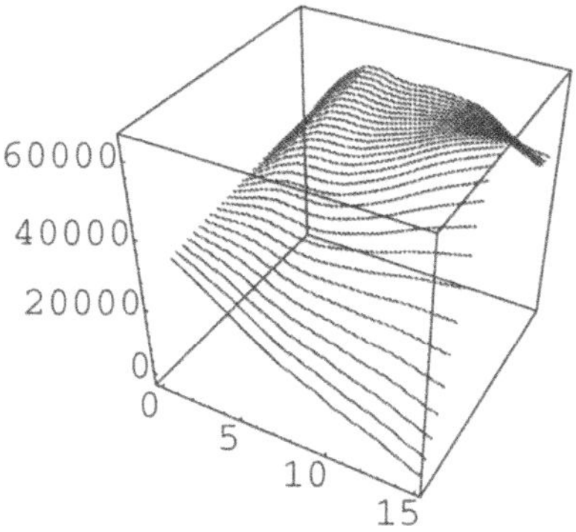

Prices :

Metallic Manufactures :

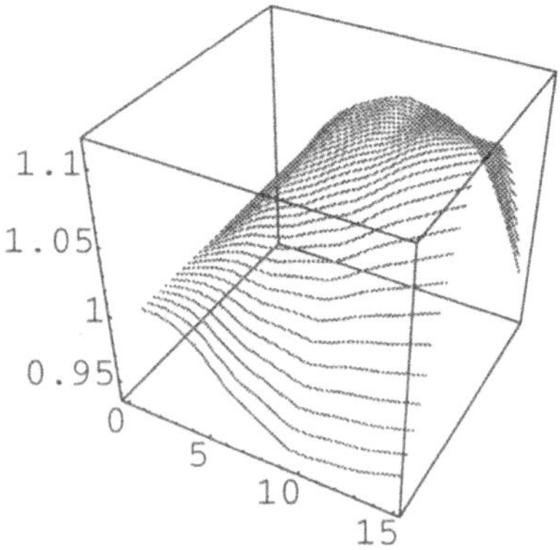

Construction :

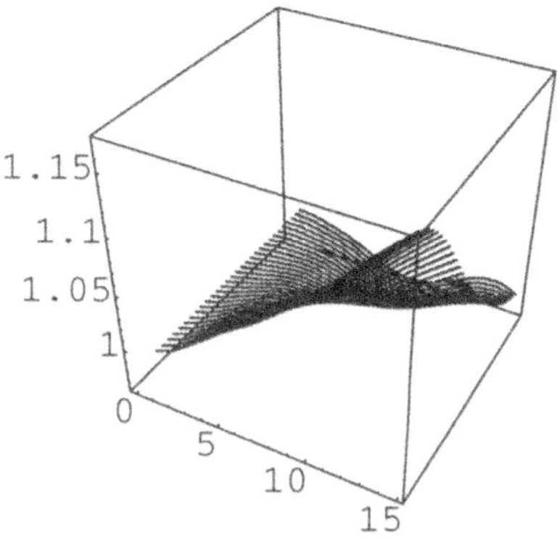

Active Population :

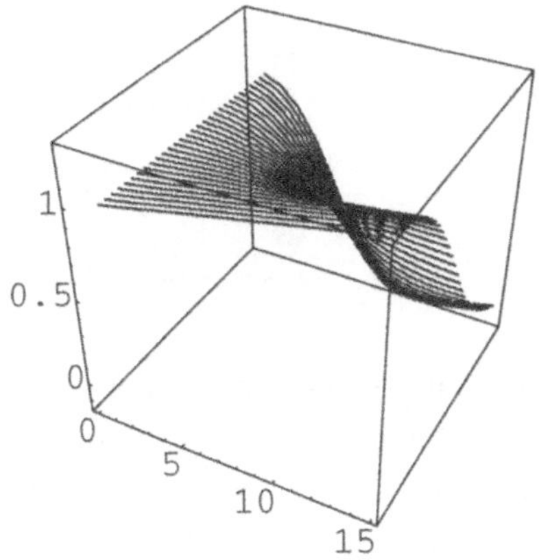

Agriculture :

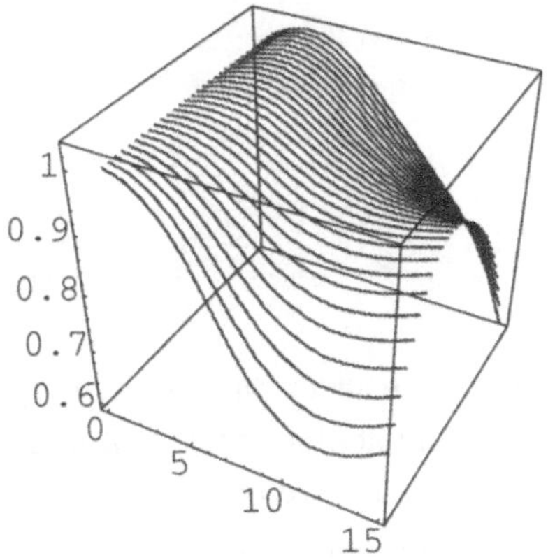

With the increase of α_3, p_3 becomes considered more and more excessive and prompts each time stronger corrective action on it, through a reduction of the w_{3j} [11]. The price-derivative of dw/dt is << 1 (reaction on w_{3j} is less than proportional to a Δprice variation because α is << 1 and the Δprice is multiplied by the w<1 and because we are dealing with the dynamic of a variable which is bounded to 1). On the other hand, the w-derivative of dp/dt is >>> 1. Now, p is bound to decrease because in this scenario supply is reacting much slower than, and to, demand changes : the perturbation comes from the demand side and has to accumulate into the buffer stocks before affecting productions and capital formation. Thus, with prices reacting much faster than w's, we would expect to observe the price p_3 to become desirable again quite soon and to stabilise the decline of w_{3j} (as displayed on figures below where the evolution of $w_{3.1}$ -- among the 12 evolutions of input coefficients for sector MM -- with α_3 = 0.015 (left) is to be contrasted with its evolution under the reference scenario (right); see curve number 3).

---

[11] this illustrates the interest and difficulty of modelling over-reactive phenomena with global endogenous models : the threshold value for the firing of the over-reaction depends on many equations and parameters (here, μ, η, π, α, ω_{3j}), whereas linear dynamics localises the impact of a variable in the partial derivative of the system with respect to this variable.

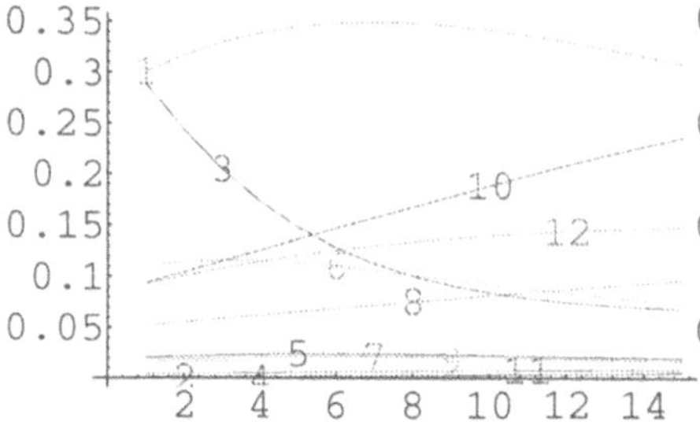

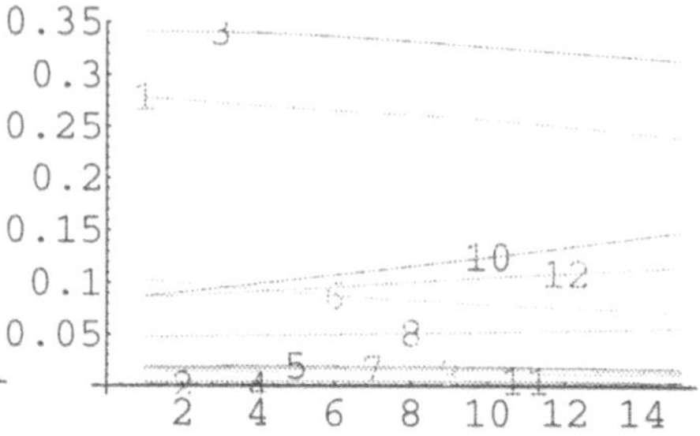

But, instead of that, something else must have happened besides these microscopic nonlinearities that might explain the sharp deflation of prices and productions that we observe for extreme values of α_3. If we take a look at the boxes below concerning derivatives of w_{3j} , $w_{12.3}$ and $w_{12.12}$, we can see that, because of the big loss of purchasing power of the population, an important cost compression initiative has been launched in order to restore some financial security as allowed by equation 5 (see Malinvaud (1981), p 56 for a more general discussion of this reaction).

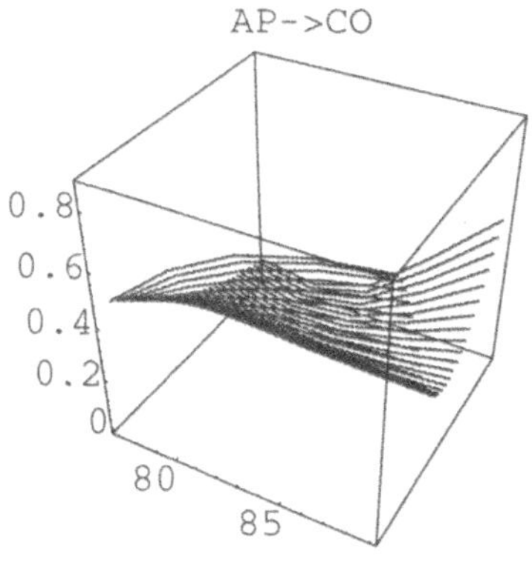

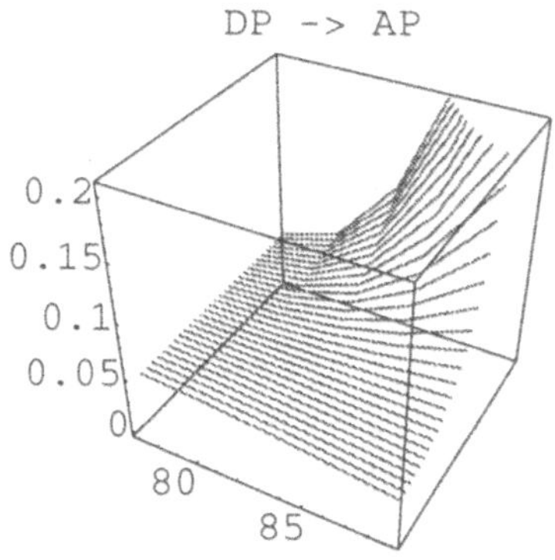

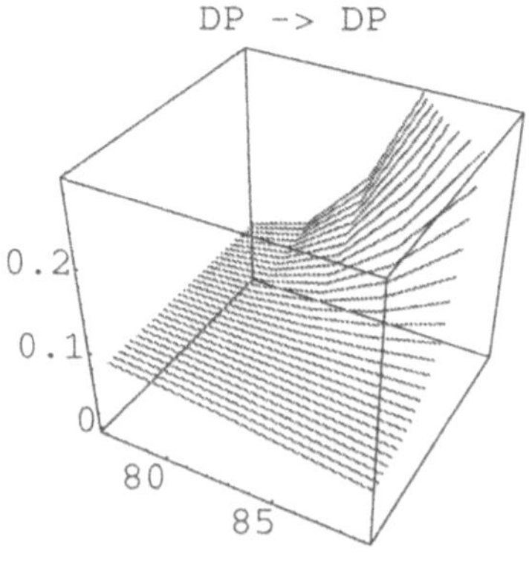

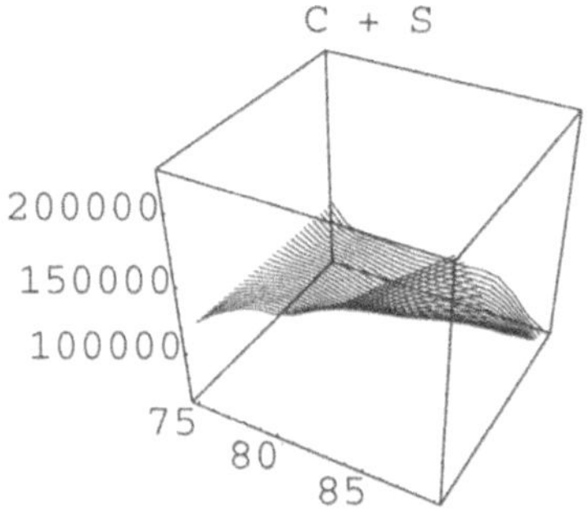

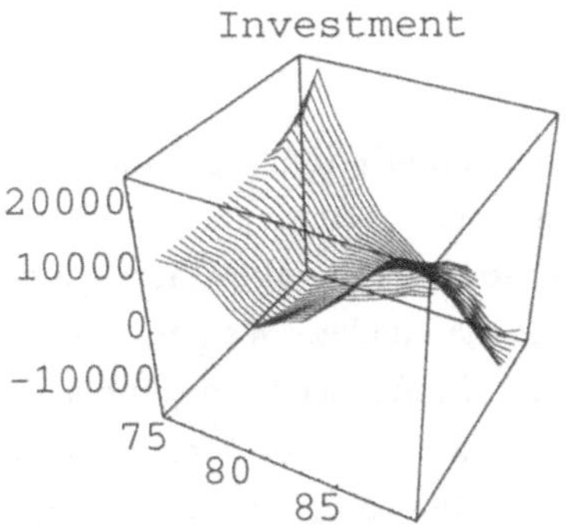

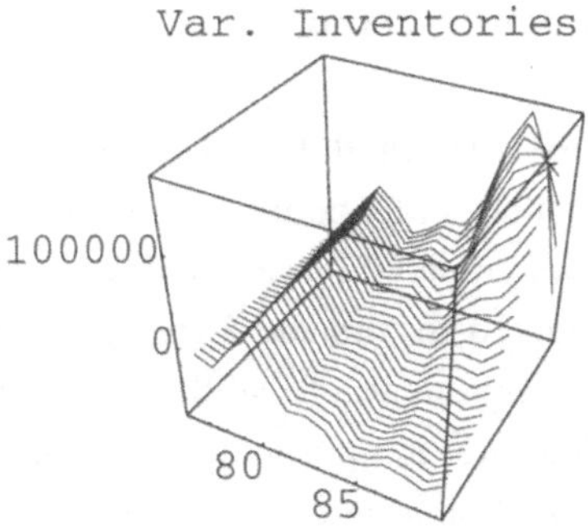

If we analyse this in terms of our welfare criterion from Section 3, (C+S), the last three graphs above show us that increasing α_3 beyond a certain level is detrimental to growth because the increased savings do not stimulate productive investments anymore, but inventories investments instead because of a too strong reduction on consumption.

This way, the capital formation that could have been stimulated by increased profit margins due to wage reductions (see Differential Equation 3) and that could have induced a lot of growth, under other circumstances, through reduced prices and thus stronger purchasing power and new demands, has been completely inhibited in this case by the volume-effect of reduced order books. That kind of growth did happen when we repeated the experiment after having disactivated saving propensity reactions to purchasing power variations (the special condition for j = ns in equation 5), as illustrated on the following graphs :

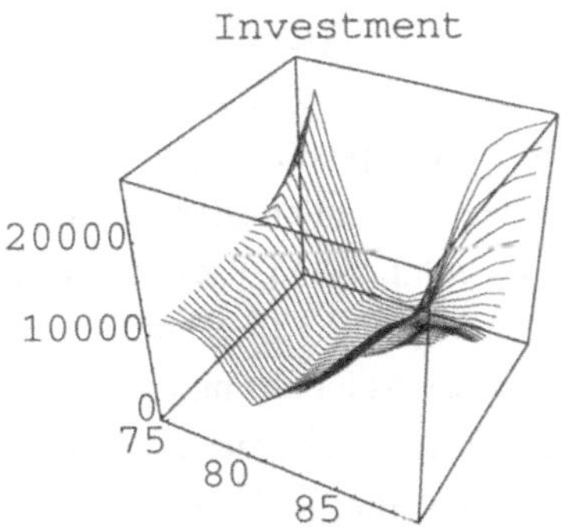

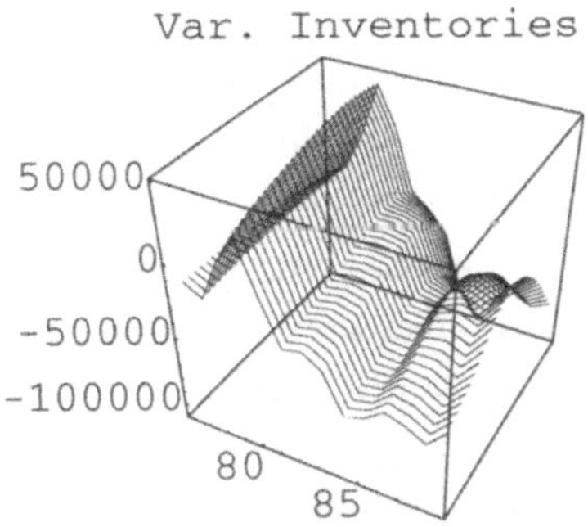

5. Conclusions

The ISIS model, where state variables are populations, productions, investments, order books, inventories, prices, savings and production technologies, has been prepared for an application to the F.R.G. from 1975 to 1989, aggregated in 12 macro-sectors and 7 regions corresponding to the Länder. We performed a first calibration as a feasibility study and framework of reference for a subsequent detailed microscopic validation with statistical assumptions about parameters, which will be necessary in order to produce reliable alternative evolutions to the historical path. Indeed, the more disaggregated the validation becomes, the more variety of contexts and behaviours is being taken into account and thus the more the model qualifies as an applied "behavioural" model, offering meaningful and interpretable parameters and alternative simulations. The only exogenous time functions and constants introduced in this preliminary calibration are the sectoral imports and exports -- which become endogenous as soon as enough countries are included -- and 178 constants taken from data sources and 10 parameters to be estimated. This low degree of exogeneity (328 parameters for 1351 state variables) and the invariance of the six basic differential equations across time, space and economic activity give our model a reasonable degree of genericity.

Although the spatial dimension has not been fully exploited in this research, previous works[12] have used it in order to study spatial synergies and also the conditions behind differentiation or uniformisation of the spatial distribution of activities. Appendix 4 displays a simplified geographical representation of growth and distribution effects of the reference scenario.

Using the semi-applied model in the German context, we discussed the role of a parameter controlling the sensitivity of production technologies to the labour cost. This enabled us to assess threshold levels where positive microscopic reactions from producers and negative microscopic reactions of consumers due to macroscopic losses of purchasing power start to compensate each other in response to decreases of labour intensity, or the reverse : the threshold levels where positive macroscopic effects on demand of increased labour intensity start to be tamed by poor microscopic results in profitability. Bifurcation analysis, though, would require a totally endogenous framework, that is, in our case, an application to a sufficiently large and integrated portion of the world economy.

---

12 see Guzzi R., Sanglier M., El Korchi D. (1996)

6. References

• Allen P.M., Sanglier M. , Engelen G. & Boon F. (1985) : "Towards a new synthesis in the modelling of evolving complex systems, in : *Environment and Planning B : Planning and Design*, Vol. 12, Université Libre de Bruxelles, pp.65 to 84.

• Allen P.M., Sanglier M. , Engelen G. & Boon F. (1984) : “L'auto-organisation des systèmes humains”, in : Y. GUERMOND (Ed.) , *Analyse de Système en Géographie*, Presses Universitaires de Lyon, pp 200-253

• Arthur W.B.(1986) : *Industry Location Patterns and the Importance of History*, Center for Economic Policy Research, Paper no. 84, Stanford University.

• Banks R. B. (1991) : *Growth and Diffusion Phenomena*, Springer-Verlag

• Biart M., Praet P (1987) : "The contribution of opinion surveys in forecasting aggregate demand in the four main EC countries", in : *Journal of Economic Psychology* n° 8, North-Holland, pp 409-428

• Fontela, Pulido A. (1991) : "Input-Output, Technical Change, and Long Waves" ; in : *Advances in Input-Output Analysis*, W. Peterson (Ed.), Oxford University Press, Oxford

• Franke R., Wegehorst W. (1988) : "Complex dynamics in a simple Input-Output model without the full capacity utilization hypothesis", in : *Metroeconomica*, Vol 39, no 1, Fev

• Guzzi R., Sanglier M., El Korchi D. (1996) : *ISIS, Interregional Socio-Industrial System: a non-linear dynamic model for multi-regional economic simulations - Towards an application to Germany*, Report concerning contract N° JOU2-CT92-0262 with DGXII from the European Commission.

• Hamilton J.D. (1989) : "A new approach to the economic analysis of non stationary time series and the business cycle", in : *Econometrica* , VOl 57, n° 2, March, pp 357-384

• Isard W. (1975) : *Introduction to Regional Science*, Prentice Hall

• Lorenz H-W. (1987) : "Strange Attractors in a Multisector Business Cycle Model", in : *Journal of Economic Behavior and Organization*, no.8, Elsevier Science Publishers, North-Holland, pp.397 à 411.

• Lorenz H-W (1989) : "Nonlinear Dynamical Economics and Chaotic Motion", in : *Lecture Notes in Economics and Mathematical System* , no.334, Springer-Verlag, Berlin.

• Malinvaud E.(1981) : *Théorie macro-économique. 1. Comportements, croissance* , Bordas, Paris.

• Malinvaud E.(1982) : *Théorie macro-économique. 2. Evolutions conjoncturelles*, Bordas, Paris.

• Medio A. (1992) : *Chaotic Dynamics. Theory and Applications to Economics*, Cambridge University Press

• Miller R.E.,Polenske K.R. and Rose A.Z. (eds.) (1989) : *Frontiers of Input-Output Analysis*, Oxford University Press.

• Mirowski P. (1989) : *More Heat than Light, Economics as Social Physics, Physics as Nature's Economics,* Cambridge University Press

• Nicolis G. (1995) : *Introduction to Nonlinear Science*, Cambridge Univ.Press

• OCDE (1993) : *Etudes Economiques de l'OCDE, Allemagne*

• Prigogine I. (1994) : *Les Lois du Chaos*, Flammarion

• Prigogine I. (1996) : *La Fin des Certitudes*, Odile Jacob

• Reiner R.(1991) : *From Micro Behaviour to Macro Dynamics. The Master Equation Approach*, Institut für Theoretische Physik, Universität Stuttgart.

• Ruelle D. (1991) : *Chance and Chaos*, Princeton University Press

• Stock J-H. (1989) : "Hysteresis and the evolution of postwar U.S. and U.K. unemployment", in : *Economic Complexity : chaos, sunspots, bubbles, and nonlinearity*, W.A. Barnett, J. Geweke, K. Shell (Eds.), Cambridge Univ. Press.

• Weidlich W., Haag G. (1983) : *Concepts and models of a Quantitative Sociology*, Springer-Verlag, Berlin.

Appendix 1 - Initial conditions (t_0=1975)

Table for the w_{ij}

	MM	CO	AP	AG	EN	BA
MM	0.28097	0.15302	0.03925	0.02864	0.03332	0.01855
CO	0.00096	0.02656	0.09897	0.00849	0.01293	0.00045
AP	0.34203	0.28326	0.00000	0.07056	0.14998	0.15368
AG	0.00008	0.00178	0.01606	0.23114	0.00141	0.00009
EN	0.01860	0.02396	0.03782	0.03745	0.39556	0.09607
BA	0.10612	0.15967	0.00426	0.00695	0.00698	0.51276
CH	0.01647	0.00288	0.00935	0.03238	0.01611	0.01556
OM	0.04740	0.08203	0.18398	0.11659	0.00895	0.02089
TR	0.01526	0.02149	0.01795	0.01723	0.02216	0.02307
MS	0.08410	0.11149	0.32149	0.12083	0.03833	0.08146
NM	0.00404	0.00358	0.22086	0.00387	0.00314	0.00306
DP	0.08398	0.13028	0.05000	0.32587	0.31112	0.07435

	CH	OM	TR	MS	NM	DP
MM	0.04121	0.02168	0.07608	0.02236	0.05865	0.03801
CO	0.00153	0.00094	0.00958	0.00600	0.01076	0.09585
AP	0.23457	0.21125	0.37928	0.24039	0.60000	0.00000
AG	0.00730	0.16215	0.00042	0.00879	0.00877	0.01555
EN	0.07632	0.02552	0.07957	0.02353	0.02525	0.03663
BA	0.03939	0.00863	0.00561	0.00214	0.00666	0.00412
CH	0.28051	0.05032	0.00531	0.01120	0.04157	0.00906
OM	0.06908	0.24676	0.03534	0.05248	0.07373	0.17817
TR	0.02812	0.02063	0.07273	0.00796	0.01008	0.01739
MS	0.07957	0.09292	0.09932	0.22295	0.12797	0.31134
NM	0.00754	0.00410	0.00610	0.01018	0.03000	0.21388
DP	0.13486	0.15510	0.23066	0.39203	0.00657	0.08000

Table for the monthly o_j

MM : 40417	EN : 11167	TR : 7392
CO : 14583	BA : 15167	MS : 65417
AP : 63583	CH : 9000	NM : 22833
AG : 7308	OM : 34250	DP : 34583

(dist(l,k)/minimum dist) :

1.41						
3.	1.833					
3.33	4.33	1.08				
6.66	7.33	4.	1.5			
5.	6.	2.33	3.33	1.33		
2.66	4.66	2.33	5.33	3.	1.	
9.	8.66	6.	2.66	5.33	7.33	1.

Table for the ω_{ij} :

	MM	CO	AP	AG	EN	BA
MM	1.0077	1.0703	0.9934	0.9921	0.9849	0.9924
CO	1.0141	1.0741	0.9930	0.9918	0.9859	0.9979
AP	1.0081	1.0814	0.9955	0.9950	0.9840	0.9920
AG	1.0128	1.0203	0.9944	0.9849	0.9413	0.9974
EN	1.0090	1.0806	1.0010	0.9964	0.9866	0.9930
BA	1.0059	1.0799	0.9944	0.9948	0.9859	0.9916
CH	1.0087	1.0873	0.9970	0.9961	0.9612	0.9944
OM	1.0089	1.0755	0.9943	0.9927	0.9755	0.9872
TR	1.0058	1.0789	0.9914	0.9895	0.9784	0.9871
MS	1.0114	1.0813	0.9953	0.9895	0.9869	0.9932
NM	1.0099	1.0814	0.9980	0.9931	0.9865	0.9931
DP	1.0103	1.0817	0.9956	0.9914	0.9832	0.9895
	CH	OM	TR	MS	NM	DP
MM	0.9902	1.0027	0.9725	0.9934	0.9938	0.9924
CO	0.9945	1.0077	0.9843	0.9985	0.9971	0.9945
AP	0.9951	1.0021	0.9890	0.9931	0.9930	0.9945
AG	0.9555	1.0008	0.9776	0.9916	0.9858	0.9934
EN	1.0000	1.0050	0.9929	0.9960	0.9953	0.9964
BA	0.9816	1.0034	0.9894	0.9937	0.9707	0.9935
CH	0.9984	1.0030	0.9855	0.9904	0.9950	0.9946
OM	0.9902	1.0034	0.9858	0.9920	0.9852	0.9933
TR	0.9907	1.0005	0.9916	0.9946	0.9922	0.9904
MS	0.9996	1.0045	0.9939	0.9939	0.9972	0.9943
NM	0.9979	1.0042	0.9912	0.9946	1.0011	0.9980
DP	0.9928	1.0027	0.9865	0.9927	1.0025	0.9946

Appendix 2 : Equilibrium between savings and investments

We would like to verify that our equations always preserve the equilibrium between savings and investments : $S = I + \Delta St + (X\text{-}M) + (G\text{-}T)$.

The last term will have to be ignored in explicit reasoning since we did not yet include public accounting in our model, but this public deficit might play an implicit role in our subsequent dynamic reasoning, as will be seen later on.

For the sake of simplicity, we will assume there is only one zone outside the considered country : zone *nz*.

Let us develop the macro-economic ΔSt from equation 1 :

$$\Delta St = \sum_{k}^{nz-1} \sum_{j}^{ns-1} - \dot{b}_{kj} = \sum_{k}^{nz-1} \sum_{j}^{ns-1} \left(o_{kj} - \sum_{l}^{nz} \sum_{i}^{ns} a_{li \rightarrow kj} \left(w_{lji}\, o_{li} + \phi_{ji}\, i_{li} \right) \right)$$

the external summation ranges need not cover k=nz nor j=ns because that would correspond to variations of stocks from abroad and they are not defined for sector DP; but the internal summation ranges DO need to be complete since demands do emanate from abroad and from distributed profits. Let us now split this sum in three : the splitting coming from the minus sign, and the second split operating inside the resulting second term : separating all terms corresponding to l=1...(nz-1) from the ones corresponding to l=nz :

$$\Delta St = \left(\sum_{k}^{nz-1} \sum_{j}^{ns-1} o_{kj} \right) - \left(\sum_{k}^{nz-1} \sum_{j}^{ns-1} \sum_{l}^{nz-1} \sum_{i}^{ns} a_{likj} \left(w_{lji}\, o_{li} + \phi_{ji}\, i_{li} \right) \right)$$
$$- \left(\sum_{k}^{nz-1} \sum_{j}^{ns-1} \sum_{i}^{ns} a_{nz.i.k.j} \left(w_{nz.ji}\, o_{nz.i} + \phi_{ji}\, i_{nz.i} \right) \right)$$

The third term (or parenthesis) represents exactly the exports from all domestic producers [k,j] to all clients i from region nz (rest of the world), and after having transferred them to the left of the equality, we can further separate from the remaining second term the part concerning i=ns , which gives :

$$\Delta St + X = \left(\sum_{k}^{nz-1} \sum_{j}^{ns-1} o_{kj} \right) - \left(\sum_{k}^{nz-1} \sum_{j}^{ns-1} \sum_{l}^{nz-1} \sum_{i}^{ns-1} a_{l.i.k.j} \left(w_{lji}\, o_{li} + \phi_{ji}\, i_{li} \right) \right)$$
$$- \left(\sum_{k}^{nz-1} \sum_{j}^{ns-1} \sum_{l}^{nz-1} a_{l.ns.k.j} \left(w_{lj.ns}\, o_{l.ns} + \phi_{j.ns}\, i_{l.ns} \right) \right)$$

we can substitute in both second and third terms the indices [l,i] for [k,j] and vice versa since they play exactly the same roles over the same ranges now, and we can collect before the new summation sign over "l" the factors that do not depend on it :

$$\Delta St + X = \left(\sum_{k}^{nz-1}\sum_{j}^{ns-1} o_{kj}\right) - \left(\sum_{k}^{nz-1}\sum_{j}^{ns-1}\sum_{i}^{ns-1}\left(w_{kij}\, o_{kj} + \phi_{ij}\, i_{kj}\right)\sum_{l}^{nz-1} a_{kj.li}\right)$$
$$- \left(\sum_{k}^{nz-1}\sum_{i}^{ns-1}\left(w_{li.ns}\, o_{k.ns} + \phi_{i.ns}\, i_{k.ns}\right)\sum_{l}^{nz-1} a_{k.ns.li}\right)$$

Now, using the fact that the sum of **a**'s over all possible destinations must be 1, we have : $\sum_{l}^{nz-1} a_{kj\rightarrow li} = 1 - a_{kj\rightarrow nz.i}$ and it all ultimately boils down to the following when we bring the last two parenthesis under the same summation over k :

$$\Delta St + X = \left(\sum_{k}^{nz-1}\sum_{j}^{ns-1} o_{kj}\right) - \sum_{k}^{nz-1}\sum_{j}^{NS}\left[\begin{array}{l}\sum_{i}^{ns-1}\left(w_{kij}\, o_{kj} + \phi_{ij}\, i_{kj}\right) \\ - \sum_{i}^{ns-1} a_{kj\rightarrow nz.i}\left(w_{kij}\, o_{kj} + \phi_{ij}\, i_{kj}\right)\end{array}\right]$$

where the second term inside the square brackets [ ] gives the purchases of all outputs i=1...ns-1 produced in region nz (rest of the world) by all domestic sectors (DP being included, j=1...ns) and by all regions from the hinterland (k=1...nz-1) , in other words, the total imports by this country, that we can now move to the left side of the equation :

$$\Delta St + (X - M) = \sum_{k}^{nz-1}\sum_{j}^{ns-1} o_{kj} - \sum_{k}^{nz-1}\sum_{j}^{NS}\left[o_{kj}\sum_{i}^{ns-1} w_{kij} + i_{kj}\sum_{i}^{ns-1}\phi_{ij}\right]$$

where the second term inside the [ ] brackets equals i_{kj} because the ϕ_{ij} are 0 only for $i \leq 2$, so that their sum over ns-1 is equal to 1, and we thus recuperate the macro-economic investment $I = \sum i_{kj}$; which gives, after having again separated the terms concerning j=ns

$$\Delta St + (X - M) + I = \sum_{k}^{nz-1}\sum_{j}^{ns-1} o_{kj}\left(1 - \sum_{i}^{ns-1} w_{kij}\right) - \sum_{k}^{nz-1} o_{k.ns}\sum_{i}^{ns-1} w_{ki.ns}$$
$$= \sum_{k}^{nz-1}\sum_{j}^{ns-1} o_{kj}\left(1 - \sum_{i}^{ns-1} w_{kij}\right) - o_{k.ns}\left(1 - w_{k.ns.ns}\right)$$

where the last term corresponds to consumption coming from DP (let us call it C_2) and the first term can be split in three by separating all terms corresponding to sector 3 (AP) as follows :

$$\sum_{k}^{nz-1}\sum_{j}^{ns-1} o_{kj}\left(1-\sum_{i}^{ns-1} w_{kij}\right) = \sum_{k}^{nz-1}\sum_{j\neq 3}^{ns-1} o_{kj}\left(1-\sum_{i\neq 3}^{ns-1} w_{kij}\right) - \sum_{k}^{nz-1}\sum_{j\neq 3}^{ns-1} o_{kj}\, w_{k3j}$$

$$+\sum_{k}^{nz-1} o_{k3}\left(1-\sum_{i}^{ns-1} w_{ki3}\right)$$

where the first term equals the classic National Income (the sum of added values), the second term, using equation 1 for AP, can be proven to be equal to

$$\Delta St_3 - \sum_{k}^{nz-1} o_{k3}$$

which yields, after we simplify this re-written 2nd term with part of the 3rd :

$$\sum_{k}^{nz-1}\sum_{j}^{ns-1} o_{kj}\left(1-\sum_{i}^{ns-1} w_{kij}\right) = N.I. + \Delta St_3 - \sum_{k}^{nz-1} o_{k3}\left(\sum_{i}^{ns-1} w_{ki3}\right)$$

Now, if we call C_1 the 3rd term, corresponding to the consumption coming from AP, we obtain, for the main equation :

$$\Delta St + (X - M) + I = N.I. + \Delta St_3 - C_1 - C_2$$

and thus :

$$\Delta St_{\neq 3} + (X - M) + I = N.I. - C = S$$

Appendix 3 : Calibration results at the national level

The following figures show, for each sector aggregated at the national level, the historical evolutions (thick line) with the simulated ones (thin line) for production, with the percentage error just in front :

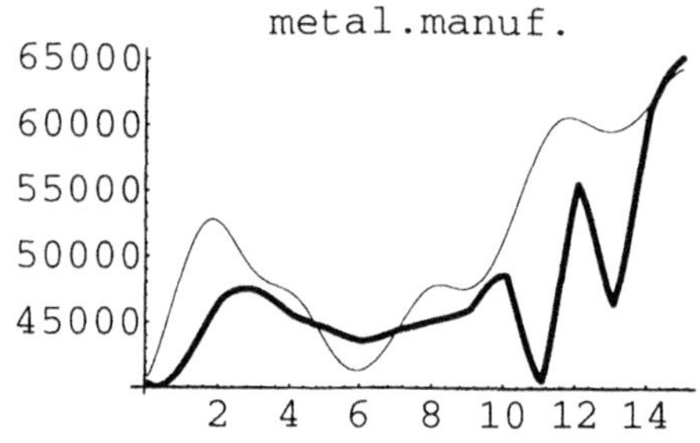

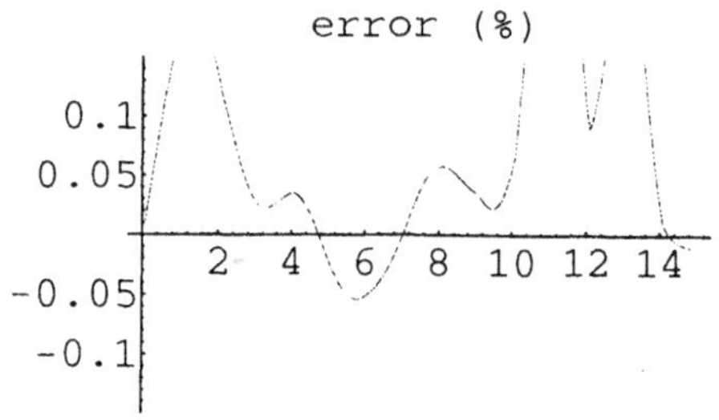

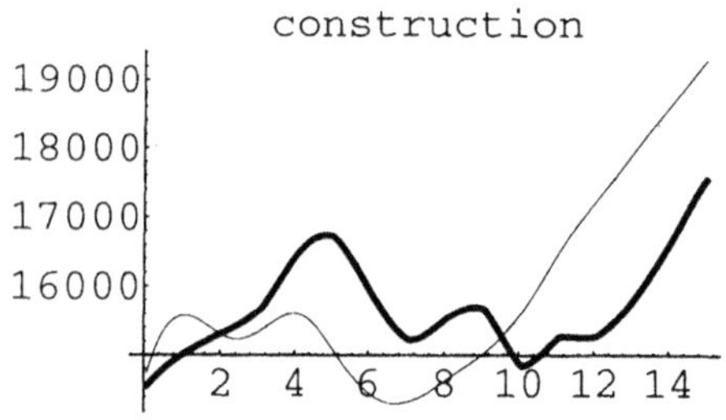

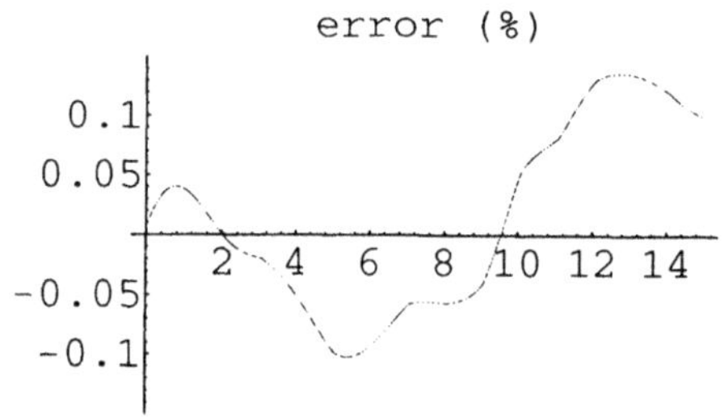

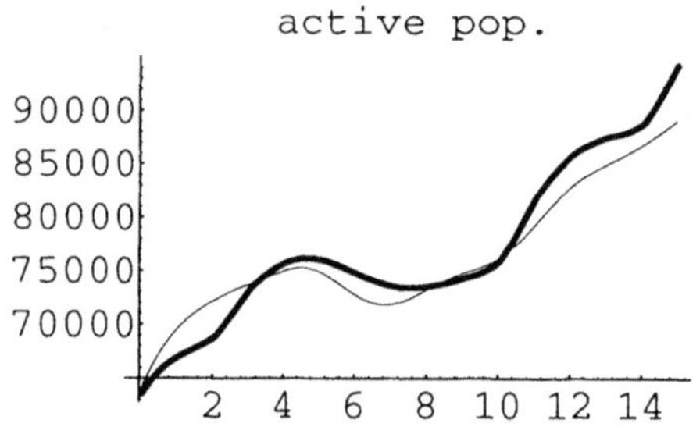

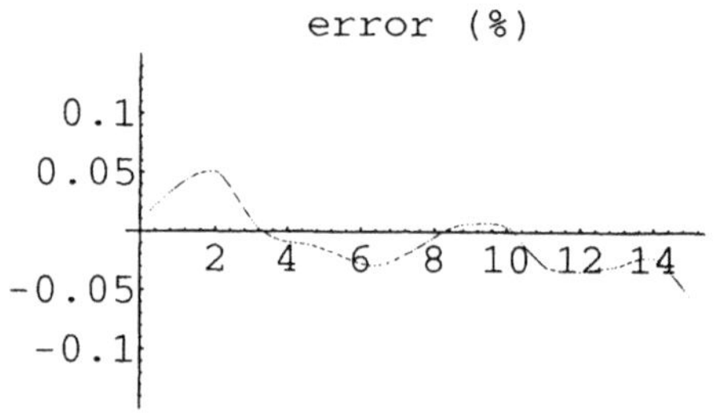

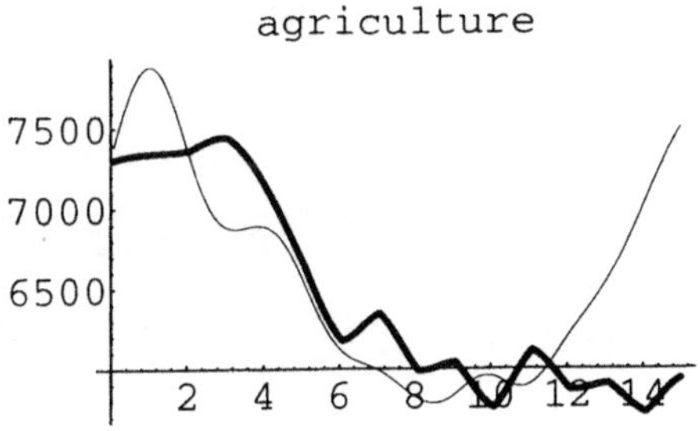
agriculture
7500
7000
6500
2 4 6 8 10 12 14

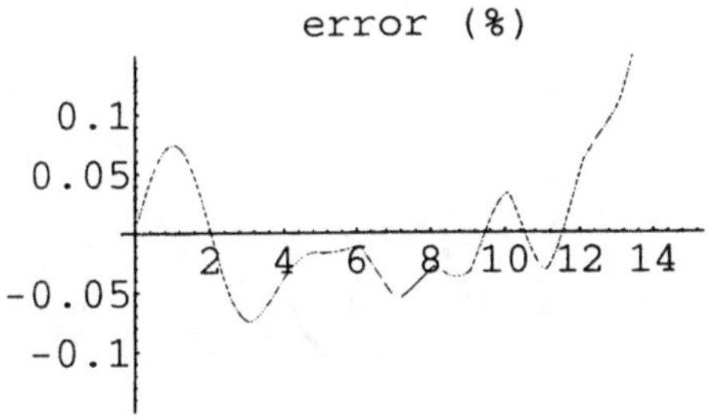
error (%)
0.1
0.05
-0.05
-0.1
2 4 6 8 10 12 14

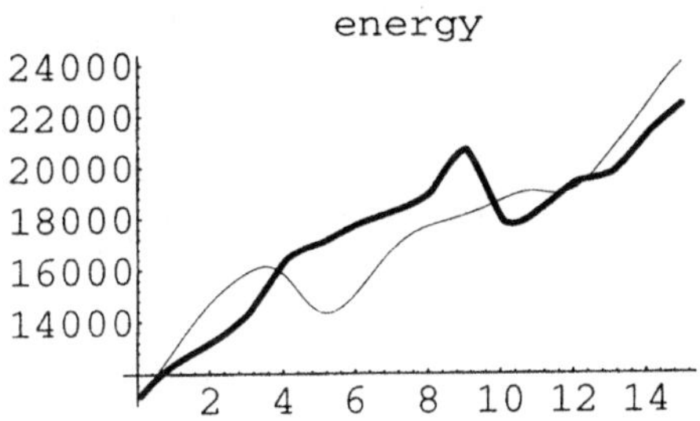
energy
24000
22000
20000
18000
16000
14000
2 4 6 8 10 12 14

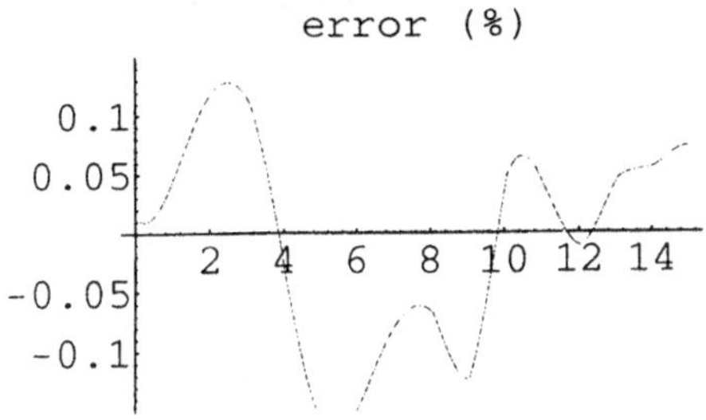
error (%)
0.1
0.05
-0.05
-0.1
2 4 6 8 10 12 14

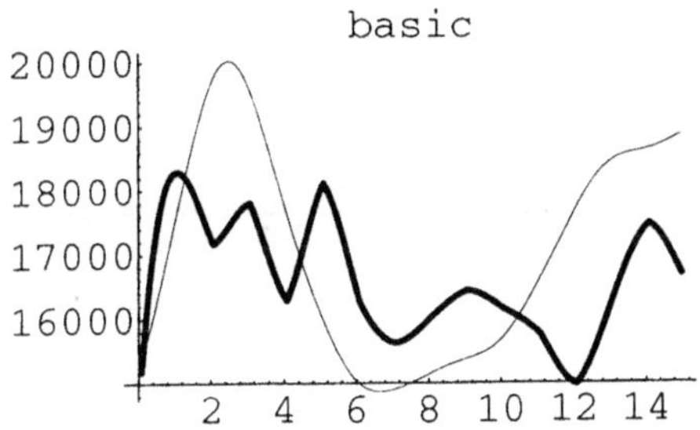
basic
20000
19000
18000
17000
16000
2 4 6 8 10 12 14

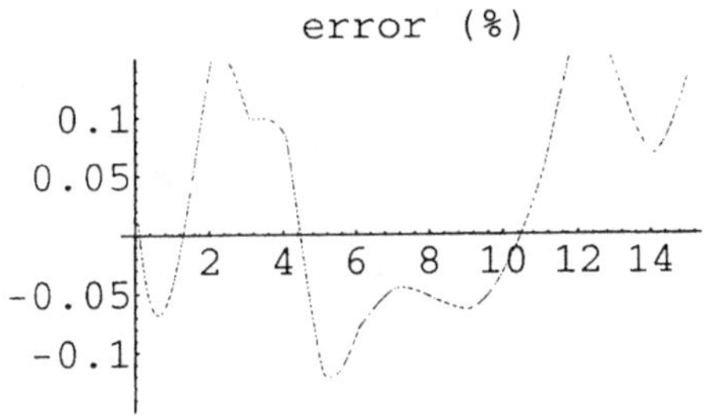
error (%)
0.1
0.05
-0.05
-0.1
2 4 6 8 10 12 14

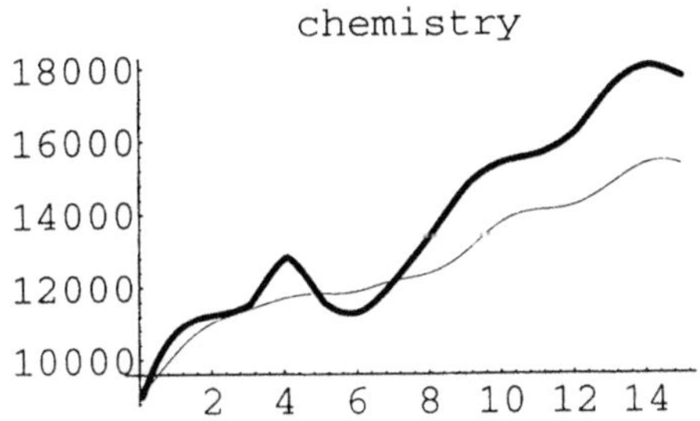
chemistry
18000
16000
14000
12000
10000
2 4 6 8 10 12 14

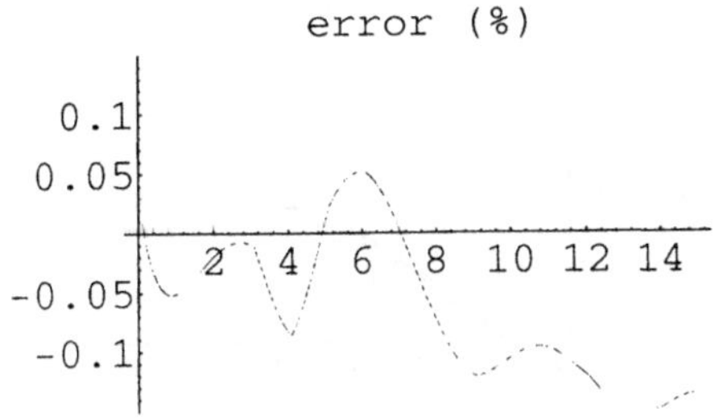
error (%)
0.1
0.05
-0.05
-0.1
2 4 6 8 10 12 14

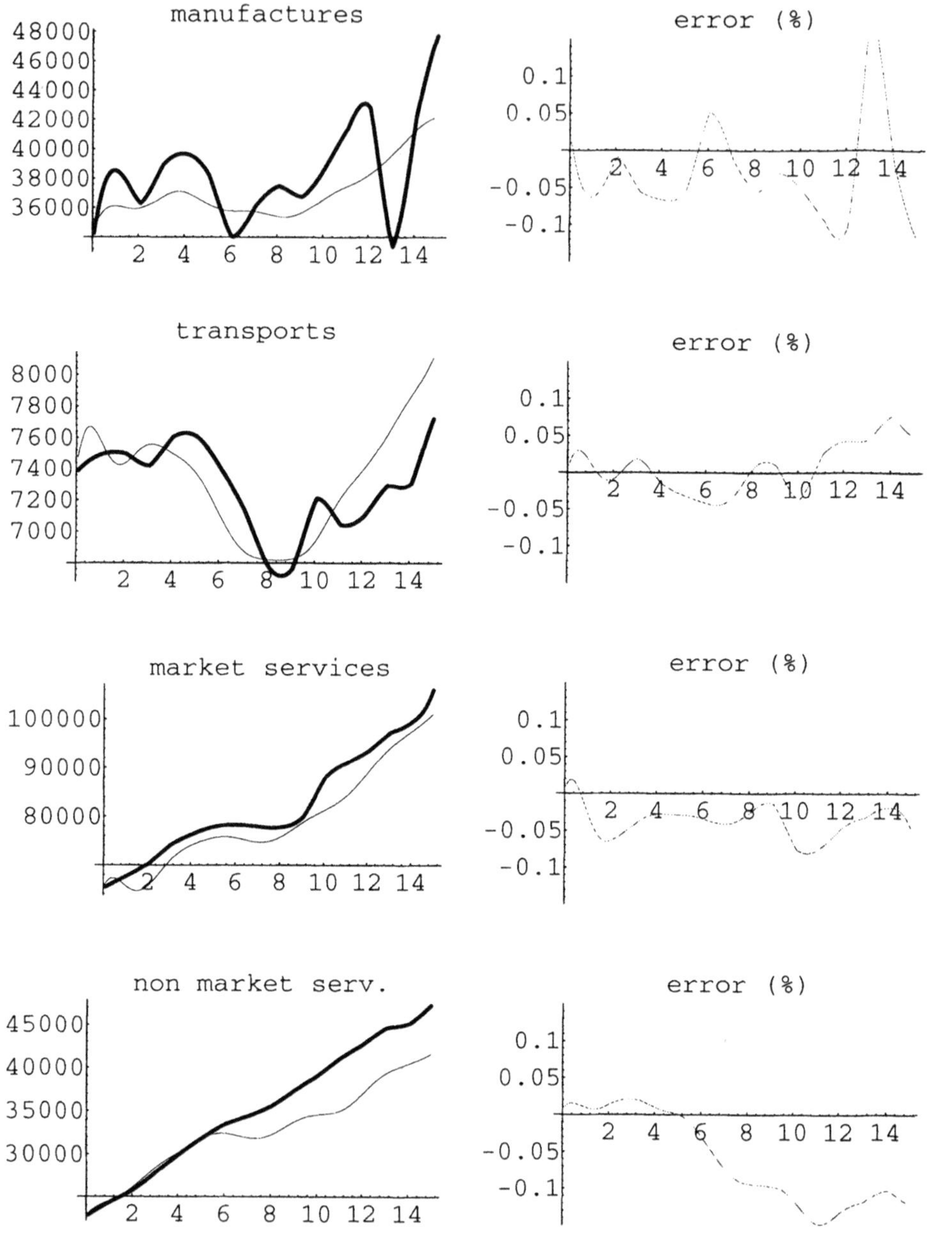
manufactures
48000
46000
44000
42000
40000
38000
36000
2 4 6 8 10 12 14
error (%)
0.1
0.05
-0.05
-0.1
2 4 6 8 10 12 14
transports
8000
7800
7600
7400
7200
7000
2 4 6 8 10 12 14
error (%)
0.1
0.05
-0.05
-0.1
2 4 6 8 10 12 14
market services
100000
90000
80000
2 4 6 8 10 12 14
error (%)
0.1
0.05
-0.05
-0.1
2 4 6 8 10 12 14
non market serv.
45000
40000
35000
30000
2 4 6 8 10 12 14
error (%)
0.1
0.05
-0.05
-0.1
2 4 6 8 10 12 14

Appendix 4 : Maps of the historical simulation

Initial production structure

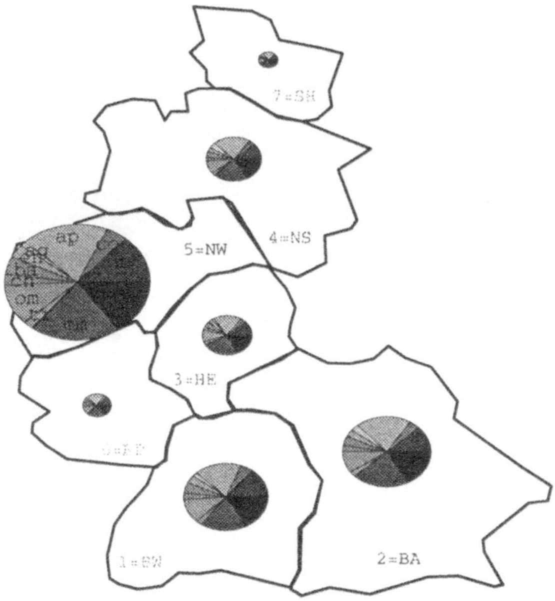

Production structure after 15 years

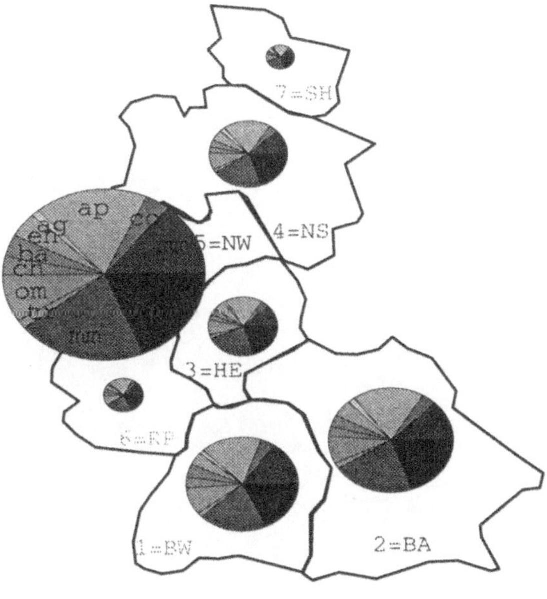

IV. Stochastic approach and data analysis

An Application of the Extended Linear Expenditure System to Pattern of Demand in the Jiangsu Province of China

Hua Ding .

International Business School, Nanjing University
Nanjing, China, 210093

1. Introduction

This paper discusses whether the Extended Linear Expenditure System (ELES) is able to analyze the pattern of demand in the Jiangsu province of China, based on the household budget surveys of rural and urban areas in the Jiangsu province from 1980 to 1990. During this period, the economy of Jiangsu province grew rapidly and went through two economic waves.

The results in Sections 4 and 5 show that the ELES could well explain the pattern of demand in the Jiangsu province from 1986 to 1990, but could not do that well for 1980 and 1981. The reason might be that, at beginning of the eighties the living standard in the Jiangsu province was lower, and goods were not rich enough to let consumers allocate their expenditures to maximize their utilities, but afterwards this situation had changed because of rapid economic growth.

Section 4 shows the estimates of parameters of the ELES. Among them, the minimum values of demand of goods were reasonable and dynamically stable from 1986 to 1990, but were not for 1980 and 1981, and the marginal propensities to consume some goods changed substantially from 1980 to 1990. It can also be seen that there was a sudden change of pattern of demand in 1988, the peak year of the economic wave.

In Section 5 various elasticities of demand are discussed. Their values calculated from estimates of parameters of the ELES for 1990 were reasonable for both rural and urban areas.

2. The Extended Linear Expenditure System

Consider the utility function

$$U = \sum_{i=1}^{n} \beta_i ln(q_i - r_i)$$
$$0 \le r_i < q_i, \quad 0 < \beta_i < 1, \quad \sum_{i=1}^{n} \beta_i = 1 \tag{1}$$

where q_i and r_i represent quantity of consumption and the minimum quantity of demand for the ith goods respectively, and β_i is the share parameter. Maximizing utility U from limited budget yields the demand functions,

$$p_i q_i = p_i r_i + \beta_i (M - \sum_{k=1}^{n} p_k r_k) \quad i = 1, 2, \cdots, n \tag{2}$$

where p_i is the price of the ith goods, and M is the total expenditure of a consumer. Demand functions (2) are called the Linear Expenditure System (LES).

Regarding the saving of the consumer as the $(n+1)$th goods, and changing the total expenditure, M, in the LES (2) to the income of the consumer, y, then the demanding functions (2) become the Extended Linear Expenditure System (ELES),

$$p_i q_i = p_i r_i + b_i (y - \sum_{k=1}^{n} p_k r_k) \quad i = 1, 2, \cdots, n+1$$
$$0 < b_i < 1, \quad \sum_{i=1}^{n+1} b_i = 1, \quad r_{n+1} = 0 \tag{3}$$

where b_i is the marginal propensity to consume the ith goods.

Obviously, only if a consumer could distribute his limited income to achieve the greatest value of utility U in (1), his demand function would be expressed by the LES (2) or ELES (3). When there is a shortage of goods in the market or the consumer's income y is as low as the minimum value of demand, $\sum_{i=1}^{n} p_i r_i$, the consumer could not distribute his income among various goods to maximize his total utility, then the LES (2) and ELES (3) could not fit the pattern of expenditure of the consumer. In Sections 4 and 5, the applicability of the ELES to the pattern of expenditure in the Jiangsu province is discussed with the empirical results.

The parameters $p_i r_i$ and b_i in the ELES (3) could be estimated with the grouped data in a household budget survey. Reforming the ELES (3) as

$$p_i q_i = a_i + b_i y \quad i = 1, 2, \cdots, n \tag{4}$$

$$a_i = p_i r_i - b_i V, \quad V = \sum_{i=1}^{n} p_i r_i \tag{5}$$

It is easy to estimate a_i and b_i in Equation (4). The V in Eq.(5), the minimum value of demand, could be calculated with a_i and b_i.

$$V = \frac{a}{1-b}, \quad a = \sum_{i=1}^{n} a_i, \quad b = \sum_{i=1}^{n} b_i \tag{6}$$

then parameters $p_i r_i$ are obtained from Eq.(5).

By partial differentiating the ELES (3), some formulae for elasticities of demand come out,

$$\eta_i = b_i \frac{y}{p_i q_i} \tag{7}$$

$$e_{ii} = -\eta_i \left(1 - \frac{V - p_i r_i}{y}\right) \tag{8}$$

$$e_{ij} = -\eta_i \frac{p_i r_i}{y} \tag{9}$$

where, η_i is income elasticity of demand, e_{ii} is price elasticity of demand, and e_{ij} is cross-price elasticity of demand. Then the price elasticities ξ_{ii} and cross-price elasticities ξ_{ij} of compensated demand are given by

$$\xi_{ii} = e_{ii} + \alpha_i \eta_i, \quad \xi_{ij} = e_{ij} + \alpha_i \eta_i, \quad \alpha_i = \frac{p_i q_i}{y} \tag{10}$$

Using the estimates of parameters b_i and $p_i r_i$, the average income y as well as the expenditures $p_i q_i$ of the total sample households, all the values of elasticities of demand could be obtained by Eqs.(7),(8),(9) and (10).

3. Explanation of the Data

The analysis in this paper is based on the household budget surveys of rural and urban areas in the Jiangsu province of China in the recent ten years. The Jiangsu province is situated in the east of China. It is one of the most advanced provinces in economy and culture, and its total output value had ever ranked the first one among all of provinces in China for some years.

During recent years, the economy of Jiangsu province has been growing rapidly. In the eighties, the average growth rate of GNP was about 11 percent. The consumption expenditure per capita increased from 265 yuan in 1980 to 456 yuan in 1989 in price of 1980, and buyer's markets for most of consumption goods have been forming gradually. Therefore, it seems that consumers are getting to allocate their expenditures to maximize their utilities more and more.

The Statistical Bureau of the Jiangsu Province conducts a household budget survey every year. The sample households are obtained by the stratified sampling method. The sample size in the rural area was about 1000 households before 1985, then increased to 3400 since 1985, and the sample size of in the urban area had been gradually increasing from 550 households in 1980 to more than 2000 since 1987. Thee data were grouped according to the level of household income per head, then, the average income and expenditures for various goods per head in every group were obtained. These grouped data were the source of the demand analysis in this paper.

Usually, the expenditure of a consumer in the urban area was classified into five categories : (1) foods (2) clothing (3) articles of everyday use, including furniture, bicycle, refrigerators and so on (4) articles of culture and entertainment (5) the others, including housing, electricity and water, services and so on. There were six sorts of expenditures in the rural area : (1) foods (2) clothing (3) articles for use (4) housing (5) fuel (6) services. The pattern of demand discussed in Sections 4 and 5 will use the above classification exactly.

4. Estimates of the ELES

Based on the household budget surveys in the Jiangsu province, the parameters b_i and $p_i r_i$ of the ELES for urban and rural areas were estimated by the method described in Sec.2. They are shown in Tables 1 and 2, where b_i and $p_i r_i$ are the marginal propencity to consume and the minimum value of demand, for the ith goods and services respectively, the subscript i is the ordinal number in the classification of expenditure in Sec.3, V is the minimum value of demand and the numbers in the brackets are the real values of corresponding items in price of 1980.

Inspection of Tables 1 and 2 shows the followings:

(1) The trends of marginal propensities to consume.
During these ten years, the marginal propencity to consume foods decreased, from 0.4278 for 1980 to 0.3640 for 1990 in the urban area, and from 0.3340 for 1980 to 0.2613 for 1990 in the rural area. Meanwhile, the marginal propensity to consume housing in the rural area increased from 0.1926 for 1980 to 0.2846

for 1990 substantially, but the marginal propensity to save was increased from 0.1399 for 1980 to 0.1956 for 1990 in the urban area. The expenditure for housing in the urban area did not change substantially, because the houses for households of the urban area were still provided by the State or working units.

(2) The sudden change in the pattern of demand occured in 1988.

The inflation rate in 1988 was 22 percent, much greater than previous years, thus, the inflational expectation of consumers made a sudden change in their expenditures. In the urban area, the marginal propensity to consume increased to 0.9754 suddenly, and consumers rushed to buy articles of everyday use, which caused the marginal propensity to consume rising to 0.2592 in 1988. In the rural area the change happened in expenditure of housing, and it caused the marginal propensity to consume housing to increase from 0.3286 for 1987 to 0.4790 for 1988. From 1988 to 1989, the economy of Jiangsu province went through an economic wave. 1988 was a prosperous year; 1986 and 1989 were depressed years. It can be seen that the greatest effect of the economic wave on the pattern of demand happened just in the prosperous year, 1988.

(3) Reasonableness of estimates of parameters.
Most estimates of parameters in Tables 1 and 2 are reasonable, but there are some exceptions. One exception is that the estimates of the minimum value of demand, V and $p_i r_i$, in urban area for 1988 were much greater than those for other years. This is due to the sudden increase of b, the marginal propensity to consume, in 1988. The estimate of b for 1988 was 0.9754, and it caused a large value of V, which was calculated by Eq.(6), therefore, the large value of V produced large values of $p_i r_i$, which were calculated by Eq.(5). Thus, it can be seen that the minimum value of demand, estimated with the ELES, is economically meaningful only when it is based on the data in the normal years of economy.

The estimates of V, $p_3 r_3$ and $p_5 r_5$ in the rural area for 1981 are negative, and they are also not reasonable. The reason will be analyzed in (4).

In Table 2 the estimates of b_4 for 1987, 1988 and 1989 are negative. In fact, the expenditure of fuel in the rural area was not related to consumer's income since 1987. Therefore these estimates of b_4 make no sense as well. However, the expenditures for other goods and services had high related coefficients with consumer's income.

(4) Suitability of the ELES for the pattern of demand in the Jiangsu province.
If the ELES is suitable for the demand pattern of the Jiangsu province, the estimates of its parameters, V and $p_i r_i$, should be in keeping with their economic sense. At first, they should be dynamically stable. Inspection of

Table 1: Estimates of Parameters in the ELES for the Urban Area

	Year						
Parameter	1980	1981	1986	1987	1988	1989	1990
b_1	0.4278	0.4302	0.2969	0.3356	0.3396	0.3394	0.3640
b_2	0.1197	0.1401	0.1263	0.1388	0.1458	0.1064	0.1093
b_3	0.1179	0.1577	0.1597	0.1687	0.2592	0.1900	0.1313
b_4	0.0785	0.0500	0.1041	0.0981	0.1382	0.1192	0.0944
b_5	0.1162	0.1282	0.2081	0.1158	0.0926	0.0871	0.1054
p_1r_1	242.8 (242.8)	152.5 (151.0)	324.4 (234.2)	378.1 (242.1)	895.2 (446.3)	527.4 (231.8)	498.9 (215.0)
p_2r_2	81.5 (81.5)	31.2 (31.5)	79.4 (82.3)	92.9 (91.4)	302.2 (258.3)	112.3 (79.0)	103.9 (67.7)
p_3r_3	40.2	13.6	52.5	73.7	421.2	89.6	60.6
p_4r_4	19.7	5.9	12.6	18.4	195.9	34.4	17.8
p_5r_5	63.9	36.4	48.7	89.2	224.1	131.7	124.6
V	448.1 (448.1)	239.6 (235.8)	517.6 (415.4)	652.3 (478.9)	2038.6 (1229.5)	895.4 (457.8)	805.8 (402.7)

Table 1 shows that the minimum value of demand, V, in urban area from 1986 to 1990 were 415.4, 478.9, 1229.5, 457.8 and 402.7 yuan respectively in price of 1980. They are rather stable except the value of 1988, 1229.5 yuan, which is abnormal as analyzed in (3). In Table 2 the estimates of V in the rural area from 1986 to 1990 were 329.9, 347.7, 327.0, 332.2 and 293.0 yuan respectively in price of 1980. They are more stable, even in the abnormal year 1988. Foods are the main consumption goods in China. Tables 1 and 2 show that the minimum values of demand of foods, p_1r_1, from 1986 to 1990, were respectively 234.2, 242.1, 446.3, 231.8 and 215.0 yuan in price of 1980 for the urban area, and were respectively 148.2, 154.1, 137.7, 147.0 and 138.7 yuan in price of 1980 for the rural area. They are also rather stable except the value, 446.3, of the urban area for 1988.

Secondly, the estimates of V and p_ir_i should be reasonable, compared with the actual expenditures of sample households. The average expenditures of all sample households in the urban area were 866, 953 , 1239, 1301 and 1339 yuan respectively from 1986 to 1990. They were compared with the corresponding estimates of V, 518, 652, 2039, 895 and 806 yuan in Table 1. The former were higher by 50 percent than the latter except that for 1988, and the estimates of V were close to the average expenditures of 10 percent of sample households, which had the lowest income. In the rural area, the

Table 2: Estimates of Parameters in the ELES for the Rural Area

	Year						
Parameter	1980	1981	1986	1987	1988	1989	1990
b_1	0.3340	0.3572	0.2363	0.1997	0.2163	0.2708	0.2613
b_2	0.1055	0.0854	0.0382	0.0344	0.0450	0.0529	0.0414
b_3	0.1926	0.3254	0.1756	0.3286	0.4790	0.3098	0.2846
b_4	0.0224	0.0071	0.0039	-0.0014	-0.0003	-0.0003	0.0003
b_5	0.0917	0.0891	0.1155	0.1116	0.1030	0.1029	0.0941
b_6	0.0135	0.0113	0.0168	0.0106	0.0151	0.0254	0.0241
p_1r_1	79.0 (79.0)	33.9 (33.6)	205.2 (148.2)	240.7 (154.1)	276.3 (137.7)	334.5 (147.0)	321.9 (138.7)
p_2r_2	14.0 (14.0)	3.1 (3.1)	36.1 (37.4)	34.2 (33.7)	38.1 (32.6)	48.5 (34.1)	43.1 (28.1)
p_3r_3	6.3	-53.8	96.4	102.5	113.6	133.8	93.9
p_4r_4	6.3	7.5	19.8	27.8	27.5	25.3	25.2
p_5r_5	10.0	-0.6	41.6	49.1	61.6	72.1	64.3
p_6r_6	4.2	3.0	12.0	19.2	25.1	34.5	37.8
V	119.8 (119.8)	-6.9 (-6.8)	411.1 (329.9)	473.5 (347.7)	542.2 (327.0)	649.7 (332.2)	586.2 (293.0)

average expenditures of sample households were 499, 579, 747, 811 and 787 yuan respectively from 1986 to 1990, and the estimates of V in Table 2 were 411, 474, 542, 650 and 586 yuan respectively. The average expenditures for 1986, 499 yuan, is just a little higher than the estimate of V, 411 yuan, and is higher and higher afterwards. These results are reasonable for the situation of economy in the Jiangsu province.

The estimates of V for 1981 are quite different from those for 1980. In the urban area, the estimate of V for 1980 was 448.1 yuan, but 235.8 yuan for 1981. In the rural area it was 119.8 yuan for 1980, but -6.8 yuan for 1981. These results are extremly unreasonable. It must due to the fact that the ELES is not suitable for the demand pattern of the Jiangsu province for 1980 and 1981. In Section 3, it was mentioned that at the beginning of eighties, the level of consumption in the Jiangsu province was lower and the goods in the market were not rich enough, thus, it seems that consumers could not allocate their expenditures to maximize their utilities, then the ELES could not fit the expenditure pattern for these years. Here, the empirical results support our guess.

Table 3: Elasticities of Demand for the Urban Area in 1990

	F	C	AEU	ACE	O	η
F	-0.5665 (-0.2025)	-0.0509 (0.0359)	-0.0297 (0.0419)	-0.0087 (0.0290)	-0.0610 (0.0345)	0.7168
C	-0.3080 (0.1509)	-0.4333 (-0.3240)	-0.0374 (0.0529)	-0.0110 (0.0366)	-0.0769 (0.0435)	0.9036
AEU	-0.4482 (0.2195)	-0.0933 (0.0658)	-0.6694 (-0.5381)	-0.0160 (0.0533)	-0.1119 (0.0633)	1.3149
ACE	-0.6103 (0.2989)	-0.1271 (0.0896)	-0.0741 (0.1047)	-0.9637 (-0.8694)	-0.1524 (0.0862)	1.7904
O	-0.2697 (0.1321)	-0.0561 (0.0396)	-0.0327 (0.0463)	-0.0096 (0.0321)	-0.3682 (-0.2628)	0.7911

5. Elasticity of demand

The elasticities of demand calculated by Eqs. (7), (8), (9) and (10) in Section 2 for urban and rural areas of the Jiangsu province in 1990 are shown in Tables 3 and 4 respectively. The abbreviations in these tables are : F (foods), C (clothing), AEU (articles of everyday use), ACE (articles of culture and entertaiment), O (others), H (housing), AU (articles for use) and S (services) respectively. The numbers in the row of foods are the elasticities of demand of the foods, and they are successively price elasticity, cross-price of the clothing elasticity, and so on, as well as the income elasticity of demand in the column η. The numbers in brackets are elasticities of compensated demand.

Inspection of Tables 3 and 4 shows the following :

(1) In the urban area the articles of everyday use, and the articles of culture and entertainment are luxuries, because the income elasticities of their demand are greater than one; but the foods, clothing and others are necessities, because the income elasticities of their demand are smaller than one.

In the rural area, housing is a luxury and other sorts of consumption are necessities.

(2) In both urban and rural areas, the price elasticity of demand was greater than the cross-price elasticities of demand for every sort of goods and services, and the cross-price of the foods elasticity was the largest among all of the cross-price elasticities. These results are reasonable to the reality of consumption in China.

(3) All of the price elasticities of compensated demand were negative and all of the cross-price elasticities of compensated demand were positive. It means

Table 4: Elasticities of Demand for the Rural Area in 1990

	F	C	H	AU	S	η
F	-0.3986 (-0.1373)	-0.0277 (0.0093)	-0.0604 (0.0441)	-0.0414 (0.0169)	-0.0243 (0.0051)	0.5686
C	-0.2313 (0.0605)	-0.2448 (-0.2034)	-0.0675 (0.0493)	-0.0462 (0.0294)	-0.0271 (0.0056)	0.6351
H	-0.5636 (0.1473)	-0.0755 (0.0253)	-0.6854 (-0.4008)	-0.1126 (0.0459)	-0.0661 (0.0137)	1.5473
AU	-0.3345 (0.0874)	-0.0448 (0.0150)	-0.0976 (0.0713)	-0.3760 (-0.2819)	-0.0393 (0.0082)	0.9183
S	-0.1698 (0.0444)	-0.0228 (0.0076)	-0.0496 (0.0362)	-0.0339 (0.0138)	-0.1769 (-0.1528)	0.4662

that any two sorts of goods are substitutes, after income is compensated. These conclusions are also reasonable.

However, for the urban area in 1980, the price elasticities of compensated demand were positive, and most of cross-price elasticities of compensated demand were negative. It means that an increase in the price of goods caused an extension in its demand, and some sorts of goods are complements to each other, after income is compensated. These results are not reasonable for the sorts of goods and services classified in this paper, and also show that the ELES is not suitable for the pattern of demand in the Jiangsu province for 1980.

References

1. Guo Jianjun (1989), *Analysis and Forecast of the Consumption of City Inhabitants using the Extended Linear Payment System Model*, Quantitative and Technical Economics, **6**, No.2, 49. (in chinese)

2. Henderson, J.M. and Quandt, R.E. (1985), *Microeconomic Theory, A Mathematical Approach*, McGraw-Hill Book Co.

A Master Equation Approach for the Modelling of Interregional Flows

Driss El Korchi, Michèle Sanglier
Instituts Internationaux de Physique et de Chimie fondés par E. Solvay, Campus de la Plaine CP231,B. 1050-Bruxelles, Belgium

Abstract. First, we design a macro-economic model which simulates a national economy disaggregated in various sectors and regions. The main endogenous variables are the sectoral production levels and prices. The demand is calculated through fixed input-output coefficients. Then, we connect each regional module with the others through a demand distribution function. A master equation approach introduced in the social sciences by Weidlich and Haag is used to model the interregional flows.

1 Introduction

This study is an attempt to model regional dynamics at both, macro and micro-economic levels. In a first step, the regions considered as autonomous entities are approached by an intersectoral model based on the input-output exchange matrix, with products and prices as the state variables. In a second step, we analyse the interactions between different regions. The connections between the different regional modules are modelled through an extention of the exchange matrix framework. A stochastic approach allows to extract the needed macroscopic information through an appropriate averaging method.

2 The macro-economic model for a single region

The macro-economic part of the model consists of input-output equations. These equations are a generalization of the dynamic Leontieff input-output models (I-O) [1]. This model generates endogenousely both the production and the sectoral price dynamic. Exports and imports are introduced in the model as exogenous variables. In the present system, the wage rate per sector and the final consumptions (domestic and public consumptions) are entered as fixed coefficients. In a further step, we develop a specific module for the wages and the consumptions.

If we consider an economy agregated in ns sectors, the (I-O) system will

[1] For applications of such a model, we can see for exemple Zhang, W.B. (1990)

be presented as a set of $2\,ns$ coupled equations (one price equation and one production equation for each sector).

The price evolutions are determined by equations which involve demands addressed to the sector and its supply (its own production here). The demands will be calculated through the input-output matrix. Indeed, the demand addressed to a given sector (D_j) will be a linear combination of the productions of the sectors from all the economy (X_j), and whose coefficients are those of the input-output matrix (ω_{ij}):

$$D_i = \sum_{j=1}^{ns} \omega_{ij} X_j$$

$$for\, i = 1 \ldots ns, \;\; j = 1 \ldots ns.$$

where ns is equal to the number of sectors considered

The gap $(1 - \frac{X_j}{D_j})$ between one and the ratio of the production to demand corresponds to an excessive or unsufficient production. These gaps will determine the evolution of the sector prices. We can write the equation for the sector i's price (P_i) as follows :

$$\frac{dP_i}{dt} = \pi_i \{1 - \frac{X_i}{\sum_{j=1}^{ns} \omega_{ij} X_j}\}$$

Let us point out that these equations for the price are only a mathematical representation of the supply and demand rule. If the supply is lower than the demand, the prices increase, while they have to decrase in the reverse case.

As for the production variation, it is proportional to the net investment (I). Globally, this investment is proportional to the difference between the production income and the production costs. If this difference is positive, the sector benefits of an increase in value which is re-invested in the expansion. On the contrary, if this difference is negative, which corresponds to a decrease in value, the sector declines. The production costs are represented by I O coefficients as follows :

$$Production\, cost\, of\, the\, sector\, j\, per\, unit \; = \; \sum_{i=1}^{ns} P_i\, \omega_{ij}$$

This allows us to write the equation describing the evolution of the production as :

$$\frac{dX_j}{dt} = \sigma_j\, X_j\, \{\, P_j - \sum_{i=1}^{ns} P_i\, \omega_{ij}\}$$

Adding on one side the demands addressed to the sectors like the consumptions (C_j) and the exports (Ex_j), and on the other side the sector input like the salaries distributed by the sector (S_j) and the import (Imp_j), the I-O equations system becomes :

$$\frac{dX_j}{dt} = \sigma_j X_j \{ P_j - \sum_{i=1}^{ns} P_i \omega_{ij} \} - S_j$$

$$\frac{dP_i}{dt} = \pi_i \{ 1 - \frac{X_i + Imp_i}{\sum_{j=1}^{ns} \omega_{ij} X_j + C_i + Ex_i} \}$$

Initially, the I-O system for one region, only considers external relations under an exogenous form (imports and/or exports). Within this study we will extend the technological coefficients to the interregional level by combining them to dynamic flow functions between regions, in order to make the system entirely endogenous. Indeed, the knowledge of the flows between the different sectors ($i\ j$ index) and the different regions ($k\ l$ index) permits to write the demand addressed to a sector i of the region l by the sector j located in the region k (D_{kj}^{li}) as following :

$$D_{kj}^{li} = F_{kj}^{li} \omega_{ij}^{k} X_{kj}$$

$$for\, i = 1 \ldots ns, \; j = 1 \ldots ns.$$

$$for\, l = 1 \ldots nz, \; k = 1 \ldots nz.$$

where nz is equal to the number of zones considered

If we gather the flow coefficients (F_{kj}^{li}) and the technological coefficients (ω_{ij}^{k}) we obtain a generalization of the I-O matrix :

$$\Omega_{kj}^{li} = F_{kj}^{li} \omega_{ij}^{k}$$

For the determination of the F_{kj}^{li}, we decided to use the master equations approach. This approach, introduced in human sciences by Weidlich & Haag (1983) offers an adequate structure for dynamical systems including a big amount of interactive agents at a "microscopic" level with visible effects at "macroscopic" levels.

3 Stochastic approach for interregional flows

Let us assume that each sector is composed of a number N of agents having the same characteristics and/or importance; each one producing the same quantity with the same technology. According to these asumptions, we are able to deduct the production for each of them as well as their needs for intermediary goods. Indeed, in both cases, we must only divide, either the total production or the total needs by the number N, to obtain the required variables.

Since the agents are free to adopt different purchasing behaviours, we can classify the agents belonging to the same sector j, and region k and purchasing an intermediary good i, from a region l, in the same group N_{kj}^{li}. By this definition of groups, any agent will belong at the same time to ns groups (the number of input sectors considered). So, we have the following configuration for each intermediary good :

$$N^i = \{N_{11}^{1i}, \ldots, N_{11}^{Li}, \ldots, N_{kj}^{li}, \ldots, N_{KJ}^{Li}\}$$

where N_{kj}^{li} is equal to the different agents of the sector j and the region k buying good i in region l.

This grouping allows us to identify the interregional flow coefficient under the form :

$$F_{kj}^{li} = \frac{N_{kj}^{li}}{\sum_{l=1}^{nz} N_{kj}^{li}}$$

and thus to determine the orders generated by each configuration.

3.1 Evolution of the Ni configuration

So the flows dynamic will be described by the evolution of the N^i configurations. The different types of individual agent behaviours must be taken into account to model these configurations. Generally speaking, by considering the situations we are studying, we meet 2 cases :

1) One agent can change of supplier, which gives :

$$N_t^i = \{N_{11}^{1i}, \ldots, N_{11}^{Li}, \ldots, N_{kj}^{li}, , \ldots, N_{kj}^{l'i}, \ldots, N_{KJ}^{Li}\} \Rightarrow$$

$$N_{t+\delta t}^i = \{N_{11}^{1i}, \ldots, N_{11}^{Li}, \ldots, (N_{kj}^{li}+1), , \ldots, (N_{kj}^{l'i}-1), \ldots, N_{KJ}^{Li}\}$$

2) An agent enters or quits a category without coming from an other group: it corresponds respectively to an enterprise birth or death.

$$N_0^i = \{N_{11}^{1i}, \ldots, N_{11}^{Li}, \ldots, N_{kj}^{l'i}, \ldots, N_{KJ}^{Li}\} \Rightarrow$$
$$N_{\delta t}^i = \{N_{11}^{1i}, \ldots, N_{11}^{Li}, \ldots, (N_{kj}^{li} \pm 1), \ldots, N_{KJ}^{Li}\}$$

The individual decision processes of agents with respect to some characteristics define the microlevel. However, a complete deterministic description of all individual patterns, which would overload the analysis with too many details is neither faisible nor desirable. We may circumvent the difficulty by introducing a probabilistic description.

The probabilistic description will be approached by a distribution function $P(N^i, t)$, which gives the probability to find the system in configuration N^i at time t. A distribution function must satisfy the condition of normalization and thus:

$$\sum_{N^i} P(N^i, t) = 1$$

where the sum is extended over all N^i configurations.

According to some general assumptions Weidlich & Haag [2] deduce the evolution equation for the distribution function :

$$\frac{dP(N^i,t)}{dt} = \sum_{N'^i} W(N^i|N'^i)P(N'^i,t) - \sum_{N'^i} W(N'^i|N^i)P(N^i,t)$$

where $W(N^i|N'^i)$ is the configurational transition probability per unit of time from state N'^i to state N^i.
The right side of this equation describes the difference between the probability flow into state N^i and the probability flow out of N^i.

The distribution function contains all information about decision processes. Unfortunately, the solution of the master equation is only possible in simple cases. But instead of solving these equations, it is possible to deduce evolution equations for the mean value of each category N_{li}^{kj} (i.e. $\bar{N}_{li}^{kj}$). These mean values $\bar{N}_{li}^{kj}$ will be supposed equal to macroscopically observed configurations.

3.2 Mean value equations

It is easy to show in our problem that the mean value equations are given by:

$$\frac{d\bar{N}_{kj}^{li}(t)}{dt} = \sum_{q=1}^{nz} \overline{W(N_{kj}^{li}|N_{kj}^{qi})} - \sum_{q}^{nz} \overline{W(N_{kj}^{qi}|N_{kj}^{li})}$$

However, in this form, we still need the distribution function in order to determine the transition rates of mean values. But, if we suppose the distribution

[2] Weidlich & Haag (1983) and Haag (1989)

function to be a regular, unimodal and sharp function, we can aproximate the mean value of a function by the function of the mean value and write :

$$\frac{d\bar{N}_{kj}^{li}(t)}{dt} = \sum_{q}^{nz} W(\bar{N}_{kj}^{li}|\bar{N}_{kj}^{qi}) - \sum_{q}^{nz} W(\bar{N}_{kj}^{qi}|\bar{N}_{kj}^{li})$$

Now, rewriting the $W(\bar{N}_{kj}^{li}|\bar{N}_{kj}^{qi})$ in terms of individual probability transition rates $(p_{kj}^{lqi}(t))$, which represent in our case an agent probability to change the origin of its input, we obtain :

$$\frac{d\bar{N}_{kj}^{li}(t)}{dt} = \sum_{q} p_{kj}^{lqi}(t)\bar{N}_{kj}^{qi}(t) - \sum_{q} p_{kj}^{qli}(t)\bar{N}_{kj}^{li}(t)$$

In a general case, $p_{kj}^{lqi}(t)$ can be decomposed to a symetric and an asymetric term. The symetric one (ν_{lq}) can represent the physical distance between two regions. The second term could involve the comparative characteristics like agent utilities (u_{kj}^{li}) to buy in a region instead of another. The following minimal requirements must be fulfilled :

1) $p_{kj}^{qli} \geq 0$, for all indices l et q;

2) $u_{kj}^{li} \geq u_{kj}^{q} \Rightarrow p_{kj}^{lq} \geq p_{kj}^{ql}$;

3) p_{kj}^{lq} must be a decreasing function of the difference $(u_{kj}^{li} - u_{kj}^{qi})$.

The most reasonable form for $p_{kj}^{lq}(t)$ satisfying these conditions is an exponential function :

$$p_{kj}^{lq} \approx \nu_{lq}\, exp\{u_{kj}^{li} - u_{kj}^{qi}\}$$

The utility functions depend on system characteristics. We set them inversely proportional to the prices of each sector.

$$u_{kj}^{li}(t) = \frac{\alpha_{kj}^{l}}{P_{li}(t)}$$

Where α_{kj}^{l} is a trend parameter which may contain exogeneous variables.

4 The global model

Combining the different parts of our model, we obtain the following nonlinear set of equations;

$$
\begin{aligned}
\frac{dX_{kj}(t)}{dt} &= \sigma_{kj}\, X_{kj}(t)\, \{\, P_{kj}(t) - \sum_{l,i=1}^{nz,ns} P_{li}(t)\, \Omega_{kj}^{li}(t)\,\} - S_{kj}(t) \\
\frac{dP_{kj}(t)}{dt} &= \pi_{kj}\, \{ 1 - \frac{X_{kj}(t) + Imp_{kj}(t)}{\sum_{l,i=1}^{nz,ns} \Omega_{li}^{kj}(t) X_{li}(t) + C_{kj}(t) + Ex_{kj}(t)} \} \\
\frac{d\bar{N}_{kj}^{li}(t)}{dt} &= \sum_{q}^{nz} p_{kj}^{lqi}(t) \bar{N}_{kj}^{qi}(t) - \sum_{q}^{nz} p_{kj}^{qli}(t) \bar{N}_{kj}^{li}(t) \\
\Omega_{kj}^{li}(t) &= \frac{\bar{N}_{kj}^{li}(t)}{\sum_{l=1}^{nz} \bar{N}_{kj}^{li}(t)}\, \omega_{ij}^{k} \\
p_{kj}^{lqi}(t) &= \nu_{lq}\, exp\{u_{kj}^{li}(t) - u_{kj}^{qi}(t)\} \\
u_{kj}^{li}(t) &= \frac{\alpha_{kj}^{l}}{P_{li}(t)}
\end{aligned}
$$

The stochastic or probalistic approach considered in this work significantly simplifies the problem. This approach allows us to determine the flow variables as the mean values of microscopic behaviour. Almost all the time, these mean values will depend on macroeconomic variables by individual probabilty transition rates. On the other hand, the IO equations are generalised to interregional. Factors as the interregional distance and the own region attractiveness, will be entered under exogeneous parameters form. The analyse of the model, according to the different values of the parameters, will enable us to test the occurent scenarios, to calibrate on the data bases and in a certain way to analyse the economical policy effects.

5 Numerical simulations of our model

In this section we discuss some numerical simulations related to two interacting regions with an economy aggregated in 2 sectors.

There are two specific cases :

1) economically similar regions;

2) economically different regions, one of them showing a less important growth than the other.

The economical differentiation of the regions and/or sectors can be made through the technological coefficients of the I-O matrix and/or by the level of the consumptions (C_j), the exports (Ex_j), the salaries distributed by the sector (S_j) and/or the imports (Imp_j), these last variables are supposed in the simulation proportional to the production level. We introduced then like parameters included between 0 and 1. In the two cases we took the next similar set of parameters for the simulation;

$$\omega_{kj}^1 = \begin{pmatrix} 0.30 & 0.30 \\ 0.30 & 0.30 \end{pmatrix} \quad \omega_{kj}^2 = \begin{pmatrix} 0.30 & 0.30 \\ 0.30 & 0.30 \end{pmatrix}$$

$$\sigma_{1j} = \begin{pmatrix} 0.10 & 0.10 \end{pmatrix} \quad \sigma_{2j} = \begin{pmatrix} 0.10 & 0.10 \end{pmatrix}$$

$$\pi_{1j} = \begin{pmatrix} 0.10 & 0.10 \end{pmatrix} \quad \pi_{2j} = \begin{pmatrix} 0.10 & 0.10 \end{pmatrix}$$

$$wages_{1j} = \begin{pmatrix} 0.204 & 0.221 \end{pmatrix} \quad wages_{2j} = \begin{pmatrix} 0.227 & 0.213 \end{pmatrix}$$

$$consumptions_{1j} = \begin{pmatrix} 0.45 & 0.45 \end{pmatrix} \quad consumptions_{2j} = \begin{pmatrix} 0.45 & 0.45 \end{pmatrix}$$

while the differentiation is introduced through import coefficients.

In the first case we took:

$$import_{1j} = \begin{pmatrix} 0.107 & 0.105 \end{pmatrix} \quad import_{2j} = \begin{pmatrix} 0.107 & 0.109 \end{pmatrix}$$

and in the second case, we took:

$$import_{1j} = \begin{pmatrix} 0.207 & 0.205 \end{pmatrix} \quad import_{2j} = \begin{pmatrix} 0.106 & 0.109 \end{pmatrix}$$

We have considered both cases for different values of interregional distance parameters and for different attractivenesses of the regions. As it has been said before, the attractiveness parameters allow to insert in the model exogeneous factors which, contrary to interregional distance, are not symetrical across regions. Factors such as borders, which play a more or less important role (e.g.customs duties, currency fluctuations or regional dynamics, advertising effects) will be entered this way in the system.

The figures 1 and 2 show respectively in cases 1 and 2, the simulated evolution of production for the different sectors and regions for non coupled systems.

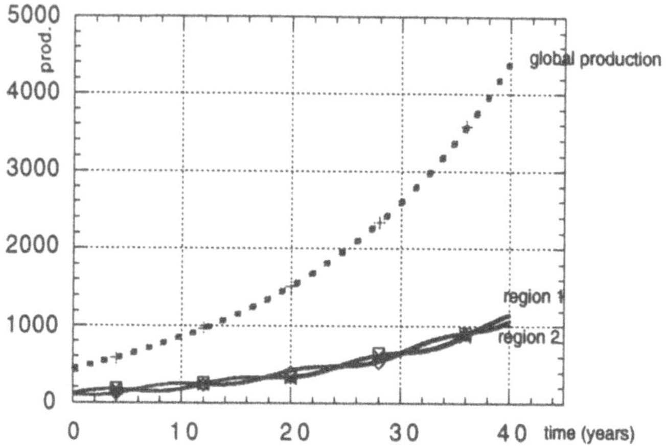

Fig 1 : Simulation in the case of two regions economically similar.
(no connection between the two regions)

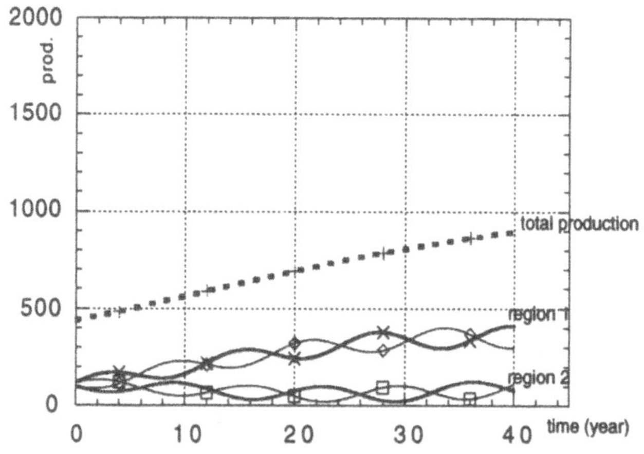

Fig 2 : Simulation in the case of two regions economically different.
The difference is induced by the technological coefficients
(no connection between the two regions)

In a system with two competitive regions , we may generally attribute a constant value to the atttractiveness of one of these regions (α_1 = constant) and let the other vary (α_2). For the simulations we set $\alpha_1 = 1$ while α_2 will vary between 0 and 2 by steps of 0.1.

The figures 1.1, 1.2 and 1.3 represent the simulation for case 1. We observe, according to the parameters values, differential evolution with a symmetry between the regions. This symmetry clearly appears if we look at the whole production evolution in function of the α_2 values (figure 1.4.). It seems that the flows between the regions is, in this case, favorable to both regions. The optimum is effectively reached when both regions have similar attractiveness.

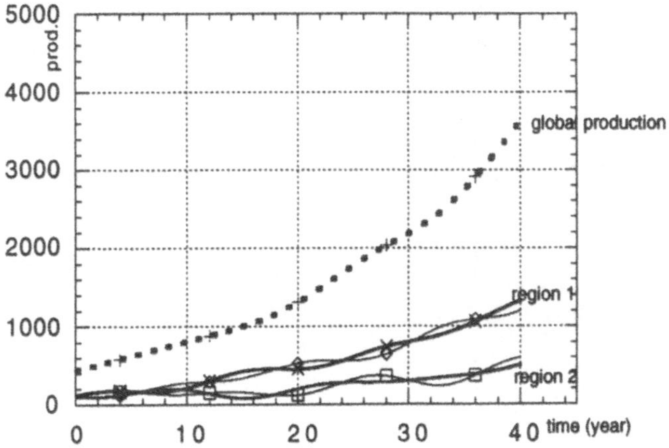

Fig 1.1 : Simulation in the case of two regions economically similar. (α1=1, α2=0.1)

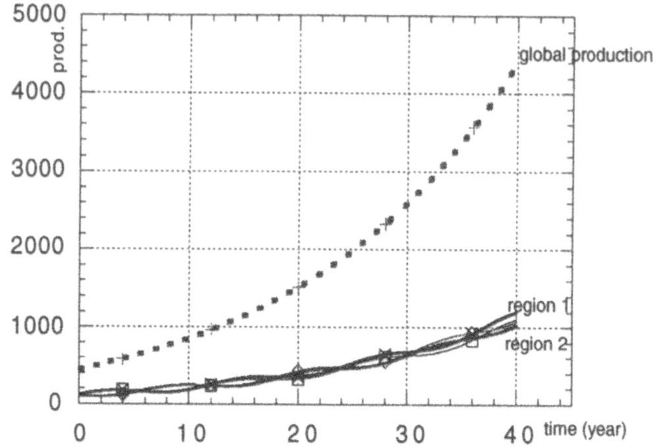

Fig 1.2 : Simulation in the case of two regions economically similar. Same attractiveness for the two regions. ($\alpha 1=1$, $\alpha 2=1$)

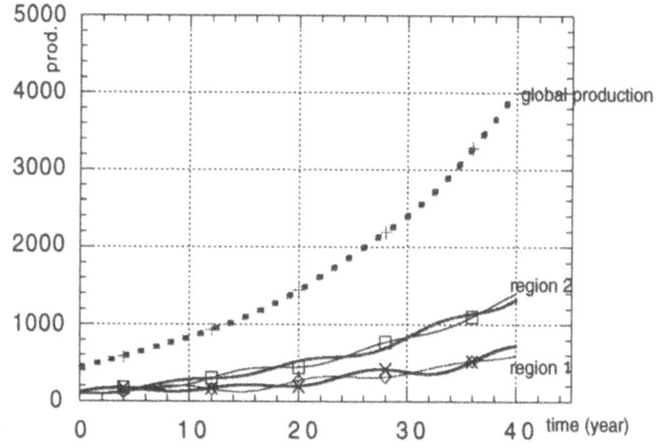

Fig 1.3 : Simulation in the case of two regions economically similar.($\alpha 1=1.0$, $\alpha 2=2.0$)

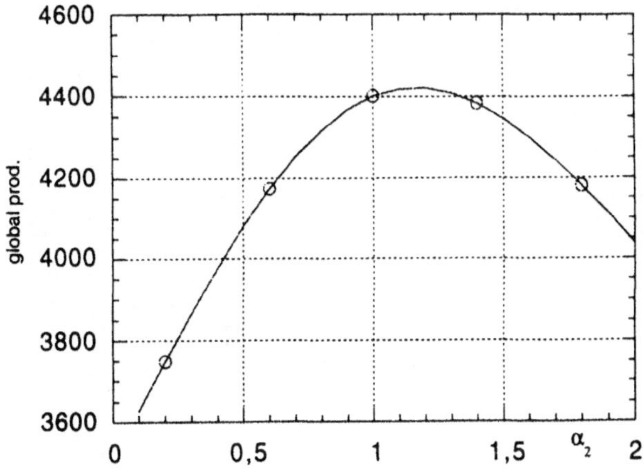

Fig 1.4 : The global production as a function of the parameter α2 (α1=1)(case 1)

The figures 2.1, 2.2 and 2.3 represent the simulation for the case 2. In that case, the symmetry between the regions disasppeared. Contrary to the first case, the whole production of the system is now decreasing as a function of α_2 (figure 2.4).

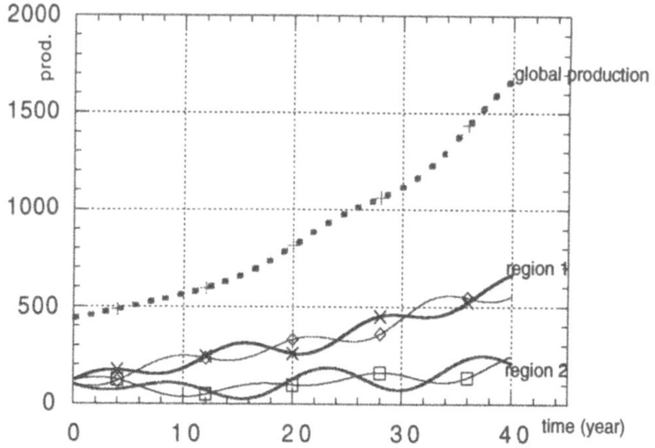

Fig 2.1 : Simulation in the case of two regions economically different. ($\alpha 1=1$, $\alpha 2=0.1$)

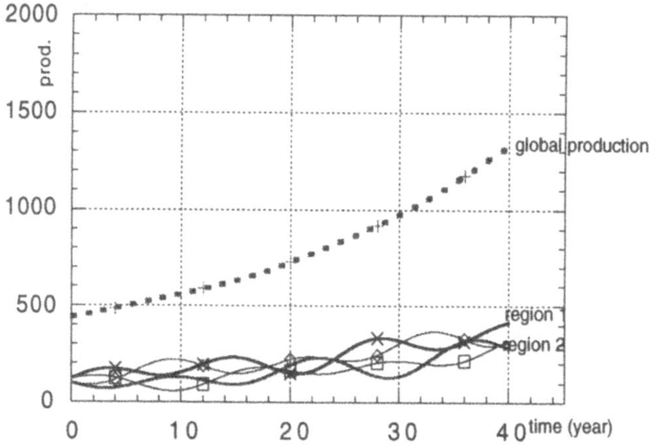

Fig 2.2 : Simulation in the case of two regions economically different. Same attractiveness for the two regions. ($\alpha 1=1.0$, $\alpha 2=1.0$)

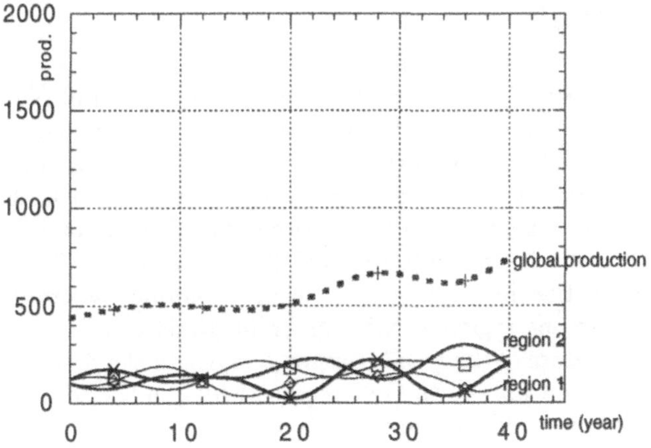

Fig 2.3 : Simulation in the case of two regions economically different.(α1=1, α2=2.0)

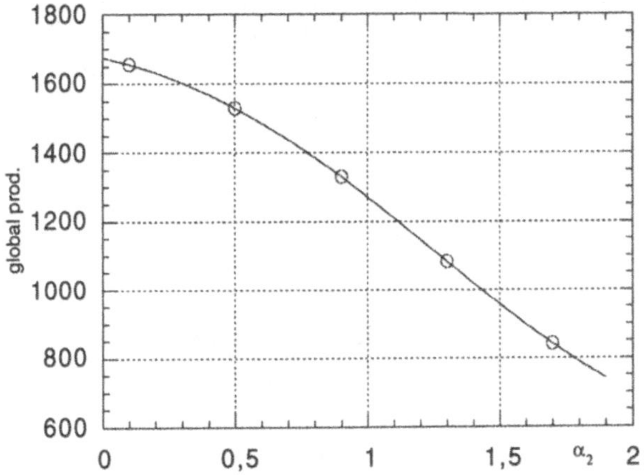

Fig 2.4 : The global production as a function of the parameter α2
(α1= 1.0)

6 Outlook

The model and the discussion above suggest the possibility of interregional modelisation which combine the classical deterministic macro-economic and the master equation approach. The first one allows us to simulate some marcroeconomic variables like prices, productions... for each region, while the second one (the master equation) combined to input ouput coefficients allows us to build some interregional flows variables. The first numerical simulations of the model in simple cases (economically similar regions, economically different regions) exibit different kinds of behaviors according to the relatives values of the trends parameters α_i. In the first case, competition seems to be favourable to the two regions while, in the second case, only the richest region wins of the competition.

7 Acknowledgements

This research has been made possible by a funding from DGXVI of the European Commission and this work is supported by the Solvay Institutes for Physics and Chemistry and l'Université Libre de Bruxelles. We would especially like to thank Rolando Guzzi for its constant interest and support.

8 References

Weidlich, W., Haag, G. (1983): *Concepts and Models of a Quantitative Sociology. The Dynamics of Interacting Populations*, Springer Series in Synergetics, Vol. 14 Springer, Berlin, New York.

Haag, G., (1989) : *Dynamic Decision Theory. Applications to Urban and Regional Topics*, Kluwer Academic Publisher, Dordrecht.

Zhang, W.B. (1990): *Economic Dynamics-Growth and Development*, Springer, Berlin, New York.

Zhang, W.B., (1991): *Synergetic Economics, Time and Change in Nonlinear Economics*, Springer,Berlin, New York.

Economic Entropy and Its Application to the Structure of the Transport System

Lu Jiang and Xiaohong Liu

Institute of Non-equilibrium Systems,
Beijing Normal University, Beijing 100875, China

Abstract: The need for a concept of economic entropy is discussed and a definition of economic entropy is given. The system of transport is described in terms of economic entropy. The structure of energy resources is examined and used in analysis of the economic development of various countries and of the characteristic features of economic entropy.

Keywords: Entropy, Transport, Evolution, Structure of system

1 Introduction

To study a complex economy system, usually, two different approaches have been developed. The first analyses interaction mechanisms in the economical system to construct various models to explain economic phenomena, achieve the goal of controlling the economy and molding its development to human needs. The second approach examines statistical data to find the underlined laws to achieve the same goal. Simple statistical concepts and definitions such as mathematical expectation, fluctuation and covariance between variables have been employed to explain a great deal of economic behavior on the basis of statistical data. An economic system is a hierarchical system in which there are complex interactions among subsystems. In a particular country, the development of one economic sector will accelerate or retard the development of others. At a world level, as trade among countries continues to expand, a change in the economic conditions of one county will influence the economic development of others. So globally understanding the economic development becomes more and more important. An efficient way is to study the structure of economic systems and the evolution of the structure with time.

Entropy has been introduced into economics by a number of economists. The distribution of the economic system and its evolution have been discussed. Interesting results have been obtained. (Willson, A. G. (1970), Theil, H. & Fiebig, D. (1981), Invernizzi, S. & Medio, A. (1991))

In our point of view, discussion of the concept of entropy in the economic system has two deficiencies. One is that entropy is discussed in a general sense and particular entropy has not been defined (Jiang, L. (1994)). The other deficiency is the adoption of the Principle of Maximum Entropy to analyze the evolution of the system(Jiang, L. (1994)). In economics the definition of entropy, usually ,is formulated as:

$$S = -K\sum_{i=1}^{N} P_i * \ln(P_i) \qquad (1)$$

The form is the same as in Shannon's information theory and in nonequilibrium statistical physics. The objects of discussion in physics and information theory are simpler; the meaning of P_i in Eq. (1) is very clear. Hence the entropy calculated from Eq.(1) can represent the distribution of subsystems in the system (the structure of the system). An economic system is complex and hierarchy. Its structure should be described in many aspects and at different levels. That means there are many kinds of entropy. Therefore, if we do not indicate the descriptive field and the variables of state, it is incorrect to conduct general discussion of entropy of the system. In the following, we will defy two entropies for one transport system to represent its structure from different aspects. One represents the structure of the system in terms of various forms of transport (rail, road, inland waterways, sea). The other represents the structure of the system in terms of the forms of energy used in transport. Those energies are hard coal and derivatives, brown coal and briquettes, aviation gasoline, jet fuels, motor gasoline, gas/diesel oil, heavy fuel oil, liquefied petroleum gases, natural gas and other derived gases, electric energy and other forms of energy . As we know, the second law of thermodynamics states that in the evolution process of a system entropy increases and gradually achieves maximum, in which the system is steady and does not change. The second law of thermodynamics requires the specific condition that within the system there is no exchange of matter and energy with the environment. Only when the isolated system undergoes spontaneous evolution does the entropy of the system increase and achieve the maximum. When there are interactions between the system and the environment, the entropy of the system may decrease, and the system may be in an orderly state with less entropy (Nicolis, G. & Prigogine, I. (1977)). This is because an economic system is a *live* system which continuously exchanges matter and energy with the environment. Some conclusions based on the principle of maximum entropy are sometimes restricted and sometimes incorrect in economy systems (Jiang, L. (1994)). In this paper , we show that the evolutionary direction of entropy of the transport system in different countries is different: it increases in some countries and decreases in some others. The increase or decrease of entropy with time reflects the different evolutionary features of the economic structure in different countries.

2. Economic Entropy Relative to the Structure of the Transport System

In this paper we analyze the data from *Annual Bulletin of Transport Statistics for Europe* (United Nations Publication, New York, 1978-1992) to discuss the concept of entropy in a specific way. We first analyze the data of drain on gas/diesel oil in various forms of transport. The results indicate the form structure of transport system and its evolution. Then we use the data of various forms of energy expended on the transport to analyze the structure of energy resource of transport.

Table 1. The drain on gas/diesel oil in various forms of transport in Germany (Unit:TJ)

Year	Rail	Road	Inland waterwy	Sea	Total
1978	21905	380030	39156	119475	560566
1979	22674	412055	42999	123873	601601
1980	22332	421876	36167	123232	603607
1981	21350	429989	35740	133181	620260
1982	21051	438529	34117	117041	610738
1983	20240	458427	32708	106536	617911
1984	19856	475678	33135	97185	625854
1985	20000	497000	30000	123000	670000
1986	19173	537786	28994	168245	754198
1987	18363	563108	25879	124357	731707
1988	16826	586169	25879	94629	723503
1989	17082	612732	25111	79155	734080

Table 2. The drain on gas/diesel oil in various forms of transport in Norway (Unit:TJ)

Year	Rail	Road	Sea	Total
1978	1544	20357	2419	43320
1979	1579	21515	19023	42117
1980	1624	21581	16286	39491
1981	1598	22012	5443	39053
1982	1099	23258	24653	49010
1983	973	24061	24696	49730
1984	1027	25384	26054	52465
1985	846	32760	27241	60847
1986	1142	46149	65057	112348
1988	1227	37882	39008	78117
1989	973	36800	34730	72503

Table 1 shows that the total consumption of gas/diesel oil has increased. The gas/diesel oil consumed by road has increased 61.2% during the 12 years. In rail and inland waterways, it has decreased, while in sea it has fluctuated. It is clear that road transport has become more and more important than other forms of transport. All these indicate that although transport in Germany has globally undergone a large-scale development, different forms of transport has developed at different rates.

When we analyze data of Norway given in Table 2, We can get similar general trend. Transport has globally developed. But All the three forms of transport are almost the same important to Norway's transport. There is no one form of transport outstandingly important

Based on the concept of economic entropy and Eq. (1) , we can give a quantitative description of the structure and evolution of the transport forms in Germany. In Eq. (1), here N=4 (there are four forms of transport in this system), P_i equals the ratio of the drain on gas/diesel oil in i-th form of transport to the total gas/diesel oil consumed. Entropy of each year is calculated and shown in Table 3. The entropy of the United States and Britain are also set out in Table 3 .

Table 3. Total drain on diesel/gas oil and economic entropy describing the structure of the drain on gas/diesel oil in transport (Unit: 100TJ)

Year	Germany		U. K.		U. S. A.		Norway	
	total	entr.	total	entr.	total	entr.	total	entr.
1978	5606	.9056	3661	.9703	27233	.6472	435	.8420
1979	6016	.8967	3791	.9761	29236	.6351	422	.8406
1980	6036	.8654	3608	.9557	28500	.6633	396	.8487
1981	6203	.8647	3340	.9217	28125	.6694	392	.8391
1982	6107	.8317	3677	1.0014	30155	.7550	490	.7845
1983	6179	.7921	3694	.9116			497	.7758
1984	6259	.7628	4117	.9374	30838	.5746	525	.7759
1985	6700	.7766	4290	.9260	30660	.5425	608	.7526
1986	7542	.7944	4543	.8626	31452	.5180	1202	.7078
1987	7317	.7134	4623	.7694			1123	.7285
1988	7235	.6432	5080	.7562	34192	.5015	781	.7630
1989	7341	.5939			35687	.4850	725	.7546
Rate%	+ 30.94	- 34.4	+ 38.76	- 22.07	+ 31.04	-25.06	+ 47.94	- 3.81
Ave.rate	+ 2.48	- 3.76	+ 3.33	- 2.46	+ 2.49	- 2.59	+ 5.75	- 0.55

From Table 3, We know that, in general, the total quantities of gas/diesel oil consumed in each country increased by more than 30%, with an annual average of 2.48%, however, the economic entropy of the countries all decreased. This decreases in economic entropy is because when using gas/diesel oil in some form of transport is efficient, this form of transport will develop rapidly. For example in Germany, Road has developed most and become more and more important than other forms. So the change of entropy reflects the change of the structure of the transport system. Also, we find that although the increase in total gas/diesel oil consumption is generally similar, the evolution of the structure of transport is quite different in each country. From table 3, We find that the degree of changes of entropy can reflect such differences. The greatest decrease of entropy in Germany shows that the structure of transport has changed most . From Table 3 , we can see that in Norway economy entropy almost did not change between 1982 and 1989, also it is shown in Table 2 that the structure of transport did not change during that period.

Above we have analyzed the transport system by considering its different transport forms. We can also analyze the structure of a transport system and its evolution from another point of view —from the energy sources used in transport.. In the following, the sorts of energy used in transport are the eleven types given by *Annual Bulletin of Transport Statistics for Europe* (United Nations Publication, New York, 1978-1992): hard coal and derivatives, brown coal and briquettes, aviation gasoline, jet fuels, motor gasoline, gas/diesel oil, heavy fuel oil (residual), liquefied petroleum gases, natural gas and other derived gases, electric energy, and other forms of energy. Table 4 gives out dateaof total energy consumed in Germany, the United States and Britain between 1978 and 1989.

Table 4. The economic entropy of energy used in transport (Unit: 100TJ)

Year	Germany		U. K.		U. S. A.	
	Total	entropy	total	entropy	total	entropy
1978	16575	0.8797	14592	1.1611	201389	.9088
1979	17404	0.9171	14915	1.1585	201363	.9544
1980	17610	0.9149	14795	1.1423	196296	.9906
1981	17163	0.9291	14252	1.1235	189704	.9772
1982	17199	0.9179	14763	1.1120	191514	.9462
1983	17433	0.9166	14923	1.0964		
1984	17834	0.9204	15705	1.0988	199436	.9618
1985	18190	0.9408	15942	1.0895	193202	.9722
1986	19570	0.9415	16877	1.0905	196652	.982
1987	19770	0.9387	17372	1.0836		
1988	20287	0.9450	18484	1.0881	208532	.9924
1989	20522	0.958				
Rate %	+23.8	+8.9	+26.67	-6.3	+3.55	+9.2
Ave. rate %	+1.9	+0.78	+2.39	-0.65	+0.35	+0.88

In Germany and U.K., the total energy used in transport has increased year by year at a rate of about 2%. During the twelve years it has increased more than 20% in Germany and Britain. Economic entropy has increased 8.9% (0.78% per annum) in Germany, but decreased 6.3% (0.65% per annum) in Britain . Changes of the energy structure in the two countries are different. When we consider more detail, we find that in Germany the more consumed energy has increased less, while the less consumed energy has greatly increased. Each component of the transport system turned to be unanimity. Thus the entropy of the transport system in Germany has increased. In Norway, things are different. The more consumed energy has increased greatly and rapidly. The structure of Norway's transport has become "asymmetry". Its entropy has decreased. Here we can see that the different trends of change of entropy represent different trends of development of economic systems. Moreover, in the United States during these ten years, total expended energy has not varied. But Its entropy has increased 9.2% showing that the structure of expended energy has varied most. The reason for the increase in entropy is that aviation gasoline and liquefied petroleum gases, both expended less per year, has decreased 32% and 67% respectively . So the change of the quantity of one type of energy consumed less can greatly affect the structure of energy in transport, although it does not greatly affect the total.

From above discussion , two entropies have been defined for the same transport system: one reflecting the structure from the point of view of different forms of transport; the other reflecting the structure from the point of view of different forms of energy expended in transport. We also find that the evolutionary direction of entropy in the economic system is indeterminate. Entropy may increase (so that entropy reflects the structure of energy sources in Germany) and decrease (so that entropy reflects the structure of energy source in Britain) with time.

3 Discussion

In conclusion , the measurement and analysis of the economic entropy of particular systems yields following conclusions.

1. Analysis of the quantitative change of economic entropy provides information on change in the structure of a system from a particular point of view: if economic entropy increases, this indicates that every component of the system generally tends to be unanimous; in contrast, the difference among each components increases.
2. Entropy is only a tool used to describe the state of a system. The relationship between entropy and other economic variables is still a problem which requires careful research.
3. The evolution of entropy with time reflect the different trends of development of different countries. And the different degree of change of entropy represent the different degree of change of the structure of the transport system.
4. Economic entropy can reflect the symmetry of economic system.

Acknowledgments

We would like to thank the University of Trento for its financial support and help with my research. We would also like to thank Prof. P. Villa and Dr. A. Belton for their useful assistance.

References

Annual Bulletin of Transport Statistics for Europe, *United Nations Publication (1978-1992)*, New York.

Wilson, A. G. (1970): The Use of the Concept of Entropy in System Modelling *Operational Research Quarterly 21,* 247-265.

Theil, H./Fiebig, D. (1981): A Maximum Entropy Approach to the Specification of Distributed Lags, *Economics Letters* 7339-342.

Invernizzi, S./Medio, A. (1991): On Lags and Chaos in Economic Dynamic Models. *Journal of Mathematical Economics 20* ,521-550.

Nicolis, G./Prigogine, I.(1977): *Self-Organization in Non-equilibrium Systems,* New York: Wiley.

Jiang, L. (1994): A Discussion on the Introduction of Entropy into Economics. *Journal of Systems Science & Systems Engineering 3,* 158-163.

Jiang L. (1994): A Note on the Maximum Entropy Approach to Economics. *Journal of Systems Science & Systems Engineering.*

Jiang L. (1994): Entropy in Nonequilibrium Phase Transition. *Journal of Beijing Normal University (Natural Science) 29*

Foundation & Prospect of Sino—European Market Combination

Xiaomei Li

Economics Department,
Huazhong University of Science and Technology, Wuhan, China

Abstract. We analyze the theoretical and realistic base of Sino—European market combination, state the bright prospect of the combination. Although there are some questions in the combination now, we propose corresponding policies.

Key words: System Reform ,Trade Deficit, Anti—dumping, Prospect.

1 Foundation of Combination

1.1 Heckscher—Ohlin Theory

Comparatively speaking, ECM has more capital and advanced technology than CM. China has comparative advantage of natural source, labor and part technology. It will benefit Europa and China even the total world that Europa and China make full use of their respective advantages of production factors. Both Advantages may complement each other. According to H—O Theory, the complementarity leads to the flow of capital & technology from ECM to CM and the refluence of primary product & part technology—intensive product from CM to ECM.

An important principal of H — O Theory is the reversibility of commodity trade and flow of production factors. Seeing from the view of geographical economics, we know Japan and America are superior in exporting commodity to China . So European Economic Community (EEC) had better enforce shifting it's technology and capital to China in order to open CM further and compensate it's disadvantage in commodity trade. Moreover, China hope to get direct investment as much as possible to produce and sale locally. This is a good oppotunity for EEC to invest in China.

According to the Theory of Product Life Cycle, it is necessary and realizable that mature product and technology in ECM spread to China. Sino — European market combination will promote the adjustment of European industry structure and give China a good chance to gain more market share in ECM than before. Especially those aging — industries in ECM, such as steel manufacture, automobile industry, and chemical industry, will develop rapidly in China.

1. 2 The Realistic Base of Sino — European Market Combination

It is well known that European production cost, tax and price are high, but China is exactly the country with low cost, tax and price. The three pairs of essential differences form the complementarity of Sino—European economy, which reveals the following:

European commodity urgently need the international market to support the slow economic recovery of Europa. On the other hand, China is a big developing market and greatly need science & technology. Generally speaking, European science & technology are advanced and Europa is glad to export her technology to China because both has not essential interest conflict. Furthermore, Europa has enough capital, and urgently seek overseas investment place. Because of high European wage level, and some shrivelled trades. Meanwhile, the development of various trades in China need lots of capital, and Chinese wage level is very low. In terms of German report, the cost of German labor is the highest in the world, that of American is it's 76%, that of Japanese is it's 80% and that of Chinese is only 1%. Therefore, European enterprises transfer their production to those countries with low salary and tax. As a rapidly expanding market with low production cost and tax, China actually has become the one of the best investment place in the world. Recently, China greatly need to speed up developing the capital construction, such as communication, transport, and energy industries. It is on the aspect of the development and management of infrastructure that Europa have their advantages of technology, and experience. It is powerful complementarity of Sino — European economy that provides realistic foundation for the combination of Sino—European market.

1. 3 External Pressure of the Combination of Sino — European Market

Sino — American economy develops unstably and easily is influenced by non — economic factors. Moreover, the rising protectionism of the NAFTA has obviously become the barrier which stops commodities of other countries from entering the North American market, and has led to a series of the trade conflict between the countries in the NAFTA and the others frequently and intensely. An outstanding example is that America reuse *The Super* 301 *Terms* in spite of the intense opposition of the international community. In fact , the direct goal of establishimg the NAFTA is exactly to resist Europa and Japan in the international competition; In the case of China, following problems are more serious: First, her economic structure and level are similar to those of Mexico and both have advantage in the traditional labor intensive industries. Second , Mexico enjoys the tariff preference of the NAFTA. So, in a relatively long period ,the products of Mexico will exclude similary products from China in the North American market. These products mainly are traditional labor intensive products such as textiles,toyes and so on . As a result ,non—NAFTA countries (areas) has begun to enforce business relation one another, and to adjust their trade policies to reduce the dependence on the North American market. I think the combination of the Sino—European market is inevitable and has internally urgent demand.

The Sino—European cooperation in the economy and technology has great achievement Since China began the economic reform. This has proved well that the Sino—European market combination benefit both. At the present ,the Sino—European cooperation has still enormous potential. Both may establish the long—term, stable and over—all cooperation relation without the essential interest conflict.

2 Prospect and Barrier of Combination

2.1 The Bright Prospect

From the aspect of the foreign trade, although the European trade value to China has been less than those of Japan and America for 15 *years, the growth of the European trade value to China is rapidly.* The Sino—EC trade value in 1993 increases 50% than that in 1992. The Sino—EC trade value in 1994 increases about 21.7% again. It is possible that the trade value of Europa to China catches up with and surpasses those of Japan and America before long if Europa keep her current developing trend in the future. ①Sino—Finnish trade value in 1993 increase by 23.4% over 1992, of which Chinese imports from Finland increase by 28% over 1992, which increase by 30% over 1991. ②Austrian exports to China in 1993 increase

① In terms of the Chinese customers statistics
② The Austrian Chamber of Commerce statistics

by 41% over last year. ③the Sino—French trade value in 1993 increase by 17% over 1992, of which French exports to China increase 10%. Sino—Swiss trade value in 1993 increase by 43. 7% over 1992. ④ German exports to China in 1993 exceed 10 billion Germany Deutsche Mark (DM) and increase almost 100% than that in 1992, which increase by 41% over 1991. In 1994, Germany gets $2. 5 billion equipment orders of communication, transport, energy industries , and other infrastructure from China. To some extent, those achievement comes from the rapid development of Chinese economy.

The growth of the direct investment in China is rapid too. According to the German report, the German investment in China has increased obviously since the end of 1991 and has reached 4 billion DM. Indeed, wholly German—owned enterprise and joint venture in China, such as the Siemens Co. and the Volk Co. , which have the huge investment in China ,almost all get quick economic returns. Meanwhile, European business of these companies has losses because of economic depression. In respect to her population and area,China is a big market, particually on the part of automobile and airline industries, China is the last big unoccuppied market. It is predicted that the total import of China from 1991 to 1995 will reach $400 billion, and infrastructure investmnt will almost need $600 billion. As has been noted ,China is a realistic big market and European enterprises will have a bright prospect of development in China. In this case,Europa had better make full use of the rapid development of Chinese economy to accelerate it's economic recovery. Moreover, the Coordinating Committee for Export Control has been dismissed on April 1, 1994. This provides more chance for Europa to benefit from exporting the sophisticated techniques to China than before, which may increase the exports of technology, equipment, and service, and also help reduce unemployment.

It is well known that the investment environment of China, hardware such as communication , transport & other infrastructure and software such as investment policies, has been improved greatly since the economic reform began. It is no doubt that this trend will still go on. China has finished drastic tariff cut in large scale and unifying exchange rate on the basis of market. *Now, China is carring out a series of bold taxation, finance, trade and investment system reforms.* These reforms greatly accelerate Sino—Foreign market combination.

In reference to the customary international practice, *China has established a new taxation* to create the circumstances of market economy for the equal competition of Chinese and foreign enterprises. The

---

③ According to the customer's satistics of France
④ The trade data from German Federal statistical bureau

transparency of new taxation is better than the old. New taxation benefits foreign enterprisers investing in China.

The reform of Chinese financial system is powerful. Uniformity of exchange rate of Renminbi (RMB) in January 1994 shows that China begin to ease her exchange control. This is the foundation of the combination of Chinese and international stock market. So, there are not technical problem for foreign capital entering the Stock A market. Maybe the uniformity of Stock A and Stock B market is not in the remote future, which will greatly accelerate drawing foreign capital in indirect way and expanding the size of drawing capital. Indeed, this will open broad investment area for huge international idle. In April 1994, China set up the first inter — bank exchange market in ShangHai to perform floating rate system and permited an American bank to try operating RMB transaction. China will finish many financial law such as Bank, Bill and Insurance Act. These reveals that China is speeding up opening market operation and China's financial management is being standardized. China will give foreign financial enterprise national treatment in predictable future and permit RMB to be exchanged free. Finally China's financial market will join in the international market.

The reform of Chinese foreign trade system shows the following:
First ,China reduces drastically her tariff, cuts her export subsity and boardens her import quota. Second, China sets up the single floating exchange system of RMB and manages it on market basis. New trade system eliminate the exchange remains of China's trade enterprises and unify exchange settlement. New system keeps abreast of the operation of international economy better than the old.

The investment system reform separates the policy financing from the business financing and opens some service business including retail, finance, insurance market and so on. We can establish the stock company utilizating foreign investment, seek BOT means of infrastructure, set up foreign investment firm and exploit foreign trust investment & fund.

These reforms greatly accelerate Sino — Foreign market combination, whose symbol is that China is a founding member of the World Trade Organizayion(WTO),and benefit foreign enterprisers from creating CM.

2. 2 **Barriers in the Combination of Sino — European Market**

2. 2. 1 **Primary Problems in the Trade**

Trade Deficit. Many countries think that China has lots of trade surplus. But China does not think so. How to solve the statistical discrepancy of Sino — European trade? I think this problem is complex. Current international statistical principle is *Origin—Consumer Country Principle* , which directly leads to the statistical discrepancy betweenChina and her trade partners. In fact, this principle interferes with forming the comparability of statistical data among nations.

At present, the primary reasons of the statistical discrepancy of Sino—Foreign trade can be expressed as follows:

Many China's export products are revalued upward greatly in HongKong. Sometimes the revaluation rate is higher than 50%. In light of the customary international practice , China thinks that the value of revaluation in HongKong should not be calculated her export value. But other countries still calculate import value from China including it in keeping with the origin principle. So, there is the statistical discrepancy of bilateral trade. China's entrepot commodity through HongKong mainly export America and Europa. Thus the statistical discrepancy about the appreciation of China's entrepot commodity artificially exaggerate China's trade surplus in Sino—American and Sino—European trade . Obviously it is not reasonable.

Besides, after China opened her door, many countries or area, for example, HongKong, America, Japan, Taiwan and so on, transfer their labor intensive industries to China. The most products of joint ventures and wholly foreign — owned firms in China are saled in America and Europa. So, China actually has not lots of exchange earnings, but has large number of surplus. This is unfair for China. Even if Europa has the deficit in Sino—European commodity trade, to some extent, the European surplus in the service trade, whose primary form is the transfer of technology, will offset it's deficit in the commodity trade. We should select the reasonable statistical principle of international trade to deal with the statistical discrepancy:

First, we should adopt the *Departure—Destination Country Principle* as soon as possible to eliminate the uncomparability of trade statistics. Second, after HongKong return to China in 1997 , Chinese statistical border will expand to HongKong. This will technologically reduce the statistical discrepancy made by the entrepot trade between China and her trade partners. Third, we should establish the coordinating institution of bilateral or multilateral trade statistics as soon as possible.

Antidumping. Recently cases that foreign countries accused China of dumping increase rapidly . The kinds of commodity investigated and taxed are more and more. Some commodity continuously are investigated and taxed in many countries. According to reports, the cases that EEC accused China of dumping goods account for 34% of the total dumping cases in 1992. We can see that Europa speeds up pursuing trade conservatism, although the chief reason is that some China's export enterprises excessively compete one another only by cutting price.

China had better research into the market of import country before export carefully to set reasonable export price and quantity to avoid being accused of dumping. Meanwhile ,China should enforce the antidumping measures, including legislation and establishment of the institution dealing with antidumping,and increase the investment to handle dumping and antidumping cases by inviting officer of WTO to give lecture and training all concerned officials. After certain product is accused of dumping, all relevant companies must actively coordinate to respond to the accusaction .

Some information tells that EEC mainly protect intraregional trade by non—tariff barrier compared with America and Japan ,especially against developing countries.

Table1. Percent of Import Commodity Influenced by Non—tariff Barrier (1984).

Name of import country	PICINB from developed countries	PICINB from developing countries
EEC	10.7	21.7
Japan	12.4	14.5
America	9.2	16.1

Source:Jan S. Hogendorn,Economic Development. P. 412

This table shows the rate that the export commodity of developing countries are influened by non—tariff barrier of developed countries is far higher than that of developed countries. In essense, the export of developing country to developed country nearly accounts for 60% of it's total export. Therefore, developing country is primary victim of new trade conservatism. It is more serious that some strict non—tariff barriers of developed countries play a dominant role in holding back the import of textile, dress, shoes, glass and so on. However, developing countries exactly have their comparative advantage in producing above labor intensive products, which are the most of finished products from developing countries. China is such a typification.

How to cope with non—tariff barrier? We hope to become a contracting member of the WTO as soon as possible and solve this problem with other countries by carring out the final agreement in Uruguay Round. Because the final agreement require that non—tariff measures of farm products be tariffized, committed and cut, and discriminating quotas of textile be abolished step by step in 10 years.

Protection of Knowledge Property Rights. The service trade, in which knowledge property rights is primary, is more and more important. Developed countries mainly export technology—intensive and knowledge—intensive products, therefore they are concerned about the protection of their knowledge property rights more and more. China has enforced the protection measures of knowledge property rights in compliance with the customary international practice. China has set a series of law such as the patent law, the copyright law and so on. But now the protection of China's knowledge property still has defect because of lacking experience, which is often complained by developed countries. This only is temporary. China is improving step by step. A outstanding example is that Chinese authority destroyed a factory that illegally imitated laser disk in ShenZhen in April, 1994.

Transfer of Environmental Protection Technology. At present, some European aging—industries, such as chemical and automobile industry, continuously are transplanted to China. It is inevitable that this kind of industry transplant will bring China environmental pollution. And it is well known that European environmental protection technology is advanced. So, Europa can create the environmental protection market in China by transfering the environmental protection technology corresponding to the chemical industry and the others.

2.2.2 Primary Problems in the Investment

European Investment in China. At present, primary European investment in China is the direct investment. The indirect investment is still at the small—sized experimental stage.

European direct investment in China makes full use of both comparative advantage and reduces the production cost, which strengthens European enterprises' international competitive power and satisfies China for getting technology. Therefore, both work hard to promote the European direct investment in China.

China should notice the following in order to draw foreign direct investment efficiently:

She should take full advantage of taxation leading the direction of foreign investment in CM, which mainly encourage foreign firms to invest in hi—technical enterprises and infrastructures, and encourage foreign manufacturers to establish joint venture with current state enterprises to avoid blindly building new factories which occupies excessive farm. Meanwhile she may exploit taxation to limit drawing enterprises with pollutants.

She should strengthen the administration upon the foreign capital.

First , we should strengthen the check and management of actually operating foreign capital. In a current random sampling survey of 1066 joint venture made by our state statistics department, we find that the actually capital input ratio of foreign enterprises' direct investment generally is relatively low.

Second, we must improve the investigation and management of foreign enterprises' evading tax and transfer of profits in compliance with the customary international practice.

Third, Chinese government should distinguish it's scope of positions and powers, and raise it's work efficiency when it exams and approves foreign investment projects, or provides service for the foreign investment.

Table 2. Agreement and actual foreign investment value

Years	Agreement Foreign Investment Value: Actual Foreign Investment Value
1987	100:62.38
1988	100:60.5
1990	100:51.7
1991	100:34.3
1992	100:18.98
1993 (1—10 month)	100:19

Source: Asian—Pacific Economic Times,(3.8.1994).

In addition to the direct investment,China must strengthen exploiting the indirect investment.

In a relatively long period,EEC has to make a great deal of investment in the East Europa (including Russia) in reference to it's strategic interest. Particularly, Germany has the heavy burden of rebuilding the East. So, it is difficult that China gains lots of European government loan or economic aid. On the other hand, EEC and America currently have the low interest rate & investment efficacy, and the smooth capital flow & slow economic growth. But they have not the tax reduction obviously. In result, a great deal of private capital outflow. ① For example, Germany lowened it's interest rate under the pressure of EEC from the end of 1991 to the middle of 1993. The private deposit, nearly 300 billion DM, was transfered to Luxembourg, Swiss, Austria and other countries for avoiding the deposit interest tax. The huge idle needs to seek a new investment place when economies of developed countries last depressed and their industry structure is adjusted. On the contrary, Chinese economy develops rapidly. The forming and opening of China's money and capital market provide a good investment chance for the huge idle.

I think, China should strengthen raising fund from overseas money and capital market as extensive as possible with various forms such as bond and fund. In the past years, China's successful experience in issuing bond and stock in HongKong, Europa and America has proved that China exploits the indirect investment is necessary and potential. Especially in building large — sized capital construction projects, which generally has the long construction cycle and slow capital recovery, we should exploit foreign direct and indirect investment together. Foreign indirect investment help China gain the long — term and large — scale financing quickly and promote the direct investment. We can draw foreign capital by flexible means. For example, we can get the bank guarantee by mortgaging the assets of company to purchase European and American advanced technology and equipment by progressive payment; we can carry on the compensation trade; we can exploit the buyer's credit and preferential loan provided by European banks as much as possible to purchase the foreign technology and equipment; we can try BOT means to combine raising fund with building in investing the large — sized capital construction project.

China's Investment in Europa. It is well known that China lacks the capital, especially the currency reserve. Therefore, China generally controls the outflow of capital except directly investing overseas for compensating her lack of some resource.

It has many advantages that Chinese enterprise directly invest in Europa, establishing wholly Chinese — owned enterprise or joint venture with local enterprises:

First, China's direct investment can take a round about the trade barrier of European market. Second, European enterprise generally has good commercial credit. So, Sino — European joint venture easily get the efficient bank support, such as easily getting the loan provided by local bank which is equal to the registered capital of the joint venture. European financial environment, infrastructure, communication and legal

① According to reports of Mirror Weekly

system are suitable for foreign investment. Particularly, on the part of enterprises managing the import—export trade, EEC provides China the Generalized System of Preferences (GSP) which is far perior to the Most Favoured—Nation Treatment provided by America.

On the other hand ,Europa lacks the attraction as a foreign investment market. First, European land price and labor cost are high. Second, China has to pay the huge environmental protection fees If directly invests in Europa. Third, the working hour of European enterprise is very short and company tax is very high. Besides, EEC limit foreign capital too strict. For instance, some products made in Europa are required to appreciate to 50%, otherwise these products are not regarded as the products of EEC. The company tax rate in Europa generally is higher than the average of the world yet in 1994 — 33%, although EEC lowen their interest rate and company tax rate to stimulate economy recovery and draw foreign investment.

Generally speaking, Chinese enterprise have not comparative advantage in directly investing ECM because of lacking capital. Therefore, now the China Europa business policy should still be *"Export—Seeking wholesaler —Investment"*.

Table 3. Company Tax Rate of Part European Countries in 1994

Name	Belgium	Luxembourg	Denmark	Norway	Finland	Portugal	France	Switzerland	Greece
CTR	39%	39.39%	34%	28%	25%	46%	33.3%	13.15—38.36%	35%
Name	Spain	Netherlands	Great Britain	Ireland	Sweden	Iceland	Germany	Italy	Austria
CTR	35.34%	35%	33%	40%	28%	33%	44.3—56.5%	52.2%	39%

Source: Industry and Commerce Times (3.7.1994)

But the applying of this policy is not absolute because the development level of whole Europa is not single. Some countries are advanced, such as Germany, France, Belgium and so on. But other countries, particularly the Eastern Europa, have relatively low productivity and their unemployment is worse than that of the Western Europa. Our productive technology and management exprience in some labor intensive industries have it's comparative advantage for taking in lots of local labors . Thus, China directly invests in ECM by annexing or purchasing the same kinds of European enterprise is possible. Futhermore, this can relatively ease the antidumping pressure upon China. At the same time, the East Europa has provided a series of preferential treatment such as the tax reduction and exemption to draw foreign capital.

Reference

Fu Donghui(1993):Anti—dumping:A Great Obstacle to China's Exports into Europe. *Intertrade*,Vol. 140,29—33

Zhang Yuching(1993): New Trend in Antidumping China's Products. *Intertrade*,Vol. 141,20.

Ke Juhan (1994):Comments on the Slow Development of West Economy. *International Finance*, Vol. 151, 5—7

Yao Sufeng(1993):EC's Protective Barriers in China Trade. *International Trade Journal*,Vol. 121,29—33

Shen Panyang (1993): EC and Responding Deal of Asian Companices. *International Economic Cooperation*, No. 1, 31—33.

LiLi(1994): China — Europe Economic Ties Strengthened. *International Economic Cooperation*, Vol. 104,5—9

Wang Zhile (1994):1993:Rise of East Asian Economy, Change of World Economic Pattern. *International Economic Cooperation*, No. 1 , 18—21.

Zheng Zhihua (1994): Group — Oriented USA — Canada — Mexica Free Trade Area. *World Economy*, No. 1, 62—65.

Zhu Xuebal (1993):The Rapid Development of Sino—German Economic Ties. *Federal Germany Research*, Vol. 7,No. 4, 14—17.

Huang Zhihui (1980): *International Economics*,Shanmin Press, 86.

A Generalized Ramsey Pricing Model with Applications to Chinese Postal and Telecommunications Services

Yang Chengyu

Institute of Nonequilibrium Systems, Beijing Normal University,
Beijing 100875, People's Republic of China

Abstract. This paper discusses the optimal pricing rule for a compound economy in which public and private firms coexist. A generalized Ramsey pricing model is introduced which is, in comparison with the traditional Ramsey model, characteristic of the mixed maximization of social welfare and self profits, returns to scale specific to good and exogenous price constraints. Finally, its applications to Chinese postal and telecommunications services are provided.

Key words: Compound Economy, Generalized Ramsey Pricing

1 Introduction

Optimal pricing for a compound economy in which public and private firms coexist is of both theoretical and practical interests. It is originated from the theory of optimal pricing developed by Frank Ramsey (1927) and later by Boiteux (1971) and Baumol/Bradford (1970) in the context of public monopolies as a second-best optimal pricing under budget constraint, and recently by Danielsen. et. al. (1990) as a third-best optimal pricing under both budget constraint and pre-specified allocation of revenue responsibilities among consumer classes. In this work, we consider a compound economy in which there are private firms whose objective is the maximization of their own profits and public firms who aim to maximize both social welfare and their0 own profits. It is assumed that some of these firms, both private and public, characteristically, may display increasing returns to scale. In this situation, it is general to say that first best optima are infeasible and it is difficult to imagine that public activities can be financed without any distortions in the economy. Given certain structural conditions that prevent prices from being set equal to marginal costs everywhere in the economy, the price distortions may be due to the government price control or to monopolistic pricing in the private sector. The analysis below shows how the pricing rules can be set on the basis of economic efficiency.

In Ramsey pricing model, the public firms' objective is simply assumed to be the maximization of social welfare, which we think to be oversimplified and unrealistic. The government is not almighty, so the public firms can not merely depend on subsidies and have to earn their own money. We assume that public firms preset the mixed maximization of social welfare and their own profits. Although most of the interesting models (Hagon/Sheshinski(1986),Danielsen et. al.(1989)) emphasize by a general constraint that the general increasing returns of scale of public sector contribute most to the deviation from marginal costs for pricing, they leave the fact that the returns of scale specific to each good differ a lot, a general constraint on the returns of scale of the whole production is unable to describe the state of every good's production and the interrelationship between production and pricing of different goods, then the inter-structure of multi-production. In this paper we define the returns of scale specific to good according to the generalized Aumann-Shapley average cost and introduce constraints reflecting every good's returns of scal.e.

In section 2 a general formulation of the generalized Ramsey pricing rule adopted by a public multi-product sector whose objective is the mixed maximization of social welfare and its own profits is provided. The public firm competes in some markets with private, profit-maximizing firms. Then the economic gradient method (Willig/Bailey (1979)) is presented as a practical approach to the calculation of the generalized Ramsey prices. Section 3 applies the generalized Ramsey pricing to Chinese postal and telecommunications services and get some interesting results.

2 The Generalized Ramsey Pricing Model

Consider a compound economy consisting of l individuals labeled h, m private firms indexed j, and a public sector. For simplicity, the public sector is assumed to consist of one public firm. There are n private goods indexed $i=1,\cdots,n$, consumed or supplied by the individuals, the private firms and the public sector. Let $x^h=\sum_i x_i^h$, $y^j=\sum_i y_i^j$, $z=\sum_i z_i$ denote respectively n-dimensional commodity vector representing consumer h's consumption plan, private firm j's production plan and the net production plan for the public sector. The technology of both private and public firms is characterized by the same cost function $C(\cdot)=F+V$, where F is the fixed cost, V is the variable cost and is assumed to be smoothly continuous on the commodity space. The returns of scale specific to each good is defined according to the generalized Aumann-Shapley average cost as follows:

$$GAC^i(C,q)=\frac{f_i F}{q_i}+\int_0^1 C_i(tq)dt \qquad i=1,\cdots,n \tag{2.1}$$

where f_i is ith good's share of the fixed cost, $f_i\geq 0,\sum_i f_i=1$. C_i denotes ith good's marginal cost. The attributable cost of ith good is $C^i=q_i\cdot GAC^i$. The returns of scale specific to ith product is

$$s_i = \frac{GAC^i}{C_i} = \frac{C^i}{q_i C_i} \qquad i = 1,\cdots,n \tag{2.2}$$

We assume that technically efficient production plans for the public sector are represented by a cost function consisting of all the returns to scale specific to good.

$$\sum_i s_i z_i C_i - C = 0 \tag{2.3}$$

The index set E represents the set of goods whose prices are under public control. Moreover, we assume that the public sector is subject to a budget constraint.

$$b - \sum_i p_i z_i = 0 \tag{2.4}$$

where $p = (p_1, p_2, \cdots, p_n)$ is a n-dimensional price vector.

We also assume that for the reasons which are exogenous to the model, some prices are subject to ceil and floor constraints given by

$$g_i(p_i - d_i) \le 0 \qquad i = i_1, i_2, \cdots, i_k, k < l - 1 \tag{2.5}$$

where $g_i = \pm 1$, $d_i > 0$.

Assume that individual consumption plans are ranked according to the strictly increasing and strictly quasi-concave utility functions $U^h(x^h)$ and social welfare is denoted by the weighted sum of individual utility functions. Public sector's objective is defined to be the maximization of $(1-\lambda)\sum_h \theta^h U^h(x^h) + \lambda \sum_i p_i z_i$, where $0 \le \lambda \le 1$ is the mixed factor.

We have the generalized Ramsey optimal pricing model as follows:

$$\begin{aligned}
\underset{(p_e, \{r^h\}, z)}{Max} \quad & (1-\lambda)\sum_h \theta^h U^h(x^h) + \lambda \sum_i p_i z_i \\
S.t. \quad & \sum_h x_i^h - z_i - \sum_j y_i^j = 0 && (\alpha_i, \quad i = 1,\cdots,n) \\
& \sum_i s_i z_i C_i - C = 0 && (\beta) \\
& b - \sum_i p_i z_i = 0 && (\gamma) \\
& g_i(p_i - d_i) \le 0 && (\zeta_i, \quad i = i_i, i_2, \cdots, i_k)
\end{aligned} \tag{2.6}$$

where $(\alpha_i), \beta, \gamma$ and (ζ_i) are the Lagrange multipliers of the corresponding maximizing problem. r^h is hth individual's income. It is easy to get the optimal conditions of the maximum by using the method of Lagrange multiplier. Then We have

$$\sum_i (C_i - p_i)\frac{\partial \hat{z}_i}{\partial p_e} = \mu z_e + (1-\mu)\sum_i\sum_j (p_i - {}^jC_i)\frac{\partial y_i^j}{\partial p_e} \qquad e \in E \qquad (2.7)$$
$$-\sum_i (s_i - 2)\frac{\partial \hat{z}_i}{\partial p_e} - g_e\eta_e - \sum_i\sum_k s_k z_k (C_{ik} + \frac{C_k \delta_{ki}}{z_i})\frac{\partial \hat{z}_i}{\partial p_e}$$

where ${}^iC_i \equiv -\partial y_1^j/\partial y_i^j$ denotes either the marginal cost of ith good ($y_i^j > 0$) or the rate of marginal substitution of ith input to the numeraire good ($y_i^j < 0$) of the jth private firm. $\eta_e = \zeta_e/\beta$ denotes the social effect of exogenous price constraints, $\partial\hat{z}_i/\partial p_e$ denotes the derivation of ith good's net market demand to the compensated price, i.e. $\partial\hat{z}_i/\partial p_e \equiv \sum_h (\partial x_i^h/\partial p_e + x_e^h \cdot \partial x_i^h/\partial r^h) - \sum_j \partial y_i^j/\partial p_e$, $C_{ik} = \partial C_i/\partial z_k$, μ is the traditional Ramsey number, explained as the shadow-price of the normalized budget constraint of the ith commodity. $\delta_{ki} = (z_i/s_k)(\partial s_k/\partial z_i)$ represents the cross elasticity of returns to scale specific to good.

If the independence of demands and constant marginal costs are provided, also, if we assume the private sector is perfect competitive and ignore the exogenous price constraints and elasticities of returns to scales, (2.7) will be simplified to a concise form:

$$\frac{p_i - C_i}{p_i} = \frac{s_i - 2}{s_i - 1} + \frac{\mu}{(s_i - 1)\xi_i} = \frac{\nu_i}{\xi_i} \qquad i \in E \qquad (2.8)$$

Here we have n ν_is specific to different goods and a traditional Ramsey number μ which has only one general value. The applications following are all based on this simplified formulation.

We can also see from (2.8) that $\partial[(p_i - C_i)/p_i]/\partial s_i = (1-\mu/\xi_i)/(s_i - 1)^2 \geq 0$, the larger the increasing returns to scales specific to good is, the larger the percentage optimal markup is. Moreover, we have $\partial[(p_i - C_i)/p_i]/\partial\xi_i = -\mu/(s_i - 1)\xi_i^2 \leq 0$, the larger the own-price elasticity is, the less the optimal markup is, this is what called the "inverse elasticity rule".

In order to calculate the generalized Ramsey prices, we choose the economic gradient method since information is available over too narrow a range to get any credible calculation of the global optimum. We then use the gradients of the relevant functions evaluated at the current point of operation and calculate the directions of change from the status quo that yields the greatest feasible local rate of increase in the objective function. Define Ramsey numbers μ_i from (2.8) that

$$\mu_i \equiv [(s_i - 1)(\frac{p_i - C_i}{p_i}) - (s_i - 2)]\xi_i \qquad i = 1,\cdots,n \qquad (2.9)$$

When the Ramsey numbers μ_i at the current point of operation are not all equal, optimality has not been reached and social welfare and public sector's profits could be increased without diminution of constraints by suitable adjustment of prices.

The critical Ramsey number μ is a weighted average of the Ramsey numbers of the goods whose prices are under consideration

$$\mu = \frac{\sum_i \mu_i (p_i z_i)^2 (1-\mu_i)}{\sum_i (p_i z_i)^2 (1-\mu_i)^2} \tag{2.10}$$

The optimal price change is decided by

$$\frac{p_i^* - p_i}{p_i} = \frac{(\mu - \mu_i)}{(\xi_i - \mu)} \tag{2.11}$$

where p_i^* is the generalized Ramsey price. Goods with Ramsey numbers larger than μ have their prices decreased in the locally best direction and inversely. In this direction, a larger proportional price change is indicated for a good having a relatively large value of own-price elasticity and having a relatively large deviation $(\mu - \mu_i)$. The percentage change Euclidean metric that measures the distance between the actual and the generalized Ramsey optimal prices is then determined by

$$\rho(p, p^*) = \sqrt{\sum_i (p_i^* - p_i)^2 / p_i^2} \tag{2.12}$$

3 Applications to PRC Postal and Telecommunications Services

We choose Chinese postal and telecommunications services (CPTS) for the applications of our model since it is a traditional public sector and is undergoing rate and structure adjustment in recent years. This study contrasts CPTS rates from 1988 to 1992 with those that are calculated to be generalized Ramsey optimal for five categories and services(all measured in RMB yuan). For each category or service, the price is taken to be the average revenue per piece, the marginal cost is assumed to be constant and equal to the average attributable variable cost, while returns to scale specific to good is calculated on a year-to-year basis. Cross elasticites of demand and elasticities of returns to scale are assumed to be negligible. Own-price elasiticities are determined over years and assumed to be constant. The optimal prices are calculated using the economic gradient method introduced above.

Table 3.1. displays the parameters and results of the CPTS Ramsey study of 1989 as an example. The percentage change Euclidean distance between the CPTS and generalized Ramsey prices $\rho(p,p^*)$=1.03 and μ=0.149. The move to the calculated optimal rates require a 19.4 percent decrease for telegram and 0.8 percent decrease for long distance telephone call and increases from 9.4 to 71.4 percent for the other services. The prices of mail and parcel post are extremely low compared with the optimal prices. This can be explained by the fact that those prices were decided by the government and have never been changed for 40 years. The prices of local phone call are measured in term of household/year.

Table 3.1. The Shift From 1989 CPTS Rates

	Actual Price	Quantity (10e6 pieces)	Own-price Elasticity	Marginal Cost	Ramsey Number	Optimal Price Change (%)
Mail Post	0.0542	5728.0	0.163	0.0317	0.139	+71.4
Parcel Post	1.744	99.4	0.163	1.024	0.139	+71.4
Long Distance Telephone Call	2.242	853.0	0.275	0.695	0.150	-0.8
Local Phone Call	215.57	4.4	0.255	67.258	0.139	+9.4
Telegram	1.644	297.3	0.340	0.511	0.186	-19.4

Table 3.2. shows the parameters and results of the CPTS Ramsey study of 1990. The percentage price change distance $\rho(p,p^*)=0.26$ and $\mu=0.145$. Because the PRC government increased the prices of postal services by over 150 percent on July, 1990, the prices of mail and parcel post are much closer to the generalized Ramsey optimal prices which can be seen easily from the table. The deviation from the optimum is mainly due to the difference between the large amount of investments i.e. the high returns to scale specific to good and relatively low existing price of local telephone call and due to the relatively high price of telegram with the largest own-price elasticity of all the telecommunications services.

Table 3.2. The Shift From 1990 CPTS Rates

	Actual Price	Quantity (10e6 pieces)	Own-price Elasticity	Marginal Cost	Ramsey Number	Optimal Price Change (%)
Mail Post	0.0607	5487.0	0.163	0.0300	0.143	+11.1
Parcel Post	2.323	96.9	0.163	0.0834	0.143	+11.1
Long Distance Telephone Call	2.371	1167.7	0.275	0.633	0.146	-0.8
Local Phone Call	236.14	5.39	0.255	62.813	0.136	+8.2
Telegram	1.819	268.2	0.340	0.484	0.181	-18.5

The comparison between actual and generalized Ramsey optimal prices of some Chinese postal and telecommunications services from 1988 to 1992 are shown in the following figures.

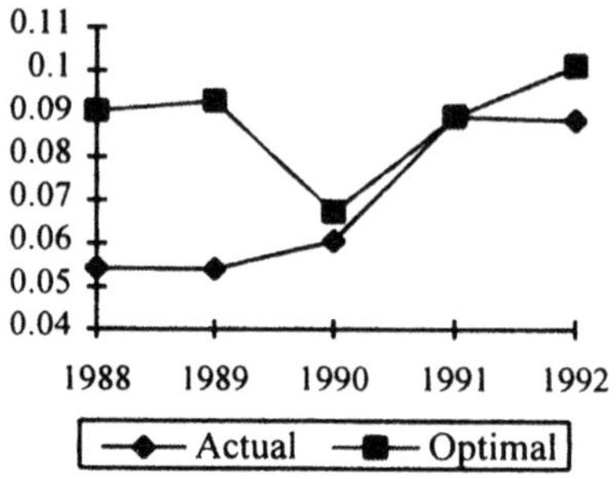

Figure 3.1. Mail Post Prices

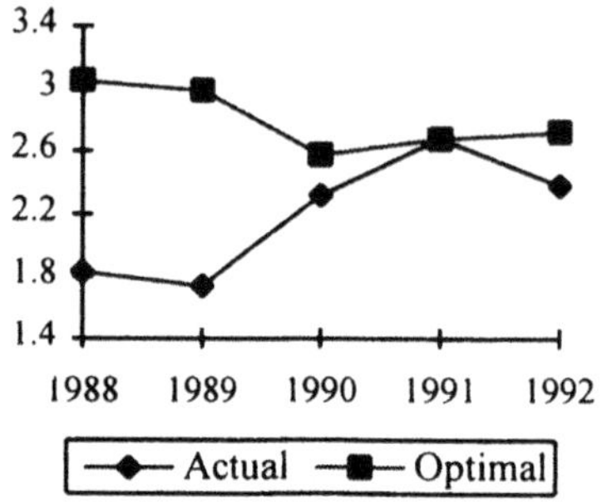

Figure 3.2. Parcel Post Prices

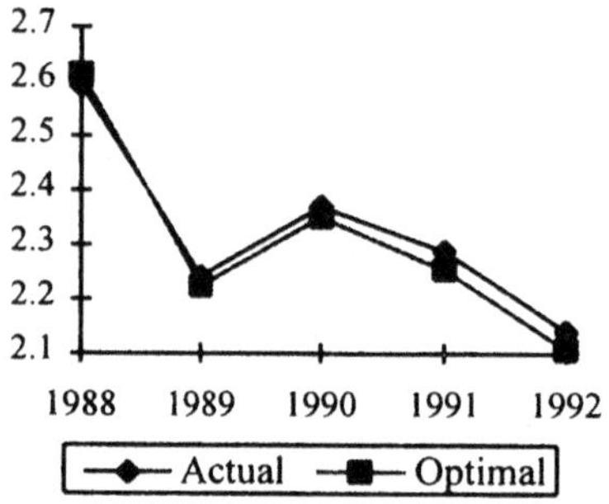

Figure 3.3. Long Distance Phone Call Prices

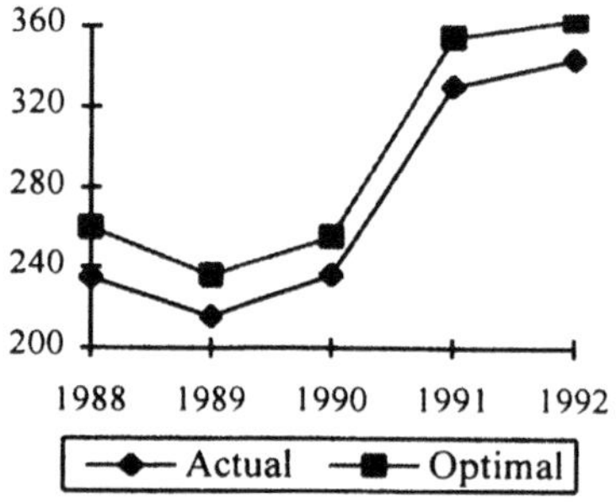

Figure 3.4. Local Phone Call Prices

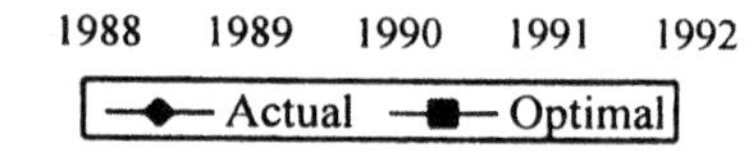

Figure 3.5. Telegram Prices

The prices of mail and parcel post of 1988 and 1989 are extremely low because they have not been changed for 40 years in spite of cost increases and inflation. This fixed pricing causes a lost more than 15 millions yuan each year. The situation is better after 1990 since the government increases the price of postal services in 1990 by 150 to 250 percent which makes the actual rates much closer to the optimum. Nevertheless, the prices move away from the optimum and become overlow again which can be attributed to the ever growing costs and high inflation rate after 1991.

Chinese local telephone service is developing very quickly in recent years, which means large amount of investments and high returns to scale. All of these make the existing price too low to meet the optimum although it has been regulated extinctly since 1991. The price of traditional telecommunication service such as telegram is relatively high and should be decreased for its high own-price elasticity.

References

Baumol, W.J./Bailey, E.E./Willig, R.D. (1979): The economic gradient method. *American Economic Review 69*

Baumol, W.J./Bradford, D.F. (1970): Optimal departures from marginal cost pricing. *American Economic Review 60*

Boiteux, M. (1971): On the management of public monopolies subject to budgetary constraints. *Journal of Economic Theory 3*

Danielson, A.L./Kamerschen, D.R./Keenan, D.C. (1990): The third best pricing rules for regulated utilities. *Southern Economic Journal 56*

Hagon, K.P./Sheshinski, E. (1986): Positive second-best theory. in Arrow, K.J./ Intriligator, M.D. eds. *Handbook of Mathematical Economic III.* North-Holland

Ramsey, F. (1927): A contribution to the theory of taxation. *Economic journal 37*

Statistical Yearbook of China 1988-1993. Chinese Statistical Pub.